OXFORD STUDIES I
SOCIAL AND CULTURAL ANTF

Editorial Board

IDENTITY AND ECOLOGY IN ARCTIC SIBERIA

OXFORD STUDIES IN SOCIAL AND CULTURAL ANTHROPOLOGY

Oxford Studies in Social and Cultural Anthropology represents the work of authors, new and established, that will set the criteria of excellence in ethnographic description and innovation in analysis. The series serves as an essential source of information about the world and the discipline.

IDENTITY AND ECOLOGY IN ARCTIC SIBERIA

THE NUMBER ONE REINDEER BRIGADE

DAVID G. ANDERSON

OXFORD
UNIVERSITY PRESS

OXFORD
UNIVERSITY PRESS

Great Clarendon Street, Oxford OX2 6DP

Oxford University Press is a department of the University of Oxford.
It furthers the University's objective of excellence in research, scholarship,
and education by publishing worldwide in

Oxford New York

Athens Auckland Bangkok Bogotá Buenos Aires Cape Town
Chennai Dar es Salaam Delhi Florence Hong Kong Istanbul Karachi
Kolkata Kuala Lumpur Madrid Melbourne Mexico City Mumbai Nairobi
Paris São Paulo Shanghai Singapore Taipei Tokyo Toronto Warsaw

with associated companies in Berlin Ibadan

Oxford is a registered trade mark of Oxford University Press
in the UK and in certain other countries

Published in the United States
by Oxford University Press Inc., New York

British Library Cataloguing in Publication Data

Data available

Library of Congress Cataloging in Publication Data
Anderson, David G.
Identity and ecology in Arctic Siberia: the number one reindeer brigade/
David G. Anderson.—[English ed.]
p. cm.—(Oxford studies in social and cultural anthropology)
Includes bibliographical references.
1. Evenki (Asian people)—Domestic animals.   2. Evenki (Asian people)—Social
conditions.   3. Evenki (Asian people)—Economic conditions.   4. Reindeer herding—
Russia—Taymyr Peninsula.   5. Human ecology—Russia—Taymyr Peninsula.   6. Taymyr
Peninsula (Russia)—Social conditions.   7. Taymyr Peninsula (Russia) Economic
conditions.   8. Taymyr Peninsula (Russia)—Politics and government.   I. Title.   II. Series.
DK759.E83 A53 2000
305.8941—dc21 99-052980

ISBN 0–19–925082–0

1 3 5 7 9 10 8 6 4 2

Typeset in Ehrhardt
by J&L Composition Ltd, Filey, North Yorkshire
Printed in Great Britain
on acid-free paper by
Biddles Ltd, Guildford & King's Lynn

FOREWORD TO THE ENGLISH EDITION

THIS book is based upon the text of my doctoral dissertation defended at the University of Cambridge in November 1995. The text has been substantially reworked and updated following return trips to Taimyr in 1995 and 1997. The original text of the dissertation has been published in microfilm format in 1996 and in 1998 has been published as a monograph in Russian translation (D. G. Anderson 1996*a*; 1998).

I shall be using a modified version of the Library of Congress transliteration system for Russian, Evenki, and Dolgan words. I will use the letter 'Y' to indicate iotized vowels when they appear at the beginning of words, thus 'Yenisei' or 'Yakutsk' and not 'Enisei' nor 'Iakutsk'. This makes the text more legible in English and has the advantage of avoiding confusion with indigenous words, such as the name 'Evenki' itself which, like so many words in this language, rarely uses the iotized vowel 'YE'. For Evenki and Dolgan, the consonants 'NG' will indicate the nasal sound 'ӈ' and long vowels will simply be doubled as in *atakii*. I will be retaining the use of the Russian soft-sign 'ь' represented by ' for both accuracy and its very important local role of distinguishing Evenki and Dolgan written surnames (Yelogirs are Evenkis while Yelogir's are Dolgans).

For ethnonyms I shall be adopting the vernacular singular as the root. Plurals will be formed by adding 's'. This will lead to some unfamiliar departures from official Russian language names. Thus I will use the terms Evenki(s), Nia(s), and Enneche(s) and not Evenk(i), Nganasan(y); nor Enets (Entsy). Yakuts shall be termed by their new official name Sakha(s).

For administrative terms, I shall use the term 'district' to refer to *okrug*; the term 'county' to refer to *raion*; the term 'province' to refer to *oblast'*, and the term 'territory' to refer to *krai*.

Much of the material for this book was gathered in and around the settlement of Khantaiskoe Ozero [Lake Khantaiskoe]. For readability, I shall call this settlement 'the Khantaika' [han-TAI-ka] making use of the common Russian phrase 'na Khantaike' used by local Evenkis and Dolgans to refer to their home.

PREFACE

THIS book is a test of the ethnographer's premiss that a small social setting, intimately described, can speak to large issues of politics and identity. At the end of the twentieth century there are not many places which are not represented on the television sets and within the journals of literate elites in the industrial heartlands. However this story, taken primarily from the lives of a family of ten people living on the Arctic fringe of eastern Siberia, is a story that has not been often told in English, or for that matter, in Russian. Although the Khantaika is a small, faraway, and no doubt exotic place for some, it is a place caught within the sweep of some of the most trying political and ecological changes of this century. While my ultimate goal will be to introduce the Evenki of Taimyr, their history, and their unique knowledge of reindeer husbandry, this book speaks generally to the issue of social and ecological change in all rural areas of the former Soviet Union, and more generally to that rich frontier of industrial expansion known as the circumpolar North. In presenting this material for review and at academic conferences I have often been questioned by historians and sociologists on how a community of six hundred indigenes far away from the cafés of St Petersburg, Paris, or New York can speak to the general issues of property, commodity exchange, nationalism, or post-Soviet society. At the outset, I wish to emphasize that a simple and perhaps unexpected case, stated strongly, provides much richer data for reflecting upon the nature of social structure than a complex case which is represented thinly or statistically. In this light, the lives of the members of the Number One Reindeer Brigade is as firmly rooted in the dilemmas produced by industrial development in the era of the end of the Cold War as are the lives of any factory-worker in Yekaterinburg or Manchester.

Some might perceive a slippage of jurisdictional terms in this work which deserves some comment. Although the fieldwork for this project was conducted unambiguously in the Russian Federation in the very first years of its post-Soviet incarnation, the meaning of all social events from marriages to barter transactions grew out of the complex institutional matrix of the Soviet period. This book, to considerable depth, delves into the meanings of social and administrative practice established under Soviet power. However, it should not be considered an exercise in social history. Without entering into the debate of whether or not 'transitional' societies have their own discrete dynamics, suffice it to say that practices forged under the peculiar forces of state socialism reappear in new and unexpected ways in the 'new' economy.

This work has developed immensely due to the generous comments of many colleagues in Cambridge, Manchester, Canterbury, Tromsø, and Edmonton; all of whom I would like to thank collectively. In particular I would like to acknowledge my supervisor, Dr Caroline Humphrey, for her guidance in learning the craft of how to delicately pull human stories from within the tangle of state socialist bureaucratic systems. I would also like to thank my students in the Seminar on Aboriginal Rights at the University of Alberta for highlighting aspects of this story of special relevance for Cree and Dene people in Canada. This manuscript benefited greatly from the comments of Dr Bruce Grant and Dr David Koester. The fieldwork for this project would not have been possible without a fellowship from the Social Sciences and Humanities Research Council of Canada and a language training fellowship from the Social Science Research Council (New York).

My road to the Khantaika and to the tundras of the Number One Reindeer Brigade was opened by many officials to whom I offer my thanks. In particular I am indebted to Eduard Anatol'evich Tumanov, Agrafena Aleksevna Mankhirova, and Liudmila Aleksandrovna Kaplina. Without the help of the Dolgan writer Nikolai Anisimovich Popov in extending my visa my stay in Taimyr would have been much shorter. I am especially grateful to Nikolai Borisovich Vakhtin, who supported my application for a research visa and introduced me to several wonderful people who helped me greatly.

I thank heartily the members of the Number One Reindeer Brigade, and in particular the brigadier Nikolai Savel'evich Utukogir, who accepted me into the company of his family.

D.G.A.

CONTENTS

LIST OF PLATES

LIST OF CHARTS

LIST OF MAPS

LIST OF TABLES

THE LEGEND OF THE KHANTAIKA

A LONG time ago, a girl lived on our lands. She had long, black, braided hair and radiant eyes. Everyone from every camp loved her for her kindness and joyous manner. A skilled hunter, who was able to fell a flying bird with an arrow, fell in love with the girl. All the people admired this beautiful couple.

However, an old, evil shaman heard of this romance and became furious. He had been planning to marry this girl. For three days and three nights he shamanized. With his song, he turned the boy into the big rock, which to this day stands near our village on the lake shore. The girl cried bitterly. Her tears became a deep lake into which she disappeared. Even then the shaman did not leave the couple in peace. Out of anger, he transformed himself into a huge mountain range encircling the lake: the Putoran mountains. The evil shaman thought he had finally separated the couple. However every year, in the spring, when the lake pours over its shores, it reaches out to hug the big rock.

Today, young people from the village walk together to the big rock to leave it gifts; tokens of respect for this great love.

A story composed by Tat'iana Vasil'evna Bolina

1
Evenkis in the Lower Yenisei Valley

THE PURPOSE OF this book is to answer the primary question of my field hosts: who are the Evenkis of Taimyr? As the following chapters will show, this is a complex question which will consider the history of a single reindeer brigade, the nature of identity when it is questioned by bureaucratized organs of power, and the utility of nationalist rhetoric for making political claims. Although Evenkis in the lower Yenisei valley are far from articulating a nationalist project in a classic sense, their recent circulation of claims to national pedigrees, exclusive territories, and kin linkages illuminate the origins of social movements focused upon national identity. Through identifying three ways in which Evenkis wield their identities, I present an ethnographic account of the everyday life, culture, and economy for Evenkis in this region of Arctic Siberia. The key foci for national identity in Taimyr are an inflated concept of nationality, a consciousness of territory, and a feeling of solidarity for one's *kollektiv*.

Arrival

There is no word in Evenki for 'blizzard' but there is a word for 'wind'—*edyn*. For the experienced *tundrovik,* who moves between the rolling hummocks of the tundra or through larch forests sheltered by foothills, there is no need to name the blinding mix of snow and wind called *purga* in Russian. A person who lives on the land learns to avoid exposed places during wind. If a hunter happens to find himself in a vulnerable open place, such as the sites of most Russian-built cities and settlements, it is easier to use the Russian term.

For the traveller who first arrives in the region of Siberia called 'the Taimyr' the differing pragmatics of how one might experience wind are not at all obvious. The airports and the regional capitals are built not in the most protected settings but in the most strategic locations to receive mechanized transport and to dispatch production to the other industrialized centres of the Russian Federation. These portholes are as practical as they are disorienting. They are designed to deliver people or freight quickly and in straight trajectories with no relation to the rhythms of the land. When gazing at Taimyr from the frosted windows of an airport baggage hall, it is difficult to know which hillside is less windy or which plain is naturally swept clean of snow. With experience one learns that the Taimyr is better imagined not as the edge of the industrialized world but as a chain of places chosen over time for their unique properties to harbour life from the winds that rage between tundra, taiga, and jagged mountain ridges.

There are two airports to which the traveller can arrive in Taimyr. The large commercial airport, Noril'sk–Alykel', hosts at least two flights a day from Moscow as well as many other Russian centres and chartered flights from Kazakhstan, Ukraine, and South Korea. It is built on a large open plateau that is popularly said to have been a 'no man's land' by indigenous Dolgans and Nenetses. The smaller airport in the district capital of Dudinka is built on an exposed island at the place where the Dudinka river meets the wide Yenisei. In 1992 it was still possible to arrive here from the territorial capital of Krasnoiarsk and then set off for any one of the smaller rural settlements, if the winds and water levels permit. Upon a December arrival at either airport one learns the meaning of *purga*. The blizzards are so constant on this large continental peninsula that pilots must search for a lull in what are often gale-force gusts to ease their jets down the ice-strip in Dudinka. When travelling from the territorial capital 1,500 kilometres to the south, you watch the clear, cold weather of the continental centre of Siberia cloud over into an almost bubbly turbulence below. The midday sunlight, still quite strong at the altitudes where jet aircraft travel, abruptly ends upon descent. It seems that you can make out the line between southern day and polar night outlined against the clouds. In your mind you know you are flying to the dark side of the globe, but for the newcomer it creates the impression that you have flown off the end of the Earth.

Upon disembarking, you immediately taste the flavour of the winds. They have a warm breath to them, although not a light one. It is the best that you can do to stay upright when walking against them. The haze created by a turbulent mix of snow and wind make the nearest mountains vanish and well-lit apartment blocks dissolve into a milky haze. In Dudinka, snow can bank up to the third storey of the centrally heated eight-storey buildings within a few hours to be removed the next morning by a patient tractor operator. During the winter of 1992–3, the Taimyr was buried under a snowfall that was four times the average precipitation for this season.

I left from Dudinka for the Khantaika on a special flight for the Department of Education earmarked to deliver snowmobiles for the school. The flight had been already delayed for over a month due to 'scheduling conflicts' (which turned out to be a refusal by the pilots to manhandle the leaden machines onto the plane). I had been assured that the flight would soon be organized, perhaps due to the increased exoticness of delivering a Canadian ethnographer. On the third day of negotiations, the conflicts were resolved when the airport supplied a fixed-wing biplane charged at the higher fee of a large helicopter (it was left unclear who received the difference). Our passenger complement included a teacher (and husband to the school director) who was overseeing the delivery of the snowmobiles; a 12-year-old boy expelled from the Dudinka boarding school for petty robbery, and a teacher from the neighbouring settlement of Potapovo. In addition to the two tonnes of snowmobiles, we took on board my trunk of cassette tapes, winter clothes, and notebooks, and the equally sizeable trunks of the teachers which, it later turned out, were filled with illegal shipments of alcohol. The Evenki boy had no luggage other than the package of gum that I gave him.

On the day of our departure we were blessed with a hard frost and no wind. It took us a couple of hours to load the snowmobiles onto the plane—during which time the reddened faces of the teachers looked close to frost-bite. After removing the protective quilts from the engine, the single propeller sputtered into action. The two pilots, their breath icing the wind-screen, urged the plane forward and back to dislodge the skis from their frozen hollows. They slapped each other's shoulders and shouted out 'with God!' over the sound of the engine. The plane slowly trundled down the ice-strip and took flight into the deep blue of the noon twilight.

After the days of anxious waiting and negotiation, the flight to the Khantaika was deceivingly quick and easy—making the settlement seem to be a close neighbour to Dudinka. The distance was not great—250 kilometres as the crow flies or 370 kilometres by the aviation corridors which weave between the mountain tops. The land gradually changed from windswept tundra to rolling hills with stands of larch in the valleys, and finally to the front ranges of the Putoran plateau blanketed in deep snow. In the short two hours that it took us to arrive the twilight was already fading. My first sight of the settlement from the cockpit of the aircraft was the single navigation light in the midst of a large white lake, and the frozen rock face to the south whose top was obscured by windswept clouds working their way down the mountain. It was this sight that worried the pilots. The *purga* always starts unexpectedly from the south and can strand travellers for weeks. Omitting the obligatory flight over the airstrip offices, the pilots hurriedly landed and bullied the local porters to quickly unload the snowmobiles and the freight. The plane was quickly turned to escape back to Dudinka.

On the ground, in the place that I had planned to reach for two years, I was immediately bundled onto an awaiting snowmobile and hauled off to the apartment of the school headmaster. A large crowd of drunk adults, children, and dogs greeted the plane, apparently anticipating the contents of the teacher's trunk (and hungrily looking at mine). That night, while making toasts with the assembled Russian intelligentsia, I was poorly placed to understand the context of my arrival. Thinking that I was simply in the company of teachers and transport employees, I could not understand why the chain of people who called by to make my acquaintance were briskly turned away. In conditions of a crumbling economy, teachers do not make ends meet with their pay-checks but on their access to centrally funded chartered flights. The local callers did not at first interpret my place in this company as part of a scientific project to extend literature and knowledge to an unknown corner (as the toasts of the headmaster signified), but instead understood that a foreign tradesman had arrived as a guest to an infamous den of bootleggers with exotic alcohols for sale. It was only several months later that I understood the significant smiles and winks that I received on the street that next day.

It became immediately clear to me that I had arrived to stay for a long time with this uneasily united group of people. What Russians describe as 'unusually unlucky weather' was to continue in the wake of a string of angry deaths. Evenkis and Dolgans say that when an old person dies, the *purga* comes from the south for the period before the body is interred (and while the drunken *pominki* [wake] is conducted). After the burial, the elder takes an infant soul with him or her. My arrival had coincided with the death of an elder to be followed, as forecast, by the death of an infant. It would be two weeks (perhaps due to a particularly successful wake) for both burials to be concluded and for the raging winds to cease and for the skies to clear. It was only then that I first discovered that this settlement, on the shores of a majestic lake, was surrounded by one of the most breathtaking range of mountains that I have seen anywhere.

The road to the Khantaika

Evenkis believe that a person's life has a trajectory. The image that they often use in conversation when discussing significant turning points in a person's biography is that of a 'road'. For me, the lower Yenisei valley, and specifically the tundra around Lake Khantaika, lay at a crossroads of many different trajectories. The predominating rationale which brought me to 'the Khantaika' (as the locals call the village) was a dry, scholarly one. My intention was to find a place and a people in the Russian sub-Arctic which bore a close resemblance to the geography and economy of a community in the Canadian sub-Arctic. This design had much to do with my biography. Before starting graduate work, and before studying anthropology, I had worked for the Fort McPherson Indian Band in the Northwest Territories, between 1983 and 1986. The Gwich'in people of Fort McPherson first gave me the taste for living on the land in an Arctic landscape which lets itself become known to people through stories, dreams, and the paths of animals. They also presented to me the problem of how a subtle relationship between people and the land becomes a troubled one when confronted with the regulation of governments and powerful mineral consortiums. Analytically, the study of an equivalent Siberian community—a community which was not presumably struggling with capitalist corporations—seemed a practical way to demonstrate that industrial development could be conducted in a different fashion. Personally, the transplanting of this Canadian experience into the Siberian frontier was an indirect way to explore an interest in Slavic cultures which I inherited from my parents.

In comparative terms the Taimyr Autonomous *okrug* [district] is an ideal field location. Although the Taimyr peninsula is geographically unique in that it extends its tundra marshes above 74 degrees North latitude (making it the most northerly continental peninsula in the world), the southern parts of this administrative district start at the more modest height of 69 degrees North latitude. Southern Taimyr is bounded by the wide Yenisei river, the mountainous Putoran plateau, and is interspersed with thick patches of larch forest. Unique to this region of Siberia is the large migratory population of wild deer which continues to provide a staple source of food for indigenous peoples. The geographical combination of rich fishing sites on a large Arctic river, a traditional economy centred on the hunt of the wild deer, and series of valleys populated with many different linguistic groups immediately suggests comparable sites in the circumpolar Arctic such as Canada's Mackenzie delta.

The cultural complexity and the rich history of the lower Yenisei valley initially drove me away from my original comparative project. I mention this aspect here since it formed a very important silent part of this work. Much of my enthusiasm for spending long terms on the land in often cold and cramped conditions came from an earlier introduction to this climate. My familiarity with cross-country skiing, with splitting wood, and fetching water from under the ice made me a clumsy but not useless companion around the camps. Finally, my stories and photographs gave a point of common contact with my Evenki hosts—for it turned out that they as well as I felt a common identity between the Canadian Arctic and the Russian Arctic and had a keen curiosity as to how life might be different across the polar sea.

An analytic curiosity is not sufficient to describe the road which led me to the Khantaika. Taimyr is a huge Arctic territory which, between 1932 and 1992, was completely closed to foreign guests and thus was a place poorly known. My attention was drawn specifically to the area around Lake Khantaika by the late Galina Nikolaevna Gracheva of the Museum of Anthropology and Ethnology in St Petersburg. She spent several decades working in the Dolgan and Nia settlements of Ust'-Avam and Volochanka and had made one trip to the Khantaika in 1976 (Gracheva 1983). One half-year before she departed on the ethnographic expedition to Chukotka which claimed her life, she surprised me by alerting me to the very existence of Evenkis in Taimyr. In January 1992 I had lazily assumed, as do many contemporary Siberianists, that the national composition of Siberian administrative districts was roughly congruent with their names. Thus, expecting to find only Nenets and Dolgan people within the 'Taimyr (Dolgano-Nenets) Autonomous District', I was caught entirely off-guard to hear of Evenkis, *sakhalar*, *argastar*, and a host of other localized identities which have puzzled many generations of ethnographers working in Taimyr. With her words in mind, I paid careful attention to what it means when people apply a name to themselves or to others. However, more importantly, it was her enthusiasm for studying this forgotten corner of the Russian ethnographic map that encouraged me to complete this project when overwhelmed by adverse circumstances and every rational reason to leave for a less troubled site.

My arrival by bush-plane on the shores of Lake Khantaika at the beginning of December 1992 followed upon a three-month period studying the Evenki language with the linguist Nadezhda Yakovlevna Bulatova. This short but intense course in orthography and grammar was conducted in the Institute of Linguistics of the Russian Academy of Sciences in St Petersburg and at the practice site of Number Three Reindeer Brigade of the Surinda state farm in the central part of the Evenki Autonomous District. From December 1992 to August 1993 I remained within the borders of the state farm Khantaiskii (with the exception of two ten-day trips to Dudinka in February and July). This nine-month period of my field project was abruptly cut short by the need to extend my Russian visa. After extending my visa, I remained in Russia until the end of December 1994 conducting library and archive research in the cities of St Petersburg, Moscow, Novosibirsk, and Krasnoiarsk. The entire length of the field project was sixteen months. Since completing my doctoral thesis, and before commencing this book, I have returned to Taimyr twice; once in 1995 and again in 1997. Both times poor weather did not permit me to fly to the Khantaika.

Although I spent much time with the fishermen, teachers, and office workers of the Khantaiskii state farm during my nine months' stay, the largest part of my time was spent with Number One Reindeer Brigade. This formally organized team of kinsmen was reputed to be the most representative collective of Evenkis and of Evenki knowledge in the settlement. From February 1994 until August 1994 our brigadier, Nikolai Savel'evich Utukogir, patiently led me through a vigorous training exercise which did not differ from that of a local apprentice herder [*uchenik*] within the brigade. In that short time I learned much about the reindeer, wood, wind, and about humility in the face of unfamiliar skills. However, before I can tell the full story of the people and their animals, and the skills and technology which mediate this relationship, I wish to discuss the identity of my hosts and of their homeland.

Evenkis and Dolgans

For reasons which will soon become clear, it is impossible to write about Khantaika Evenkis without also discussing those from whom they distance themselves. Like many places in Inner Asia and the circumpolar North, identity here sports a relational quality which makes it difficult to draw hard and fast lines between people. To be Evenki on the Khantaika means to be an Evenki living among Dolgans, Russians, and to a lesser extent, among Sakhas and Enneches.

Although Khantaika Evenkis may have been forgotten by many professional ethnographers, they have chosen to ally themselves with one of the widely dispersed and widely known nationalities in eastern Asia. Contemporary Evenki populations can be found in a wide arc starting at the northern edge of Kamchatka, descending along the Pacific interior into Manchuria and eastern Mongolia, and then ascending northwards along the Yenisei river valley into Taimyr. Within the centre of this arc, Evenki (and their Eveni cousins) live side by side with Turkic-speaking Sakhas. In the 1989 census their population within the Russian Federation was 29,901 (with 311 living in Taimyr). Taimyr represents the most northerly point of their settlement and, with the exception of Sovetskaia Rechka (Turukhansk County) and the settlements in Tomsk Province (Siminov 1983; Vasilevich 1931*a*; 1931*b*), it is also the westernmost fringe of Evenki settlement (see Map 1). The sum total of the published work devoted to the Evenkis of the lower Yenisei valley and the Putoran plateau can be found in Rychkov (1917–23), Lebedeva (1960), Tugolukov (1963; 1985), and Vasilevich (1951; 1972). In English-language anthropology and classic Russian literary works, Evenkis are known as Tunguses.[1]

Evenkis are generally known to ethnographers as the domesticators of the reindeer, speakers of a language of the Tungus-Manchurian family, and masters of a mixed economy of hunting, fishing, reindeer herding, and trading exclusively within taiga regions. Almost every ethnography stresses their extensive use of land and their wide knowledge of the customs and languages of their neighbours. They are perhaps best known to the English-language reader for their *hamanil* [shamans] who had privileged knowledge of the spirits of animals, people, and places (Shirokogoroff 1935). Khantaika Evenkis are no different in their traditions or their lifestyles from the 'classic Evenkis' of the literature. Until the late 1960s, Evenkis at Lake Khantaika used saddled reindeer to hunt, fish, and trade with neighbouring Sakhas, Enneches, Russians, and Evenkis. Their language is that of the northern dialect of Evenki spoken in Ilimpei County (Evenki Autonomous District). The extent of their historic land use went no further than the fringe of the larch forest high in the rugged Arctic valleys of Taimyr. Although there is little talk today of shamanism, the reticence to speak of deceased shamans combined with the large number of abandoned (and feared) ritual sites suggest that the skill of seeing deeply into the souls of living beings was

[1] There are additional rich sources of unpublished ethnographic material in the archives of K. M. Rychkov (AIV fond 49), Tugarinov (ARAN fond 135) and A. A. Popov (AMAE fond 14) as well as in the notes of Soviet Territorial Formation workers (AMAE fond K-2; GAKK fond R-1845). Notes on the region surrounding Lake Khantaika can be found *passim* in Stepanov (1835), Middendorf (1869), Kastren (1860), Czaplicka (1914; 1917; see Collins & Urry 1997) and Tret'iakov (1869). Recently, Ziker (1996) has published his account of a short visit to the Khantaika. Portions of my field research have been published as articles and chapters (1994; 1995; 1996*b*; 1996*c*; 1997).

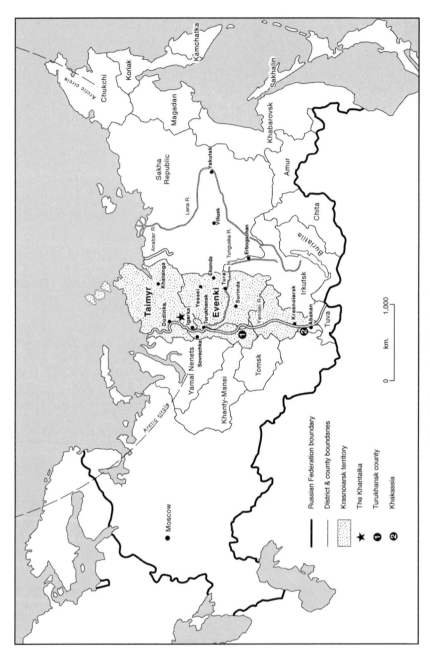

Map 1. Krasnoiarsk Territory, Russian Federation

Plate 2. Innokentii Tasachi and Anna Gavrilova preparing his saddle-reindeer for sable hunting on the territories of the Surinda state farm

no less developed here. At this most northerly and westerly extent of Evenki settlement, one finds occasional borrowings from Sakhas and Enneches in technology, mythology, and lexica.

In direct contrast to the wide and ancient pedigree of Evenkis, Dolgans are reputed to be among the 'youngest' of the Siberian nationalities. In most official and vernacular presentations of Dolgan identity, Dolgans are said to be a 'mixture' of Sakhas, Evenkis, Nias, Enneches, and Russian Tundra-Peasants. Dolgans can be found exclusively within the territories of Taimyr and Anabar County of the Sakha Republic (which was once contiguous with Taimyr). Their cosmopolitan origins open the possibility of comparing Dolgan sub-groups to each of their 'component' nationalities—a technique which carries much potential for political positioning in everyday village life. Like the ripples in a pond, easterly Dolgan groups are said to have a dialect and consciousness which reflects that of Sakhas. As one moves westwards, the Sakha elements of the culture dampen and become interlaced with lexica and skills which are represented as *tongus* ['Evenki-like']. Specific Dolgan clans who have been more closely concerned with trade, and who usually

Plate 3. Vladimir pilots his *balok* above the Sukharika river

locate themselves close to major rivers like the Yenisei, the Dudypta, and the Kheta, are often said to have an appearance and behaviour which is Russian. In the 1989 census the population of Dolgans within the Russian Federation was 5,584 (with 408 living in the Sakha Republic). Ethnographic and linguistic work on Dolgans is thin but authoritative. It is associated with the names of Popov (1934*a*; 1954), Dolgikh (1963), and Ubriatova (1985).

Dolgan ethnography tends to distinguish this people by qualities which resonate with more recent political concerns of the Russian state. They are often portrayed as 'leading' or 'advanced' people in Taimyr, having an interest in trade, and a closer relationship to Christianity than to pagan beliefs (for an exception see Popov 1958; 1981). Dolgans are said to have adopted domesticated reindeer-breeding from Evenkis and to have modified it into a more intensified, 'efficient' form. The best illustration of their 'modern' outlook is the invention of the *balok*, a light, mobile, furnished structure which can be pulled behind harnessed reindeer to facilitate comfortable travel across the tundra. Classically, their folklore displays a mixture of themes from each of their 'component' nationalities (but shows a great debt to Sakha oral style). Both their language and musical culture display Sakha features most prominently with lexica and motif being contributed from other cultural areas. Like Evenkis, they tended to trap fur-bearers and to keep their reindeer within the embrace of the boreal forest but characteristically close to those rivers which were the arteries of trans-Siberian trade.

The above descriptions of Evenki and Dolgan practice already foreshadow some of the more contentious issues involved in ascribing culture and nationality. As is the case in the relationship of both Canadian Metis and Peruvian mestizo to their 'pure' indigenous neighbours (Slobodin 1966; Gow 1991), assigning an identity to an individual immediately implicates that person's attitude towards tradition, profession, or his or her relationship to a colonizing nation. Rather than affirming the national distinctions which have become part of official Russian ethnography, this book will encourage the reader to consider Evenki and Dolgan identity positions as part of a continuum. In this manner it will be possible to understand what it means when people choose a life trajectory which advertises either the flexibility of 'mixing' of cultural practice or instead choose to display the dignity of an ancient and fixed pedigree.

Mapping the tundra

The entity which is most closely involved in the politics, economy, and identity of both Evenkis and Dolgans in Taimyr is the landscape surrounding the settlements. People speak of 'the tundra' as a place where one makes one's livelihood, follows one's life road, or makes a political point of the self-determination of one's nation. It is important to point out from the outset that these places are not technically tundras of twiggy bushes, rock outcroppings, and lichens. *Tundra* stands for any place which is not built, wired, and measured by the apparatuses of the Russian state structure. The 'tundras' where most Dolgans and Evenkis travel lie at the borderline where thick stands of larch merge into arctic and alpine expanses devoid of trees. This patchwork alteration of ecological zones in fact constitutes the places which are good for hunting, travelling, and coveting.

The tundras which are important for this story can be found within a large region which I call the lower Yenisei valley (Anderson 1996b). This region, composed of the tree-line areas along both the left and right banks of the Yenisei river, is known on official maps by some four administrative parcels, the largest of which is the Taimyr (Dolgano-Nenets) Autonomous District (see Map 2). Other than the obvious ecological marker of the Yenisei river itself, the valley is characterized by the transition of three ecological zones. The major part of the Taimyr peninsula is located in the tundra zone, which is not now permanently occupied (with the exception of a handful of scientific and military outposts). Here one can find the short shrubs and lichen-covered hummocks that in the spring and summer support the Taimyr population of wild tundra deer [*Rangifer tarandus sibiricus* Murray] and a wide variety of waterfowl which migrate yearly from as far as Africa. The permanent points of settlement of Russians, Dolgans, and Evenki are located to the south within the reach of the central Siberian taiga. Here one can

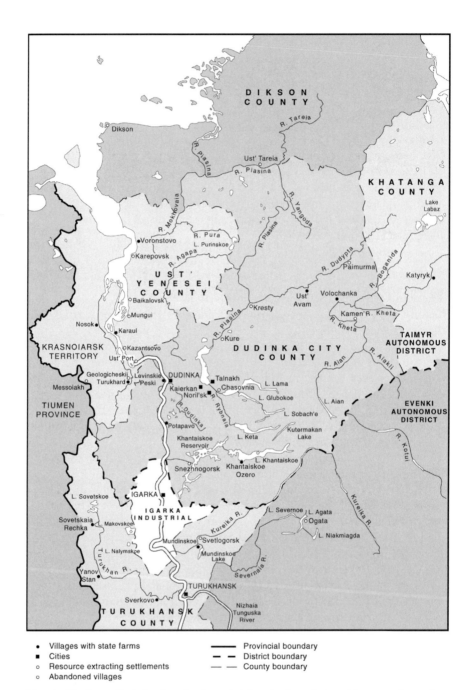

DIKSON
COUNTY

R. Tareia

Dikson

Ust' Tareia

R. Piasina

KHATANGA
COUNTY

Lake
Labaz

R. Mokhovaia

R. Yangoda

R. Pura

L. Purinskoe

•Voronstovo

R. Piasina

R. Dudypta

Paimurma

R. Boganida

Katyryk•

•Karepovsk

R. Agapa

UST'
YENESEI
COUNTY

Ust'
Avam

Volochanka

○Baikalovsk

○Kresty

Kamen'R. Kheta

R. Kheta

○Mungui

R. Piasina

TAIMYR
AUTONOMOUS
DISTRICT

Nosok•

• Karaul

○Kure

KRASNOIARSK
TERRITORY

○Kazantsovo

Ust' Port

DUDINKA CITY
COUNTY

R. Alan

R. Aiakli

EVENKI
AUTONOMOUS
DISTRICT

Geologicheskii

Levinskie

DUDINKA

Talnakh

L. Lama

Messoiakh

Turukhard•

•Peski

Kaierkan■

○Chasovnia

TIUMEN
PROVINCE

Noril'sk■

L. Glubokoe

L. Aian

R. Dudinka

•Potapavo

Khantaiskoe
Reservoir

Kutermakan
Lake

L. Keta

R. Kotui

L. Sobach'e

R. Rybnaia

IGARKA

L. Khantaiskoe

L. Sovetskoe

Snezhnogorsk•

Khantaiskoe
Ozero

IGARKA
INDUSTRIAL

L. Severnoe

L. Agata

Kureika R.

Sovetskaia
Rechka

•Makovskoe

○Ogata

Kureika R.

L. Niakmiagda

L. Nalymskoe

Mundinskoe○

○Svetlogorsk

Turukhan R.

•Mundinskoe
Lake

Yanov
Stan

Severnaia R.

TURUKHANSK

Sverkovo•

Nizhaia
Tunguska
River

TURUKHANSK
COUNTY

•   Villages with state farms
■   Cities
○   Resource extracting settlements
○   Abandoned villages

———   Provincial boundary
– – –   District boundary
— — —   County boundary

Map 2. The lower Yenisei valley showing administrative boundaries, cities, extensive settlements, and abandoned villages, *circa* 1993

Plate 4. Guiding the Number One herd through a *laida* near the Gorbiachin river

distinguish two zones. At the intersection of the tundra and the taiga there is a wide area of relatively dense forests of larch and pine interspersed with large patches of tundra and marsh. The latter are of primary importance for hunters and herders. These *laidil*, which one finds dotting the landscape, are the primary feeding places for both wild deer and domestic reindeer. The speckled distribution of differing micro-ecological areas along the tree line is also an ideal haven for fur-bearers such as the Arctic fox, forest deer [*Rangifer tarandus valentinae* Flerov], and other large mammals such as moose and bear. The majority of the traditional native settlements are located, as is popularly said, 'along the forest's edge' [*v krae lesa*]. The third zone starts suddenly along the right bank of the Kureika river and to the north of the port of Igarka. Here one finds the start of the classic Siberian taiga of fir trees and cedars with luxurious fur-bearers such as the sable.

What is unique about this region is the Putoran alpine plateau. These mountains, which start as isolated, box-like, foothills and get progressively more rugged as one moves east, have the ecological effect of pushing the tree-line zone unusually far past the Arctic Circle. This geographical factor alone has made the region along the edge of the Putoran plateau—the region corresponding to the headwaters of the Piasina and Kheta rivers—a very rich and comfortable place to hunt wildlife and to raise domestic reindeer. Not only does the existence of wood and fur-bearing animals make life on the land possible, the varied terrain created by these flat-topped mountains allows one to change ecological zones quickly by simply changing altitude as well as moving laterally. Although much of the Russian-language literature portrays the lands of the lower Yenisei valley as harsh and uninhabitable, the biodiversity and variety created by the rapid succession of ecological types makes this area a very rich and secure one for those who know its secrets. The rugged valleys also cover some of the richest lodes of strategic and precious metals in Asia—the mining and smelting of which pose the most significant threat to the ecology of the region.

One of the most significant wildlife resources for the local economy is the migratory population of wild deer. All of the aboriginal peoples of the lower Yenisei valley invested much effort and enjoyment in taking wild deer from the land for fresh meat, to make dried meat, and to sew winter clothing. Within the Putoran mountains, herders could take advantage of the rapid alteration of ecological zones in order to harness domesticated reindeer in order to approach quickly and silently the pastures where migratory wild deer fed. Wild deer also provided an invaluable breeding source for domestic reindeer breeders. Since the 1970s, for reasons which are a mystery to biologists, the Taimyr population of wild reindeer began to explode in population, jumping within a decade from a rough estimate of 100,000 head to nearly half a million (Syroechkovskii 1990). This explosion was also accompanied by unpredictable changes in the migration trajectories. Some observers blame the expanding ring of heavy metal pollution from Noril'sk for poisoning traditional pastures (Shideler *et al.* 1986; Klein 1971). Local people blame the lack of respect shown to migrating herds at the dozen points along the Piasina and Dudypta rivers where hired marksmen from the *gospromkhoz* [state economic enterprise] Taimyrskii efficiently but unceremoniously slaughtered thousands of migrating deer with automatic weapons (Yakushkin *et al.* 1971; 1984). The change in migration routes has made it difficult for both local people and Russian marksmen to anticipate where the deer will go and more importantly made it difficult for herders to shelter domestic populations of reindeer from large flows of wild deer blackening the horizon. From 1973 onwards, several waves of chaotic migrations have steadily stolen away the local populations of domestic reindeer from Kresty, Ust'-Avam, and Volochanka and now threaten herders within villages in Khatanga County and Ilimpei County of the Evenki Autonomous District (Klein 1980; Geller 1984; Gracheva 1980; Syroechkovskii 1984). People in these communities still hunt the wild deer, but they do so with snow machines or on foot. The Khantaika today is one of the last havens of domestic reindeer-breeding in the lower Yenisei valley and one of the last places where domestic reindeer are used to hunt wild reindeer.

The location of Evenki and Dolgan places within the rural areas of the lower Yenisei valley could at one time be explained by their proximity to major trading routes established along corridors which intersected the migratory paths of the Taimyr population of wild deer. This is rapidly changing as state-enforced relocations, pollution, and transportation bottle-necks change the human geography. The Yenisei river itself provides a major transport artery. The tree line along the edge of the Putoran plateau was also a major historic overland transport artery into eastern Siberia known as the Khatanga Way [*trakt*]. Those settlements located within the embrace of the Putoran mountains have been located along routes of easy overland travel across the distinctively long lakes which fill valleys of the region. The left-bank communities similarly provide convenient staging points for overland travel to the Ob' river system (see Map 4 in Chapter 6).

Moving across the land for Evenki and Dolgan has much to do with taking advantage of the opportunities that the tundra offers and classically does not respect externally imposed measures of time and space. This flexible manner of 'knowing' the tundra has been under attack throughout the period of Russian colonization, but especially during the Soviet period. Instead of responding to the movements of wild deer and the changes in the distribu-tion of fur-bearing species, Soviet officials encourage people to imagine the landscape as a series of bounded spaces fitting one within the other. Instead of knowing the tundra, contemporary hunters and herders are expected to map the tundra—or at least to understand and respect how government officials imagine and enclose space. While having little to do with the dynamics of living on the tundra, these maps are by far the easiest way for the reader to initially situate Taimyr and the Khantaika.

The political geography of the lower Yenisei valley is unusually Byzantine. The greater part of the space has been mapped as the 'Taimyr (Dolgano-Nenets) Autonomous District'—a jurisdictional unit created in the Soviet period on 10 December 1930. It takes its title from the peninsula which fills its boundaries and the Russified ethnonyms of the nationalities that made up the largest part of its population at this early date. The valley is also enclosed by the two smaller territories of the Turukhansk County and the Evenki Autonomous District, and two small but wealthy industrial enclaves: the Noril'sk Industrial County and the Igarka Industrial County. The contem-porary demographic indicators of these units are given in Table 1.

During the Soviet period, all of these units were part of the immense Krasnoiarsk Territory. In the cybernetics of Soviet administration, counties had the lowest authority to be followed up the rungs by districts, provinces, and territories. However, the political ecology of administration in the lower Yenisei valley was even more intricate than the standard Soviet template. During the fever of centralizations in the 1950s and 1960s, several rural counties of Taimyr were restructured with two (Dudinka and Avam counties) becoming a huge rural frontier to the Dudinka City Council. Of greater political importance is the odd constitutional status of the territories encom-passing the cities of Igarka and Noril'sk. Due to their strategic significance,

TABLE 1. Population statistics for the Sparse Peoples of Taimyr

Population	Total	Aboriginal					
		Total	Dolgans	Nenetses	Evenkis	Ngan asans	Enetses
Taimyr TOTAL (1992)[A]	53,100	8,585	4,851	2,465	316	844	109
Dudinka City County[B]	36,769	2,592	1,543	751	298	727[A]	65[A]
Ust'-Yenisei County[A]	3,800	1,906	51	1,800	6	5	44
Khatanga County[A]	9,200	3,679	3,539	24	4	112	0
Urban Centres (1992)[A]	35,900	N/A	N/A	N/A	N/A	N/A	N/A
Dudinka[B]	32,180	505	385	191	30	N/A	N/A
Noril'sk[B]	179,757	146	83	40	23	N/A	N/A
Igarka[B]	26,506	66	16	6	44	N/A	N/A
Rural Settlements (1992)	17,200[A]	N/A	N/A	N/A	N/A	N/A	N/A
Selected from Taimyr (1990)							
Khantaiskoe Ozero[C]	540	476	242	0	229	1	4
Potapovo[C]	509	252	26	142	68	4	12
Volochanka[C]	942	756	373	7	8	368	0
Levinskie Peski[C]	467	233	199	11	0	11	0
Ust'-Avam[C]	701	637	325	3	11	296	0
Selected Settlements from Neighbouring Districts (1988)							
Sovetskaia Rechka[D]	148	146	0	0	0	118	0
Chirinda[D]	336	300	(30)	0	262	0	0
Yessei[D]	799	746	(778)	0	21	0	0
Tutonchany[D]	554	219	0	327	0	0	0

N/A Not available.

[A] Administration of the Taimyr Autonomous District, Internal Memorandum, January 1992.

[B] Goskomstat (1991). These data are for Jan. 1991. The cities of Noril'sk and Igarka are not jurisdictionally part of the Taimyr, thus their populations do not contribute towards the total for Taimyr. The Noril'sk Industrial District also includes the cities of Talnakh and Kaerkan for which I have no statistics.

[C] Petrushin (1992). A copy of this manuscript is in the library of the Scott Polar Research Institute.

[D] Department of the North and the Arctic, Administration of Krasnoiarsk Territory for Jan. 1988. The Yakut-speaking population of the Evenki Autonomous District, although related to Taimyr Dolgans, is statistically registered as Yakut.

these cities were placed in special postage stamp counties which have direct relationships with Moscow and Krasnoiarsk but absolutely no legal relationship with those districts (such as Taimyr) whose tundras enclose them. This pattern of encapsulated governance wherein strategic urban sites live a charmed existence independent of their 'autonomous' rural neighbours creates extreme paradoxes. For example, most people wishing to arrive in Taimyr have to pass through one of the airstrips or ports which are located on territories 'outside' of Taimyr; a difficult journey in the days before 1991 when special permits were required by all to enter and leave each of these 'closed' jurisdictions. The most tangible paradox is the bifurcation of wealth between the well-supplied and well-built brick and marble city of Noril'sk and the poverty of the rural terrains from which it draws its wealth. Finally, of central importance to this book is the paradox of assigning national identifiers to a tundra which resists classification. The result is that the mapping of Dolgan and Nenets identity over a large rural space masks the complexity of real identity at the local level.

Since the dissolution of the Union of Soviet Socialist Republics (USSR) in 1991 each of these administrative fragments has been vying for various forms of sovereignty in a struggle for control of budgets, peoples, and resources which, at the time this book goes to press, is not yet clearly resolved.[2] For the purposes of this ethnography it is sufficient to understand that each of these units, be they districts, counties, or territories, continues to possess a powerful administrative imprint on people such that the level of wages, the reliability of public services, and even the possibility of travelling between one unit and another may differ wildly between each unit. The speckled political geography of the lower Yenisei valley, like that of its tree-line ecology, implies great differences of opportunity for traders and entrepreneurs who know how to profit from its administrative disjunctures.

The fact that maps of the tundra have been administratively created and invigorated will be a point that I will return to often. It is impossible to justify Taimyr's southern or eastern border on ethnographic lines since Dolgans, Sakhas, and Evenkis have shared land-use and kinship lineages across the boundaries. Geographically there is little to distinguish the alpine plateaus of the Putoran mountains in northern Evenkiia and southern Taimyr. However, the recently created boundaries have come to be meaningful in terms of trade links and transport as well as in the imaginations of people. This is to the credit of the efficacy of the state in defining and realigning social practices and movements along the patterns that it itself authorizes.

---

[2] The history of administration in this region from Tsarist times to the present can be found described in Anderson (1996a: 24–7). The present district of Taimyr was formed out of the Tsarist administrative unit 'Turukhansk *krai*'. In 1975 the word 'national' was dropped from its original title and replaced with the ambiguous adjective of 'autonomous'.

Since 1991 the relationship between Taimyr and Noril'sk has gone through a number of trials. In 1995 Taimyr had taken a strong stand on its own autonomy such that it refused to participate in territorial elections and even threatened to challenge in court the legality of the administrative decision [*ukaz*] which severed the Noril'sk Industrial County from Taimyr in 1940. In Nov. 1997 the Governor of Taimyr attempted to settle a growing feud through a treaty with the President of the Russian Federation and the Governors of Evenkiia and of Krasnoiarsk Territory. In somewhat ambiguous language, this treaty recognized that Taimyr will possess a separate administration and would receive its budgetary finances directly from Moscow as a 'subject' of the Russian Federation. However, Taimyr would remain part of the transportation and trade networks of Krasnoiarsk Territory and the urban enclave of Noril'sk would remain jurisdictionally separate. Local commentators hoped that this document would help in obliging Noril'sk to pay several billion roubles in unpaid rent, taxes, and fines for environmental degradation to Taimyr.

2
The Number One Reindeer Brigade

UPON ARRIVING IN Taimyr, my professed desire to learn about Evenkis was met with some confusion. In the district capital of Dudinka many Russians and members of the native intelligentsia alike told me with authority that there were no Evenkis in Taimyr. The more anxious among them suggested I get back on an aeroplane and travel to the Evenki Autonomous District where, judging by the map at least, I should be able to find Evenkis. Those with a deeper understanding of the history of Taimyr politely informed me that if there were any *tungusy* left in Taimyr they were very few and had most certainly 'forgotten' their culture. These practically minded advisers invited me to study Dolgans, Nenetses, or Nias—all of whom are classically associated with Taimyr. At Khantaika, the place where most of Taimyr's Evenki population is officially registered, the reaction to my project was even more polarized. Dolgans who worked in the office of the state farm, at the school, or for the village council laughed at the thought that 'the *tongustar*', as they are called locally, could offer much of interest to a foreigner. Once again I was invited to learn about old legends from Dolgan elders or to study the beadwork of Dolgan seamstresses. To my surprise, many Evenkis to whom I was introduced initially repeated the same trope by emphasizing that their language was forgotten, that the 'old people' were now all gone, and that their people had all but vanished. Using the last resort of a desperate student, I pleaded with my hosts that I had to learn some Evenki words or at least understand a bit about Evenki pastoralism since I had travelled so far to write a project for my school. With greater sympathy, I was then told by Dolgans, Russians, and village Evenkis alike that the only people who could help me were *tundroviki*—the 'people who live on the tundra'. Among *tundroviki* the place to start, they said, was with the Number One Reindeer Brigade; the 'most Evenki brigade' on the territory of the Khantaiskii state farm.

The most Evenki brigade

In Euro-American popular culture, reindeer pastoralism carries a certain romance bound up with ideas of Christmas gift-giving as well as a flavour of gentle primitivism. In Siberia, reindeer herding is a modern profession, which in the early Soviet period at least, was considered to be a strategically important sector of the economy. Rural institutions in Taimyr, as elsewhere in the territories of Soviet influence, have been nationalized, mobilized, reorganized, modernized, and cleansed for political and national purity in what has been called aptly a 'century of perestroikas' (Grant 1995). A reindeer 'brigade' consists of a set of individuals who have been selected by the state for their skill and reliability in delivering a fixed quota of meat at a selected place and time. Any other quality or skill which makes a particular brigade more 'traditional' or more 'Evenki' is reproduced external to the system of state-regulated reindeer pastoralism and, for many administrators, represents a threat to efficiency. Thus, in contrast to the stereotype, brigade-type reindeer management in its pure form has very little to do with a tradition-bound social setting.

In 1992 the state farm [*sovkhoz*] 'Khantaiskii' was responsible for the production of four reindeer brigades, each one distinguished here, as all over Siberia, by a militaristic numeric designator (First, Third, Fourth, and Fifth). The Number One Reindeer Brigade [*pervaia brigada*] was reputed to be the most productive and most disciplined. In contrast to the other brigades, it was the only brigade to be composed for the most part of a single family—which made it the most 'progressive' according to the then current rhetoric of economic reform (Humphrey 1989; Vitebsky 1990). Although there were only ten Dolgans in the farm's entire complement of twenty-nine brigadiers, herders, and apprentice herders, it was often pointed out that only in this brigade could one find a family made up entirely of *khantaika* Evenkis. In a happy harmony of circumstance, the fact that this family respected many tenets of Evenki pastoralism was seen by the present farm director as a guarantee of their effectiveness (although this was not the case with previous directors). At the time of my apprenticeship, the brigade had nine full members: one brigadier, five herders [*pastukhi*], two female tent-workers [*chumrabotnitsy*], one local apprentice [*uchenik*]. The core of the brigade, with the exception of two men, was composed of the sons, cousins, and in-laws of the brigadier Nikolai Savel'evich Utukogir mimicking an Evenki lineage structure of the 'classic' Evenkis of the ethnographic literature (see Chart 1).

I initially understood the special 'Evenkiness' [*samaia evenkiiskaia brigada*] of this team of state reindeer managers to be a statistical distinction. However, with time it became obvious that the Evenkiness of the First Brigade was a product of much deliberate cultivation. To be an Evenki herder in this state farm had as much to do with one's loyalty to the farm and to the regulated dictates of planned reindeer husbandry as it did to one's access to the lore of this nation which reputedly first tamed the domestic reindeer. Furthermore, I learned the fact that this brigade was the *most* Evenki brigade implied that in a different time and place a different national allegiance might have been selected. As the following chapters shall show, in order to understand why being the 'most Evenki' brigade was a rare and valuable distinction, one has to understand much about the politics of reindeer pastoralism, Soviet nationality policy, and the chaos of the recent economic reforms. As a prelude to this voyage, it is sufficient to understand a little of the biographies and the practice of each of the members of the brigade.

Nikolai Savel'evich was one of the most experienced reindeer herders in the community. He was raised as an orphaned son to Fedor Mikhailovich Yelogir, a brother of the rich herder Mikhail who, in 1939, endowed his reindeer to the collective farm. Both the brigadier and his stepbrother *starik* ['senior kinsman'] Momi Fedorovich Yelogir were the first members of the Communist Party from the settlement. They were both referred to as 'the Communists' by settlement residents. The proud Yelogir pedigree can also be sensed in the reindeer themselves. Modest-sized but well-proportioned rein- deer are known as the Yelogir 'type'. When Momi Fedorovich retired, 'his' herd was combined with the 'Number Two herd' of the deceased brigadier Agata Filipovich Utukogir (a first cousin—Chart 1) to create the Number One herd: a herd with a new number but with many familiar reindeer.

Nikolai Savel'evich's bearing was characteristic of both his people and his profession. When we first met in the office of the director of the state farm, I somewhat stiffly presented my research theme, my greeting card, and my request to become part of his brigade. Nikolai Savel'evich patiently listened. He smiled now and again. And then nodded his assent with a wide, silent (and drunken) grin. I had initially understood that I was being humoured. For a month and a half the three members of the brigade who had made the long trip to the village for the autumn slaughter seemed more concerned with celebrating than escorting a foreigner several hundred kilometres to their pastures. First the herdsmen celebrated the fulfilment of their meat contract, then they participated in a string of wakes, the New Year had to be greeted, and then, of course, Orthodox Christmas and finally the Orthodox 'Old New Year'. However, on one day towards the end of January, as agreed by Nikolai Savel'evich's nod, a silent herdsman arrived at my door on a sled with two harnessed reindeer to escort me and my bags ten kilometres on the first stage of a journey southwards to the Number One herd which would take a month.

Although humble in formal settings, Nikolai Savel'evich excelled in life on the tundra. Blind in one eye due to an unanticipated jolt from a bull reindeer, he could detect the motion of either wild deer or stray reindeer on hillsides several kilometres away. Despite his age (50 years), he could chase down and lasso most bulls, calves, and nervous cows in the herd. Using a knife hand- crafted from a discarded ball-bearing race, he was an excellent craftsman of sleds, *baloks*, and harnesses. In his view of the world, any skill can be learned if one watches carefully enough, and, most importantly, if one has a keen desire to learn. Thus, according to his generous philosophy, any Evenki, Dolgan, or even Canadian can be made into a successful apprentice herder. When asked why he spent an entire life as a herder when he had the opportunity to be a fisherman or even to advance in the Party hierarchy he answered simply, 'Who would feed the village?'

Surrounding Nikolai Savel'evich is a large complement of sons, nephews, and daughters-in-law. Among the sons, Viktor was the eldest at 29 years. At

Plate 5. Nikolai Savel′evich Utukogir planing a *kurei* used for directing reindeer in harness

the time of my apprenticeship, he was the only married herder (other than Nikolai Savel′evich) and was preparing to assume control of the Number One herd. This meant he spent much time making equipment for himself: lassos, sleds, and *baloks*—all skills at which he excelled. At different times of the year he would take direct responsibility for large portions of the herd, such as the troublesome cohort of cows and calves in the spring, or for the animals presented for counting in late spring and early autumn. Unlike his brother Konstantin, or his cousin Vladimir, he served in the Soviet Army at Petrozavodsk—an experience upon which he reflects often as a contrast to his life on the tundra. While in the army he picked up a facility for working with weapons of all types, a taste for strong cigarettes [*paperosy*] and vodka, and a belligerent pride of his own nation (the honour of which he had to defend more than once in brawls). When he returned from the army he spent a few seasons in the settlement before choosing a strong, directed road out onto the tundra where he takes pride in raising and delivering reindeer, as he says, with military precision.

Viktor's wife Natasha married into the family from the large and well-known central Siberian Evenki family the Chempogirs. She was an unlikely recruit for the wife of a reindeer herder. She spent most of her youth living in a tuberculosis hostel in Tashkent and thus had been isolated from learning many basic skills. She had also picked up a taste for the refinements of life in a major city. Both of these aspects were seen by the male herders as obstacles to life on the tundra. When deciding herself which road to take upon Viktor's invitation to marry, her mother advised her strongly to take the road to the tundra for both its wholesomeness but also for the direct access to meat, reindeer, and the right to choose the best quality skins from which to sew. Given the rapid crumbling of the post-Soviet economy this very traditional advice may have been prescient.

The herder with whom I spent the most time was Vladimir Yermolaevich Utukogir (aged 27), a nephew to Nikolai Savel'evich. He was my constant companion since I was assigned to his *balok* and most often given his reindeer to harness. Vladimir was a proud man who enjoys 'doing things right' and for better or worse often points out what his companions do 'wrong'. In his account of his life, he used to be an angry youth who wandered the village 'getting into trouble' when Viktor took him on as an apprentice. Working with the Number One Brigade opened up a wide road of independence and an opportunity to excel in difficult and respected skills. Within the brigade Vladimir was known as the best blacksmith and an exceptional hunter of wild deer. Like all members of the brigade he also took great pride in being Evenki and often checked my notebooks to ensure that I spelled his surname right or had recorded the accurate meaning of Evenki words. His knowledge did not end at his acquaintance with Evenki and Russian culture. From reading magazines extensively he collected knowledge about honey farming in Latin America to the trials of the British royal family. From his father, he also knows much about Sakha and Dolgan culture (and had strong opinions as to the differences between them). He was regarded as a bit of a braggart, but was given a silent respect since it was obvious that he was still a young man and that he perhaps more than most has a clear opportunity to become a *tundrovik*. In this respect his position as a herdsmen was somewhat liminal. Although it gave him access to reindeer and the chance to know the tundra, it was clear that authority and responsibility for the animals would pass to Nikolai Savel'evich's sons. Upon the retirement of Nikolai Savel'evich in 1996 he eventually left the brigade to hunt alone, living in a log cabin several days' travel from the village.

A central figure, if not *the* central figure, of the brigade was Nikolai Savel'evich's wife Liubov' Fedorovna (aged 47). As the senior housekeeper and mother or aunt to many of the herdsmen, she directed the packing and unpacking of sleds, the management of skins for sewing, and often the distribution of meat between the *balok*s. Liubov' Fedorovna exemplified what urban intellectuals identify as the 'direct and open' mannerisms of people who live on the land. In the course of a few minutes she switched from gossiping about her neighbours in the village in a speech peppered with swear words to quiet reflections on how times have changed since the days of her youth. She had an opinion on everything, including on topics which are considered to be closed to debate. Of special interest to me were her views on the relationship between Evenkis, Dolgans, and Sakhas. She married into the Utukogir family from the Kashkarev lineage—a group of kinsmen which boasts descent from Evenki, Sakha, and Russian roots. In other parts of Taimyr, Kashkarevs are generally considered to be Dolgans. Indeed, Liubov' Fedorovna's knowledge of Dolgan at times seemed to me to be quite fluent. However, officially she registered herself as Evenki and waives off any suggestion that there was any significance to her identity at all—unlike her sons and in-laws who tend to deny any common descent with Dolgans. Like all senior women on the tundra she was a master seamstress and very knowledgeable about the nature of animals both alive and undressed. Her special passion was for all kinds of knowledge about spells and fortunes; often quizzing me about the meaning of horoscopes and supernatural phenomena from psychic healers to alien abductions. Of all the members of the brigade she was the most 'superstitious' (as her husband would say), being careful to respect age-old rules of behaviour on the land regarding the spoken word and offering gifts to the 'invisible' masters of the land.

At the time of my stay on the tundras of the Number One Brigade, there were two other groups of herders which were loosely tied to the brigade: the

Plate 6. Liubov' Fedorovna Utukogir (Kashkareva) preparing bread and pastries in her *balok*

Plate 7. Old Man Yeremin preparing to lasso his private harness deer

Potapovo Evenkis and the young herder-apprentices. The most notable in terms of skill and experience was the group known jokingly as the 'Potapovo Gypsies': a set of older Evenki herders who moved to the Khantaika when reindeer herding was restructuring in the experimental farm at the neighbouring village of Potapovo. Formally, Leonid Men′ko was a full herder in the brigade. At the time of my stay he was joined by a guest; his uncle 'Old Man' Yeremin (Sergei Sergeevich). Both Leonid and the Old Man showed considerable independence of attitude within the brigade and for good reason. Up until the flooding of the Khantaika Hydroelectric Reservoir in 1972, they travelled the lands which are now being used by the Number One Brigade. The huge reservoir flooded most of their traditional lands thus giving them the choice of abandoning their reindeer altogether or moving to the unfamiliar territories on the left bank of the Yenisei river.[1] They both

[1] The Ust′-Khantaika Hydroelectric Station was opened in 1972. It is the most northerly hydroelectric dam in the world supplying 441 megawatts of power over 160 km. of transmission lines to the industrial enclave of Noril′sk. The reservoir, which is also the largest polar reservoir in the world, flooded much of the hunting and herding areas of the Potapovo, Khantaika, and Igarka Evenkis, Enneches, and Dolgans. At just over 2,000 sq. km., it has twice the surface area of the lake but at its deepest point is only fifty metres deep. At the site of the dam the intensive settlement Snezhnogorsk was built to house the builders and operators of the station. To the south, on the Kureika river, the energy outpost of Svetlogorsk was established in 1975. In the spring of 1993 the banks of this river began filling with the reservoir of a second hydroelectric station (see Map 4 below). Both stations have been built and financed by the combine which operates the Noril′sk smelter.

chose to move higher into the foothills of the Putoran plateau to join the state farm 'Khantaiskii' and the Number One Brigade. When moving across the tundra, Nikolai Savel'evich often would talk quietly with Old Man Yeremin either asking advice or diplomatically discussing the landscape. The Old Man seemingly knew all of the places we were to visit from his childhood. He would often enigmatically point out to me features such as a chiselled stump or an old vodka bottle hung on a tree branch and say with a smile 'it is almost as if someone was here before'. The other herders gave Leonid an ambiguous respect as one of the most knowledgeable folk veterinarians of reindeer but also one of the more infantile members of the brigade. Viktor, in his struggle for authority, often observed that Leonid had only a few grades of schooling and was functionally illiterate (and thus could not make an effective briga-dier). Others laugh at the fact that he preferred the company of men to that of women and thus at 44 years old had no family. This was seen as 'childlike' behaviour. Both he and the Old Man also differed from the other herders along the lines of technique. Having had close friendships with Enneche herders, they and all Evenkis on the left bank of the Yenisei river harness their lead reindeer from the left side of their sleds and wore the Enneche-style *malitsa* fur clothing when the hard frosts hit. Although this may seem to be merely a matter of preference, it implied that they had to struggle to train and reproduce distinct herds of reindeer which would respond to commands from the left side, and would have to maintain separate networks of kinsmen in order to obtain new clothing. On some evenings when the reception was clear, he and the Old Man would have somewhat melancholy conversations in Evenki with their kinsmen herders some three hundred kilometres on the other side of the wide Yenisei river over the ghostly electronic channels of the bush-radio. The knack for maintaining independent supply-lines is a long tradition for the Evenkis of both Potapovo and Igarka. In both places many families never had their reindeer collectivized into state institutions. The radical independence of these 'free-holder' *yedinolychniki* is also a point of suspicion for the 'Communist' herders of the Number One Reindeer Brigade.

During my nine-month apprenticeship on the tundras above Igarka, a number of youth came in and out of the brigade. None had yet chosen a solid commitment to the tundra, although several would later become independent herders and even brigadiers. From within the Utukogir family, the middle son Konstantin spent the spring with the Number One Brigade. He was known for his facility in using mechanized equipment such as electric gen-erators and snowmobiles. He had an unsettled aspect to him which drove him to travel anxiously across the territory of the farm visiting friends, hunting, or scouring storage sites for misplaced spare parts. At the time of my stay he proudly refused to drink alcohol. Liubov' Fedorovna was then hoping that a successful marriage would give him the discipline to choose a single direction in his life. In 1997 he was still unmarried but had become brigadier of the Number Five herd along with a large cohort of young, unmarried men. The next eldest son to Viktor, Andrei, had only recently returned from the army and was drawn to the company of his friends in the village. He appeared in the brigade only during the hectic time of the spring count. He eventually would marry a daughter of Old Man Yeremin in 1995 and become a full-time herder under the command of his younger brother Konstantin. In the brigade there were also two young Evenki 'relatives' who spoke Dolgan and Russian but not a word of Evenki. Mikhail Yelogir', who was 'a cousin somehow' to Nikolai Savel'evich, was overjoyed at being accepted as a herder in the brigade. He had suffered through an uncomfortable apprenticeship in the Number Three Brigade, where, according to his account, 'people just kept quiet and didn't tell you anything'. Having been given an opportunity to have his own reindeer, responsibility for piloting a *balok*, and a chance to actively share in the herding process in this brigade was seen by him as a mark of great generosity. I am grateful to him for sharing his growing knowledge with me on how to make speedy repairs to tools and sleds when others more senior in the brigade could not be bothered to fix the things I broke. Finally, there was a 13-year-old youth, Andrei Vereshagin, who was taken into the Brigade 'to teach him something useful'. He was the eldest son of Liubov' Fedorovna's sister Valentina (who is a Dolgan) and had recently been in trouble for quitting school and leading small groups of village youths in drinking and petrol-sniffing. Within the brigade he went by the name 'Smokey' [*kuragin*—a play on the Russian verb 'to smoke' and his surname] for the fact that he was determined to chain-smoke his way through the brigade's considerable reserves of cigarettes. Although forced by necessity, this invitation of an uncle 'helping' a young nephew by taking him as an apprentice recapitulates a long tradition of Evenki pedagogy.

At the time of my apprenticeship, the First Brigade was struggling to assimilate many changes. Within the brigade itself, the older generation of herders was on the verge of retirement, raising the question of whether or not the sons and cousins would have the discipline, the knowledge, or even the state's permission to manage the herd. Although it may at first seem that the internal politics of the Number One Reindeer Brigade are that of a traditional pastoral lineage, in fact the lines of authority here only happen to resonate by chance with the lineal authority structure of Soviet institutions (see Humphrey 1983). The fact that elder sons can position themselves to inherit resources in this brigade, and in the brigades before it, has less to do with the hegemony of Evenki jurisprudence than the fact that Soviet techno-crats were unable to gain control of how people come to 'know reindeer'. Despite several decades of instruction in the methods of Soviet pastoralism, the strict pedagogy of how to respect the tundra and the people and animals which live upon it is a skill taught by older kin to younger kinsmen (most often uncles to nephews). Those few who hold the knowledge of reindeer pastoralism de facto inherit the reindeer since both the herders and the farm require individuals who are interested in 'feeding the village'.

Surrounding the brigade, the state farm system was collapsing, threatening the very existence of brigade-style reindeer pastoralism and collectivized farming. The year 1992–3 was the first year that wages were not paid on time and the bimonthly supply of food, medicine, and equipment by helicopter had practically ceased. The long-wave radio stations *radio Rossiia* and *radio Maiak* both carried long, propagandistic programmes about the virtues of something called privatization. These odd events made the members of the brigade even prouder that they were 'maintaining Evenki traditions' in the face of the collapse of Russified economic organization. However, these events also raised many uncertainties.

The troubling question which faced the brigade was whether Evenki knowledge would enjoy as much currency in the market economy as it did in the Soviet economy. Linked to this anxiety was the fact that the tundra itself seemed to be changing. Since 1965 the Yelogir and Utukogir-run reindeer brigades have been moving steadily south escaping the expanding ring of heavy-metal pollution of the Noril'sk smelters. In 1992–3 they would spend their second spring on their new pastures on the headwaters of the Sukharika river, approximately 250 kilometres from the village on lands which were technically outside of the Taimyr itself. This distance was so great that the village itself was barely audible on the farm's single-frequency bush-radio. Although Potapovo Evenkis knew these lands as those of their childhood, the younger Utukogirs revelled in this unfamiliar landscape of fir trees and sable tracks as if they were now brave Evenki pioneers exploring lands far from the security of helicopter transport and regular communication with their village-bound kin. However, this isolation also became the brunt of a bitter humour. During the critical federal election of 1993 when President Yeltsin put his programme of privatization to the Russian electorate, the First Brigade in vain tried to hail the village on the weak radio to discover if a helicopter would be sent to collect their votes. In the end they had to settle with relaying a message through a nearby fishing point: 'just tell them that the First Brigade is behind Yeltsin!' The crackling radio answered with the ironic laughter of the Russian fisherman. For several generations, exclusive access to Evenki ways of knowing was a guarantee of success within the state farm system. In the eccentric setting of a privatized administrative economy, the refined skill of being the 'most Evenki brigade' seemed now to be greeted with indifference.

Herders and tundroviki

In official terms, a herder is 'set into' [*ustroen*] a reindeer brigade by the executive decision of the director of the state farm; a decision which should ideally take into account that person's paper qualifications and work record but may or may not consider the desires of the worker or those of the other members of the brigade. However, from the point of view of *tundroviki*, what determines whether or not a person can remain with the brigade is whether or not the tundra 'takes' [*vozmet*] him or her. To be a successful herder [*pastukh*] requires a certain respect for the administrative landscape of the farm with its quotas, delivery dates, and time clocks (Kwon 1993). To be a successful *tundrovik* requires a special type of knowledge, which includes a wide repertoire of technical skills, but most importantly involves a respect for the ethical imperatives which govern the relationship between people, animals, and tundra. The farm can formally assign a person to a brigade, but without first becoming a *tundrovik*, that person cannot physically fulfil the designation. The rich and respectful knowledge of a *tundrovik* is not a sufficient base with which to be a successful herder. One must add an element of discipline, loyalty, and the canniness of how to manipulate the institutional structures of the farm. To be a herder one must both 'know reindeer' and 'know' how they are useful.

'Knowing reindeer' on the Khantaika is a difficult skill to define since it is very rarely described by herders and combines many contradictory strategies. The primary paradox of reindeer husbandry here, as in many places of Eurasia, is the simultaneous cultivating of 'wild' and 'tame' elements in the behaviour of the reindeer themselves. 'Wild' reindeer are those which anxiously strut about when people come near, or worse, unpredictably bolt into the tundra; sometimes leading with them a sizeable segment of the herd. Tame or 'trained' *uchenye* reindeer are said to 'know' their home, a set of commands and tasks, as well as the roads upon which people travel. It is said that a good, trained lead reindeer can return a hunter safely home in a blinding blizzard when absolutely nothing is visible. In order to raise a healthy herd, both 'wild' and 'trained' qualities are needed. Unlike cattle, reindeer are not kept in enclosures nor fed, but instead are expected to crater through the packed snow of the *laida* in search of lichen [*engkel* (Ev.); *Cladonia rangiferina*]. The fattest and healthiest reindeer are those which are entrepreneurial enough to break away from the company of people to find the best feeding spots. However, if the reindeer use this entrepreneurial strategy to excess they become 'wild ones' [*dikie*] through shunning the company of people and eventually blending into the various wild populations of migratory deer which biannually scour the landscape. On the other hand, in order to keep a herd, Evenkis rely upon that aspect of reindeer behaviour which propels them to social settings. The 'gregarious instinct of *Rangifer*', as biologists call it (Baskin 1970; 1984; Bykov & Slonim 1960), allows the herder each morning to approach the herd on skis and, with a melodious call, patiently assemble the herd to 'bring it home' in a single-file march across the tundra. To recognize both wild and tame aspects of a reindeer's behaviour is

Plate 8. Viktor and Vladimir
Utukogir carefully trimming the
antlers of a trained reindeer

an applied psychological skill. As Vladimir once explained to me, 'I like
working with reindeer because they are like people. Each one is different
and they act differently everyday'.

While knowing the 'wild' and 'tame' aspects of reindeer is necessary in
order to keep them, reindeer are also kept for contradictory purposes. Most
herds of the Soviet era are composite in nature since they are kept to appease
different masters. To be a good 'herder' implies that a population of reindeer
is regularly culled to keep a majority of cows. In this manner, official
economists reason, the herd can reproduce quickly and thus can produce
the maximum number of animals for meat for a minimum number of
'remunerable man–days' (Anderson 1995). To be a real 'Evenki herder'
according to the members of the Number One Brigade, implies also keeping
a small number of bulls in an intimate form of domestication such that they
can be harnessed and most importantly saddled. This training represents a
special partnership between the *tundrovik* and a special set of reindeer which
gives a person the ability to travel widely and securely to take advantage of
either the wild animals offered by the tundra for hunting, or opportunities

offered by the farm for remuneration. These specially trained reindeer are typically seen as belonging to a specific herder.

The Number One herd is neither a completely intimately trained transport herd nor is it an industrial herd shepherded about for meat. In a classic example of Caroline Humphrey's (1983) 'manipulable resource', the Number One herd can be simultaneously a 'real Evenki herd' and a 'Soviet productive herd' depending how it is organized, counted, and presented either to state authorities or to other Evenkis. To be a herder-*pastukh* implies that one can recognize which reindeer can provide safe transport for a junior apprentice, which reindeer are expendable for slaughter, and which reindeer are best left alone lest chasing them makes them so nervous that they quit the company of the herd altogether. A successful herder cultivates a herd such that the reindeer prove to be useful in a variety of situations.

To distinguish the various tasks of domestication, it is significant that the herders of the Number One Brigade speak of reindeer in a variety of languages. When comparing the attitude, markings, or genealogy of a particular reindeer, they prefer to use the Evenki language, which is rich in such distinctions (see Table 2). When speaking of how a reindeer is best used, how it is best classified as taught or untaught, harnessable or wild, or as the charge of a particular person (or just a 'farm' reindeer) the herders tend to use the language of Soviet state pastoralism—Russian. When using Evenki, the herdsmen rarely use a word which identifies a single population of reindeer as having a fixed and set identity (but may use the Russian word *stado* [herd] for this idea). They instead speak actively of 'bringing reindeer together'

TABLE 2. Evenki terms used for distinguishing reindeer

Evenki Term (Plural)	English Translation
GENERAL AGE/SEX CATEGORIES	
Oron (Oror)	domestic reindeer
Khonngiaachan (Khonngiaachar)	newborn calf
Enngeeken (Enngeeker)	one-year calf
Eepkan (Eepkar)	young bull
Khiru (Khirul)	rutting bull
Ngemii (Ngemikhaal)	domestic cow
Irgingo (Irgingol)	pet reindeer (hand-raised)
HARNESS REINDEER	
Gilge (Gilgel)	domestic male (castrated)
Iuk (Iukil), Ini (Inil)	domestic cargo reindeer
Vangai (Vangail)	sterile female reindeer
APPEARANCE	
Kongemen, Karochen	black colour
Choorokan	spotted colour
Chelko	white colour
Tepor	without antlers (bald)

[*takhakhin-mi*]. By managing the nervous wild behaviour of reindeer with their gregarious desire to stay together with their human companions, Evenki pastoralists *make* herds for a variety of masters.

A final paradox is the complex amalgam of technique with which one interrelates with reindeer on the Khantaika. The Number One Reindeer Brigade prides itself on its Evenki heritage. Thus, here one can find ten to twelve reindeer which are trained to carry a rider *verkhom* 'upon a saddle'. These reindeer are distinct from the approximately one hundred reindeer which are used in harness with sleds [*uprazhnie*]. Beyond this specific badge of proficiency, this brigade is rather famous for resisting state directives to hold a large number of female reindeer. Instead, reindeer are valued for their potential of providing transport (and only reindeer which are untrainable are offered for slaughter). In the long run, the herders argue, their 'rate of retention' of reindeer is higher with a trained herd since these predominately male reindeer who 'know the rope' provide a calming effect on the herd; in effect encouraging them to remain together. Thus of the one thousand and thirty reindeer officially registered in the spring accounting of 1993, approximately 40 per cent were cows.

Although the herders of the Number One Brigade see all of their practice as being Evenki, there is much in their day-to-day activity which could be comfortably used in Nenets, Dolgan, or even Saami reindeer brigades. The brigade has four dogs which chase the reindeer during the daily round-up— as in Nenets and Enneche herds. One of the most valued herding dogs was a gift from a Nenets brigadier. Although some reindeer can be saddled, the vast majority of the trained reindeer are put before a high, hand-carved wooded sled both winter and in summer, as in Samoed practice. To protect the sled runners from the abrasion of the rough rocky terrain of the foothills (unlike the marshy summer tundras of the Nenetses) the herders affix thick plastic strips to the sleds scavenged from the discarded tubing of the Snezhnogorsk Hydroelectric Station. There is no 'classic' Sakha type of reindeer husbandry. However, much of the lexica used in the Number One Brigade to identify different age-sets within the herd and different types of reindeer is of Sakha/Dolgan origin. The practice of keeping herds of reindeer which number over six hundred head is one historically associated in this region with Sakhas but not Evenkis. Arguably, the practice of using trained reindeer for specific assignments such as long-distance travel, trapping, hauling fish or other freight, or just the reproduction of the herd stems from the strategy of Sakha traders. These special-purpose reindeer are often marked by cutting the proprietary brand of their trainers into their fur on the rear flank (a design which then sheds the next spring making it possible to change the reindeer's owner and designation). Finally, some of the most time-consuming practices in the brigade can find their roots in the cosmopolitan nature of the Soviet economic system. The practice of building biannual corrals [*korraly*] in order to make accurate counts of reindeer was first used in a Nenets reindeer brigade in 1925 and then was spread across the north of the USSR as an effective accounting technique (Lenartovich 1936). It would seem that the practice of making cuts in the ears of the reindeer of each brigade (instead of just 'recognizing their face') stems from a Soviet-Saami administrative adaptation. Finally, the idea that reindeer are good not only for riding, or for admiring, but also for counting, is an idea which has a longer history with Russian measures of status than Evenki notions of husbandry.

When I was invited to join the Number One Brigade to learn about Evenki pastoralism, these paradoxes of local husbandry proved very disorienting. Having read Bogoraz-Tan (1933), Vasilevich & Levin (1951), and Vainshtein (1970), I had hoped to instantly 'classify' reindeer pastoralism in this area as either stemming from a Tungusic or Samoedic tradition. Instead I discovered that these herders governed their lead reindeer both from the left and the right sides of their sleds, kept reindeer both for harness and for meat, sometimes marked them with brands or with ear-marks and sometimes took offence at my suggestion that an unmarked reindeer should be marked (since they prided themselves on their ability to recognize a reindeer's face). Initially, I assumed that all reindeer were rather tame, but in trying out my lasso I soon learned the humiliation and sometimes the fear of entangling the wrong bull, or worse, a 'wild' calf. Finally, I had rather assumed that the appellation of 'brigade' implied a certain consistency to the herd. Instead I learned that small parts of the herd belonged to senior women, other trained deer were for the exclusive use of certain herders, some reindeer were illegally 'borrowed' or were being kept for old people in the village, other 'farm reindeer' could be slaughtered with indifference. Most troubling was the fact that each of these parts was not clearly defined, as one might expect of Western property relationships, but instead would blur one into the other. Thus a reindeer which would be a favourite for harnessing for several days would suddenly be declared to be 'useless' and then be unceremoniously slaughtered for dog food. At times it seemed as if the herders, like me, were learning to know their reindeer anew. Young and old alike complained that with each year the herd was becoming wilder. They were more difficult to collect in the morning, and certain reindeer were becoming more difficult to catch at all. The reindeer of the past were always referred to as being stronger, healthier, more disciplined, and more Evenki-like. In the year of my apprenticeship, the nervousness of the herd was amplified due to a level of snowfall which was four times the average. This necessitated a daily search for new accessible pastures for the hungry animals in a landscape which was unfamiliar to the majority of the brigade's workers. To be a 'herder' in this time of transition implied a resignation for managing an imperfect and imperfectible breed of reindeer in a manner which satisfied the director of the farm and proved profitable in cash or in kind for the families of herders.

An Evenki pedagogy

While 'knowing reindeer' and becoming a herder is ultimately a personal journey, one is helped, prodded, and cajoled along this road by the strict tenets of the Evenki pedagogy. To a person schooled in a formal academic setting, how one 'learns' to be a useful herder comes as a bit of a shock. Knowing reindeer is achieved in a harshly organic manner without tuition, or words. An apprentice is expected to learn by close observation and through experience. Instead of being given long explanations and insightful descriptions of what to expect and what to notice, a fortunate apprentice will be handed a tool and a task and then be chided with humour for the smallest error. An apprentice who has exhausted the humour of his seniors might not be told anything at all. He or she will be expected to find useful things to do all by themselves, and then have their faults mercilessly exposed with insults.

Many young Evenki apprentices were attracted to the Number One Brigade for its atmosphere of collegiality in the sharing of knowledge and of opportunity. However, the fact that one would be given the freedom to learn did not absolve one from the criticism of others. During our blizzard-bound journey from the village to the pastures of the Number One Brigade in January 1993, I learned much about the need for observing practice with fine detail, as this passage from my diary attests:

I am constantly attributed with childish mistakes: 'Your leggings [*bakeri*] are all wet like a child's', 'Don't use that axe or you'll chop your leg off!', 'Don't bother trying to catch reindeer with your lasso—better to try to lasso a bush!' I am accepting all of this slightly unfair advice with patience. I don't point out that others in the group CONSTANTLY give me contradictory advice. The men NEVER explain anything but will quickly do up a harness or wind a lasso even twice [as a demonstration] before getting frustrated. If a harness on my sled is not done up right I will suffer laughter even if another [herder had] pushed me aside and did it up himself. I am now being tortured over [tying] knots. After the night on the [river] Mahin when the reindeer got into the bread supply everyone with little tact kept loudly repeating the importance of tying things right. The Old Man keeps tying everything to my sled, pushing me out of the way. Also, if I can't tie up the freight harnesses right they impatiently do it themselves and only show me the finished result: 'That's how!' I am on the verge of getting angry.

The sharpness of the Evenki pedagogy was no doubt exaggerated for me since I had missed the more gentler aspects of learning about the tundra in childhood. For my age, incompetence in the use of a one-sided Evenki axe or in how to approach a reindeer so as not to frighten it was seen as an inexplicable clumsiness. All of my fellow herders, including the 14-year-old boy 'Smokey', had spent most of their days up to the age of 7 or 8 living out on the tundra with their parents where they were exposed to basic skills. It is also important to note that the other competing models of formal training available to Evenkis, such as the residential school system or the army, are not notably polite or articulate (and are often physically violent). Thus, by contrast, the Evenki pedagogy as exercised on the Number One Brigade was strict and thorough, but not unusually aggressive.

Exposure to the Evenki pedagogy, while often unpleasant, is nevertheless a limited resource on the Khantaika. In answer to my queries about why more people did not live outside of the village with its chronic problems of supply and its polluted water, I was often told that it was not that easy to go out on the tundra since one needs relatives to learn about the land. A case in point is that of the young Mikhail who joined the Number One Reindeer Brigade only in the spring of 1994. Until this time he had worked for two years in the Dolgan-speaking Number Three Brigade. Here, instead of being under constant watch, these distant kinsmen ignored his presence, often hiding from him knowledge of the plans of the brigade or not offering coveted foodstuffs or tools. In contrast, he found the atmosphere of the Number One Brigade to be open and nurturing. He rejoiced equally in being given a bit of partially worked metal with which to make a knife as in being told which marshes or hills to avoid on his travels on the tundra. In an act of anxious desperation to avoid exasperating his new comrades, he even shot his prized hunting dog to ensure that it would never again chase the wrong reindeer during the daily round-up.

The strict nature of the Evenki pedagogy also turns some youths away from life in a brigade. These individuals tend to speak as if becoming a 'herder' in fact betrays some of the responsibility and the joy of being a *tundrovik*. The biographies of these young men were often very similar to those of the herders of the Number One Brigade. In their childhood they had grown up with well-known *tundroviki* and had in their youth tried to live in various brigades. In the case of one young man, the death of his father, who was a widely respected brigadier, caused him to leave the Number Four Brigade. This young man found he could not put up with the constant chiding of people who were not kinsmen and who he thought managed a herd in a manner which he found to be improper. In his case, the strict self-reliance bred into him at an early age sent him on a different trajectory of becoming a state farm hunter using snow machines and a string of cabins instead of the flexible technology of reindeer traction. The same trajectory would later be chosen by my *balok*-mate Vladimir after the retirement of his uncle Nikolai Savel'evich.

These instances of individuals who chose diverging trajectories point to a harsher, and somewhat colonized side of the Evenki pedagogy. Although a training in the techniques for living with reindeer carries a host of skills which can be applied in any situation on the tundra, there is a distinct set of skills which are peculiar to Soviet-style industrial reindeer herding. During the years from 1937 to 1989, when reindeer management was carefully monitored by the state, the loss of animals in these large socialist herds was first considered to be a criminal offence punishable by imprisonment or death, and then fined severely through deductions from a herder's salary. In this sense, the aggression and diligence with which herders are taught to approach reindeer and to husband them reflects the atmosphere of culpability before the state commonly bred into the older generation of herders. The anxiety or 'nervousness' with which herders notoriously approach their task may be a symptom of the fact that contemporary herders are finding it more difficult to strike a balance between the competing forces, ecological and economical, which affect the fate of their herds. In instances such as these one can identify a subtle form of surveillance buried within the contemporary Evenki pedagogy as applied within the Number One Brigade which drives away more independently minded youth.

Despite its excesses, there are several qualities to this strict training which contribute to a special type of knowing. What the Evenki pedagogy lacks in encouragement it gains in robustness. As Jean Briggs (1983) argues, in an unpredictable Arctic environment the most dangerous attribute that one can develop is the arrogance that there is a single authoritative answer to a given problem. Thus, the Evenki pedagogy is designed to develop a cautious self-reliance. The ceaseless insults that the elders heap upon the young encourage humility, a knack for understanding through empathy, and an eye for subtleties of context. In this manner, each person discovers his own method of thinking through a problem instead of mimicking a procedure by rote. Here, as Robin Ridington (1990) notes for Dunne-Za of the Canadian sub-Arctic, mediated or articulated knowledge is considered suspect and potentially dangerous.

The fact that the spoken and written word is avoided when learning about reindeer makes it doubly difficult to write about life in a reindeer brigade. As the senior herdsman of the Number One Brigade often exclaimed to me with exasperation, 'Why do you waste time writing? If you want to know reindeer you should be out there beside them!' Nikolai Ssorin-Chaikov (1991) struggled with a similar problem when he wrote that Evenki herders in the Evenki Autonomous District disdain all accounts of events be they historical, prognostic, or even just gossip. In his evocative language, all spoken or written accounts are by definition *ulo* or 'lies' to Poligus Evenkis. A fully respectable account is that which is properly done or demonstrated. The most startling visual demonstration of the anger and insult which elders can throw upon the young for a job poorly done is in a scene from the award-winning film, for which Ssorin-Chaikov was a consultant, where an old man verbally rips apart his young nephews or grandchildren for not assembling his tent correctly (Lappalainen 1992). The strictness of the Evenki passion for a proper demonstration of knowing drove Ssorin-Chaikov to conclude that all written accounts, including his own presumably, can only have the status of a 'lie' in the Evenki life-world.

In the Number One Reindeer Brigade, the 'lie' [*ulo*] is also an important category for herdsmen; however, it stands for a rather narrower range of phenomena than Ssorin-Chaikov lists. Thus I would argue that written accounts such as mine (and his) have a place within both Evenki and Euro-American ways of knowing. To 'lie' in this brigade means not to represent through words but to deliberately provide misleading information to manipulate a herder to choose an incorrect action. Thus, a raven might 'lie' when he flies in the direction of a particular hillside giving the herders the misleading message that they might expect to encounter wild deer on its slopes. Alternately, a dog might *uloderin* when it points and howls unexpectedly at a point on the tundra as if to indicate a dangerous predator which, upon inspection, does not exist. In this book, these words point to my own experience in living with knowledgeable Evenkis and in reading numerous accounts about Evenkis. They intend to give an accurate account of what a person might expect if they followed the same road as I did through numerous academic institutions to the Siberian tundra. In the Evenki world, I expect they would find a place among other types of 'talk' [*gundera*] such as a trip to the city, a story in the district newspaper, or the story of one's stay in the army. To Khantaika Evenkis this account might seem a bit more boring than most since most of the events it describes would be 'obvious', but it would be at least reliable. Thus, in contrast to Ssorin-Chaikov (1991), I argue that accounts need not enjoy universal authority in order to be valuable. As an honest account of my journey, these words are more than 'lies', something closer to a crafted, formal account [*istoriia*] but are less than 'knowing'; which can ultimately only be demonstrated in practice.

This position has broad implications for the entire debate on what is variously described as 'indigenous knowledge' or 'local knowledge'. Unlike many advocates who study and write about non-Western ways of knowing, I insist that experience taken from other situations and pedagogical traditions represents something more than a missing footnote in a library of scientific works. As Colin Scott (1996) articulately argues for the case of how James Bay Crees know how to hunt geese, the sum of local knowledge is much more than those aspects of myth or practice which are sifted, sorted, carved, and then translated into the language of wildlife biology so that they provide exact homologues to a set of rather mundane conclusions in the Western canon of goose biology. The training in ethics and in self-reliant living that one may gain in a reindeer brigade tells us something about the 'carrying capacity of pastures' but more importantly provides a model for how to make judgements and to live a proper life in a certain ecological setting. Certain moments of the *habitus* of the Number One Reindeer Brigade will always remain inchoate (Bourdieu 1990). Writing about inchoate ways of knowing is not an insignificant shadow of real experience, but instead, like a truthful raven, points to a trajectory whereupon those who hunger for knowing can find a different dimension of experience.

State nomadism

Despite their distant pastures and the changing economic climate, the yearly round of the Number One Brigade remains much as it had been since the last rationalization of reindeer herding in the late 1960s. The herders have accepted, on the whole, the dictate of state managers to maintain a large, well-disciplined herd which is populated with a large number of cows. In order to provide this large nervous herd with grazing areas, and to provide the settlement of meat, the brigade is obliged to make frequent migrations from pasture to pasture and from pasture to settlement. This industrial regime of a constant search for forage and a constant accounting before farm officials, gives a certain flavour to life 'in the brigade'. Although Evenkis are famous in the ethnographic literature for having the most unpredictable and far-flung regimes of motion, ironically the calling to be a state herder implies a nomadic pattern which is unprecedented in Evenki history. The task of being set into the profession of the 'state nomad' implies a constant vigil of attentiveness to the needs of the reindeer which often overrides private desires such as the passion for hunting wild reindeer or even forgoing regular contact with one's family.[2] The 'wild' lifestyle of the herder is underscored by an environment stocked with hand-fashioned or scrounged goods, privations in terms of a varied diet or a comfortable dwelling, and an overall ethic of being clever enough to get by.

In contrast with life in the settlement, the most noticeable aspect of life on the tundra is the lack of industrially finished goods. Despite the integration of reindeer herding into an industrial economy, the herder has little access to the benefits of this division of labour other than the binoculars, canvas, and rifles which are supplied to brigades. While villagers are supplied free of charge with housing, electricity, heat, and often food and clothing, herders are expected to be extremely resourceful. In the winter they live in their handmade mobile caravans with a hand-fashioned wood-burning tin stove. An alternate dwelling is the traditional Evenki tent [*chum, diu*] which consists of a conical portion of tanned reindeer skin mounted on a conical frame with an open fire in the middle. In the summer, canvas tents will be chosen for their lightness, but the *chum* will be constructed for relief from mosquitoes and flies and for its coolness. The bulk of the transport, apart from a rare

---

[2] I am grateful to Dr Ian Whittaker of the Scott Polar Research Institute for suggesting the term 'state nomadism' for the structural privations of regulated Evenki pastoralism.

helicopter flight, is provided by the animals themselves on a home-carved sled. When searching for the reindeer, herders make use of wide wooden skis which are handmade from pine and covered with reindeer skins, or begged or borrowed from a rare shipment to the village of similar factory-produced skis. Most of the herder's cold-weather clothing is sewn entirely from specially prepared reindeer skins. The herders themselves maintain that to live on the tundra they require no more than an industrially produced rifle with ammunition, an axe blade, and discarded metal for a knife. The time of my apprenticeship coincided with an extreme dearth of commodities. Number One Reindeer Brigade went through a six-month period without shells with which to hunt wolves. This was combined with the usual lack of building material with which to repair stoves of the caravans and to sew harnesses, the lack of batteries for the two-way radio, or the lack of kerosene for the lamps. Typical of the frugal style of the profession, the brigadier would place things in perspective by reminding us that during the war the 'old-timers' would sew nets out of unravelled flour sacks and make harnesses out of old boots. The collapse of the administrative distribution system seemed to approach that troubled time. Discarded bearing races, plastic tubing, the instrumentation of a crashed weather balloon, and bits of scrap lumber all became invaluable building materials. When familiar with the ingenious frugality of the herder, it tests one's patience to listen to the complaints of the state farm economist regarding the unproductivity and unprofitability of reindeer herding. To be generous to the state managers, they no doubt felt that their accounting methods inflicted no measurable hardship on the *pastukhi* while many professed an endearing faith in the romanticism of an occupation wherein 'you do not need anything' [i.e. like a radio]. Nevertheless the industrial culture of socialist reindeer herding can be defined by an extreme degree of fidelity to the state farm in the use of labour time and to production quotas combined with an almost absolute level of subsistence in consumptive goods.

State nomadism has very specific implications for the life careers of herders. Not only would it become physically difficult to continuously set and strike a comfortable Evenki *diu* every day as the pace of the orbits increased, but the wider orbits required by unruly herds forced herders and their families to be in infrequent contact with their neighbours. The tendency of this pattern of production to promote an asocial existence limited the profession's attractiveness to only the most unsettled bachelors and made it unappealing to young women who risked being entrapped within an impoverished, small, and continuously moving domestic space devoid of community with other women (and in complete dependence on one's in-laws). Given the implications of rationalized management it is not surprising that the most common complaint from the accountants, party activists, and economists is of the 'undisciplined' characters of *pastukhi*.

An average day in the brigade starts with lighting carved kindling [*luchinki*] in the stove, melting ice with which to wash, having several large cups of strong tea, and then donning skis to search for the herd. Finding the herd depends equally upon the herder's knowledge of the local terrain and weather as well as his understanding of the mood of his charges. A well-fed, calm herd might feed and lie close to camp while a hungry, anxious herd might travel as far as twelve kilometres. Once the animals are 'brought home' in a single-file march headed by a charismatic lead reindeer, the harness reindeer are caught with lassos and prepared for the daily migration [*argish*]. While the men run after the skittish reindeer swearing at each other or at the dogs, the women boil wild deer meat for lunch. When the caravan is assembled, the brigade has its lunch and then sets to the trail. At the new site (typically up to ten kilometres away), young herders (and ethnographers) set out on skis to collect dry larch for firewood and ice for water. The senior person in each *balok* chooses a wide log for a doorstep and prepares tea. Once the camp is established, the harnessed reindeer are released to forage in their new pastures. After supper of boiled meat with macaroni, the young men gather to listen to the radio, play cards, or to read magazines and newspapers by the light of kerosene lamps. The women may sew or prepare skins. If the airwaves are clear of magnetic static the brigadier's *balok* might whine with the sound of the tuning signal [*nastroika*] and the aspirated voice of the two-way radio. The next morning starts afresh with the first speech of the day, '*Idu oror?* [Where are the reindeer?]'

The productive calendar of the state nomad is framed by the annual trip to the settlement in November for the annual slaughter [*zaboi*]. Using a circular corral made of larch, a complement of one hundred to two hundred deer are selected for slaughter. Approximately forty castrated transport deer are also selected to pull the sleds bearing provisions and pulling the caravan that serves as a living space. Depending on the location of the winter pastures, the trip to the settlement may take between three days to two weeks. The slaughter is conducted in the space of two days. A majority of the brigade will choose this time to come to the settlement leaving only one or two members to tend the herd. After the slaughter, the women will purchase food for the coming year [*ottovarovat'*] and the men will conclude contracts with the farm for the next year's production, receive licences for trapping, receive shells for their guns, and ideally receive their back-pay. In between these negotiations can be a long period of drunkenness (from two weeks to three months) until either a dry period in the supply of vodka or unanimous community censure (often including that of the bootleggers) will coax the herders back to the tundra. The dark periods between the November slaughter and the exit back to the tundra in January or February are either endless riotous nights of drink or a time of much sleep. For the two or three young herders left at the herd [*v stade*] this is also a time of minimal migration and a chance to sleep, listen to the radio, carve new sleds, or work on a knife.

Once the brigade is reunited, it is not long before the busy spring season starts. In April, just before calving time, another wooden corral is built for the annual audit of the herd and to divide the herd into bulls [*molodiaki*] and pregnant cows with their one-year-old calves [*vazhenki*]. This is a time of much frantic activity. The pregnant cows, behaving 'nervously' reportedly because of their condition, are liable to stray away from the herd. Those that stray away often encounter the hungry wolves awaiting them. Any free time that appears as the days get longer is invested in hunts for the migrating wild deer [*dikie, baiur*] along the crests of the mountains—one of the great passions of the herders. From November until April 1992–3 during a particularly hard winter, only five reindeer were slaughtered for food—the remainder of the food being wild deer meat.

After the division of the herd, the brigade separates once again with one half tending to the male herd and one half tending to the female herd. The two fractions may be up to twenty kilometres away at any one time—yet there are often occasions for members to travel to visit each other [*gostovat'*]. As the snow gets softer, the two fractions of the brigade head in the direction of the summer pastures, which, in the case of the Number One Brigade, lay to the south across two swollen rivers. In order to take advantage of the frost when the spring sun dips below the horizon for a few hours—both fractions invert their daily regime to sleeping by noontime and running and travelling on the frozen snow at night. With the movement to the south out of radio distance of the settlement and with the adaptation of a separate time regime, the distinctiveness of the life of the *tundrovik* becomes quite pronounced. The brigade may go for weeks without contact with the settlement. The base [*baza*] of the brigade is achieved by late May or early June, just as the rivers swell and overflow and the snow pack is reduced to islands in between inundated marshes. At this point there is no longer a concern for keeping the herd separate. The brigade will live together for a few weeks.

The calving season is hectic for its responsibilities. Herders keep a daily vigil to watch for cows with an obstructed birth or for abandoned calves. Weather plays an extremely important role in a successful calving season. A sharp change in weather from steadily increasing warmth to a harsh blizzard can kill off the new cohort over night. Herders also keep watch for wolves. Some young reindeer are adopted when it seems that their mothers have abandoned them. Raised by children, or women, these reindeer achieve the status of 'pets', losing their interest in the company of reindeer and following their adopted parents around, often to the extent that they will enter the caravans in search of bread or salt.

The herd becomes increasingly difficult to manage as the grasses green and the twigs bud out producing a plethora of easily available food. There is not much concern with keeping the herd close together for the swollen rivers provide a natural barrier to movement. Until the mosquitoes 'fall' [*ngingartyn burure*] the long days of June may provide a time for sitting in the sun, fishing, or preparing the summer tents. As soon as the swarms of bugs well inside the eyes and ears, people return to the shelter of the smoky tent and the deer automatically seek the comfort of colder, windswept ground. As the herders say, the 'mosquito is the best herder'. It is only at the end of June that the herd gathers itself high on the plateaus at their summer pastures.

At this point the brigade will split a third time with the young men taking a portable tent with them to the top of the hills and the women staying at the base-camp to cook bread which the men will collect at occasional intervals. The young men will remain separate until the first snows of September. This is a period of great freedom for the men, for in the endless days of the summer they can catch reindeer to ride from brigade to brigade, cut off velvety antlers to roast, or fish for grayling in the high river sources. Once the first snows arrive, the reindeer themselves seek lower ground where some clear patches of pasture may remain. The men follow them down, becoming more vigilant to stray reindeer. As the domestic reindeer move down the mountain the high plateaus fill with migrating wild deer once again. During the rut of October, the men must balance a day and night regime of guarding the herd with a desire to hunt the wild deer. The domestic herd must be kept out of the path of migrating wild deer or risk being swept away. By the time that the wild deer migration is finished and November arrives, it is time to build another corral in order to divide out the reindeer for slaughter. A caravan is assembled and the herders return to the settlement to demand their back-pay, meet friends and relatives, and to enjoy a taste of vodka.

The yearly round performed by herders is certainly distinctive when compared to the measured life of the villagers, who negotiate a maze of controversy and paperwork within the built environment of their village. The life of a herder may even appear to be romantic when compared to the life of an urbanized Muscovite. However, it is important to emphasize that the constant vigilance by which the herder keeps reindeer is a new innovation in what can only be understood as an industrial form of pastoralism. At the turn of the century, as the following chapter will outline, Evenkis kept much smaller herds and were specialists in a much wider range of activities ranging from freelance trading to fishing and trapping. Perhaps more importantly, the tundras were well populated with small groups of people travelling, hunting, and fishing. Evenkis at this time travelled extensively (some often covering thousands of kilometres) but they did so within a landscape populated with many familiar human and non-human souls. The productive 'orbits' [*marshruty*] of the state nomad are mapped out chiefly to ensure that the reindeer are well nourished and protected, and not to feed the curiosity and initiative of the people keeping the reindeer. Most importantly each orbit begins and ends with periodic returns to a industrial focal point of the counting corral or the accounting office where the journey of the previous half-year is measured and validated. Although Evenki herders do know the tundra well and find much adventure in the interstitial moments of their productive regime, their life-world has been harnessed to the needs of the Russian industrial economy. Although the image of the herder stands for a stubborn repository of tradition for both Evenki nationalists and casual readers of Russian ethnographic literature, the state nomad on the Khantaika, and indeed all over Russia, measures a significant proportion of his status in terms of statistics, figures, and time horizons rather than the more relational imperatives demanded of him by the tundra.

3
Feeding the Village

HERDERS AND *TUNDROVIKI*, Evenkis and Soviet state managers, are united by a common concern for feeding society. Each of these agents, however, approaches this task differently. Officials in the various state agencies responsible for rural economy [*sel'skokhoziaistvo*] have a substantive interest in ensuring that set hundred-weights [*tsentara*] of meat or fish reach distribution points in the expected quantities and at the proper time. This interest tends to manifest itself empirically as a hunger for production indicators, statistics, and invoices. *Tundroviki*, beyond their hunger for knowledge, have a substantive interest in ensuring that they, their families, and their village are well fed. They also take responsibility for feeding a wider social setting than that ordinarily recognized by agents of state bureaucracies. The hungry, non-human persons whom they serve obviously include their reindeer but also the invisible 'masters' of the tundra who are fed small but sincerely offered gifts of wild deer fat or coins when *tundroviki* arrive at fresh pastures. Each of these interests converges within the institution of the state farm Khantaiskii, which through the action of its employees sates the village's hunger for meat, the land's hunger for gifts, and the state's hunger for figures.

The history of the state farm, like that of all collectivized agriculture, is a complex mixture of tragedy and heroism. The displacement of local ways of organizing production radically shifted the careers of generations of kinsmen and the ecology of the region. It is a central argument of this book that the processes of territorial formation and collectivization best account for the change in the identity of people from being *tundroviki* to being advocates of one or another discrete nation. Much more sobering is the fact that the building of a planned economy on the tundra resulted in the methodical construction of a wild terrain wherein the movement of animals can no longer be understood. However, the building of collectives also left an important human legacy. Fifty years of state attention and investment on the Khantaika gave people a lifelong interest in building a community which approached the standards of comfort and refinement in the Russian centres of high culture. The threat poised to these built communities by the current programme of privatization underscores most emphatically the contemporary resistance to reform on the Khantaika, and by analogy, in many areas of rural Russia. In order to understand the radical effects of the collectivized economy on the fate of people and their landscape, it is necessary to view 'the building of collectives' [*kollektivizatsiia*] as a process which continued long after the central edicts of the 1930s and which has precedents within the administrative practice of the Tsarist era. A necessary first step towards this end is to assimilate a vocabulary of collective actors in Taimyr, each engaged in feeding one or more human or non-human masters.

Building collectives

Before there was a need to feed the surveillance needs of the Soviet state, Evenkis on the Khantaika organized their activities through groups of kin who were governed directly by the tundra's rules of reciprocity. Unlike the multi-generational Evenki estates classically described by Shirokogoroff (1933), Evenki households on the Khantaika at the turn of the century did not include many people nor many reindeer. Small aggregates of five or six kinsmen, remembering their kinship for up to four generations along the paternal line, moved extensively throughout the Putoran plateau with herds of reindeer rarely exceeding forty head. It is difficult to know how people named their groups at this time, but following Karlov (1982) and the statements of elders it is likely that they understood each other to be *dial* ['ours' or 'our own']. They referred to each other by distinctive Evenki clan appellations ending in *-gir*; appellations which would later be reified by Orthodox missionaries as written surnames.[1] Reindeer were used exclusively for transport in order to take hunters into the mountains, to hunt migratory wild deer, or to haul smoked or salted fish twice a year to Russian trading posts [*faktorii*] along the Yenisei and Nizhnaia Tunguska rivers. At these posts, hunters would pay their yearly tribute (*yasak*) to the Tsarist state, trade for flour, salt, and tea, and perhaps christen their children if a missionary happened to be visiting. Although Evenkis travelled widely, accounts from the Khantaika affirm that they did not travel randomly. Most families preferred to return to familiar valleys and mountain tops where they would meet 'their own' kinsmen, encounter 'their own' micropopulations of migratory wild deer, and tend to the appetites of 'their own' masters by offering wild deer fat to their home fires or feeding coins, shells, and other trade goods to special carved idols [*saitanil, khomdisar*], boulders, lakes, or mountains.

In the lower Yenisei valley of the late nineteenth century, Evenki hunters were not considered to be wealthy subjects of the Tsarist state. They paid their tribute at the lowest statutory rate of thirty squirrel skins, four ermines,

---

[1] Some of the surnames/clan names common to the Khantaika are Utukogir, Yelogir, Chempogir, Kilmagir, and Typtogir. These clan appellations came to be used as surnames in the first half of the 19th cent. presumably under the agency of missionaries working out of a chapel based at the mouth of the Khantaika river. In addition to clan/surnames, Khantaika Evenkis used so-called 'Evenki names' until the 1930s. These names are classically associations given to a person at the time of birth and usually refer to natural features such as *khulaki* [fox], *atakii* [spider], *orokta* [reindeer faeces]. Popular Evenki names of the second half of the 19th cent. were derivations from Orthodox Christian names *Bahilii* [Vasilii], *Barvara* [Varvara], *Prokospii* [Prokopii]. It was common for Evenkis to have more than one name.

Plate 9. Sergei Yarotskii and Aleksandr Bolin show an old wooden idol (*khomdisan*) near their hunting territory

or one arctic fox pelt (GAKK R1303–1–121: 2). Although missionaries made an effort to register Evenkis as individuals with biblical names and patrilineal surnames, the Tsarist state knew Evenkis by the place where they paid their *yasak* through a legal institution known to contemporary historians as the 'administrative clan'. Khantaika Evenkis were primarily registered as the Fourth 'Summer' Tunguses.[2] The large territories enclosed by administrative clans would later, in the 1920s, form the basis for the first Soviet civic districts and the first collective appellations.

Not all of the travellers of the lower Yenisei valley at the end of the nineteenth century were poor. Wealthy Yakut-speaking herders bisected the entire Putoran plateau with trade caravans, managing long interregional trading corridors with the use of reindeer herds numbering upwards of two

---

[2] In the 17th cent., *yasak* collection points were established at Turukhanskoe, Letnee, Yeseiskoe, Turyzhskoe, and Ilipeiskoe. 19th-cent. documents indicate additional *yasak* points on the Kureika, Khantaiskoe, and Dudinka rivers (Bakrushin 1955; Dolgikh 1960). Evenkis travelling along the Khantaika and Kureika watersheds paid their tribute as the Fourth Summer Tungus Unit [*IV Letnyi*] at the mouth of the Kureika river (Dolgikh 1960: 154–5; Tugolukov 1963: 9, 1985: 198). Orthodox missionaries travelled from Tomsk to the lower Yenisei valley in the 18th and beginning of the 19th cent. After a hiatus of several decades, the lower Yenisei valley was 'remissionized' by the Krasnoiarsk epiarkhy in the second half of the 19th cent. Suslov (1884) gives a lively account of his adventures christening Evenkis, Dolgans, and Sakhas in the region in 1870. Until the firm establishment of Soviet power in the region in 1930 (AMAE K2–1–127: 12), written records on the activities of Evenkis at the Khantaika are almost non-existent. There are fragmentary reports of the existence of census material dating back to 1896 and 1914 which are seemingly lost (Anderson 1996a: 53).

thousand head. In the pre-Soviet period, a person's wealth was calculated by ease of access to the only means of transport available—harnessed reindeer. These 'rich ones', as they were known to Evenkis [*baiil*], would recruit local kinsmen to train and manage their reindeer, to take small herds of reindeer on special tasks such as maintaining a network of deadfall traps for fox, and to 'help out' those who were poor. This local arrangement of mutual aid wherein labour was exchanged for access to reindeer (and often brides) was known as *posobka* ['help', 'welfare'].

Stationary Evenkis were not the only agents dependent upon richer herders for access to trade goods and the means of motion. The Tsarist state also depended heavily on these 'princes' [*kniazi*], who for two centuries would be delegated responsibility for collecting tribute, transporting missionaries, and, towards the middle of the nineteenth century, transporting the first ethnographers. The Tsarist organic engagement with rich Sakha herders created a dilemma for the first Soviet organizers who arrived in the lower Yenisei valley in 1920. Without access to reindeer transport, the entire Turukhansk tundra effectively remained in control of Yakut-speaking 'bandits' and 'counter-revolutionaries' thought to report directly to Admiral Kolchak, the leader of White resistance in eastern Siberia (Smele 1997; Snow 1977). To negotiate access to the interior of the Putoran plateau and the Taimyr peninsula, the first Party workers built their initial alliances with the poorest Evenki and Dolgan hunters and fishermen. As the Soviet state developed an appetite for intensive forms of production, its interest shifted away from the modest loyalty of small-scale Evenki hunter-fishermen towards courting, once again, the highly mobile Sakha herders. The story of how the Sakha *baiil* formed an alliance with the Soviet state sets the stage for the rise of national rivalry in the region.

From the point of view of Bolshevik planners, the feeding of Evenki and Sakha tundra-people into the Soviet industrial economy was organized, as it were, in two courses. During the first course, from 1927 to 1932, territorial formation officers established the civil organizations of 'clan' [*rodovie*] and 'nomadic councils' [*kochevie sovety*] to replace the administrative tribute units of Tsarist times. To Soviet organizers, the nomadic councils mapped the loyalty of rural producers to the new regime onto discrete parcels of land. They also gave administrators an appetizing taste of their productive potential. The main course, which ran from the early 1930s to 1968, was devised to revolutionize the tundra in a new sense. With the inscribing of a new set of rural economic institutions [*kolkhozy*, *sovkhozy*] within nomadic councils, *tundroviki* were encouraged to imagine their sentient ecology to be a landscape of expropriated state property and state production indicators. Reindeer were not to be seen as gifts of the land but instead as a transport resource which could be harnessed first to build the factory-city of Noril'sk and later to feed its hungry workers. This new way of understanding the land was most intimately felt by the change in local practice. Whereas during the nineteenth century, Evenki and Sakha hunters had to be concerned with sating the tundra and the occasional appearance of tribute-demanding princes, the intensification of collectivization into the day-to-day labour process implied living in a clamorous social setting where one or another master was constantly making demands on one's activities.

The charting and surveillance function of the early nomadic councils is best illustrated by the paper records they kept. The chairman and secretary of each council would compile yearly accounts of the national and demographic composition of each human household, establish the age and sexual composition of their associated reindeer herds, and enumerate other significant assets (such as boats, nets, or weapons). Using the Leninist template of social stratification, adapted to Siberia by the ethnographer Innokentii Suslov (1930), territorial formation officers divided the population into 'rich' [*kulak*], 'middle' [*srediak*], and 'poor' [*bediak*] segments. Formally, producers having less than forty reindeer were considered 'poor' while those with more than one hundred head were considered 'rich' [*kulaki*]. Shamans were singled out into a special category and were categorically forbidden from participating in the political life of the council. The accuracy of the stratification system was severely constrained by the deductive ability of the officials. Throughout Siberia, and especially on the Khantaika, literate accountants were brought into native communities from the outside and were given the task of guessing how various kinsmen used the reindeer around them. The accounting of wealth in reindeer to individuals is a very inexact science. Although there are impressive reams of papers within offices and archives giving numbers on property in reindeer, they are often contradictory and incomplete. The environment of Taimyr is such that portions of herds can be 'presented' for counting while larger fractions can be kept in rugged valleys a few kilometres away invisible to all but those who understand the signs of the tundra. Similarly powerful knowledge was also diffusely distributed among the population in a manner no doubt unfamiliar to a person versed in the Russian formal education system. Very few individuals immediately presented themselves as shamans and in fact Party organizers were later dismayed to learn that some of their best cadres could with equal ease be classified as shamans. The difficulties in understanding the more flexible strategies and ways of knowing of Evenki *tundroviki* implied that the reach of the state into Evenki pastoralism in the early days of Soviet power was limited to periodic counts and representations of herds on paper.

When the fledgeling state apparatus developed a greater hunger to control the use of land, water, and reindeer, the households registered in nomadic councils formed the nuclei for increasingly complex rural institutions

ranging from the 'simple work-units' [*tovarishchestva; artely*] of 1929 to the
state farms [*sovkhozy*] of the 1960s.[3] Each of these economic enterprises,
formed within discrete nomadic councils, were administrative tools for keeping closer accounts of productive activity and reforming the way in which
labour was performed. Work-units were established first along the banks of
the Yenisei among Nenets, Russian, and Enneche fishermen, and then were
gradually extended inland. The official literature proclaims that all rural
residents of the lower Yenisei valley were made members of simple work-
units by 1939. Factually a substantial number of large-scale Sakha herders
managed to live independent of the collective institutions until 1941, and
many smaller 'freeholders' among Nenetses and Potapovo Evenkis never
surrendered their reindeer to the state accountants.

   Although both nomadic councils and work-units were administratively
weak when compared to the regimented form of the state farm, they did
effectively encapsulate and harness the lives of rural Evenkis in Taimyr, as
elsewhere in Siberia. However, what every *tundrovik* implicitly understands
is that every act of feeding a powerful master induces an act of reciprocal
respect. The first formal appropriations of land and productive resources
were consolidated with the introduction of several important collective
designations which would prove to be strategically useful to Evenkis. For
example, the nomadic councils were expected, by statute, to be nationally
homogenetic. The national 'purity' of each of these civic organizations was in
fact written directly into their titles such as the 'Khantaika-Tungus Clan
Council' or the 'Avamo-Nganasan Nomadic Council'. Further, the rationalization of practice into discrete types of economic activity also implied the
building of the first 'labour collectives' [*trudovye kollektivy*]. The division of
labour between 'communities of producers' in the early *artely* of the lower
Yenisei valley was simple. Up to ten individuals were employed in administration, accounting, or in the school, while the remaining sixty adults would
be members of one or two productive communities such as trappers or

---

[3] In most parts of rural Russia, there existed a regular evolution in types of rural institutions from
'simple work-units' such as *tovarishchestva, artely*, and the PPOs [*Prosteishie Promyslovie Ob'edinenie*;
simplest hunting unit] to collective farms [*kolkhozy*] and state farms [*sovkhozy*]. According to the
template, simple work-units involved collective labour but were not built upon the expropriation of
animals or tools. In collective farms, all capital assets were owned collectively, tasks were assigned
collectively, and profits, consumption goods, and pensions were distributed collectively. In the state
farm, all assets were owned by the state and workers received salaries, pensions, and orders from
centrally appointed authorities often with high rates of subsidization (see Kuoljok 1985; Sergeev
1955; Slezkine 1994; Humphrey 1983; and Nikul'shin 1939). The lower Yenisei valley is an exception
to this pattern due to its distance from urban centres and its history of armed resistance. In archival
documents for this region, *tovarishchestvo* [work-unit] and PPO [simplest hunting unit] are used
interchangeably, as are the terms *kolkhoz* [collective farm] and *artel'*. For practical purposes, most
producers experienced a shift in their lives when they became members of one of the three types of
'simple work-units' from 1929 to 1937, and again when these units were reorganized into state farms
from 1958 to 1968. For greater detail on the evolution of these organizations see Anderson (1996*a*:
54 ff. and appendix 3).

fishermen. In terms of identity, Evenkis began to experiment at this early date with various national and professional allegiances which would eventually eclipse the use of clan-based appellations such as *dial*, 'Evenki names', or the more formal 'administrative clan'. These two types of communities, productive communities and national communities, in the late 1980s would become the units which would be presented to state officials as collective identities worth defending. This important binomial equation of nationality and profession forms the heart of what can be identified as the Soviet citizenship regime (Anderson 1996*b*).

The taste of Soviet planners for mapping the landscape and its people first into civic parcels, and then into productive parcels, at times reached levels of fanaticism. While territorial formation officers on the Yamal peninsula won their fame by revolutionizing reindeer herding with the counting corral, officers in the lower Yenisei valley dreamed of distinguishing themselves by creating a single 'Reindeer Farm' [*olen'sovkhoz*] for a district the size of Great Britain. The Orwellian connotation of the name was unfortunately matched with practice. Writing in 1928, Lebedev (1929) bragged that Taimyr would soon become a 'laboratory' of socialist reindeer herding with the establishment of a single farm with over twenty thousand animals. In 1930 territorial formation officers mapped out official pastures for the Reindeer Farm on the north bank of the Khantaika river within the contemporary territories of the Potapovo and Khantaika village councils on lands now submerged under the Ust'-Khantaika reservoir. The seed stock of 300 reindeer came from an expropriated private trading organization in Dudinka. By 1931, four thousand reindeer had been forcibly expropriated from richer herders (although most would die that same year due to an epidemic). To rebuild their numbers, officials from the Department of Rural Economy were poising themselves in the spring of 1932 to expropriate a forecasted forty thousand head of reindeer between the posts of Avam, Dolgany, and Volochanka when local Evenkis, Dolgans, and Sakhas took to arms. The Volochanka rebellion claimed the lives of 4 'rebels', 20 Party members, and left 14 Party members injured.[4] The direct result of the rebellion had an interesting turn. Instead of repressing the participants, the State Political Police arrested the head of the Reindeer Farm with a

---

[4] Archival material on the plans for the Reindeer Farm can be found in AMAE (K2-1-124; K2-1-127). Published accounts of the Volochanka rebellion are limited to one newspaper account (Troshev 1993) and several archival sources (KTsKhIDNI 28-2-28; RTsKhIDNI 17-114-305). The dream of one big Reindeer Farm did not end in 1932 but was redirected into the revolutionizing of the reindeer phenotype. In 1948 the territory and reindeer remaining on the farm's official pastures along the Khantaika river was converted into the Potapovo 'Experimental Industrial Farm' [*Opytnnoe Promyshlenoe Khoziaistvo*]; an organization which would experiment with different 'scientific' strategies, feeds, and inoculations for increasing the size of reindeer bodies. It is rumoured by herders on the Khantaika that the tampering with the reindeer form led Potapovo Evenkis to once again take up their hunting weapons to chase off zealous veterinarians in the early 1970s.

charge of theft. Later that year there was a significant refinement in Party policy in the North which forbade expropriation without the gradual establishment of collective institutions in which people could work and live (O rabote 1932). Arguably, the nightmare of the Volochanka rebellion can explain the odd fact that only a handful of the simple work-units [*artely*] of Taimyr were ever legally transformed into proper collective farms [*kolkhozy*] as central templates dictated. The present reticence of current administrators to experiment with breaking up state farms may also reflect the fear of instability on the tundra. The most important lesson of this collectivization debacle was that expropriation of land or animals had to be reciprocated through the creating of allegiances to certain civic institutions fractured by nationality and by *kollektiv*.

Most accounts of the building of collectives in the lower Yenisei valley are much less dramatic. In the majority of cases, collectivization involved the collaboration of the poorest producers in the early days of involvement with Soviet officials. Early work-units then were invigorated through a contract with one or more wealthy *kulak* producers. The story of collectivization on the Khantaika followed a standard pattern for Taimyr. The first written description of Khantaika Evenkis, composed by the Territorial Formation Officer who came to authorize boundaries around the 'Khantaika-Tungus Clan Council', stressed the poverty which initially attracted Soviet organizers:

The Khantaika Evenkis are an extremely closed and isolated group of producers . . . Very rarely, not more than two or three times a year, they go out to sell the results of their hunting to the Yenisei trading posts—mostly the Plakhino Factory . . . Their wealth in reindeer . . . is very low. Their main instruments of hunting can be distinguished by their primitive character and their insufficient quantity. If we count the complete subsistent economy, the complete lack of cultural and medical assistance, their distance from markets, and the harshness of their nomadic lifestyle, then it becomes completely clear why this group of Evenkis have come . . . to be in their well-known crisis [of dying-out]. I should add that here one finds only 7.4% speak Russian and not a single literate [person] (AMAE K2–1–127: 4).

The forty Evenki households living along the shoreline of Lake Khantaika were among the last to be reached by the Soviet state due to the difficulty of their geographic location.[5] They lived entirely outside of the gaze of the first Party workers who arrived in Dudinka (GAKK R1845–1–224: 55). They were not canvassed in the polar census of 1926/7 (Sibirskii 1928), and once targetted to become a nomadic council in 1928 only one-quarter of their one

[5] Instructor Turenko, who wrote this report, undoubtedly spent his time with 25 of the poorest families in Dec. 1930. The wealthier and more mobile families had probably left for hunting areas further south. It is ironic that much of his writing, like those of most people who visit the Khantaika, complains of the harshness of weather which delayed his return home by several months.

thousand reindeer had became state property by 1939 (GATAO 2–1–27). The bloody repressions of the late 1930s did not seem to have a memorable impact on Khantaika Evenkis (unlike, for instance, on the Avam tundra), perhaps due to their poverty and isolation. Indeed most contemporary stories of the *gulag* genre tend to be action sagas of young men and women cleverly avoiding the threat of escaped prisoners from the labour camps at Noril'sk, Dudinka, and Igarka.

The relative isolation of Khantaika Evenkis from the Soviet industrial economy did not shield them long from the tempo of change all over rural Russia. When Party Instructor Turenko left the Khantaika in February 1931, he took with him a map and an inventory of the tools and reindeer of nine 'poor' and the one 'middle' household. On the basis of this data, the association 'Red Trapper' [*tovarishchestvo 'Krasnyi Promyshlennik'*] was formed with nineteen members and 110 head of reindeer (GATAO 2–1–12: 1). The name chosen for the work-unit featured an inspired lexical error which was none the less prescient of the changes awaiting these families. A *promyshlennik* in literary Russian refers to an industrialist or manufacturer (while a *promyslovik* is a hunter or trapper). The root of both, *promysl*, is an old word with sacred connotations referring to the providence which comes of acting in the world typically by harvesting wealth from the earth. The slippage of meaning from religious notion of 'providence in nature' to the directed notion of industrialism captures nicely the transition to the second stage of collectivization.

The association was upgraded to the work-unit 'Red Trapper' [*artel' 'Krasnyi Promyshlennik'*] in 1939 when a wealthy Yelogir household 'gave' their herd of 391 reindeer to the farm. The exact conditions governing this transfer are difficult to determine. The contemporary Yelogirs on the Khantaika are rumoured to be descended from a rich ancestor. Most stories of their wealth have a mythic quality. Almost every elderly man told me with a glint in his eyes of the great lost riches in gold and fur which the Yelogirs buried on the far side of '[Treasure] Chest Mountain' [*sunduk gora*]. The knowledge of this rumoured wealth was taken to the Upper World when two Yelogir brothers perished as heroes during the Second World War. Nikolai Savel'evich, a grandson to the 'rich' Yelogirs through his mother, spoke once to me of the awe he experienced as a young boy (*circa* 1938) when he saw a 'huge' herd of reindeer blacken the frozen surface of Lake Khantaika until the face of the lake collapsed under the weight of the herd. Whether or not the herd that Nikolai Savel'evich remembered was the *kulak* herd is difficult to say, but his image and the date are appropriate. None of these individuals would speak to me about exactly how many reindeer their forefathers had or indeed how it came to be that these reindeer were 'given' [*daril*] to the farm. Guessing from the date of this 'gift', it is likely that the Yelogir family cannily turned over a portion of their herd to the state only when it became completely obvious that the carefully woven net of nomadic councils and collective farms had finally fallen upon the Putoran mountains. Up until 1939, there are fragmentary records of wide travels of rich herders from Lake Yessei, to the Kamen' trading post, and finally to Lake Khantaika—a triangle of several thousand kilometres.[6] By being the first to 'donate' a large herd, the Yelogir family and thereby the Khantaika Evenkis both placated Soviet organizers but also made a substantial investment in the new collective organization. It is not without reason that Nikolai Savel'evich and his kin look upon the contemporary incarnation of 'Red Trapper', the state farm Khantaiskii, as 'our [Evenki] farm' thereby echoing older ideas of posses-siveness for a certain social setting.

Although 'Red Trapper' was fully within the administrative framework of the Soviet rural economy by the Second World War, it functioned indepen-dently of its official administrators in Dudinka. From 1937 to the 1960s the farm fed the state with furs (sable and arctic fox), leased reindeer for hauling freight, and provided wild deer venison and fish to the hungry sedentary employees of the settlement offices. During this era before snowmobiles and helicopters, the mobile economy was supported by reindeer bred, trained, and kept especially for transport (and not for meat). This necessitated a herd structure favouring a higher number of castrated male reindeer and a lower proportion of breeding females (Table 3), which in turn implied a specific division of labour. Castrated male reindeer would be kept in the winter by households, widely dispersed across the tundra, in order to service a large network of deadfall traps set on windswept hummocks [*pasti, langil*—Ev] (Plate 10). To give an example of the extent of this network, an archived map within the office of the state farm enumerates the locations of some 1,800 deadfall traps in 1957 which had to be constructed out of hand-hewn logs, kept clean of snow, and checked every two days. When the trapping season ended, the reindeer would be released at whatever spot the trappers estab-lished their summer camp. The reindeer, by the force of an instinctive fidelity to their birth pastures would regroup themselves by gradually making an unaccompanied journey of ten to one hundred kilometres high up to the cool, windswept plateau. A small group of young men would meet the herd at the expected time and place for the summer to guard it from predators and to lead it on to desirable pastures. Below, on the banks of lakes and rivers, their older male and women kin would catch, clean, and salt fish for exchange to

---

[6] In 1941 there were five Yelogir households registered to the Khantaika, each privately holding the legal maximum of 25 head of reindeer. If one assumes that the donated reindeer herd was used collectively, it is possible that the Yelogirs once controlled a herd of approximately 541 head. The Yelogirs most likely continued to use portions of the collective herd of 391 head for transportation and may have been given responsibility for pasturing the herd. In archived accounts of the 1926/7 census expedition there is reference made to a rich 'D'elegir' family living in the interior of the Putoran plateau with 300 head of reindeer some 500 km. from the Khantaika (TsGARF A310–18–67: 100–1).

TABLE 3. The structure of reindeer herds on the Khantaika in approximate five-year intervals, 1930–1993

Year	% Cows/ Total	Transport Bulls	Cows	Calves	Total
PPO RED TRAPPER					
1930 Total	22.1	632	179	⇐	811
Kulak herds (1 case)	22.0	86	24	included	110
Middle herds (15 cases)	24.8	360	119	w/cows	479
Poor herds (21 cases)	16.2	186	36	⇐	222
Average (31 herds)	23	17	5		22
WORK–UNIT RED TRAPPER					
1937 Total	46.1	232	460	212	998
Kulak herds (2 cases)	59.3	53	184	57	310
artel' Members (total)	36.4	213	326	206	896
high example	37.0	10	30	25	81
low example	42.9	3	3	0	7
average (41 herds)	36	5	8	5	22
1942 Total	40.1	327	452	209	1,127
In private use	44.9	216	297	96	661
[1947 No Data]					
1952 Total	47.9	N/A	1,089	963[A]	2,275
1957 Total	50.8	N/A	1,504	985[A]	2,961
1962 Total	46.8	N/A	1,778	1,271[A]	3,800
1967 Total	47.4	282	1,965	1,349[A]	4,032
SOVKHOZ KHANTAISKII					
1969 Total	44.8	307	1,414	689	3,156
Transport brigade (No. 1)	53.3	122	345	96	647
Production brigade (No. 3)	40.5	66	440	89	1,084
1972 Total	61.2	257	1,986	580[A]	3,243
[1977 No Data]					
1982 Total	45.7	N/A	1,778	1,023[A]	3,888
1987 Total	43.8	N/A	2,150	N/A	4,904
1993 Total	35.9	548	1,575	885[A]	4,385

N/A Not available.

[A] These figures were extrapolated from percentages.

Sources: 1930: GAKK 2275–1–22; 1937: GATAO 2–1–8: 5 & 2–1–27; 1942: GATAO 85–1–22; 1952, 1957: Otdel (1961); 1962: Staticheskoe (1967); 1969: GATAO 92–1–1: 29–32; 1967, 1972: Nauchno (1976); 1982: Administratsiia Taimyra; 1987: Petrushin (1992); 1993: *sovkhoz* 'Khantaiskii'.

the state trading co-operative. In the autumn, after the breeding season, the older castrated bulls and four-year bulls would once again be separated from the summer herd to travel the tundra as transport reindeer. One or two families would be assigned to tend to the herd of females, young bulls, and the calves over the winter. Such a division of labour of people and animals maximized the mobility of individuals across a vast territory and thus minimized the capacity of the state to control the structure of the work-unit, the number of reindeer, and the uses to which they were put. The decades of the 1950s and 1960s are remembered with fondness as a time when the tundra was filled with small family groups using harnessed reindeer to trap and fish.

Plate 10. Deadfall traps above Lake Khantaika with a wild deer hunting party in the background

Elders remember travelling with sleds or on saddles to visit kinsfolk all over the contemporary territory of the state farm, and in many other communities to the north, south, and in the rugged interior of the Putoran plateau. The relative flexibility of a trapping and hunting economy was dramatically different from the industrial economy introduced in the late 1960s with its long orbitals in the company of proud but lonesome bachelors ending in rowdy returns to the village to count the reindeer and to purchase supplies.

During the heyday of the mobile hunting economy, the built environment of the Khantaika Evenkis was very transitory. Hunters, travelling by harnessed reindeer with small portable conical tents, would choose a new campsite every two or three days and only periodically return to the settlement. Today the peninsulas and estuaries along the shore of Lake Khantaika are still dotted with abandoned tent frames, underground huts [*golomol*], idols [*khomdisar*], and burial places marking dozens of former home sites. The conglomeration of built institutions that Russian label as a village, was also scattered along the shores of the lake until the early 1960s. The most intense sedentary site was the boarding school located at the mouth of the Khakancha river with a full-time teacher, a local support person, and approximately twenty students. The one-room trading post 'Taimyr Factory' was located some ten kilometres away at the site of the present village. Seven kilometres across the lake on the opposite shore was a warehouse dug into the permafrost. The Khantaika Nomadic Council from 1936 to 1952 consisted of two officers who moved alongside other hunters. In 1952 the nomadic council became a 'village' council [*sel'skii sovet*]. To fulfil the legal title, brigades of labourers originally deported from the Germanic Volga, from Poland, and from the Baltic states built the structures of the present settlement. With the moving of the school, log by log, to the settlement site in the mid-1950s one might say that the settlement came to resemble a bounded locus of activity and a focus for the growth of a national sentiment.

The process by which collectives were built—collectivization—is commonly understood to be the bald dispossession of property from indigenous users (Osherenko 1995; Fondahl 1998). Although sentient resources such as land or harness reindeer were fed into a complex bureaucratic system, it is important to emphasize that local people also received a certain status as belonging to particular productive communities and to particular nations. While both the reindeer and the territory of the Number One Reindeer Brigade belonged formally to an amorphous state hierarchy, the actions of the herders demonstrate that they are at least relatively autonomous managers of this 'resource' if not de facto 'owners'. Of particular interest here is the fact that during the Soviet period, the sense of entitlement to these spaces and animals became encapsulated to particular collectives, on special territories, and of unambiguous national designations. On one level, this form of 'socialist land enclosure' can be directly compared to similar processes of land rationalization within the global capitalist economy (Anderson 1991; Fondahl 1998). However, socialist enclosure was legitimated on several other levels unique to a state socialist economy such that producers found themselves 'belonging' not only to territories but to special cultural projects and to special kinship groups.

Industrial parochialism

Ernest Gellner's (1983) classic statement on nationalism correctly correlates the growth of national identity with the creation of a 'mobile, literate, culturally standardized, interchangeable population' linked to a discrete political unit. Communities which are founded upon the exchange of commodities and a specialized division of labour are thought to experience a peculiar type of social interaction where contact between persons is fleeting and often mediated through roles authorized by formal education or legal contracts. A recent restatement of this modernist vision is representative of many accounts which place an optimistic accent upon the liberating effects of specific technologies which overcome the presumed parochialism of the pre-industrial age:

the power of the nationalist idea—that people should share a culture and be ruled by someone co-cultural with themselves—seems historically novel. The crude logistics of most societies in history—bereft of effective mass communication and cheap transport—meant that most human beings were stuck in highly particularized segments, quite unable to share a sense of destiny with people they had no chance of meeting (Hall 1993: 3).

The history of the lower Yenisei valley, like that of other places at the margins of Europe (Wolf 1982), empirically contradicts this faith in the novelty of a cosmopolitan modern age. Before the development of hierarchical civil institutions, mechanized but centrally allocated transport, and heavily regulated sources of mass communication, Evenkis and Sakhas travelled extremely widely, maintained a network of kin over thousands of kilometres, and traded stories in several languages. The dominant pattern stamped upon rural Siberia with the increasing tempo of industrial development, rather than cosmopolitanism, has been a narrowing of the space available for movement and a restriction in opportunities for advancement and social intercourse. By the mid-1960s, the villages and work-units first founded in 1938 came to be anchor points for the 'highly particularistic segments' known as *kollektivy*. As Gellner's prescient formulation suggests, formal education and most importantly formal *regulation* fed the flames of nationalism even in this weakly urbanized periphery of the Soviet industrial state. However, these vague sociological processes beg the question of which social segment should be the flag-bearer of the nationalist sentiment. The irony of Soviet statecraft was that although a solidarity to the international working class was overtly prescribed (and loyalty to the Fatherland overtly implied), the politics of day-to-day life necessitated a stronger sense of allegiance to localized communities of producers with their own peculiar national destinies. Soviet administrative and territorial forms effectively recentred the allegiance of Evenkis from 'their own' clans, lands, and tundra-masters to a highly localized understanding of an Evenki nation. This 'liberation' from their reliance on a complex living landscape can only be described as an effect of an industrially produced parochialism.

The production of tightly organized national communities in Siberia was paradoxically connected to the process known as the 'consolidation' [*ukrup-nenie*] of economic enterprises. Although the rhetoric of the day identified this as an 'evolution' in productive activity, the experience of living in a state farm tended to involve an 'involution' of practice within increasingly smaller parcels of land and smaller groups of people (Geertz 1963). This book argues that tight spaces and directed networks of Soviet industrialism fostered a form of inward-looking solidarity among people who were once skilled in forming extensive alliances. The roots of national resentment can be found in the industrial reforms of the early 1960s and 1970s.

Consolidation implied several subsidiary processes which had far-reaching effects on people's biographies and on the local ecology. First and foremost among the new policy initiatives was the centripetal process of forcibly resettling people into relatively large, fixed villages. This campaign, known as the 'transition from nomadic to sedentary life', has been described in a barrage of authorized government texts (for example, see Lashov & Litovka 1982). A secondary but significant development was the centrifugal process of instilling a complex division of labour wherein tasks were specialized among a diverse spectrum of professions. This had the latent effect of specializing tasks among nationalities, and creating a population that was divided between strictly sedentary segments and highly nomadic ones.

Among stories of forced resettlement and urbanization in Siberia (Chichlo 1981; Vitebsky 1992; Fondahl 1996), the creation of the village Khantaiskoe Ozero stands as one of the more dramatic cases. Up until 1968, the Khantaika was a predominantly Evenki community concerning itself with low-intensity reindeer husbandry and extensive travel over a wide landscape. Within five years a diffuse population, living in an arc 800 kilometres wide along the front ranges and interior of the Putoran mountains, was resettled onto a thin peninsula in the middle of Lake Khantaika. As a result of consolidation, the population of the area would double, the structure of economic activity would shift towards intensive forms of reindeer husbandry and fishing, and a crowded built environment would become the locus of activity for the majority of people. Among the more fateful aspects of consolidation was the wholesale resettlement of an entire community of Dolgan, Evenki, and Sakha from a different watershed and in a different ecological zone. The literal dropping of this community by aircraft onto the banks of Lake Khantaika created social and economic challenges which to a great extent are still being fought out in the community today.

The newcomers, who will be called the Mountain People,[7] originally lived in the environs of the trading post [*faktoriia*] Kamen' some 400 kilometres north-east on the Aiakli river drainage (see Map 2). The word *kamen'* is the vernacular Russian word for the escarpments of this region of the Putoran plateau which provide hunting grounds for wild deer in the spring and autumn and cool insect-free pastures for domestic reindeer in the summer. The Mountain People [*kamentsy*] were a heterogeneous collection of Evenki, Dolgan, and Sakha hunters and reindeer herders (Vasilev & Tugolukov 1960). Their territory, activities, and genealogies at one time had interwoven closely with those of Evenkis on Lake Khantaika, but after the strict establishment of authorized boundaries and fixed settlements in the 1950s the paths of these two groups intersected with less frequency. This was to change in 1969 when a Russian 'with a loud voice' gave the Mountain People a single day to pack two bundles of possessions into awaiting military cargo planes. It

---

[7] Those people who were born in the region of the Kamen' trading post are called locally by Evenkis as *kamentsy*—a word which has no satisfactory English equivalent ['mountaineers', 'highlanders']. The phrase 'Mountain People' comes closest to representing the name of the village but runs the risk of indicating that Khantaika Evenkis also do not live in a mountainous area.

was announced that the state had allotted them new houses and hunting areas
in a settlement much more consistently supplied with trade goods than their
trading post on the shallow-bottomed Aiakli river. Reindeer herders were
given the special exhortation to take their reindeer overland with the promise
that they would be empowered to instruct the Khantaika herders in how to
manage the larger herds. The former homes of the Mountain People were
abandoned and their hunting territories along Lake Aian were turned into
the Putoran Protected Area, a zone into which no unauthorized native family
was allowed to venture. It is a sadly predictable tragedy that the settlers
arrived to find that no houses had been built for them, that the Khantaika
store was poorly stocked to cope with such an influx of settlers, and that local
Evenkis took poorly to instruction.

Urbanization and resettlement is not an uncommon policy option in the
circumpolar North or developing regions (Honigmann 1966; Kennedy 1985;
Cernea & Guggenheim 1993). A unique quality of this process in Siberia was
the somewhat contradictory desire of economists to use urbanization as a
strategy to intensify *rural* production. As in all places, the necessity of
resettlement was justified on the practical grounds that the consolidation
of the population made it more 'efficient' and 'cost-effective' to deliver
services such as schooling and electricity. However, the actual selection of
which populations to crowd together was driven, once again, by the vision of
creating an industrial form of reindeer husbandry. Archival documents show
that as much as Khantaika Evenkis were understood to be loyal servants of
the socialist order, they were thought to be 'undisciplined', 'unproductive',
and 'uncultured'. The solution to their retraining was to import a population
of large-scale herders from Kamen' in order to 'raise the level of culture' of
the local population. In Party documents, the Mountain People were lauded
for their skills in keeping large herds. By contrast, local Evenkis were
criticized for their lack of discipline in increasing herd size:

For the removal of serious deficiencies and for the significant increase in the
qualitative indicators of reindeer ranching [*olenevodstvo*], the administration and
party organizations of the [Khantaiskii] *sovkhoz* are to assemble all reindeer brigades
with experienced reindeer ranchers from the ranks of the reindeer ranchers from the
Kamen' division of the Volochanka *sovkhoz* and other enterprises. They are to take
decisive measures for the intensification of productivity, the discipline of the reindeer
ranchers, and the strengthening of control over the respect of all zoological-
veterinarian regulations (A. Rosliakov, Oct. 1970, GATAO 92–1–6: 3).

When the Mountain People arrived on the Khantaika, they were immediately
given posts as professional herders while all of the local herders were pushed
into positions as fishermen. Within six years it became evident that the skills
of the imported herders were not sufficient for a terrain that was much more
densely forested and endowed with the salt licks and mushroom growths

which drive herds of reindeer to distraction. After importing over 1,000 Nenets reindeer between 1970 and 1973 into the new *sovkhoz* 'Khantaiskii', only to have them lost during the summer or during the rutting season, the state eventually permitted local Evenkis to work as herders. Although the skills of the Khantaika herders were vindicated, the sour taste of enforced competition made for an uneasy acceptance of the newcomers. It also underscored the importance of having control over one's own productive community.

In the late 1960s similar statistically inspired resettlements were repeated all over Taimyr. By 1968, the twenty-five work-units of the lower Yenisei valley were transformed into six large state farms [*sovkhozy*] specializing in reindeer herding. It might be said that this was the date when the collectivization process was completed by finally turning Taimyr into one big laboratory of socialist reindeer husbandry. The best proof of this tendency is geographical. The interlocking territories of these six enterprises, which encompass the entire landscape of the lower Yenisei valley, are ironically roughly the same size and shape as the original territories mapped out for nomadic councils by Territorial Formation Officers in the early 1930s (Tables 4 and 5).

Although the great resettlements of the late 1960s brought people into dense proximity, radical reforms in the division of labour set them off on diverging trajectories. Until 1968, Khantaika Evenkis governed their relationships through kinship institutions and a deep intertwining of a person's biography with land. The spectrum of official professions supported by the work-unit 'Red Trapper' probably did not exceed ten formal job descriptions (although factually all people were engaged in multiple, overlapping activities). Following the formation of the state farm 'Khantaika',

TABLE 4. The titles, locations, populations, and territories of the First Rural Institutions in the lower Yenisei valley, *circa* 1937

Nomadic Councils	Central Location	Population (% Native)	Territory (ha)
Khantaiskii-Evenkiiskii	Taimyr Factory	139 (N/A)[A]	2,197,536[A]
olen'sovkhoz	Potapovo	N/A (N/A)	1,172,793[A]
Noril'sk-Piasinskii	Chasovniia	306 (N/A)[A]	3,819,253[A]
Luzinskii	Luzino Station	46 (N/A)[A]	639,995
Karasinskii & Khantaiskii	Karasino Station	506 (N/A)[A]	6,365,828[A]
Ust'-Kureiskii	Lake Munduiskoe	140 (N/A)[A]	N/A
Plakhino-Evenkiiskii	Plakhino Factory	75 (70.0%)[A]	1,330,582[A]
Taimyrskii	Lake Taimyr	102 (100.0%)[B]	N/A
Dolgano-Zarechenskii	Dolgany Factory	315 (82.5%)[B]	406,691[A]
Avamo-Nganasanskii	Avam River	301 (100.0%)[B]	N/A

N/A Not available.

[A] TsGARF A310–18–21[1932].
[B] AMAE K2–1–129 &130 [1939].

TABLE 5. The titles, locations, populations, and territories of the contemporary state farms in the lower Yenisei valley, 1990

State Farm & Settlement Council	Central Location	Population (% Native)	Territory (ha)
sovkhoz Khantaiskii, Khantaika Council	Khantaiskoe Ozero	540 (88.1%)	1,973,423
OPKh Potapovskoe, Potapovo Council	Potapovo	509 (49.5%)	1,379,121
sovkhoz Yenisei, Levinskii Council	Levinskie Peski	467 (49.9%)	13,894
sovkhoz Volochankskii, Volochanka Council	Volochanka	942 (80.3%)	4,130,805
GPKh Taimyrskii, Ust'-Avam Council	Noril'sk	701 (90.6%) [in Ust'-Avam]	562,514
sovkhoz Piasino, Dudinka City Council	Dudinka	N/A	1,813,627

N/A Not available.

tasks and resources became parcelled out according to paper credentials, performance indicators, and eventually by nationality. Beginning in 1970, the entire state stock of 4,000 reindeer was divided into separate herds to be managed by professional brigades. Ideally, brigades were to function as task-oriented units disciplined to achieve high production indicators and not to be distracted with subsidiary concerns such as service to relatives, fur-trapping, or wild deer hunting. Herds were to have a 'progressive' structure with a preferred population of 60 per cent cows to calves, transport deer, and breeding males. This necessitated a culling of highly trained male reindeer used for transport. The remuneration structure was changed for these newly designed professional units so that herders would be paid by the number of reindeer that they kept (and not by the value of meat, furs, or transport provided). In fact, if one examines accounting ledgers, the line items for reindeer used for clothing or for food for the herders are labelled as losses. In effect, people were assigned to herds in order to ensure the reproduction of the animals instead of herds being kept to assist in the reproduction of human units (cf. Humphrey 1983: 258 ff.).

To both villagers and planners, one of the most fundamental differences in the new state farm was the burgeoning professional structure. According to rural economic statutes, state farms were obliged to have a large number of specialists in various sectors, all of whom were to hold formal qualifications. Thus, from 1970 onward not only were the Mountain People injected into the local community, but large numbers of 'newcomers' [*priezhie*] were hired to fill the statutory positions. According to a document produced by the personnel officer for the farm Khantaiksii in 1992, the farm employed 191 individuals in 43 different occupations corresponding to the following official 'sectors': (1) the Administrative Apparatus; (2) the Fur-Farmers; (3) the [Barge] Fleet; (4) the Motor Park and Power Stations; (5) Construction; (6) Reindeer Herders; (7) Tent-Workers [*chumrabotnitsy*]; (7) Fishermen; (8) the Fisher-Hunters; (9) the Hunters [*okhotniki-promysloviki*]; (10) the Labourers; (11) the Seamstresses. Each sector had its own administrative structure and, most importantly, its own understanding of *kollektiv*. For example, the employees of the Motor Park, Construction, and the Barge Fleet, who were primarily seen as newcomers, had their own exclusive executive member in the Administrative Apparatus. The fur-farmers, reindeer herders, and hunters, the majority of whom were Evenki or Dolgan, were overseen by the animal technicians [*okhotovod, zootechnik*]. In the case of the reindeer herders, each local *kollektiv* was administered by a brigadier (who was not a member of the Apparatus).[8] The tent-workers, labourers, and seamstresses, the vast majority of whom were native, were all administered by the personnel officer. Although the new professional structure generated a complex network, within which native producers were poorly placed to compete, one overriding fact made the division of labour seem particularly lopsided. Until 1989 the ledger books of the state farm clearly show that the payroll of the farm was highly weighted in favour of services provided by newcomers; ranging from house construction to book-keeping, the sub-sidized delivery prices set by the state implied that the net income of the farm came exclusively from the sale of primary products from the tundra, of which reindeer meat was one of the most important. Although between 1960 and 1992 the proportion of *tundroviki* in the adult working population declined from approximately 60 per cent to 35 per cent, their labour under-wrote the income of 90 per cent of the working population. While the rhetoric of the day encouraged all *khantaiskie* to think of themselves as part of a single farm, it is quite clear that phenomena such as state nomadism and the subsidized disjuncture in income placed various groups within this tightly packed community into distinct solitudes.

The objective of consolidation, with its emphasis upon fixed communities and a baroque division of labour, was classically modernist. The tasks per-formed by any individual on the Khantaika, be they a *pastukh* or a teacher, bore some relation to the same sets of practices performed by a cattle herdsman in Kazakhstan or a teacher in Odessa. However, the centralized nature of the redistributive economy created its own peculiar barriers to the vision of an interchangeable population of workers. In addition to the fact that opportunities of formal education were allocated according to tight social

---

[8] The brigade form of labour organization for a short period of time had also been used for the hunters and fishermen. By the mid-1970s it had been discarded in favour of contracts privately adjudicated with primarily Russian fishermen and the director of the state farm.

networks, the industrial transformation of the landscape created physical roadblocks to mobility. The most obvious ecological changes have been produced by the mining and smelting conglomerate at Noril'sk now known legally as 'Noril'sk Nikel' and simply called locally 'the Factory' [*kombinat*]. In order to feed this major smelting enterprise several energy corridors were constructed. The three features of most salience to the Khantaika are the natural gas pipeline from the left bank interior to the city of Noril'sk, and the two hydroelectric reservoirs (one on the Khantaika river) with their electric transmission lines. Of equal if not greater impact are the concentric rings of heavy metal and sulphur dioxide pollution coming from the factory (see Map 3). The effects of industrial development are complex but can be roughly described as an expanding ring that leaves the land barren of human activity within its compass. One of the more dramatic impacts of this zone of polluted land has been a shift in the migration routes of the Taimyr population of wild deer such that they no longer intersect the chain of native villages in a north/south trajectory but migrate east/west into lands where they are not expected. With respect to local domestic reindeer, the results of pollution and obstructions have forced native hunters and herders (as well as Russian hunters) to search out new lands along the peripheries of their former territories exaggerating the patterns of their nomadic orbits around the village. The fact that the territory in between the Khantaika and any major centre can no longer provide pastures for domestic reindeer in effect starved out any locally controlled means of transport. Thus, since the 1960s, one can sketch out a change in spatial activity from a network of small, evenly spaced communities arranged along traditional transportation routes to a pattern of peripheral settlements, cut off from one another by pollution and energy corridors, serving as centres for nomadic hunters and herders.

   The building of the settlement from the early 1950s to the 1970s has left its mark on the daily practices of the people. Physically, the settlement became the focus of social life due to the dependence of both schoolchildren and many of their parents on housing, electricity, and the central agencies of redistribution. Professionally, the activities of people have been organized into occupational categories which have a great impact on the way that people rank themselves. Ecologically, the intensified use of particular territories was to have the most far-reaching implications for the health of the people as well as their flexibility in trying to reorganize in the wake of the abdication of the central bureaucracies. The inflated national categories in circulation within the village can be understood as an attempt to advertise to the distant agencies that Evenkis and Dolgans still live on the Khantaika and deserve to be better treated.

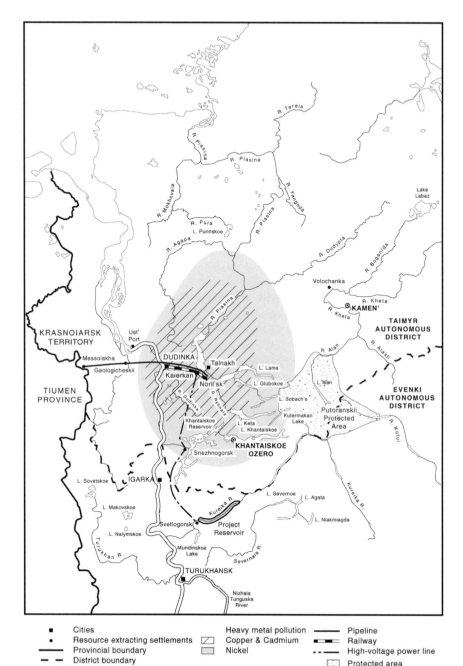

Map 3. The effect of industry and resettlement: approximate areas of heavy metal pollution and energy corridors, *circa* 1993

The 'villagers'

Upon each arrival on the Khantaika, one is constantly struck with the crowded living conditions of the village. With the eyes of a newcomer arriving from Dudinka, it was surprising to traverse several hundred kilometres of mountain plateau and forest to find an enclave harbouring six hundred people on a peninsula that was no more than forty hectares in area. The same dense quality of life is also a surprise for the person returning to the village after several months on the tundra. From the point of view of a *tundrovik*, however, the village seems teeming with activity and conviviality as if it were a metropolis in its own right. For the members of the Number One Reindeer Brigade the village is nicknamed 'the City' to emphasize its intensely social nature in comparison to that of life on the land.

The physical appearance of the present settlement reflects its stages of development. Nearest to the north bank are the old schoolhouse and the two rows of log houses built by the deportees. Until 1968 the village started and finished with these dozen structures (Tugolukov 1963). The buildings which date back to the formation of the state farm form the third row away from the bank. Here one finds the new school, the long offices of the farm and settlement administration [*kontora*], a statue to the productivity of the farm, and a series of four-apartment bungalows. The most noticeable construction extends further inland down into what was (and often becomes) a marsh. Following the forced resettlement of the Mountain People, a series of new houses were built in the 1970s which form the rows perpendicular to the lake. The amount of construction within the thirty years since the resettlement reflect poorly on the comfort of its residents. The old houses are single-family dwellings of modest size (approximately 20 square metres). The new houses are divided into four apartments of approximately fifteen square metres. Aside from these closely packed dwellings, families could also be found living in rooms of the old schoolhouse subdivided by makeshift walls and curtains until this structure burnt to the ground in 1995. There are three public outhouses located on the periphery in each of the main divisions of the town. They tend to be more frequently visited by hungry village dogs than by residents, who prefer to use a special pail in the shelter, warmth, and security of their own homes. The contents of these chamber buckets are then tossed in the open spaces between the houses where they await the spring thaw. The most memorable aspect of life in the village is the contrast between the bite of the winter winds as one negotiates the treacherous spaces between the homes, and the busy, cramped, and warm atmosphere of people's homes.

There are several social hubs within the settlement, which become active at various times of the day corresponding to the social rounds of different groups within the settlement. The central public spaces are the school, the building housing the settlement administration and the offices of the state farm, the bakery, and the store. In the morning, the trodden paths become alive with bundled clusters of children weaving their way skilfully around pools of garbage and sewage, and over or under utility corridors, on their way to school.[9] If it becomes known that the state farm's economist has returned from Dudinka, hunters and fishermen may queue in the frigid corridors of the state farm office to receive their back-pay and with a proud but quiet manner trade plug-cigarettes and recent news. At the end of the month, if the wind permits aircraft to land, pensioners may gather at the post office or single mothers may go to the settlement administration to receive their cash payments. At 11 a.m. children who happen not to be in school will collect fresh bread at the bakery to bring home to their parents. If a cargo aeroplane lands, women gather in the local store to examine the new products or clothes. As the noonday darkens, a scattering of young men might kick a ball around the only lit area of the settlement in front of state farm offices. In the shadows of the central beacon, groups of drunken men shuffle from door to door searching for cash before circling down to the house by the lakeshore, avoiding the tethered angry dogs, where everybody knows the bootlegger lives. Occasionally, the day-to-day business of settlement life is interrupted by the light of a snow machine on the horizon of the lake announcing the arrival of a hunter with the fresh meat of a wild deer—or more dramatically by a caravan of harnessed deer bringing the reindeer herders to town. On the Orthodox All Souls' Day and on the anniversaries of the deaths of individuals, mourning relatives walk over the small hill crowned by the fur farm to visit those who have passed on to the 'other settlement'. By the grave sites they gather to drink with the dead and to bring them their clothing, food, and personal items—all of which are ritually broken and left by the graveside— before exactingly, almost anxiously, retracing their steps back over the hill to face the sobering breeze.[10] In midsummer, the adolescents of the village hike beyond the cemetery to the 'big rock' jutting out from the lakeshore where they make campfires, gather berries, paint their names on the stone, or feed the rock gifts of coins in the manner of the elders.

The village depends on 'the Lake' for both its name and many of its daily routines. In the scale of the former Soviet Union, the deep volcanic beds of

---

[9] On the Khantaika, as in Arctic villages the world over, the permanently frozen layer of earth (permafrost) makes it impossible to provide central supplies of heat in underground pipes. The half of the settlement which is supplied with steam heat is connected to the central boiler by a system of overground pipes insulated in box-like utility corridors [*teplotrassy*]. In the heart of winter, most recipients of central heating also augment their comfort by firing their brick and mortar stoves [*russkaia pechka*] twice a day. Central heating and wood for the stoves is supplied by the state farm for a token fee.

[10] According to Evenki cosmology, the spirits of those in either the Upper World or the Lower World remain close by graves. If one circles a grave, the 'shadow' of the dead person will be able to 'catch' your trail causing illness or death. Dead souls are notoriously greedy for company and will stop at nothing to take the living with them. Graveyards are best avoided, but if entered, one is advised to always trace one's journey back the way one came.

Plate 11. Village youth playing ball by the productivity monument in front of the farm offices

the lake make it the fifth deepest (387 metres) and the third largest after lakes Baikal and Issyk-Kul (Dolgin & Romanov 1983: 68). In every season, fishermen draw tonnes of fish from its waters for household consumption and to balance the accounts of the state farm 'Khantaiskii'. In the summer, the twenty-four-hour daylight reflects off the lake's surface and along its agate beaches into the windows of every home. The lake also has a moody and unpredictable side. Since the construction of the hydroelectric dam and reservoir on the Khantaika river, the lake's sole outlet, the water is liable to either flood or strand the community behind an expanse of mud several metres deep. Travel to the outside world is delayed until the November freeze-up when the fogs relent and an ice landing strip can be prepared to receive aircraft. All trips onto the land start and end with a trip across the lake—and in the summer and autumn it characteristically claims the lives of some of those travellers. The older Evenki women know the lake as 'bad' and as 'greedy' since it takes bodies without surrendering them. New travellers, such as myself, are exhorted to feed it with a coin or a button before the journey starts.

The clearest social problem in the settlement (excepting alcoholism) is the lack of resources to adequately heat, house, and provide light for over 600 individuals on a narrow peninsula. Those who grew up on this home site recall how the spit was once covered with berries in the summer and stands of easily accessible wood in the winter before the resettlement of the Mountain People overpopulated the space. Presently, a state farm tractor operator ploughs an ice road ten to fifty kilometres up the nearby mountains to pull firewood into town. In high summer water is plentiful. In the winter snow machines, reindeer, and a single state farm horse are harnessed to haul water from the centre of the lake. In the springtime the pools of kitchen waste drain off into the lake causing gastrointestinal illness, parasitic infection, and the occasional outbreak of epidemic diseases.[11] The yearly shipments of building supplies, fuel, and wood, by river barge have become increasingly difficult to organize due to the uneven water level of the lake and the hazards of waterlogged stumps tearing themselves free from the drowned forests under the reservoir. The shortages of material are felt in every sector of settlement life from the lack of lumber to build, the shortage of wood for heating, and the interrupted supply of electricity from the power station. These shortages underscore the dependency of villagers upon the various state institutions whom they feed and from whom they expect service. This dependency contrasts remarkably with the self-reliant but modest life of *tundroviki* out on the land.

National rivalry

The arrival of the Mountain People on the Khantaika is still the source of many significant tales, especially when it comes to reflecting upon the various shortages which afflict the village. Filled with enthusiasm for their mission to raise the level of 'culture' of the *tongustar*, older women today still speak disparagingly of the lack of national pride the Evenkis displayed by dressing themselves in store-bought Russian clothing and by being shy to speak their own language. Evenki local historians speak of their shock of having to queue for the first time in their own store behind people dressed 'in skins' speaking 'rudely' in a private language. These polemical tales disguise the history between these people before the 1950s. Young Khantaika Evenkis today react with surprise when a Mountain elder switches from speaking Sakha to a fluent Evenki of the northern dialect.

Statistically, it is somewhat difficult to divide these two communities, although it is clearly divided in the minds of local residents. The two secretaries charged with keeping the settlement's household registries counted 536 individuals (49 per cent male) registered on the Khantaika in January 1992. If one takes only the native population (85 per cent of the residents), the villagers divide themselves almost equally with 41 per cent

---

[11] The head of a sanitary-epidemiological expedition in 1989, A. N. Borisov, wrote somewhat dramatically in his report that the 'serious housing and sanitation problems force the majority of the villagers to live in conditions degrading to human dignity'. His report identified 88 cases of dysentery and 33 cases of intestinal worms. In his estimation 88 individuals required new housing. There have been occasional outbreaks of hepatitis B and typhoid fever on the Khantaika. Tuberculosis is considered to be a problem in this village, as in most Siberian native villages.

officially registered as Evenki and 44 per cent registered as Dolgan (see Table 6).[12] However, local understanding of identity is much more subtle, taking into account indigenous language use, genealogy, place of birth, and the particular skills displayed when on the land. When Khantaika Evenkis are shown the official statistics of nationality they declare them to be a 'lie'. In their perception, 'real' Evenkis are in the minority and Dolgans are in the majority. Indeed if one divides the population between those 'native' to the Khantaika and those native to or descended from adults from the Kamen' trading post, the proportions shift. Although Evenkis are statistically as numerous as Dolgans, the numbers vastly favour the incoming Mountain people if identity is defined by place of origin (see Table 7). One could confirm this perception with a well-established technique in the toolbox of Soviet ethnography for measuring 'internationalism'. An analysis of marriage statistics shows a high degree of intermarriage between Evenkis and Dolgans (Anderson 1996a: 84). However, if intermarriage is stratified by vernacular group, one finds the near absence of intermarriage between Khantaika and Mountain Evenkis and the most number of marriages between each of the Mountain sub-groups. This phenomenon is symptomatic of the conflicts between the local and resettled factions.

It is tempting at first to explain this division in sentiment upon the clear competition over resources. As is explored in depth below, it is clear that newcomers, Mountain People, and local Evenkis compete unequally in the various sectors of the state farm. More globally, the trauma of resettlement is even visible in the demography of the community. The distribution of the population by age is weighted in favour of ages 15 to 30 with modest burgeoning of the infant groups (see Table 8). While progressive population structures are a characteristic of areas with recently established settlements (i.e. 'developing areas'), the population structure of this settlement is much more stable than many aboriginal settlements in the circumpolar Arctic (Milan 1980), North America (Young 1994), and in developing areas of Asia in the present and of Europe in the past (Chesnais 1992: 284–301). This has been accredited to the successes of health organizations in keeping down the infant mortality rate even as the rate of accidental, violent, and suicidal deaths of adults and children was high.[13] If the age and sex pyramid

---

[12] It has become a local bureaucratic tradition to record Evenki nationality for men and women as *evenk* and *evenka* instead of *evenkiiskii* and *evenkiiskaia*. This has led one historian (Popova 1991) and some central government tabulations to report the presence of Evens living on the Khantaika. Despite the administrative changes of 1959, some Dolgan individuals prefer to use their ethnonym when speaking Russian: *sakha*. Thus in Table 5 there is one Sakha individual who is from Taimyr and a one *yakut* individual from the Sakha Republic.

[13] Since 1990 there has even been a general tendency for the classically stable Soviet Siberian population structure to become regressive with a rise in violent adult deaths and infant mortality— although this scale of change is not yet visible in these tables (Pika & Prokhorov 1994: 162–77). On the Khantaika the common causes of death in the younger age groups are from diarrhoea or influenza

TABLE 6. Declared nationality of residents on
the Khantaika, 1992

Nationality	Count	Percentage
Evenki	223	41.6
Dolgan	237	44.2
Russian	52	9.7
Azerbaijani	7	1.3
Tatarin	4	.7
Enets	4	.7
Yakut	2	.4
Nganasan	1	.2
Sakha	1	.2
Moldavian	2	.4
Chuvash	1	.2
Ukrainian	1	.2
Polish	1	.2
TOTAL	536	100.0

for 1992 is compared to those for 1978 (Tables 8 and 9), it can been seen that the demographic structure has become less stable and more progressive. This shift in age seems to have more to do with an increased adult mortality rate than an exploding fecundity. In both tables, the higher mortality of males is quite noticeable as are the periods following critical events in the history of the settlement such as the resettlement of the Mountain People (1969–72), the Second World War (1945–50), and the Russian Civil War (1923–7). The forced resettlement seems to weigh as heavily upon the demography of the village as much as the two wars.

Khantaika Evenkis, however, tend to use symbolic arguments to explain what they interpret to be their weakening hegemony over their lands. People reflect upon what might be termed the 'aggressive' or 'impolite' character of the Mountain People. Khantaika nationalists often point out that instead of 'giving' their reindeer to the Soviet state, the Mountain People were forcibly expropriated through military force. Archival data tend to confirm at least a part of this story. A few years after the crushing of the Volochanka rebellion in 1932, Party workers discovered with some surprise that several extended Sakha families had managed to keep three large herds of reindeer hidden from the gaze of the state within the embrace of the Putoran mountains.

from polluted water. For the middle age ranges, death comes with murder, freezing, or drowning (all three related to alcoholism). In the above-50 age groups cancer, tuberculosis, and heart attacks (alcohol related) are common ailments. I was not able to get definite numbers for the causes of death in the settlement over time since, as the head of the regional medical service in Dudinka confided to me, there is often not enough money to confirm the exact cause of death. In the calendar years 1992 and 1993 there were 33 deaths. Drowning claimed 8 lives. Freezing claimed 3 people. The causes of 12 deaths were rumoured to be due to various illnesses from cancer, heart attacks, and tuberculosis. Five people perished in accidents (including one family in a house fire). One death was recorded as old age. Ten of the deceased were pensioners. Five were children under the age of 5.

Feeding the Village

TABLE 7. Nationality fractured by place of origin for
couples and single household heads, 1992

Nationality	Count	Percentage
KHANTAIKA GROUP		
Khantaika Evenkis	66	12.3
Potapovo Evenkis	7	1.3
Khantaika Dolgans	4	.7
Russian Settlers	7	1.3
MOUNTAIN PERSON GROUP		
Mountain Dolgans	117	21.8
Mountain Evenkis	50	9.3
NEWCOMERS		
Russian Newcomers	29	5.4
Azerbaijanis	5	.9
Moldavians	2	.4
Tatars	2	.4
Ukrainian	1	.2
Polish	1	.2
Chuvash	1	.2
OTHER SPARSE PEOPLES		
Enets	1	.2
Nganasan	1	.2
Sakha	1	.2
Yakut	1	.2
CHILDREN AND OTHER DEPENDANTS	240	44.8
TOTAL	536	100.0

Reputedly, the first surveys of this herd seem to have been done by a pistol-carrying 'veterinarian' sent to make inoculations (GANO R1072–2–3). Whatever the content of his negotiations, in 1941 5,238 reindeer suddenly appear on the books for the three neighbouring work-units of Spark [Kamen'], Stalin [Volochanka], and Shmidt [Volochanka].[14] As might be expected, the same set of events serve as a unifying myth for the Mountain People. The memory of the Volochanka uprising and of the way in which the state was deceived serves as a mobilizing symbol for resistance to the state and for unity between themselves.

Like many social facts in this region, the division in the community is more evident in action than in speech. In 1992 and 1993 there was war in

[14] The work-unit 'Spark' was first formed in 1939. According to B. O. Dolgikh, working as the Territorial Formation Officer in 1935, there were 27 'poor' households at Kamen' with 334 reindeer (average 13 reindeer per household), 22 'middle' households with 2,029 reindeer (average 92 reindeer per household), and 3 'rich' households with 3,155 reindeer. Of the *kulak* households the single Evenki household Elogir [*D'elegir*] had 300 reindeer, the two Yakut households Katyginskii and Maimago had 1,390 and 1,465 reindeer respectively. The work-unit was merged first with the Volochanka *sovkhoz* in 1966 as an independent unit [*otdelenie*] before being legally united with the *sovkhoz* Khantaiskii in 1968 (and physically united in 1969).

TABLE 8. Age and sex pyramid for the Khantaika, 1992

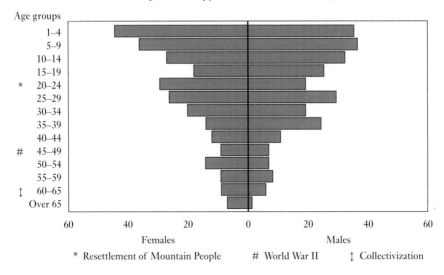

* Resettlement of Mountain People   # World War II   ‡ Collectivization

TABLE 9. Age and sex pyramid for the Khantaika, 1978

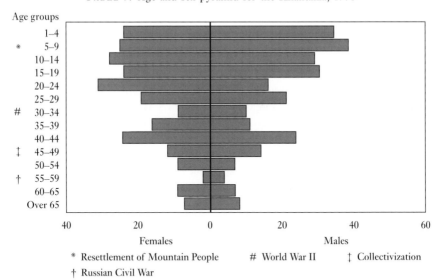

* Resettlement of Mountain People   # World War II   ‡ Collectivization
† Russian Civil War

Armenia and Georgia, a simmering dispute between Ukraine and Russia over
Crimean sovereignty, and two fatal brawls on the Khantaika over the issue of
who was Evenki and who was Dolgan. In relative terms, alcoholism and
unsafe housing kill more people in this remote settlement than national

rivalry. However, it is not the scale of conflict which makes the politics of nationality a striking phenomenon here. Unlike in Ukraine or the Caucasus, the history of the lower Yenisei valley is not one of battles to annex territory or the hearts and minds of people but instead the creative use of kinship and barter to form linkages over large territories. This is not to say that in this history there were no distinct identities. Before the arrival of ethnographers and other state agents there were many overlapping identities used to mark differences between people—but none of the distinctions were such that within a lifetime a person could not move from one to another or even hold several simultaneously. What is interesting about this case is that in a region far removed from other epicentres of nationalist conflict, but having a long history of contact with the same redistributive state, similar struggles are being acted out albeit on a modest scale.

Overt confrontations within the settlement are infrequent, but serve to accentuate a general climate of unease between the tightly packed villagers. In addition to violent fights, the sentiment of nationality can be openly expressed in a series of labels. Dolgans refer to both Mountain Evenkis and Khantaika Evenkis as *tongustar*—a label which, as the next chapter will show, has complicated connotations. While this term in some contexts may be used in a technical capacity, some Khantaika Evenkis take it as an insult; as meaning 'lower' [*nizhe*]. Evenkis for their part occasionally use the word *tehol*, which they take to mean 'foreigners' or 'outsiders'; or with a sharper tone point out that these settlers are 'merely Dolgan' with a pedigree less distinguished than peoples such as Yakuts or Russians. The labels are used in concert with a series of generalizations on national character. One or the other group will be said to be unclean, to speak Russian poorly, to be arrogant or unhelpful. A typical statement charged with national distinction might be a whispered accusation directed against a particular family seeking to take land away from 'our' state farm for private use; or a suspicious account of women plotting in 'their language' while waiting in a queue for food or social security cheques. I do not see a need to list these unpleasant generalizations in detail since it would create a misleading impression of the verbal intensity of this practice. Nationalist rivalry may slip out unexpectedly in conversation, as in this discussion on bootlegging with the young tent-worker Natasha in the Number One Reindeer Brigade:

Once after the [November] slaughter [*zaboi*] we had a lot of money. I wanted to do something with the money so that we could get ahead. I thought of going into business. After all, the *kamentsy* do it. I was going to buy some vodka and then sell it. But you see I would only sell to Evenkis. I don't like it the way that people just drink with anyone in the settlement. Evenkis should just drink with Evenkis. I would even give the vodka free to our relatives. But Vitia was against all of this. In the end the money just went.

For the most part the national division of the settlement takes the form of a frozen confrontation which is understood without elaboration. One finds that when in the company of Evenkis one rarely encounters a Dolgan. Mixed hunting teams between Dolgans and Evenkis are not assembled. When food is brought from the land it is distributed between Evenki and Dolgan households. Although it is impossible to design a table or questionnaire to show the scale of national rivalry in this settlement, the tensions in the store, the state farm office, and on the streets marked this phenomenon as the key social issue on the Khantaika during my fieldwork.

When the brittle peace of the settlement is broken upon a brazen display of favouritism within the office of the state farm, or after a drunken fight, the term that is used to describe the lack of balance is *natsionalizm*. Unlike the English word 'nationalism' this does not necessarily indicate a vision to create a sovereign political entity. Rather it is a pejorative term which signals that the formal rules of civil behaviour, distribution, or opportunity have been bent in an exclusive way. As in many parts of the former Soviet Union, residents of all nationalities on the Khantaika remark that 'before' national rivalry was not a problem in this settlement. Only upon the final days of the Soviet state and the new adventure into a reformed economy did the politics of national identity come to be a factor to be negotiated from day to day. Yet, until the tragic fire which foreshadowed my sudden departure from the settlement, the residents of the Khantaika took pride in the fact that their settlement was not as bad as others. The mixed Dolgan, Nia, and Evenki settlement of Ust'-Avam was often called 'Little Karabakh' in recognition of its heightened violence and the link of national rivalry in Taimyr to other outbursts of tension within the former Soviet Union.

In each of the following chapters the paradox of *natsionalizm* is elaborated in terms of the history of the people of the region and in terms of the peculiar problems which it creates when attempting to imagine the future. The formation of national rivalry is evident in the adherence to exclusive identities, territories, and an unsuccessful policy of national endogamy. Each of these three aspects is unseemly given the local history of the region and yet understandable given the history of the state. Through this detailed exposition of the history and contemporary practices of Evenkis and Dolgans on the Khantaika I show that national rivalry is a tragic but useful political strategy which does not feed upon archaic or 'pre-modern' sentiments but instead becomes practical within an ordered administrative system. By tracing the rise of this local phenomenon alongside the history of state practice of the region, this book draws from the very particular experience of this settlement to gain insights which may be applied to achieve a greater understanding of national identity in many other regions of the former Soviet Union.

4
The State Ethnographers

UNDERLYING THE SPECTACULAR mountains surrounding the Khantaika, there are said to be rich lodes of valuable metals. Their precise location is a secret known only to certain *tundroviki* who have long ago moved on to the Upper World and the brusque geologists who map these veins for eventual sale on foreign markets. Nevertheless the effects of the buried metals are pervasive. According to local rumour, the radio static which blocks communication between the settlement, the city, and neighbouring communities for days on end emanates from magnetic anomalies hidden below the surface. A less subtle impact of the metal ore is in the oxide taste of the north wind wafting down from Noril'sk.

The politics of national identity are not unlike the geology of the area. The divisions lying closest to the surface, and those most easily counted, are those official definitions of nationality mapped by ethnographers in the employ of the state. These are the veins which are exploited first in exchanges with official institutions. The richest deposits in day-to-day politics are those submerged in recent lived memories, such as in the memory of a newcomer or one of the resettled Mountain People. However, in-between these reserves there are still rarer vernacular compounds, which when examined and understood, show the contingent nature of the official terms which lie exposed at the surface.

It has become common to link the flavour of different ethnographic traditions to the interests of empires or of nation-states (Kuklik 1991; Stocking 1986, 1991; Slezkine 1994). The history of Russian ethnography can be understood to represent an extreme variant of this phenomenon, where the major part of the ethnographic record, especially in the Soviet period, has been commissioned, directed, and edited by state officials. The pronounced influence of the state does not invalidate the ethnographic record. Rather, it marks the existence of a unique administrative ideology whereby ethnography was wielded as a primary instrument of social power. Through ethnographic practice, state ethnographers created peoples, and made peoples disappear. Whether clumsily or skilfully applied, the national categories of the Tsarist and Soviet periods are key terms within the 'evocative transcripts' used in the struggle for resources (Humphrey 1994). In order to demonstrate the power of categorization in the lower Yenisei valley, this chapter suspends the governing assumption of Russian state ethnography that a single individual must unambiguously belong to a single nationality. By deriving the value of national labels, it will become possible to analyse the harsh speculation and inflation of identity which has so much inflected post-Soviet politics.

Sparse peoples and the Russian state

Great nations always intend to assimilate small groups, all of which potentially are the heirs of the great nations, and, consequently, dangerous . . . The ethnographers' intention to show the 'inferiority' of these small groups and the need of 'protecting them' results from the general attitude of the great nations and at the same time they work directly for the elaboration of such ideology; while they seek impartial truth, they are thus preparing the most perfected weapon for the ethnical struggle in the future. This is the reason why ethnography and anthropology are nowadays becoming fashionable—the extension of the inter-ethnic struggle requires a superior knowledge of neighbours (S. M. Shirokogoroff 1933: 168).

In the Russian ethnographic literature it is now considered proper to refer to aboriginal Siberian nationalities as 'less-numerous peoples' [*malochislennye narody*]. This phrase directly corresponds to the idea of there being demographically 'burgeoning' peoples [*mnogochislennye narody*] who, like Russians, do not count their numbers in thousands but in millions. These contemporary categories, which blend demography with identity, are significant for understanding Siberian politics. In contrast to similar designators in circulation world-wide such as 'natives', 'aboriginal peoples', or 'first nations', the terms used to speak of rural Siberians do not make explicit reference to a people's privileged relationship to a landscape. Instead, their special status within the Russian Federation is correlated directly to their population density. Within Russia, the most evocative quality of 'sparse' Siberian peoples is not so much their aboriginality as the demographic threat that they may cease to exist altogether. Rather than focusing political debate upon aboriginal lands, the 'endangered' quality assigned to Siberian peoples highlights the nationality of peoples, their purity, and the paternalistic responsibility of the state for their protection. While in Canada or Australia the discourse of aboriginality invigorates the legal procedures with tremendous political significance, the discourse of endangered identity in Russia endows a similar gravity to those responsible for counting and delineating rural nations—the state ethnographers.

There is no single people in Siberia which has escaped the shaping and careful categorization of ethnographers in the employ of the state. Although any text can be read for elements of categorization, within Russian texts one finds a heavy concern for specifying national boundaries, distilling the story of the origin of discrete peoples [*etnogenesis*], or ranking of peoples according to a quality of civilization. Typically, in addition to being authors of scholarly texts, the state ethnographers advised Commissars of Nationalities, took instructions from state committees, or guided the pens of cartographers who inscribe boundaries between administrative jurisdictions.

The recent idea in Russian politics that a people can be 'less-numerous' than they could or should be is an elaboration upon an old and demeaning

ambiguity within Russian ethnography. Within Imperial Russian ethnography, Siberian peoples were first distinguished as 'aliens' [*inorodtsy*] or
'infidels' [*inovertsy*] who potentially threatened the project of Imperial expansion (Slezkine 1994). As Russian hegemony over Siberia became firmly
established, political discourse shifted to the tragic motif that Russian
civilization might lead to the 'dying-out' [*umiranie*] of Empire's natives
(Gekker 1898; Patkanov 1911; Rychkov 1914*b*). Early Soviet rhetoric
modified both sides of the Imperial heritage with the paternalist idea of there
being 'small peoples' [*malye narody*], diminutive in *both* world-historical
importance and population. Instead of aggressively distancing themselves
from Siberian peoples, or passively watching their disappearance, the hallmark of Soviet ethnography was to analytically separate peoples [*narody*] who
were destined to be the leaders of scientific and cultural progress while
ensuring that those 'diminutive peoples' [*narodnosti*] relegated to supporting
roles were appropriately classified and protected (Stalin 1913; Kriukov 1989:
9–12; Kozlov 1992). The contemporary idea of Siberian peoples being
merely 'less-numerous' has jettisoned the Soviet and Russian Imperial ideal
of there being greater or lesser destinies to nations while continuing to
problematize the question of a people's persistence. The implication of this
special idiom is that a proper respectful relation between the state and the
nationalities will allow the smaller nations to grow, while an indifferent or
incompetent administration can be measured by the dilution or disappearance of its component peoples. Since this idiom privileges the idea of
population density over the idea of destiny (or that of aboriginality), the
term 'sparse peoples' will be used in referring to the less-numerous nationalities of Siberia.

Within the lower Yenisei valley, the state presently distinguishes eight
sparse nationalities by means of distinct Russian-language designators: *nentsy*
[Nenetses], *dolgany* [Dolgans], *entsy* [Enneches], *nganasany* [Nias],
evenky [Evenkis], *yakuty* [Yakuts], *sel'kupy* [Shol'kups], and *kety* [Ostyks].[1]
Despite the various concerns about the extinction of these sparse peoples, the
numbers for most of these nationalities have remained remarkably stable over
time. Rather than dying out, the sparse peoples of the lower Yenisei valley
have been transformed since 1928 into a statistical minority within arbitrary
administrative districts through the massive immigration of newcomers from
all parts of the former Soviet Union. The disproportion of newcomers to
natives in Taimyr, as in all northern regions, does not necessarily imply a
radical swing in the historic fate of these peoples. When considering statistical snapshots like that presented in Table 10, one has to keep in mind three

---

[1] Before 1928 these nationalities were known by the following overlapping terms: *samoedy*
[Nenetses, Enneches, Nias, Shol'kups], *ostiaky* [Nenetses, Khantis, Shol'kups], *yuraki* [Enneches],
tungusy [Evenkis, Evenis, Dolgans], *dolgany* [Dolgans], *yakuty* [Yakuts, Dolgans], and *yeniseitsy*
[Ostyks].

TABLE 10. Historical population dynamics of the lower Yenisei valley, 1926–1997[A]

Official Name	Vernacular Ethnonym (pl.)	Population						
		1997	1992	1979	1970	1959	1940	1926[B]
Dolgan—Total	Sakha (*Sakhalar*)	4,878	4,850	4,338	4,344	3,871	2,785	1,231
Taimyr		4,878	4,850	4,338	4,344	3,871	2,785	
Yakut—Total	Sakha (*Sakhalar*)	N/A	N/A	53	64	63	1,183	1,826
Taimyr		N/A	N/A	53	64	63	1,183	
Nenets—Total	Nenets (*Nenetsia''*)	2,419	2,452	2,345	2,247	1,789	1,704[C]	2,730
Taimyr		2,419	2,452	2,345	2,247	1,789	1,704	
Evenk—Total	Evenki (*Evenkil*)	450	467	444	413+	413+	1,121	832
Taimyr		292	316	338	413	N/A	563	
Turukhansk		158	151	106 (1988)	N/A	413	558	
Nganasan—Total	Nia (*Nia'*)	820	844	746	765	711	822	[867]
Taimyr		820	844	746	765	711	822	
Enets—Total	Enneche (*Enchu*)	130	105	N/A	179	18	—	[378]
Taimyr		130	105	N/A	179 (1966)	18	—	
Ket—Total	Ostyk (*Ostygan*)	762	718	78	N/A	N/A	N/A	{751}
Taimyr		0	0	0	0	2	0	29
Turukhansk		762	718	78	N/A	N/A	N/A	183
Sel'kup—Total	Shol'kup (*Shol'kupmyt*)	288	262	45+	N/A	N/A	N/A	{1,662}
Taimyr		0	0	N/A	N/A	N/A	N/A	18
Turukhansk		288	262	45	N/A	N/A	N/A	59

N/A Not available.

[A] Data for 1997, 1992, 1988, 1979, 1966, and 1959 are from working documents in the Department of the North and Arctic, Administration of Krasnoiarsk Territory. Data for 1940 come from the archives of the Administration of the Taimyr Autonomous District. Ethnonyms are taken from several native linguists who work as curriculum consultants for the Taimyr Teachers' College.

[B] All 1926 data are from *Materialy Pripoliarnogo Perepisa 1926–27* (Novosibirsk, 1929). This census used pre-Soviet geographic categories. The totals for Dolgans, Yakuts, Evenkis, and Nenets should correspond to contemporary boundaries. Working from the original source I estimated new totals for Kets and Sel'kups {in curly brackets} which represent their 1926 populations in Turukhanskii *krai excluding Tazovskaia volost'*. In this census the Enetses and the Nganasans were poorly distinguished from the Nenetses. Their totals [shown here in square brackets] are from Levin & Potapova, *Narody Sibiri* (Moscow, 1956). The total for Nenetses for the year 1926 probably includes those people who would now be classed as Nganasans or Enetses.

[C] In 1940 the total for the Nenetses probably includes the Enetses.

factors. The extremely directed nature of Soviet-era immigration has resulted in the situation that Siberian sparse peoples are massively out-numbered in compact urban areas but tend to remain in the majority over the vast expanses surrounding these enclaves. Second, although the absolute number of living representatives of the sparse peoples is small at any one time, their birth rates and death rates are at least four times that of the Russian average (Pika 1993). This implies that the number of souls entering and departing the environment (and thus populating the landscape with names, legacies, and memories) is much higher than traditional statistics might indicate. Finally, as Table 10 shows clearly, there is also considerable inconsistency in counting certain categories such as those of Enneches, Sakhas, and Dolgans due to an indecisiveness on the part of state officials on how best to apply nationality categories to particular groups of people. It is tempting to dismiss inconsistent tallies as the product of poorly trained clerks. However, the puzzle of who belongs to which official nationality is much more intricate. Whether one traces language use, territoriality, or kinship, the threads of national identity tend to intertwine in the lower Yenisei valley such that one is led to question whether some statistical categories, such as those of 'Evenki', 'Sakha', and 'Dolgan', have been manipulated so as to transform certain burgeoning peoples into sparse ones. The following case study of state ethnography in the lower Yenisei valley can be equally applied to Evenki, Even, Enneche, Nenets, or Sakha ethnology.[2] It will suffice here to focus upon the varied interpretations of Dolgans. This is not an arbitrary choice since several generations of state ethnographers have focused upon the boundaries between Dolgans and their neighbours, thus also defining the limits of each of the other groups.

Dolgan ethnology has both a rich Imperial and Soviet legacy. The first mention of the term 'Dolgan' can be found in the records of Cossack tax-collectors in 1818.[3] After this date, the term appears often in the titles of Tsarist administrative units formed by Aleksandr Speranskii in 1822.

---

[2] The question of ethnonyms for people of the Samoedic language family is particularly complex and serves as an excellent example of the arbitrary embrace of authorized nationalities. Within the ethnography of Taimyr, not only does the *enets* nationality appear and disappear in official state statistics, but different fractions of *entsy* appear to be separate 'peoples' (Vasil'ev & Simchenko 1963) or, as a 'clan group' intermarrying with Nias (Afanas'eva 1990). The authorized term *enets* was chosen by the Taimyr Executive Committee in August 1961 and is admitted by V. N. Vasil'ev to be 'artificial' (Vasil'ev 1963).

[3] Boris Osipovich Dolgikh collected the 1818 record during his expedition of 1938. It consists of a 'receipt' given to an 'unbaptized Tungus of the Dolgan clan' (Dolgikh 1963: 100; AMAE K5–1–291: 10). The next written record is a tax receipt to 'the Dolgan Oka' in 1851 (Dolgikh 1963: 100). There is at least one earlier record typically left out of official Dolgan history—that is the log-book of Lieutenant Laptev (1851), who entered the lower Yenisei valley by sea between 1734 and 1742. He gives a long description of christened and unchristened Yakuts, Evenkis, and Russians. He does not use the term Dolgan, although Soviet state ethnography assumes that this people should have been in the region by this date.

Distinct 'jurisdictions' such as the Dolgano-Yeseisk or Dolgano-Tungus *upravy* displayed the term Dolgan prominently in their title until 1925, irrespective of whether or not the individuals living within these units registered themselves as *dolgany*, *yakuty*, or *tungusy* (Dolgikh 1963: 101–3, Gurvich 1977: 22–5).

From 1835 onwards in both administrative as well as in scholarly circles there was a growing debate on how the people producing the term *dolgan* should be best classified. In an action which foreshadows the later practice of Soviet ethnographers, academic K. M. Ber charged the German naturalist A. F. Middendorf and the linguist M. A. Kastren to devote part of their time in Turukhansk Territory to clarifying a confusing overlap of the peoples inhabiting the lands between the Lena and the Ob'. In the written accounts of the expeditions of 1843 and 1846, Dolgans [*dolgany*] appear for the first time as an object of ethnological interest rather than as a source of tribute (Middendorf 1869: 688–98; Kastren 1860: 338–64). In both Middendorf's and Kastren's classifications, Dolgans are identified as one of the Yakut 'tribes' [*plemia*] on the basis of language and physiognomy, but both acknowledge that their identity is mixed in the minds of scholars and non-scholars alike with *tungusy*.

Since Middendorf and Kastren, many generations of Russian intellectuals have continued to struggle with the question of the affiliation of fractions of Dolgans to either the Tungus or the Yakut. It is not surprising that the Imperial Russian Academy of Sciences would have started this quest. Since the rationalizing of Siberian administration in 1822 by Speranskii, every people in Siberia was classified and placed on one of three steps: settled [*osedlie*], nomadic [*kochevye*], or wandering [*brodiashie*] (Raeff 1956). The hitherto elusive reports on Dolgan situated them in an ambiguous position between established ranks. Yakuts were considered a nomadic people (with tendencies to settlement) while Tunguses were thought of as a wandering people (with a tendency to regular nomadism). What is striking in the literature on this topic is not the skill with which typologies were applied, but the extreme effort invested in forcing people into one (and only one) category. The two main interests of a century of Russian and Soviet state ethnography are divided between a concern with determining if Dolgans represent a discrete people, and then ranking this people with respect to the other known peoples of Siberia.[4]

The concern with ranking is evident from the first mention of Dolgans in the scholarly literature. In 1844 Kastren is bluntly asked by the Imperial Russian Academy of Sciences 'What sort of people [*chto za narod*] are those

---

[4] In addition to confusion concerning the proper status and taxation duties of Dolgans there was a similar dispute in this region regarding the 'Chapogir people'. This group, which is now held by state ethnography to be an Evenki clan, was thought to be a separate people right up until 1927 (Keppen 1845: 114; GANO R354–1–156).

Dolgan inhabiting the northern part of the Yeniseisk *okrug* and paying their taxes at the Khatanga Parish?' (Keppen 1845: 125). Attached to this query is the request that Kastren locate the people on a 'level of citizenship' [*stepen' grazhdanskogo obrazovaniia*] and a 'level of enlightenment' which the Academy saw as corresponding to Speranskii's three-step classification system.

The endeavour of ranking clearly served purposes other than tidy administration or the sating of scholarly curiosity. Perhaps the most blatant interests implicit in the ranking were the goals of Russian settlement and colonization. Descriptions of indigenous technology, social organization, and trading patterns served as quick guides to whether or not lands were suitable for grain production or livestock, or contained surface deposits of gold. In a more classical genre of exploitation, the categories 'nomadic' and 'wandering' also helped to determine the style of extraction the Tsarist state could apply. Wandering peoples were subject to tribute paid once a year in fur at a fixed point within their administratively fixed tribal area. Nomadic or settled peoples could expect requests to pay taxes in silver, but were allowed to continue their own local legal traditions or would even be granted a charter recognizing their occupation of certain lands (Samokvasov 1876; Riasanovsky 1965). Orthodox missionaries also showed great zeal in classifying populations not only to bring native people within the fold of Christianity but also within reach of the state. The missionary Mikhail Suslov, who visited the lower Yenisei valley in 1870 and 1883, always recorded in his diaries the number of native people present, his impressions of their movements, and occasionally his advice to the state on how best to find those who were avoiding paying tax (Suslov 1884). A curious regulatory institution associated with the practice of ranking was that of the grain supply-house [*khlebnyi magazin*], which could be used to monitor and enclose the movements of the wandering peoples. Cossack warriors at these distribution points would allocate grain to natives in exchange for furs or debt payable in furs or labour. This precursor to the redistributive state, which had the explicit aim of preventing starvation, had the additional effect of making natives dependent on food commodities and anchored them to fixed points (Tugarinov 1919).

There is a distinct change of tone in the ethnography of the beginning of the twentieth century. Although these Russian ethnographers were perhaps the most independent from the influence of state policy, they did not abandon the practice of ranking but instead used it as a rhetorical device to emphasize the duty of the state to protect its citizens. The short report of Vasil'ev's expedition through the lower Yenisei valley to the Anabar district in 1905 is the first of a series of ethnographies to contrast the poverty of Tungus fishermen to the wealth of the Tungus and Yakut herders (Vasil'ev 1908: 61–2). Through vivid descriptions of the Tungus's 'monotonous and unvarying lifestyle' consisting of raw, frozen food, isolation, and illness, Vasil'ev's words contrast implicitly with the comforts of urban life in the cities. In these descriptions the traditional placement of the Yakut and the Dolgan above the Tungus is inverted by portraying a Tungus as 'honest and good-natured' in the face of a 'sullen, hard, and arrogant' Yakut (pp. 72–3). The themes of poverty and illness would be expanded upon by the revolutionary Rychkov, who was exiled to the lower Yenisei valley in 1908. His stay in Taimyr coincided with a widespread epidemic of small pox which he renders in a shockingly graphic style (1908: 78) as a literary weapon against the Tsarist state. His few published writings refer dismissively to the ethnographic controversy over the Dolgan by classing them as half-breeds [*metisy*], denying them any particular status linked with their national identity (1914*a*: 106). However as with populist writings all over Central and Eastern Europe, Rychkov's contrast of stoic hardship in the face of an indifferent and corrupt state carried a clear message that these 'vanishing peoples' are deserving of study and protection because they are unable to defend themselves.

Although the link between rank and identity is muted in the writing of Vasil'ev and Rychkov, clear concerns over economic stratification and cultural levels would once again become central issues to Soviet state ethnography. Soviet ethnography is famous for its concern for teasing out evidence of exploitation by rich Yakut households of poorer Tungus households. However, state ethnographers were also concerned with identifying cultural complexes which were closest to the Soviet ideal of civilization. Dolgans, a people who were once praised for being the lead bearers of Christianity in the nineteenth century (Suslov 1884; Laptev 1851; Vasil'ev 1908), came to be seen as the most progressive of the diminutive peoples of Soviet Taimyr. In Dolgikh's early work (1929: 63) Dolgans and Tundra Peasants would still be categorized as 'the most cultured layer' of Taimyr by their strong faith in Russian Orthodoxy and use of Russian names. Dobrova-Yadrintseva (1925: 80) would distinguish Tunguses from the other peoples of Taimyr by their 'instinct of wandering'. The legacy of ranking would culminate in Popov's 1931 description of the Dolgans as the 'avant-garde people' [*peredovoi narod*] of Taimyr (KTsKhIDNI 28–1–24: 1).

Soviet ethnography and the 'origin' of Dolgans

Ranking was applied in concert with the craft of consolidating people into discrete nationalities. Although the grouping of peoples within administrative units also has a long history within the Tsarist and various Inner Asian Empires, the division and identification of people under specific national terms would be the hallmark of Soviet state ethnography from the mid-1920s onwards. Much as the Tsarist state collected its tribute from taxation areas distinguished by allegiance to a nationally specific 'administrative clan', the new Soviet state established new administrative units based on nationality in order to channel the distribution of central state subsidies. In Soviet rankings, 'territorial administrative autonomy' would be established consonant with the ethnographic rank of a nationality. 'Peoples' [*narody*] were given autonomous republics while 'diminutive peoples' [*narodnosti*] were given national districts or national counties (Kaiser 1994).

With the post-revolutionary reordering of administrative units, the status of Dolgans once again became difficult. If Dolgans indeed belonged with Yakuts then it followed that the Yakut Autonomous Soviet Socialist Republic should control most of the territory between the Yenisei and Lena rivers—a prospect which would make Yakutiia as large in size as Kazakhstan or the Russian heartland itself. If, however, Dolgans were considered to be part of the Tungus then it would be reasonable to construct a large national district along the Yenisei river equivalent to the contemporary territories of Turukhansk County, the Evenki and Taimyr Autonomous Districts, and perhaps also incorporating portions of Irkutsk Province and the Yakut Republic (Map 1 above). Despite extensive research in state archives, I have found no officially recorded anxiety over either Yakut or Tungus imperialism. However, there are numerous contradictory proposals for the grouping of one portion of this territory to one or another administrative district and evidence of an officially adjudicated struggle over the western boundary of Yakutiia (see Chapter 7). Whether or not the Soviet state was particularly concerned about nationalism at this early date, it is significant that below each one of these proposals one could find the names of well-known figures in Russian ethnography.[5]

The question of making a clear, sharp boundary between Dolgans and other sparse peoples was raised first with the expedition of Andrei Aleksandrovich Popov from Dudinka to Khatanga in 1930. Popov encoun-

---

[5] The centre of policy-making and territorial formation between 1924 and 1935 was the Committee of the North (Grant 1993; 1995; Slezkine 1994; Kuoljok 1985). The head of this Committee was P. Smidovich, a former populist revolutionary who, like Bogoraz and Shternberg, tasted the lifestyle of Siberian native peoples during exile. Between 1925 and 1930, the period of the formation of national territories, the St Petersburg intellectual V. N. Vasil'ev was head of the Commission for the Study of Yakutiia. Lev Shternberg was active in the Commission for the Study of the Tribal Composition of Russia. The papers in Bogoraz-Tan's personal archive indicate that he was well connected to the Academy of Sciences committee which funded scientific expeditions [*Glavnauk*] and the Administrative Commission of the Committee of the North which drew up boundaries. Bogoraz-Tan (1925) was also the author of an influential article on the administration of native peoples (wherein he describes the tasks of Soviet cadres in the North as those of missionaries). The Novosibirsk ethnographer, Dobrova-Yadrintseva, was head of the Committee of the North for all of the Siberian Territory and active in the question of determining the boundary between Taimyr and Yakutiia. The Krasnoiarsk ethnographer Innokentii Suslov (grandson of the activist missionary Mikhail Suslov) was head of the Eastern Siberian Committee of the North. According to archival data, he drafted an ambitious plan in the 1920s for the massive resettlement and consolidation of all Evenkis from East Asia to the Evenki National District. Fortunately the plan was not executed on the scale originally suggested.

tered the 'Dolgano-Yakuts' for the first time at Chasovnia after walking the Dudinka–Chasovnia road (now a railway) in the company of two hundred Russian labourers about to lay the foundation for the city of Noril'sk. He returned to Petrograd in the spring of 1931, five months after the Central Executive Committee had chosen the boundaries and the title of 'Dolgano-Nenets' for the new district (Popov 1931; AMAE 14–1–151). Though once again there is no written record of an instruction to Popov to distinguish a people called 'the Dolgan' there is evidence of an official interest to this end. In his presentation to the Priorities Committee of the Turukhansk Branch of the Communist Party in Dudinka, Popov describes the goals of his expedition as one of consolidation:

The Dolgan, one of the most advanced [*peredovoi*] diminutive peoples in terms of culture, inhabit the territory between the right bank of the Yenisei and the Khatanga river. Up to the present time they remain a riddle of ethnographical science. One scholar tends to think of them as Yakutized Tunguses. Others see them as puzzling remnants of Paleoasiatics who never have been thought to have settled this area. In order to clarify the complicated question of the origin of the Dolgan I was seconded in the spring of 1930 by the Academy of Sciences. My goal . . . has been to link the Dolgan to [one of] the Turkish, Tungus-Manchurian, or Paleoasiatic groups (KTsKhIDNI: 28–1–24: 1).

That Popov took the Dolgan as one of his main subjects of ethnographic writing is quite well known; however, his writings show a lack of enthusiasm for the goal which he announced before the Party bureaucrats. His first publications would be on kinship and material culture of Dolgans (1934*a*, 1935, 1937*a*, 1937*b*, 1946) but he conspicuously avoided the high ground of Soviet ethnography—the issue of ethnogenesis. A careful reading of his unpublished writing on the question of identity shows a canniness in using collective ethnonyms other than identifiers related to kinship: *dongoot*, *ytyyn*, *bilar*, *tahaa*, the term 'Dolgano-yakut population' [*Dolgano-yakutskoe naselenie*] (AMAE 14–1–151) or even once the term 'Dolgano-tungus' (AMAE 14–1–89). The printed versions of his work (unlike the unpublished drafts) refer to 'the Dolgan' with a single unhyphenated word, but even here with curious qualifiers and very conservative population estimates.

Popov's most authoritative account of the Dolgan was in the heavily edited volume *Peoples of Siberia* (1954). Here one finds the orthodox definition of the Dolgan—a definition that any student of ethnography in Moscow or any government worker in Dudinka would be able to recite:

The Dolgan are a special population of the Taimyr National District. At the present time the Dolgan speak a special dialect of the Yakut language. They were formed from groups of differing origin. In particular, the Dolgan are made of four clan groups of Tungus origin—the dolgan, edzen, karyntyo, and dongot. The Dolgan call themselves *dulgaan*. This ethnonym is one of the clan groups of the nineteenth century that was common to all Dolgans . . . Before, they did not have a general ethnonym . . . Sometimes the Dolgans called themselves the Tungus, but distinguished themselves from the local Evenkis of the Taimyr and Evenki National Districts. They do not consider themselves Yakuts and differ ethnographically from the latter (1954: 742).

In this formulation one reads the authoritative unity of a single ethnonym, a pedigree for the ethnonym, clear division between neighbouring groups, a link to a territory which has been recognized by the Soviet Union, and a strong tone which suggests that without the help of the state and scientific ethnography they would have remained confused about their identity. In the archive of the Museum of Anthropology and Ethnography in St Petersburg there are four annotated versions of this text dating back to 1932 which show signs of marked disagreement (AMAE 14–1–141; 14–1–151). The most interesting is the third version (n.d. [1933–7]: 17–54), wherein the above passage is rendered very differently:

The Dolgan have no ethnonym of their own . . . The officially recognized name for the Dolgan *sakha* is awkward; [clause 1] since it has been accepted by the Dolgan with reluctance [*neokhotno*]; [clause 2] since the historically shaped ethnonym *dulgaan-dolgan* does not seem to be insulting to them as much as the term *sakha* creates misunderstandings. From their ethnic origin the Dolgan can be linked to the Tungus group of peoples, from their language they are related to the Turkic group (Yakut) (pp. 17–18; the two clauses are the author's handwritten alternatives).

The handwritten annotations of Prokopiev in his capacity as sub-editor of *Peoples of Siberia* (pp. 91–100) directly attacked the phrase that 'the Dolgan have no ethnonym' with the remark that the writing could be 'improved'. The clause stating that the term 'Dolgan' was 'not insulting' was deleted with great emphasis. To polish the document a number of tidy phrases were suggested, such as the Dolgan 'are the most advanced proto-people of the territory'—suggestions which did not appear in the final version. The final suggestive evidence of political pressure on Popov is in the stenograph notes of the Siberian sector of the Institute of Ethnography on 8 January 1939 (pp. 103 ff.). After reading the fourth version of his text on the Dolgan, both Lipskii and Prokopiev immediately addressed the question of the lack of a clear ethnonym and accompanying pedigree. In particular Lipskii, an ethnographer of Evens, presented what must have been a very carefully prepared statement of the undoubted origins of the ethnonym 'Dolgan' from the lexica of Evens in Primor Territory. Lipskii's careful exegesis also did not appear in the final text, but it is curious that passages similar in style and content to Lipskii's pointed critique were to appear later in Dolgikh 1963 (107–8, 131) and authoritative linguistic texts (Vasilevich 1946; Ubriatova 1985: 10).

It would be the contemporary of Popov—Boris Osipovich Dolgikh—who would instead assume the task of firmly, even belligerently, authorizing a distinct nationality called the Dolgan. The foundation for Dolgikh's writing on the Dolgan came from three expeditions through Taimyr in 1926–7, 1934–5, and in 1938–9, and numerous periods working in the state archives of the Russian Federated Soviet Socialist Republic. During his first two expeditions he served as census taker and collectivization economist respectively. Only upon his third trip did he officially become an ethnographer for the Krasnoiarsk Provincial Museum. Like Popov, his knowledge of Yakut from childhood helped him organize transport and to conduct interviews in what was a widely used lingua franca.

Dolgikh's published and unpublished works are remarkably diverse on the question of identity. What makes him the best example of a state ethnographer is the fact that his ethnographic analyses overlap precisely with the three stages of the formation of the Taimyr (Dolgano-Nenets) National District. Before the creation of this administrative district (and before Popov's officially sanctioned expedition), Dolgikh published a field report (1929) as a census employee where, like all Taimyr ethnographers, he puzzled over a complex vernacular matrix of identities which was difficult to fit within precise analytic terms. The anomalies of this work, which Dolgikh would repudiate in print in 1963, will be considered carefully below. Instead of exploring the multi-dimensional structure of identity he had stumbled upon, Dolgikh showed an early penchant for grouping peoples together. In 1929 he was one of the first ethnographers to group people into 'cultural-economic' types which yielded a curious picture of the district in terms of populations and identities (Dolgikh 1929: 76):

1) *samoedy-tavgiitsy*	220 families
2) *dolgane* (or *yakuty* of the tundra)	417 families
3) *tungusy*	80 families
4) *yakuty* (or *yakuty* of the forest)	80 families
5) riverbank *samoedy*	40 families
Total	837 families.

This model is interesting for, when compared to Table 10, it shows an elastic boundary between Tungus, Yakut, and Dolgan populations. In addition, its distinctive ecological appellations can be linked to relational identities which may have existed at that time. Dolgikh himself found this typology valuable for different, administrative reasons: '[This new] schematic is useful in that if there is to be a census of the whole of the Soviet North then the data of these five groups can be collapsed into wider categories such as: the Samoed-General category, the Yakut-General category, or the Tungus-General category' (p. 76). His passion for grouping and categorizing would become much more striking four short years after the formation of the district (and three years after the Volochanka rebellion) when he recommended in a report sent to Provincial Party officials that any mention of the Dolgan be removed from scientific classifications and from administrative names:

It would be most correct to call [the Dolgan] Yakutized Evenkis . . . However since such a detailed division of the sparse natives of the North will cause great difficulties in cultural-educational work, and also bearing in mind the linguistic similarities between these groups, it seems possible to consolidate the Yakut, the 'Dolgan' [*quotes in original*], and the Tundra peasants into one national group: the Yakuts (TsGARF A310–18–67: 97–8).

The Provincial Party officials were evidently persuaded by his advice for in the same year the category 'Dolgan' disappeared in all administrative instruments (except the official name of the district) in favour of the term '*sakha*'. In a strictly worded circular written by the Secretary of the Taimyr District Communist Party, all workers were urged to use 'modern' terms such as *sakha*, *evenk*, and *nenets* instead of the 'old' terms *dolgan*, *tungus*, and *samoed* which were seen to be tainted with 'imperial chauvinism' (KTsKhIDNI 28–4–7: 2).

Dolgikh's final word on the authorization of the Dolgan would occur following the thirtieth Anniversary of the Taimyr (Dolgano-Nenets) National District (1960) and upon the Soviet state's initiative (1958) to raise the 'level of culture' of all rural areas of Siberia.[6] 'The Origin of the Dolgan' (1963) has become the classic work that defines the history of the formation of a new diminutive people for students, state administrators, and nationalist activists. Through the detailed analysis of Imperial and Soviet archival documents, Dolgikh follows the consolidation of the Dolgan from the nineteenth century to the 1950s with a martial thoroughness capturing clans and often individuals one by one within the paragraphs of his text. In this complicated and well-referenced work he establishes that most of the total Yakut-speaking population of Taimyr, as well as some residents of the Anabar district of Yakutiia, were set to form a coherent and bounded people identifiable as 'the Dolgan' by the middle of the nineteenth century. The distinctive mechanism which generated the Dolgan, in Dolgikh's view, was the establishment of the overland trading route known as the 'Khatanga Way' (Map 4) between the mouth of the Yenisei and the northern tundras of Yakutiia. Using the Faustian imagery of the nuclear age, Dolgikh described this trading corridor as, 'a unique reactor which melded into a single mass as Dolgans the most different of peoples with the most different of histories' (p. 96). According to Dolgikh, the fundamental elements of the Dolgan are the Yakut-speaking peoples of

---

[6] There is some evidence that Dolgikh was active in exerting pressure to recover the category 'Dolgan' as early as 1954. In recently published excerpts from the reports sent to the Central Committee, as part of the Institute of Ethnography's annual policy paper on nationality issues, Dolgikh complains of the ignorance of Party workers of the nationality and languages of native peoples (1993a: 134 (1954)) and of the fact that the Dolgan are incorrectly called *sakha* (1993b: 150 (1959)). For a discussion of Dolgikh's (1949; 1960) well-known classificatory scheme of 'tribal divisions' see Anderson (1996a: 133).

three Tsarist tribute units (42%), several Evenki clans (45%), the Yakut-speaking Russian peasants of the Tundra Order (11%), and certain Enneche clans (2%). Excluded from the reaction are Evenkis living on the Khantaika (although they are posited to be reserve material for future amalgams) (pp. 98 fn., 123). Perhaps most tellingly, Dolgikh concludes that not only have the Dolgan appeared in the history books under the gaze of ethnographers, but that the fundamental changes of collectivization finally consolidated them as a socialist people (pp. 135, 138).

The most distinctive aspect of Dolgikh's version of Dolgan history is its nominalism. In the opening sentence of the article, Dolgans are cited as *already* the most numerous of the native peoples within the Taimyr (Dolgano-Nenets) National District. The body of the text consults archival sources in order to account for what is a posited 'ethnographic fact' by 1926 (pp. 97, 137). That the people themselves did not always call themselves 'Dolgan' in 1926 and 1927 is treated by him as an empirical anomaly which only establishes that the Dolgan are a nation in the process of creation (pp. 105–6). That many Yakut-speaking individuals in 1959 did not identify themselves as 'Dolgan' is discounted by the projection that the Dolgan will be fully consolidated in the future (pp. 99, 129–30). That other ethnographers and administrators did not count Dolgans as a separate people, or that they counted them as a fraction of their proper numbers is interpreted as erroneous or as a narrow perspective on a historical process that was yet unfinished (pp. 101–3, 106).

The accuracy of Dolgikh's detailed interpretation of the 'origin of the Dolgan' could be a matter of long debate.[7] What is important for this portrait of state ethnography is the principle of his analysis, which also marks the work and practice of state managers. Dolgikh's nominalist technique of organizing empirical evidence represents an elaboration of an old view in Russian state-craft that not only must groups be ranked, but that subjects or citizens must unambiguously belong to one particular people. This conviction may make for

---

[7] Dolgikh's argument hangs upon a peculiar interpretation of the ethnographic literature. He cites a battery of twelve works which provide relevant observations of the groups who (in Dolgikh's view) were to become the Dolgan during the course of the 19th and early 20th cents. (Stepanov 1835; Middendorf 1875 (1869); Kastren 1856 (1860); Mordvinov 1860; Krivoshapkin 1865; Tret'iakov 1869; Patkanov 1911; Rychkov 1915 & 1917–23; Dobrova-Yadrintseva 1925; Dolgikh 1929; Popov 1934a). According to Dolgikh, the following classified Dolgans as exclusively *tungus*: Stepanov, Mordvinov, Krivoshapkin. The authors Middendorf, Kastren, Tretiakov, and Patkanov placed Dolgans exclusively with *yakuty*. Rychkov, Popov, Dobrova-Yadrintseva, and Dolgikh (1929) divided Dolgans between both groups. In verifying all of his citations, I have concluded that Dolgikh (1963) incorrectly reads the existence of Dolgans as a group separate and independent from their neighbours in Middendorf (1869 edn.), Kastren (1860 edn.), Rychkov (1917–23), and Dobrova-Yadrintseva (1925). All of these authors either carefully identified compact Dolgan groups or did not write of a seamless border between Dolgans and other groups. In addition to Dolgikh's list, I would add the works of Isachenko (1913), Kostrov (1855), Ostrovskikh (1904), Tugarinov (1919), Tugarinov & Lappo (1927), and Vasil'ev (1908), who all also write of complicated relationships between *tungusy* and *yakuty* where particular groups (but not *all*) are distinguished as Dolgans.

simple administration, but it is a striking departure from the heart of the ethnographer's craft, which is typically founded upon identifying and elaborating difference, rather than assimilating it.[8]

Dolgikh's project was intertwined with state practice not only at the heart of his analysis, since his source of data is from tribute or census records, but in the contemporary state practice surrounding the publication of his work. 'The Origin of the Dolgan' came off the press following the return of a special ethnographic expedition assembled to mark the occasion of the Taimyr's thirtieth anniversary. Among recommendations on how best to centralize collective farms, the head of the expedition, Yurii Strakach complained to Party officials (with a copy to Dolgikh) that national classifiers were in want of tidying:

Resulting from the lack of respect for scientific methods in enumerating the native [*natsional'nogo*] population in the records of the All-Union census of 1959, there is a complete lack of data on the leading national group of the Taimyr (Dolgano-Nenets) District—the Dolgan. Our questionnaire of the population has shown that a significant part of the Dolgan use the ethnonym *sakha* but do not recognize the clear Yakut character of this term (*sakha = yakut*) . . . [Similar problems in the definition of Enneches are reported]

Instead of recommending a more subtle approach to the question of identity, Strakach characteristically recommended that the temperature of the reactor be increased:

As a correction to this situation it is necessary to:
— initiate a widespread campaign of clarification using the press and the radio.
— to conduct a fundamental scientific recounting of the Nenets-Nganasan-Enets and the Dolgano-Yakut population (GAKK R1386–1–3820: 57 [Sept. 1960]).

Although the full scientific study recommended in this letter never occurred, the spirit of the resolution came into effect very quickly. By 1 January 1961, in the yearly statistical reports for the Taimyr Autonomous District the number of Dolgans jumped from zero to 3,943 (including, evidently, some former Yakuts and perhaps some Evenkis) (GAKK R1386–1–3820). On 15 January 1961 the first article in Dolgan appeared on the pages of the district

---

[8] In a precursor to the authorization of the Dolgan, the pages of *Sovetskaia etnografiia* hosted a confrontational discussion on the status of the 'Reindeer Yakuts' living on the territory of Anabar County. P. E. Terletskii (1951) pointed out that many individuals classified as Yakuts within the Western borderlands with Evenkiia and Taimyr considered themselves as *tungusy* in the 1897 and 1926 census and that their present status as *yakuty* was a statistical error. A series of articles by Gurvich (1950*a*, 1950*b*, 1952), Dolgikh (1950, 1952*a*, 1952*b*), and Suslov (1952) established that ethnonyms are contingent on the territory of residence and not what informants may say. Despite Terletskii's early point that terms such as *tongus* may not be equivalent with nationality, Dolgikh (1950: 171) concludes that historical classifiers must be interpreted unambiguously: 'Either [the population of Lake Yessei] is all Yakut or Evenki (Tungus). No other solution is possible.' Gurvich's monograph (1977) provides the authorized history of the Reindeer Yakuts.

newspaper *Sovetskii Taimyr*. In the same year the official statistics of the Taimyr District Communist Party reported all members formerly listed as *sakha* as *dolgan* (KTsKhIDNI 26–34–98: 160). The first study on the linguistics of the Dolgan language was published in 1966 (Ubriatova 1966). In 1967 the secretaries of village councils in the rural areas changed the entries within household registries from *sakha* to *dolgan* (GATAO 73–2–13–14; 73–2–17–20).

The beauty of the authoritative style of state ethnography is that it can simultaneously spin etymologies while weaving new meanings into words. Dolgikh in 1963 (p. 106) nicely captures this practice in Taimyr:

Since 1935 the ethnonym of the Yakuts has been used in the Taimyr National District as the name of the Dolgan as an official term. The use of this term in Russian is awkward since for the real *sakha*—the Yakuts of the Yakut Autonomous Soviet Socialist Republic, there has existed for a long time in the Russian language the word *yakut*. For this reason there was even less necessity to use this term [*sakha*] in the Russian language for the Dolgan who, although from linguistics and origins are similar to the Yakuts, nevertheless represent a separate diminutive people . . . Only in 1959 [*sic*] in official documents, in the press, and on the radio within the Taimyr National District did the term *dolgan* appear again—the correct term of this diminutive people for the Russian language.

There is no one better placed to give the history of the twentieth-century usage of the word *dolgan*. As documented above, in 1935 Dolgikh himself wrote to Territorial and Party officials to complain of the lack of consistency in the use of ethnonyms and presented a well-argued case for assimilating the term 'Dolgan' with the terms 'Yakut' or 'Evenki' (TsGARF A310–18–67: 95–8). From September 1960 onwards, the term *dolgan* did appear again, but this time not as a marker of a group defined by kinship or as a marker of tribute—but as an authoritative term for a nationality.

The above examples from Dolgan ethnology demonstrate how the method of state ethnography, which involves the ranking of peoples and their sorting into discrete ethnographic units, melds seamlessly into an administrative paradigm. In Tsarist times these practices served to facilitate taxation and social control. In Soviet times, these instruments were used to place people within what can be called a 'citizenship regime' (Anderson 1996c). As in the methodology of contemporary physics, the search for fundamental elements which prove the origins of people turns quickly into an act of creation. Although the interest in classifying peoples is an old one, the documentary record suggests that the authorized nationality of 'the Dolgan' is a distinctive product of Soviet state ethnography. Only during the Soviet period did this term become linked with material privilege and with an administrative ideology with policy towards specific sparse peoples. Although authorized nationalities are connected with specific programmes designed to preserve

Siberian peoples, they also ensure that these peoples remain sparse. As the statistics in this section show, increasingly narrow classification systems which place people within circumscribed categories can expand only at the risk of dissolving the marker which gives them a place in the citizenship regime. With the wave of resettlements at the beginning of the 1970s, bearers of the Dolgan nationality would come to live in especially enlarged settlements beside other individuals who had been given different authoritative markers. In these rationalized, built surroundings, the paper category of the Dolgan came alive in the experience of real individuals both capturing the sense of belonging of certain individuals to an 'advanced' nationality as well as negatively shaping what it meant to be Evenki.

Taimyr's 'wondrous mosaic'

This frontier strikes [one] as a wondrous mosaic made up of many different diminutive peoples; each completely unstudied. For some strange play of circumstance, they have been left outside of scholarly attention. Usually on the ethnographic maps these nationalities are known by the broad terms the Tungus, the Samoed, and so forth. But upon closer acquaintance with them, they divide themselves into many different groups [*gruppy*] often differing very sharply from each other in language and lifestyle. I sincerely would like to believe that the All-Union Academy of Sciences . . . will devote its attention to the colourful and dappled nationalities [living] in this forgotten oasis between the Yenisei and the Lena [rivers] (A. A. Popov, in a letter V. G. Bogoraz-Tan [Dudinka, Nov. 1930] (AMAE 14–1–149: 6)).

The words of Andrei Aleksandrovich Popov capture an ardent curiosity but also puzzlement with the diversity of cultural practice then widespread in Taimyr. The number of ethnographic explorers in the lower Yenisei valley have been few, but all who have voyaged there have been impressed with the same diversity—even if this diversity is poorly reflected in their published work. This diversity can be read in certain anomalies of their writing which suggest that the terms collected, ratified, and ranked sit uncomfortably with the richness of their own material. In examining the plurality of identities implicit in Soviet state ethnography, it will be argued that this region is not unique for the fact that anomalous individuals confuse their own nationality, but instead that authoritative categories are anomalous to complex senses of belonging.

The difficulty of the fieldworker in understanding identity is perhaps most honestly described by the geographer A. Ya. Tugarinov, who after meticulously matching official tribute lists to living individuals in the forests of the upper Yenisei valley, was confronted with the untidy cosmopolitanism of the lower Yenisei valley in 1923:

If for some researchers the mixed origins [of Dolgans] are debatable, and for others [they are] obvious, then it follows that the amounts of cultural influence or the traces from the proto-peoples who were mixed together are also not equivalent. Therefore, it is almost necessary to conduct an individual study of each native . . . Here there is the additional problem of the artificiality with which natives have been woven into administrative clans [*administrativnye rody*] made up of individuals placed in groups to which they have no blood relation. In practice there are constant difficulties for administrators and missionaries to divide one or another family between *dolgan*, *yakuty*, or finally *tungus*. It is sufficient only to start to talk with a *tungus* and then to learn with surprise that he counts himself as *dolgan* (ARAN 135–2–305: 17).

In this frank passage, Tugarinov raises the issue not only of the loose correspondence between Tsarist administrative rankings and local identities, but the puzzling phenomenon that a single individual may have a dual identity (or even a 'mix' that varies from person to person). This phenomenon will be termed a 'relational identity' since identity in Taimyr has rarely been expressed as an unambiguous declaration of belonging but instead was crafted especially for the convenience of the observer. Using the works of state ethnographers it will be shown that identifiers, which are often understood to be bounded ethnonyms, are often juggled in order to communicate across languages, ecological zones, and occupations. Since each of these aspects can change over the course of a person's life, one encounters the phenomenon that wherever one finds a Yakut, one is likely to find a Tungus (or another regional variant such as *even*, *dolgan*, *asia*, or *betu*) (Vitebsky 1992: 225). In this respect, the taigas and tundras of eastern Siberia look like the homelands of the Kachin and Shan of Highland Burma, where one group transforms into another when different social, political, and ecological parameters are considered (Leach 1964). This relationship also appears similar to the 'situational identity' analysed by Okamura (1994).

Ironically, it was the authorizer of the Dolgan—B. O. Dolgikh—who was the first to struggle with this paradox during his work as a census enumerator in 1926 and 1927; only to a less pluralistic conclusion. After expressing an initial frustration with the lack of overlap between established administrative boundaries and the people who moved within them and across them (p. 70), Dolgikh (1929) calls for the critical analysis of the inexact terminology of local Russians (p. 62), the names of tribute units (p. 70), and the categories that native people use themselves when speaking Russian (p. 60). In applying his search for a group's 'ethnographic specificity' [*individual'nost'*] (p. 63), Dolgikh provides a very revealing hearsay ethnography:

At first glance, it is difficult to consider Dolgans as a separate tribal group. In conversations in the Dolgan language they call themselves *khaka* (or *sakha* in the more easterly portions of the Khatanga *trakt*), which means *yakut*. If one questions them in Russian, they call themselves either *dolgany*, or *tungusy*, or perhaps just simply use a clan name . . . To the question of their tribal affiliation, the [clan *dolgan*] always answer 'Dolgan'. They do not like being called *tungus*. But after long, detailed discussion they affirm their *tungus* origin . . . If one calls the natives of the clan *dongot* 'Dolgans' the majority would not agree with it. They prefer to call themselves *dongot*, lending to this term a shade of a tribal name. But in the majority of cases they immediately explain that they are really [*sobstevenno*] *tungus* and that *dongot* is only the name of their clan . . . The majority of the natives of the clan *edian* call themselves *tungus* and only rarely *dolgan*. But in the latter case if one asks a second time they will immediately correct themselves and say *tungus* . . . Finally, the natives of the clan *karanto* . . . almost always call themselves *tungus* and rarely *karanto* giving their clan name a tribal definition like the natives of the clan *dongot* . . . Thus it is now clear that all four clans (*dolgan, dongot, edian, karanto*) present themselves as a whole ethnographic group, the division of which into *dolgan* and *tungus* would be a serious mistake. In addition, it follows that the name *dolgan*, which the Russians have carried over to the entire people, is not the name of an entire tribe but only one of its component clans (pp. 60–2).

Here Dolgikh signals that the term *dolgan* has a different circulation depending on the language being spoken. He suggests that its ultimate core meaning is in a clan name, but the term has secondary and tertiary meanings as both a 'tribal name' or, for local Russians, as the name of an 'entire people'. The anomalies in the usage of *dolgan* and *tungus* are clearly related to Dolgikh's own questioning and requisitioning as the speaker tries to adapt to the idiom that the literal-minded census enumerator would understand. Later in this article, he writes of a similar relational quality to the word *tungus*:

In the vocabulary of the Russian vernacular [*zhargon*] in the Khatanga tundra the word *tungus* has, aside from its straight sense, another specific sense which it would be best to render as 'aborigine' [*aborigen*]. Also, in the language of the *samoed-tavgaitsov* the word *assi* means first of all *tungus*, and then all of the other native peoples (p. 64).

Anticipating his later work, Dolgikh moves on to recategorize the plethora of terms confronting him into analytic categories in the form of 'cultural-economic types' which are not encapsulated within a single tribute unit. Here, Dolgikh explicitly declares the importance of making language a 'cultural mark' of an overarching nationality [*natsional'nost'*] rather than local distinctions of tribe or clan (p. 72). As we have seen above, Dolgikh (1963) would eventually use this criterion to capture all people who spoke Yakut as either a first, second, or third language for the Dolgan people. However, the terms that he uses in this early article are not purely linguistic terms but refer to cultural types stratified by ecological zones: 'Yakuts of the tundra', 'riverbank Samoed', 'Yakuts of the forest' (pp. 70, 74). I wish to consider that the ecological denotations in these terms are not chance titles but cast additional meaning to specific problems of classification which Dolgikh encounters.

In collapsing the hearsay terms into ecological groupings Dolgikh makes constant reference to the Khatanga trade corridor (pp. 51, 60, 72, 74)—the cultural 'reactor' of his 1963 article—running to the north of the very

division between the tundra and taiga. Dolgans (or tundra Yakuts) are the
stewards of this corridor, entering into complex relationships with Russians,
samoedy, and *tungusy* to the north and south of them. The 'cultural mark' of
these contacts are differing degrees of 'Dolganization' [*dolganizatsiia*]
measured in use of the Yakut [*sic*] language:

Thus the *tungusy* of Taimyr can be broken into three cultural groups: the completely
'dolganized' along the stations of the Khatanga *trakt*; the 'dolganized only at the
surface' in the more distant stations and the mountainous valleys [*kamen'*] close to
them who have retained their own language and a number of *tungus* everyday traits;
and, finally, the 'almost completely pure' *tungusy* in the deeper areas of the mountains
[this corresponds to the trading post 'Kamen''—D.A.] (p. 65).

If this is read not as the author's assessment of ethnographic purity but as an
index of contact between groups, it is possible to imagine that terms such as
dolgan or *tungus* arose in a relational manner when people from different
regions and with different tongues encountered each other and tried to
communicate.

   If Dolgikh's (1929) ethnography is read more closely, it becomes possible
to divide these hearsay terms of identity between different types of activity
that one might expect to find on the tundra, in the taiga, or in the
mountainous valleys of the 'plateau' [*kamen'*]. For example, the 'dolganized'
tungus spend their summers in the high tundra while the 'completely pure'
tungusy exercise the opposite strategy of spending their summer deep in the
mountains [but undoubtedly on the cool, windswept mountain-tops—D.A.]
(p. 74). Similarly, the wealthy Yessei *yakuty* take their reindeer onto the high
tundra (perhaps with the 'dolganized' *tungus*) while their poor cousins stay
along the banks of the river Kheta to fish (p. 66). A few paragraphs later we
learn that the former call themselves the 'Yessei Tunguses' [*dekhei tunguster*]
even though Dolgikh finds their cultural type to be that of Yakuts. Although
nowhere in this text is the following conclusion explicit, it seems that the
relational term of *tungus* was associated with those individuals who directly
accompany large herds of reindeer into the cool and windswept pastures of
the high tundra, while terms such as *dolgan* were relationally applied to those
who managed the trade.

   This speculative conclusion of a culturally marked division of labour could
be reinforced by the logical fact that an arduous midsummer journey north
into the tundra would only be necessary with extremely large herds of
reindeer (upwards of two thousand head). A large herd of reindeer of the
tundra variety would require at least six adult men to tend to it. Although it is
possible that both *dolgany* and *tungusy* might jointly tend to the herd, the
nature of stratification in this period was such that there were usually rich
owners and poorer workers. It would be not unreasonable to expect that
'reindeer people' were identifiable not only by their activity but by their

status. This situation is confirmed in the highly detailed work of Dobrova-Yadrintseva (1925). Dobrova-Yadrintseva organized the cultural groups of Taimyr not by their languages but by their movements in differing ecological zones. Thus, she placed Yakuts, Dolgans, Tundra Peasants, and Tundra Tunguses together in one category, noting that 'there is not any distinction between their trails' (p. 63). In the lower Yenisei valley she noted, like Dolgikh above, that both tundra Tunguses and Dolgans spend their winters together in the Noril'sk area but go their separate ways in the summers. Tunguses moved to the high Arctic along the headwaters of the Agapa river while Dolgans stayed at the coast. Although she does not link the parting of these people in the summer to economic strategies, it seems reasonable that the coastal position gives better trading opportunities for Dolgans while the high tundras would be the appropriate pastures for reindeer during the bug-infested summers.

Turning to the writings of the first official Soviet state ethnographer to visit Taimyr, Andrei Aleksandrovich Popov, one can learn more about the vernacular terms *tungus* and *dolgan*:

A general tribal ethnonym did not exist for Dolgans until very recent times. If one asks a Dolgan which diminutive people he belongs to (by using a Yakut word which is known to him—*omut*) he calls himself by the name of his fratry (*ordy* or *biis*) [in the following manner]: 'I am *dongoot*' or 'I am *edzheen*'. It is true that Dolgans sometimes also call themselves *t'a kihite* which means in Yakut 'a man of the forest'; or [they call themselves] *teegee* which means 'people' in the Tungus language. These terms are used rarely, especially the latter which is in use only in the area of Noril'sk. The first term is used by Dolgans not only in relationship to themselves but also to the neighbouring peoples. Sometimes Dolgans may call themselves *tungus*. However it is known to us that among the Viliui Yakuts, the neighbours of the Dolgan, the word *tungus* is often used not as the name of a people but as the word for 'of the reindeer' [*olennogo*] in general without reference to what tribe the person belongs to. For this reason Viliui Yakuts, who own cows and horses, call the Tundra Yakuts with reindeer—*tungus*. The latter, when they meet Dolgans, only call themselves *yakuty*. It is not difficult from this to see that, obviously, when a Dolgan says that he is *tungus* this word means not his ethnic affiliation but his occupation [*zaniatie*]. The word *dolgan* is the name of one fratry and has become used as the name for a whole people by Russians and has come to find great acceptance and use today amongst Dolgans themselves (1934*a*: 133).

The relational quality of the terms *tungus* and *dolgan* are most striking in this passage, especially when compared to the long quotations from Dolgikh above. The Russian term *tungus* is recorded in a variety of contexts when differing native producers hail each other in Yakut [*tongus*]. A number of connotations are used in this passage. Most apparent is that the classifier which indicates greater 'reindeerness' is produced with some reluctance to both Dolgikh and Popov since it might have indicated a lesser status. The reasons why it might be less prestigious are not alluded to in this article but it is most likely that those who work with reindeer were thought to be poor or dependent. It is also possible that those who were classified as Tungus by the Imperial Russian state were branded by the 'uncivilized' aspect of being a member of a 'wandering' people. The term *dolgan* [*dulgaan*] is produced only upon contact with Russians. Thus, Russians may have called all Yakut-speaking native people in this region *dolgan*. In turn, native groups may have been using *tungus* to make finer distinctions of occupation and perhaps status. This aspect is confirmed by the parallel use of the term 'forest people' [*t'a kihite*] which described all people engaged in the same endeavour of living on the land: Evenkis and Dolgans together.[9] Popov uses this passage to provide a pedigree for the word *dolgan* which by this date had been given some recognition as a collective label. It seems much more interesting instead to exploit this anomaly in order to mark that the relational terms were very different from the bounded authoritative definitions which were being ratified by state ethnographers at this time.

The final curious anomaly in the works of the state ethnographers is the question of scope. During the period from 1929 to 1963 not only was the label identifying the Dolgan ratified but so was the extent of their national territory. At the early part of this period both Dolgikh (1929: 76) and Popov (1934*a*: 117) circumscribed a very small group onto which they mapped their ethnography: 417 families and 449 individuals respectively. By 1959 this number was to grow to the authorized figure of well over 4,000 people inhabiting all of Taimyr and a small portion of Yakutiia. The specific archival materials used to justify this exponential growth are very difficult to interpret.[10] Suffice it to say that the inclusion of every individual into the body of the Dolgan who either articulated the word *dolgan* or understood Yakut demonstrates the dramatic territorial expanse over which the *dolgan/ tungus* relation was articulated.

It is a well-worn practice in social anthropology to use analytical categories

---

[9] The term *tya/tyalar* or *tya-kikhi/tya-kikhiler* indicates a sense of rurality. It is variously translated as 'of the forest', 'of the village' (Popov 1934*a*; Dolgikh 1963: 105) or 'all who take on Dolgan habits' (Ubriatova 1985: 11). P. E. Ostrovskikh, a Krasnoiarsk geographer who made many expeditions to Taimyr between 1899 and 1904 (Ostrovskikh 1902; 1903; 1904), confirms that the term *haka* is often used by Dolgans but adds the term *tekhol'*, which, he says, is the term used by Tunguses to refer to Dolgans.

[10] The statistical inflation of the Dolgan is most evident in Dolgikh (1963). Within this article there are three different counting systems which are associated with his consolidation of the Dolgan in 1926/7 [my additions]: (1) by tribute unit [3,728] (pp. 93–4, 128); (2) by territorial group [4,391] (pp. 95–9); (3) by clan [*rod*] [4,082] (pp. 107–28). Depending on whether the reader agrees that Evenki-speaking Yakuts or Yakut-speaking Evenkis are equally Dolgan, these numbers can be recalculated to a low of 1,313 'pure' Dolgans or a middle figure of 3,591 Yakut-speakers of mixed origin. Dolgikh gives the highest figures possible for each case. In making my recalculations I have used Dolgikh's own figures since I have not been able to find the original census source cards from which he quotes. A fourth counting system can be found in the article discussed above (Dolgikh 1929) which Dolgikh later repudiated.

to discuss people's identities which may be far from the vernacular terminology in circulation. In the above analysis I have searched classic ethnographic texts for evidence of identities which would be applied differently
depending upon how important it was for the speaker to stress the nature of
his or her activity, language, or homeland. I have also indicated that the
technicians of state ethnography were not so interested in the way in which a
person would express his or her being but were more interested in identifying a single population to which an individual should belong. That state
ethnographers and reindeer herders place different stock in how identity is
ascribed would not be an issue if it were not for a question of power. As the
movements of the people become increasingly centred around rural centres
and the offices whose tasks were to regulate activity and, in turn, to account
for authorized national identities, the 'wondrous mosaic' of Taimyr came to
be fused by the peculiar forces of the Soviet cultural 'reactor'.

5
National Inflation

CONTEMPORARY NATIONAL RIVALRY on the Khantaika is expressed in murmured accusations over tea or as a cold acknowledgement on the street. People demonstrate their group of belonging through the company that they keep, the guests whom they entertain, or the choice of a partner for a voyage on the land which may last several months. Sometimes, always after the consumption of much alcohol, differences erupt into a fight with fists, knives, or hunting weapons. In such instances it is difficult to assign a reason for an injury or death, but recently these fighters have often cited nationality as their cause. It is not an unusual phenomenon that a community recognizes difference between its members. Difference was felt and expressed on the Khantaika well before the resettlement and political reforms of the last two decades. However, the current political context now encourages people to imagine their differences vociferously, using categories crafted by ethnographers and statesman rather than achieved in practice. It has now become thinkable to demand the expulsion of a particular nationality or to divide land exclusively amongst certain residents. The possibility and indeed the necessity of the division of a common territory between groups only arose with the privatization initiatives originating from the centre. Perhaps for the first time in the history of the lower Yenisei valley differences of origin, accent, and behaviour imply solidarity with others living apart at great distances and also differing rights to territory and goods to those who live side by side.

Like the angry winds which, following the death of an elder, create a new landscape of immovable three-metre drifts or solid, barren expanses, the contemporary social space on the Khantaika has been shaped by a vortex of identity politics. Contemporary categories of identity, when compared to the identities held by the older generation, or those of the recent past, can be characterized as vociferous, or inflationary. This is not the same as arguing that they are imaginary or transitory. Identity is now wielded differently in order to draw attention to the fact that social entitlements, once guaranteed through the redistributive state, have been choked by fractions now concerned with parcelling entitlements into a privatized economy. In contrast to what is commonly attributed to the post-Soviet space, I argue that while national rivalry may incite specific memories of the Soviet past, it draws its passions from the insecurities and disrespectfulness of the new market economy. It is this passion which alternately buries or exaggerates relationships between people.

Authorized and relational identities

> The rumour of my fame will sweep through vast Russia,
> And all its peoples will speak this name,
> Whose light shall reign alike,
> For haughty Slav and Finn and wild Tungus [*dikii tungus*],
> And Kalmuk riders of the plain.
>
>> (Aleksandr Pushkin, 'Unto Myself I Raised a Monument',
>> 1836)

Thirty years ago, in the office buildings of Dudinka and Moscow, the technicians of state ethnography selected the identifiers, from a wide assortment of vernacular terms, by which the peoples of Taimyr would be known in official documents, on the media, and in literature. From 1960 onwards, the residents of settlements like the Khantaika began to consider how these authorized national terms could be best assimilated into their lives. Despite official certainty that identity had been scientifically ascribed, and perhaps because of it, in 1993 the issue of who was properly *tongus*, *khaka*, or *dolgan* was still a matter of great debate in the settlement.

Vernacular identities on the Khantaika, such as the key term *tongus*, have a relational or dialogic character linking them to the pragmatic context. This quality is not uncommon in the circumpolar North. For example, as is commonly reported among Inuit people, the name of each local group is relationally linked to the landscape such that a group of people must be known as being of a particular river or being consumers of a particular species (Nuttall 1992). Harald Eidheim's (1969) classic work on Saami identification demonstrated how the production of an ethnic 'boundary' depends upon the people present in a particular encounter. Catherine McClellan's 'hearsay' ethnography of the Yukon Territory (Canada) applies well to the relational diversity of the lower Yenisei valley:

Most of the native terminology is highly relative, depending on the particular vantage points in time and space of both classifier and classified. Also, various modes of classification cross-cut each other. . . . the Yukon Indians frequently prefer to think in terms of selected individuals rather than of total geographically bounded groups. . . . Older informants almost always scoff at the idea that one's place of birth or residence counts much in determining how one is best identified. They repeatedly point out that in the old days 'the people were always walking around' (1975: 14, 16).

The contingency implied by vernacular terms does not sit well with state managers and state ethnographers whose task is to describe populations in an unambiguous manner. The selection of official national descriptors by state agents is designed to strip meaning out of particular encounters. One of the more radical examples of this process comes from the Canadian North, where social welfare administrators reduced complex Inuit names into unambiguous numbers printed on disks (Alia 1994). However, the fact that states label their subject populations does not just bury pre-existing identities. It also releases a new term into circulation which, as Marcus Banks (1996) aptly puts it, can be 'appropriated', 'filled in', or 'manipulated' to local ends. An understanding of identity on the Khantaika requires a sensitivity to the way that state-created identities can be wielded creatively.

The official terminology which qualifies the precise meaning of Soviet citizenship can be best described as 'authoritative discourse' (Bakhtin 1981; Verdery 1991). Instead of highlighting those aspects of a person's character which may be relevant in a particular dialogue or situation, the objective of authoritative discourse is to edit out all extraneous meanings which do not contribute to the stability of a certain political order. The local effect of authorized discourse is much like that of the high language of Russian poets. As Puskhin confidently declared, terms and texts become monuments around which people can orient themselves. While the legitimacy of authoritative identities are adjudicated in exclusive jurisdictional spaces, and are rarely amended in conversation, they can be alluded to, asserted, or ignored as the situation demands. Much like the toponymic local identifiers of Inuit, fixed authorized identities can be circulated in such a manner as to situate a person in a legal landscape. On the Khantaika, nationality labels may be traded strategically in a Barthian fashion (1969), jingoistically asserted in order to channel allocation (Verdery 1991: 209–14; 1993), or 'evoked' in a bid to underscore a particular set of entitlements (Humphrey 1994). However, like monuments in the landscape, despite the creative ways that an authorized identity may be used or misused, it can never be completely removed. Similarly, the task of authorizing identities through ethnography or statistical accounts becomes a war of position wherein the state must create and enforce the contexts where the new identities are useful.

The Russian state has had a long history of using authorized identities such as 'administrative clan' and approved Christian surnames. The unique contribution of the Soviet period was the concept of 'nationality' [*natsional' nost'*], which implied specific citizenship rights in a complex redistributive hierarchy (Hirsch 1997). The meaning of nationality goes beyond that of mere 'ethnicity' for it was an understanding that was carefully adjudicated by state agents. Nationalities could not be freely coined but had to be selected from a list crafted and maintained by various Commissars and Ministers of Nationality in consultation with state ethnographers (cf. Vainshtein 1993). In the latter part of the Soviet period, one's nationality would also be con-spicuously stamped in an 'internal' passport, which served as a pass to various privileges and restrictions within the system of civic entitlements. What distinguishes the category of nationality from other instruments used in the circumpolar North (such as Canadian Indian 'status' or occupationally derived Saami ethnicity) is the fact that it applies equally to Russians and other newcomers. Despite the fact that Russians might refer disparagingly to members of the sparse peoples as *natsionali* ['ethnics'], all actors in the former Soviet Union were forced to negotiate the same legal landscape.

In writing the history of the use of authorized terms on the Khantaika, I employ the metaphor of circulation to mark which identifiers are in use among differing fractions in the settlement. This term is an extension of Pierre Bourdieu's concepts of 'symbolic capital' (1990) and 'cultural capital' (1984) which draw upon the imagery of the capitalist market system. The idea of circulation has the advantage of going beyond a description of how identities become minted and accepted as if they were currencies, but can be subject to local battles wherein their significance becomes 'inflated'. On the one hand, it would seem to be inappropriate to use terms designed for capitalist market economies with a fixed money supply in a context which although recently privatized remains dominated by bureaucratic allocation. On the other hand, prominent ethnographers of state socialism draw on market metaphors to describe the manipulation of cultural and political status in a system with a finite number of administrative positions (Humphrey 1983: 366–73; Verdery 1991: 87–97). Ethnographically, I consider the market imagery of circulation and of 'nationality inflation' to be an appropriate rendering of the possessiveness displayed towards identities in the crumbling allocative economy. These terms convey well the anxiety that people feel as their identities, careers, as well as their incomes, become swept away in the rouble hyperinflation of the early 1990s.

The circulation of identities on the Khantaika is fractured both generationally and spatially between settlements and their surrounding territories. Over time, it is possible to identify a reduction in the diversity of terms within the discursive community on the Khantaika. While there is a strong argument to make that the practice of state ethnographers and administrators is responsible for a greatly impoverished vocabulary of identity, this does not imply that the authorized national terms are false or meaningless. State-ratified words have not only increased in circulation, bankrupting older terms, but have been valuable in struggles over the distribution of state resources.

The circulation of identities

The place in the settlement where official nationalities are imprinted and registered is the office of the settlement administration. Here, in multi-volume household registries the national identities of individuals are recorded for statistical purposes and are kept available for inspection by state officials or visiting researchers. The exact same data can be elicited from residents by the question 'Who are you by nationality?' [*Vy kto po natsional' nosti?*] As the secretary of the village administration explained, the nationality of a child is declared by the mother a few months after birth. At the age of 16 the child has a right to choose the nationality that will be printed into his or her internal passport. She could not recall a case of a young adult choosing a different nationality from that originally registered by the parents. When asked if it was possible to register oneself as *sakha*, *tongus*, or *kamenskie* she replied with laughter. Similarly, she thought it would be 'messy' to enter multiple terms such as 'Dolgano-Yakut'. Neither could she recall that there had been any official debate on the relative meaning of the terms *sakha* or *dolgan*. However, she did find it both possible and interesting to work through the list of surnames in the registers in order to explain to me to which vernacular group (such as Mountain, Khantaika, or newcomer) a person 'belonged' [*otnosilsia*].

As the clerk's informal advice confirms, the circulation of terms outside of the settlement administration is wider than the official list of nationalities. A list of the hearsay terms in circulation is presented in Table 11. From the large variety of terms in this table it is at first difficult to see that the state had any impact at all on the types of identities in circulation. However, many of the vernacular terms are in such limited use that they are only remembered by a few individuals. Unlike state ethnographers, or some local informants, I do not interpret these archaic terms as in any way giving an insight into primordial Evenki or Dolgan identities. However, an analysis of them is important in order to demonstrate that the circulation of identities has indeed changed over the past thirty years. An analysis of the vocabularies of the older generation compared to the younger generation implies that a richer variety of identities were once available, and that in the recent past more than one term could be applied to a single individual.

The fraction within the community with a rich vocabulary of identity is the generation of 50 years and older who were relocated from Kamen'. Within this community, the eldest 'Dolgans' will call themselves only *haka/hakalar* but will expect Russian-speaking investigators (like myself) to call them *dolgan*. Those who originally settled in Kamen' late in their lives will also use terms like *arga* ['from behind/from the South'] to distinguish Yakut-speaking settlers from the area of Lake Yessei from those who live along the Khatanga Way.[1] Typically, those elderly 'Evenkis' who had spent their lives working with reindeer are called *tongus/tongustar* even though they may prefer to speak only Yakut. The majority of this group are registered officially as Evenkis. Younger Yakut-speaking individuals (25 or above) will produce the term *kamenskii* [Mountain Person] in recognition of their birth place. However, as a sign of their education and of their

---

[1] Local people note certain lexical differences between Volochanka Yakut-speakers and *arga* Yakut-speakers: *agaal!* vs. *egœl!* [speak!]; *cherke* vs. *tanang* [white]; *arga* vs. *koshe* [back] (see also Gracheva 1983).

TABLE 11. The circulation of authorized and vernacular terms on the Khantaika,
1992–1993

Term (pl.)	Contexts	Definition
Evenk (*Evenki*)	Academic, Administrative, Literary Russian, Conversational	The authorized term for the indigenous people of central and eastern Siberia speaking one of many dialects of the Evenki (Tungus Manchurian) language. It replaced *tungus* in scholarly circles in 1926. It is in common use among Evenkis, Dolgans, and Russians alike.
Russkii (*Russkie*)	Academic, Administrative, Literary Russian, Conversational	The authorized term for the people indigenous to the European part of Russia speaking the Russian language. It is in widespread use in all circles.
Dolgan (*Dolgany*)	Academic, Administrative, Literary Russian, Conversational	The authorized term for the indigenous people of Taimyr speaking a dialect of Yakut. The term first appeared in *yasak* registries in the 17th century. It appeared in academic use and as the name of an administrative territory in 1930. Since the 1960s it has come into widespread use amongst the people.
Yakut (*Yakuty*)	Academic, Administrative, Literary Russian, Conversational	The authorized term for the indigenous people of the Sakha republic who speak the Yakut language. It has recently been replaced by *sakha* as an authorized term. It is still used in contemporary ethnology and colloquially as the Russian-language term for these people.
Dulgan (*Dulgalar*)	Administrative, Literary Dolgan	The authorized term for the Dolgan nationality in the Dolgan dialect. It has appeared in school textbooks since the late 1980s.
Sakha (*Sakhalar*)	Administrative, Literary Yakut, Conversational	This is the vernacular term which Dolgans use to identify themselves. It is understood by all generations. It served as the authorized term for this people until 1960. It is now the authorized term for the Yakut-speaking peoples indigenous to the Sakha republic.
Tongus (*Tongustar*)	Literary Yakut, Conversational	In the Sakha republic and in Taimyr, this term is used by Yakut-speakers to refer to Evenkis. In Taimyr it carries the connotation of being connected to reindeer breeding.
Evenki (*Evenkil*)	Literary Evenki, Conversational	In most Evenki-speaking regions, this is the term used by Evenkis to refer to themselves.
Yako (*Yakol*)	Literary Evenki, Conversational	This is a widely used Evenki term for Yakuts. On the Khantaika it refers to 'proper' Yakuts and not the Yakut-speaking people of the Taimyr.
Lus'a (*Lus'al*)	Literary Evenki, Conversational	A widely used term by Evenkis to refer to Russians. It is often used on the Khantaika.
Toho (*Tohol*), *Teho* (*Tehol*)	Conversational	A vernacular term for 'a people', 'foreigners (non-Europeans)', or 'a people that is unknown to the Evenki language'. It is used on the Khantaika to refer to Dolgans. See Vasilevich (1970).
Khempo (*Khempol*)	Conversational	In the Potapovo region, this term refers to a group of intermarrying clans who consider themselves to be a people. See Tugolukov (1985).

Term (pl.)	Contexts	Definition
Tyhaa (*Tyhaalar*)	Conversational	This vernacular term means 'People of the bush/tundra' or 'People from the periphery'. Evenkis and Dolgans of the older generation use it to speak inclusively of all people who live on the land (non-European). It is also used in the central regions of the Sakha republic to refer to Yakuts living in the north of the republic. See Popov (1934*a*) and Dolgikh (1963).
Liucha (*Liuchar*)	Conversational	The term used by Dolgans on the Khantaika to refer to Russians.
Tungus (*Tungusy*)	Conversational	A common vernacular Russian term for Evenkis. Before 1926 it served as the official administrative and scholarly term for this people.
Priezhii (*Priezhie*)	Conversational	A Russian term used chiefly by indigenous people to refer to Russians, Ukranians, and other peoples from the European part of the Russian Federation who have come to live in Siberia for a short time.
Sibiriak (*Sibiriaki*)	Conversational	A widely used term to refer to anyone who has lived in Siberia long enough not to be considered a newcomer. It usually is not used to refer to members of the indigenous peoples.
Silduka (*Silduki*)	Conversational	A term used vernacularly by Russians born in the lower Yenisei valley to refer to themselves.
Hokhol (*Hokhli*)	Conversational	A widely used pejorative term for Ukrainians.
Yurak (*Yuraki*)	Conversational	A widely used Russian term used by Evenkis for Enetses.
Khami (*Khamoedy*)	Conversational	A term used by Dolgans and Yakut-speaking Evenkis to refer to Nganasans.
Mestnii (*Mestnye*)	Conversational	A Russian term used by indigenous people to refer to themselves, irrespective of nationality.
Natsional' (*Natsionali*)	Conversational	A pejorative Russian term used by Russians to refer to members of the indigenous peoples of Taimyr.

consciousness of their legal status they will prefer the words *dolgan* or *evenki* to describe their nationality. Their children, born already on the Khantaika, will recognize only two terms: Evenki and Dolgan.

The same decreasing diversity of terminology is apparent within those strictly of the Khantaika community. The 50 and above generation tend to identify themselves using the word *evenki* inflected with the marks of Evenki phonology [*æw'nki*] and in the vernacular singular form (i.e. not the Russian form *evenk*). Those individuals over 25 will tend to use the Russian official term *evenk*. As an example of the pride that the younger generation takes in knowing their proper official identity, one young Evenki villager, who works as the director of social services in Dudinka, proudly showed me her passport where she forced the clerks to type her nationality as *evenkiiskaia* instead of with the spelling error common to Taimyr: *evenka*.[2]

The older Khantaika generation may in rare instances produce the word *khempo* to refer to persons who are now grouped around Potapovo but in the past travelled the lands encompassed by the southern arc of the ring of pollution from Noril'sk. Leonid Men'ko of the Number One Reindeer Brigade described the *khempol* as 'a kind of people' [*oni narod takoi*]. In terms of authorized nationality they are either Enneche or Evenki. In vernacular terms they are an exogamic group which intermarries with *yuraki* and *tungusy* (and thus are both Enneche and Evenki). The state ethnographer Tugolukov, who worked in Potapovo, was sufficiently convinced of their independent provenance as to term them an independent 'ethnographic group' (1985: 211). Vasil'ev (1963: 38) defines the 'group' *khempo* living in Potapovo as three families of Sapozhnikovs and one family of Men'kos. The existence of interval identifiers such as *khempo*, *tongus*, and to a certain extent, *dolgan*, stand as proof of the arbitrary nature of official nationality lists.

Of the archaic terms, there are two words which are explicitly inclusive and not oriented to a particular nationality. Their declining circulation may be due to the increased nationalism in the settlement. Among the terms that one encounters by chance are the cosmopolitan categories like 'forest people' *tiaa/tialaar* or 'the other people' *tehol* (Vasilevich 1970; 1972). In the words of one elderly informant the former Dolgan term means:

This is all of the people . . . kind of everyone out there . . . the tundra people both *evenki* and *dolgan* . . . it's everyone together . . . you don't hear it any more.

A young Evenki hunter defined the latter term for me with an ironic smile:

They are called *dolgan* now but really they are all *tehol*. This is what the old people say. It means foreigners—people who are incomprehensible in the Evenki language [*neponiatno evenkiiskomu yazyku*] [*smile*].

Both of these terms which once had a broad reference are now not only little used but are evidently reinterpreted in the light of the current conflict between the Mountain People and the Khantaika locals.

The unsteady slippage of connotation of vernacular terms between different groups is best illustrated by the controversial Yakut term *tongus*. The older reindeer stewards, resettled from Kamen', produce this word as a definitive term and often with a sense of pride. It is a term which is quite distant from

---

[2] Another Evenki woman spoke to me of the confusion she faced when she was placed in an Even language class at the Faculty of Peoples of the North at the Hertzen Pedagogical Institute. She had landed in the class because her passport labelled her as *evenka*. For the first two months of class she could not understand how it was that she could not understand a word when she had always assumed that she spoke her native language well.

genetic heritage as testified by the fact that I was once hailed as a *kanadskii tongus* (a Canadian reindeer-man) with a wide smile by one old herder as I walked the paths of the settlement dressed in my reindeer-skin *bakeri* and beaded fox-skin hat. In the usage of these older herders, *tongus* retains the classic ambiguity of meaning both individuals who handle reindeer and individuals who use Evenki cultural practices. Amongst the Kamen' group, the Russian word *tungus* also serves as a synonym for the Evenki language ('I don't understand Evenki': *Ya ne ponimaiu po tunguskii*).

It its most benign usage, *tongus* is a powerful adjective which indicates a hardy and untameable character which grows out of a close connection to reindeer and to the tundra. Among the member of the Number One Reindeer Brigade, a younger herder could jokingly be called a *tongus* if he spent too much time roaming the land on his skis by himself. Of all of the *tongus* characters, the favourite butt of stories was the brigadier Aleksandr Ukocher of the Number Three Reindeer Brigade. In the years preceding his retirement in 1993, he became very cavalier with his state farm reindeer. It was rumoured that he gambled away dozens of head of state reindeer in high-stakes card-games with other Mountain People. Nikolai Savel'evich, although he tended to frown upon the improper use of state farm property, had tried hard to introduce me to the crusty brigadier. During his last attempt to find him on the tundra, Nikolai Savel'evich had hoped to make use of my visit to bring up the matter of several reindeer that Aleksandr had 'borrowed' several years before. After spending two days following the tangled paths of the Number Three herd, we came across a site with a smoking campfire and a set of tracks which suggested that Aleksandr and his herd of 800 had scaled a nearly vertical incline. Older Khantaika Evenkis use the word rarely but exclusively to refer to behaviour (and with a slightly pejorative tinge). In discussing his behaviour with Old Man Yeremin, the two *tundroviki* came to the conclusion that Aleksandr was a real *tongus*:

He is the real wild Tungus [*dikii tungus*—a reference to the Pushkin poem—D.A.]. Look at his trail! It runs just like a bear trail. He goes from one thick bit of forest to another. Wherever you find thick forest that's where you find him.

The connotations of 'wildness' and 'reindeerness' in these quotes support the interpretation in the previous chapter that the word *tongus* is a relational identifier referring to an activity or an occupation. However, the humour in the discussion conveys respect for a certain untamed wilfulness, captured in the Imperial-era phrase of the wild Tungus and its implication of an un-predictable 'wandering' lifestyle. As admirable as this sense of liberty is, it works towards ends opposed to Soviet productivism. By 1997, the Number Three herd had all been traded away. The remnant 300 head of reindeer which had been lost in the hills above the River Koliumbe were officially 'turned over' to the Number One Brigade.

The most common context for the word *tongus* is between the younger generations of both the Khantaika and Kamen' groups. Those young Evenkis whose families are native to Lake Khantaika take bitter offence at the term.

I.A.   I don't like it when they [*kamenskie*] call us *tongus*. They should call us *evenki*.
D.A.   What does *tongus* mean?
I.A.   I don't know, it is like we are lower [*nizhie*] or something. I think they do it to insult us.

This new pejorative understanding of the term is directly tied in with the violent conflicts that characterize the birth of nationalism in the settlement. It is a telling example of the nationality inflation which strips the base value of complex relational terms.

The changes in the vocabulary of identity between generations display not only a reduction in diversity but also a reduction in the number of terms applicable to a single person. Older informants to this day identify with a variety of terms. For example, the 50-year-old Dolgan store clerk from Volochanka, who provided a home for me during my first month in the settlement, identified herself at various times as *sakha*, *dolgan*, *arga*, and *tiaa*. Her daughter only recognized the term *dolgan*. A well-respected retired reindeer herder regularly used the terms *tongus*, *evenk*, *evenki*, and *tiaa* whereas his son recognized the terms *kamenskii* and *dolgan*. Between individuals, as in the household registries maintained by the laughing settlement secretary, there was a narrowing array of openings within which complex identities could be attributed to a single person in the year of my fieldwork.

Although the number of categories in circulation had been reduced, a number of skilful individuals proved to be quite adept at manipulating those categories which were still in circulation, at 'tuning between' different authorized nationalities and thus preserving the relational environment of the past. Among the most experienced nationality traders were the members of the 'the most Evenki' Number One Reindeer Brigade. If asked, the senior tent-worker Liubov' Fedorovna would always declare herself to be Evenki. However, her more cosmopolitan heritage often slipped out informally. One spring day, after listening to a Dolgan shaman's song on Taimyr radio, she unexpectedly blurted out a translation of the lyrics:

L.F.   He's saying 'people are not to blame'. He just repeats that.
D.A.   [*surprise*] You understand Dolgan?
L.F.   [*pause*] Of course! There are all sorts of people speaking all kinds of languages. Everyone understands Dolgan and Evenki.
D.A.   What about the Chempogirs or the Yarotskiis?
L.F.   Those sisters [Chempogirs] are just like wild people [*dikari*]. They were always far from the settlement. That's why they don't understand. The others are kind of village-centred so they speak it.

D.A. Can the Mountain People speak Evenki then?

L.F. The *kamenskie* are so brazen [*naglie*]! Maia told everyone in the bakery that the First Brigade lost all their deer when actually all the other brigades lost their deer to the First Brigade! . . . They are all the same whether they are *sakha* or Evenki.

D.A. How does Misha fit then? [who recently joined Number One Reindeer Brigade] He doesn't speak Evenki yet he is a relative. [a second-cousin who speaks Russian and Dolgan]

L.F. Well, that family has a nature tuned-in to Dolgan [*natura nastroena na dolgan*].

Liubov′ Fedorovna's image of being able to tune between nationalities like one tunes a two-way radio is a very apt one. All across Siberia reindeer brigades and hunters communicate with one another by means of high frequency two-way radios set to a single authorized frequency. Radio sets were designed for communication between the outlying trap lines and brigades and a single dispatcher (in this case the dispatcher of the state farm 'Khantaiskii' code-named 'sunbeam'). Possessing a multi-frequency transmitter was possible only if one built it oneself; but this was a strictly illegal activity. Switching frequencies was about as easy as changing the landscape; but it was not impossible. If one wanted to communicate with other people on other exotic bands one had to change the entire technology of one's allegiance such as moving to a different community or a different district. This, in effect, is what Liubov′ Fedorovna had done many times. What she never said to me, but I learned from others, was that her own descent (see Chart 2) was classically Dolgan for the area of the Noril′sk lakes. In her background were relatives of five lineages, which would be today distinguished as nationalities. She was born in Valek (now the site of an airport near Noril′sk) to a family of Tundra Peasants who spoke Evenki. Her mother later sent her to live with relatives in Kur′e, where she spoke Yakut. When she moved to the Khantaika as a young woman she registered herself as *sakha*. In 1965 in step with administrative changes all over Taimyr, her registration became *dolgan*. After several unspecified but unpleasant incidents following the resettlement of the Mountain People, she changed her official registration in 1972 to *evenka* (and presumably stopped advertising that she spoke Dolgan) (GATAO 73–2–1–25). Her sister, who lives in the village, married to an Evenki hunter from Kamen′, is registered as Dolgan.

A similar story was recalled to me fondly by a pensioned hunter-fisherman with whom I tended nets for the months of January and February 1993. This registered Evenki spoke both Evenki and Yakut fluently. In the days when he worked as a state farm official, he would enjoy travelling to different cities in Taimyr, Evenkiia, and Yakutiia, slipping from one table to another at banquets drinking first with Evenkis and then with Yakuts. In either company he would portray himself as variously Evenki or Yakut. Although both of these examples are rather playful, they also hint that the days of trading nationalities are over. The contemporary political situation on the Khantaika has necessitated a firm solidarity to one or another nationality.

Tempering the narrowed terminology of recent times are two other Russian terms which have meanings similar to the old relational meaning of *tongus*. The categories *tundroviki* and *pastukhi* are applied broadly without respect to whether one is Dolgan, Evenki, Russian, or even Canadian. The inclusive nature of these terms stems from the fact that these terms are linked to observed practice and not the authoritative system of state ethnography. Performative terms for identity were circulated most frequently among the young and old living out on the land. As the caravans of Number One Reindeer Brigade moved further and further from the settlement, the most common declarative statement of identity was 'man-of-the-tundra' [*tundrovik*] rather than Evenki or Dolgan. If a discussion over tea moved backwards in time to broach the topic of those who lived before, my queries about the identity of the people would either be an irritated silence or that Evenkis lived 'everywhere' before. A true *tundrovik* it seemed would be a person who spoke many languages and would be a master of many skills.

In contrast to the limited contexts where ascribed identity was used, the performative contexts of identity were quite rich. The use of the national designator came up most commonly in adjectival forms. 'In Evenki [*evedyt*] this would be *huka* [axe]'; 'In Canada, do you use a Russian axe or an Evenki [*evenkiiskii*] axe?'; 'Let's use Evenki napkins to cook this fish [*wrapping the fish in newspaper and placing it in a stove*]'. Apart from asking, at the beginning, if Evenkis lived in Canada, the only most commonly repeated phrase to me with the word *evenki* was 'If you keep [tying, braiding, chopping] in *that* way you will never become Evenki!' In a harsher vein, the younger herders would make fun of my strict attention to harnessing technique (which, according to Russian ethnography, is a tell-tale clue to national identity). As I practised throwing my lasso, Konstantin would comment approvingly that only *real* Evenkis throw lassos with their left hand (presumably to see if I would then record this in my notebook). The quality that herders seemed to value most in a *tundrovik* was the ability to perform a task well in a manner that would suit the context. This could include mixing Yakut words with Evenki words for describing reindeer. It could mean mixing words of different Evenki dialects. Perhaps the least successful experiment I performed was to read out my Evenki glossary (Kochneva 1990) to test if terms from the southern literary dialect were in use in this northern frontier of Evenki settlement. Of two hundred terms, including forty which I myself noted were not in daily use, the obliging brigadier replied that he knew each one or had heard someone speak it at some time. The conclusion of this exercise was that Nikolai Savel'evich had witnessed, or could imagine, a context, where the use of a southern term would be legitimate. What would characterize my apprenticeship would be a steady relaxing of my ethnological fixation upon ascribed terms to a more subtle appreciation of how identity could be displayed.

My eight-month experience on the land and several months in archives suggests to me that the last thirty years has had a deep effect on the categories of identity in the territories surrounding Lake Khantaika. Comparing the discourse of the older to younger generation shows a reduction in the diversity of terms to indicate identity. When the statements used by *tundroviki* are compared to those used by villagers, one finds that performative indicators of identity are spatially limited to non-urban contexts. Finally, it seemed that inclusive terms of identity ranging from *tiialar* to *tungus* were gradually becoming rarer currencies, or had been changed into derogatives. These changes in context and connotation suggest a refocusing of identity away from a person's performed sense of being to rather encapsulated sense of belonging. Nevertheless, the idea of belonging to a nationality can also be used as a rich idiom with which to make political claims. This in part explains the phenomenon of 'tuning oneself' into one authorized identity or the more exotic examples of switching channels. The usefulness of authorized identities explains their expanding and inflated circulation in everyday life.

Inflationary strategies

Yesterday they sent [my brother] Denis to prison. He killed the Chuprin boy in a fight. The real issue was again being a *tungus*. Denis was sticking up for the rights of the Evenkis. He didn't like it that they called us that name. The funny thing was that in the passports Denis is Dolgan and Chuprin was Evenki. Of course it was all connected with vodka (Letter from the Khantaika, Dec. 1993).

In the previous section, a diverse list of vernacular identities was contrasted with the unambiguous and narrow official terminology which has been ascribed to persons by state ethnographers and administrators. Among those terms, the richest store of identities remains in the minds of the older generation or within the practice of the *tundroviki*. The burgeoning adolescent and young adult population (and the villagers in general) were shown to divide their social world with a narrow range of terms which, if presenting any vernacular elaboration at all, had been turned into pejoratives. In post-Soviet Khantaika, authorized identities have become stretched to include a greater number of people and to be used in a wider number of contexts. The use of authorized identities to foment nationalist rivalry is a case of 'national inflation'.

The metaphor of national inflation carries the connotation that a value is asserted for particular categories which is greater than is justified by the original definition of the term. Unlike with monetary currencies, it is both impossible and inappropriate to establish an essential base value to national identities. In the preceding two sections documentary and ethnographic evidence was used to show that the various vernacular identities of this region were not minted in limited editions but were interrelated in complex ways which took into account the actions, lifestyle, and status of both listener and speaker. On the other hand, the authorized identities introduced by state socialism were limited, officially sanctioned, and valuable. With the collapse of the centrally administered social contract, people have turned to these national categories to make political and social claims in a vociferous manner which goes beyond the tightly regulated administrative and ethnographic system under which these terms were originally issued.

National inflation on the Khantaika has not affected Evenkis and Dolgans equally. The rise of a sense of belonging to an Evenki nationality is by far the more recent phenomenon.[3] The most common examples of inflation are the subsuming of complex identities under Dolgan coinage. The quote at the start of this section is a dramatic and complex case in point. The irony in this tragic account is that the officially registered Dolgan combatant, who was imprisoned, most probably learned his nationalist convictions from his strong-willed Evenki mother born on the Khantaika. Although the boy's father was officially Dolgan (a Dolgan of Lake Yessei Yakut heritage), the boy felt obliged to avenge the insult of being called a *tongus*. The insult here had a double barb. On the one hand, it devalued the attachment that Denis felt to the nationality of his mother and his kin. On the other hand, it denied that his paternal heritage gave him entrance into the Dolgan community. There is also a second layer of irony. The boy who called him *tongus* was an officially registered Evenki with roots extending back to Lake Yessei to a generation which would have perhaps proudly called themselves *tongus*. This incident is a complex example of an accusation which devalues Evenki heritage and nationality while inflating the value of Dolgan identity. What makes the letter tragic is not so much the ironic mismatch between authorized identities and each boy's passionate feeling of belonging, but the insidious logic of a nationalist confrontation where the sense of belonging to one nationality can only be properly savoured by negating the other. The forgetting of a common bond between both Evenkis and Yakuts—an element which often goes along with nationalist rivalry (Renan 1990)—is a common theme in the nationalist rhetoric of this settlement.

Reactions to national inflation are usually expressed in more subtle ways in both the settlement and out on the land. In both cases, *tundroviki* and villagers stress the mismatch between sentiments and official categories.

---

[3] In other parts of Siberia, the Evenki identity is hegemonic. Heonik Kwon (1993: 129) notes that on Sakhalin island Evenkis are thought by Orochons to be 'more developed' and 'closer to Russian culture' than themselves: 'this is what makes several genealogically *orochonskie* women claim that they are Evenk'.

However, their plea is not for more numerous categories of identity but for fewer.

Although the characteristically silent idiom of *tundroviki* is ill-suited to nationalist discussions, I did encounter other examples of concern over official identities which were perceived to be inappropriately circulated. As with my rigorous training in household and herding skills, some of the richest conversations seemed to be provoked by what were regarded as careless mistakes on my part. If this topic arose at all with the usually taciturn Brigadier Nikolai Savel'evich, it would be if our paths happened to cross during long hikes across the land in search of reindeer.

N.S. See, up on the rise. That's an old *chum* [teepee]. Some hunters were here. . . . [*long pause*] . . . Maybe it's that shaman's place . . . Ptarmigan [*kurapatka*].
D.A. Is that his name? [N.S. *affirmation*] How do you say it in Evenki?
N.S. . . . [*long pause, then quickly*] . . . *khulaki.* . . . To this day his relatives say *kurapatka* because they are scared.
D.A. . . . [*after a few minutes' walk*] . . . The Kurapatovs are his relatives then.
N.S. [*with impatience*] Don't mix up names and surnames! Besides Kurapatov is another one of those made-up [*pridumannaia*] surnames. The same goes for Ul'man [a Mountain Evenki surname]. It is supposed to be Vereshagin. The Proshkins are supposed to be Tul'skie. It's all like that. In general there are no such people as Dolgan. It's all made up!

Two days later at the base camp, uprooting trees with a pick-axe in order to carve runners for a new *balok*:

D.A. You know—I was reading that story on Dolgans [Dolgikh 1963]. It seems that their name switches from *sakha* to Dolgan on paper all the time.
N.S. It's just like that with the *kamentsy*. When they came they called themselves *yako* [Yakuts]. Some kind of *yakol* they are! They are not *yakol*. It's all been mixed up!

In a context where a silent performance is the most convincing statement, it is difficult to deduce a strong declaration of resistance to the changing circulation of identities. Part of the frustration evident in these statements can be understood as a concern with the inappropriate replacement of performative categories by authorized terms. In other contexts Nikolai Savel'evich would describe statements concerning the Dolgan as 'gossiping' [*boltavania, ardia*] or as 'lies' [*lozh*]. Part of the resentment in these quotes comes from the burning memory that several wealthy Yakut families went so far as to change their surnames in order to disguise their wealth and their nationality from Soviet organizers.[4] However, beyond the frustration is also a

---

[4] According to representatives of both Mountain and Khantaika groups, Dolgan individuals with the contemporary surnames 'Katyginskii' and 'Espok' are related to Yakut families remaining in the Evenki Autonomous District with the surnames 'Maimago' and 'Botulu'. Both surname groups can be identified within archival records as controlling large herds of reindeer in 1927.

directed attempt to assert that in this discursive community there is space only for the circulation of Evenki or Yakut identities. In these statements the Dolgans as a group are defined out of circulation.

The similar tack of negating the existence of the Dolgan as nationality was taken by my *balok*-mate Vladimir, a young man who was also a member of the same clan as the brigadier:

There is nothing special about them. They are just a mixture. They are Yakuts mixed with Evenkis who went too far North. . . . My father spoke Yakut and Evenki. And Filip belonged [*otnosilsia*] to the Yakuts—but to the real Yakuts—none of their mixture.

Grammatically, *otnosit'sia* carries a passive mood which connotes a weak sense of grouping. The passive sense of Vladimir's statement gains an elective dimension if one knows the Utukogir genealogy (see Chart 3)—a genealogy which reveals the inter-braiding of Evenki and Yakut partners through marriage. For example, the belonging of Filip to the Yakut, as understood here by his nephew, cannot be deduced by genetic descent alone. Although Filip spoke Yakut, so did many of his brothers, sisters, and cousins. His cousins in particular (shown in this genealogy as members of the Khutukagir' clan) are thought to belong to Dolgans—or members of the 'mixture' of which Vladimir spoke. In this statement, Vladimir seems to have elected to associate his uncle with an official nationality—and a prestigious one—as if to indicate that the category Dolgan is a debased or a forged currency.

Within the settlement, the inflation of the Dolgan community of belonging is typically expressed in small ironic incidents. One common example is the surprise that some villagers express in learning of the officially marked Evenki heritage of some of the Kamen' settlers. The case of one marriage was told to me first by the young Evenki bride and then a few months later by her father:

L.S. When I first came here [from Potapovo] I didn't know much about the *kamentsy*. Then I married. I thought it was okay being married. We got along fine. One day I found his passport and it said *evenk*. I showed it to him and asked him if he was Evenki and he said he was. Isn't that funny?

As with the tragic story above, this humorous story contains within it a subtle irony when one learns of the complex history of the father's identity.

S.S. You never know who is an Evenki around here. Here my daughter married a Dolgan and then you find out that he's Evenki. You might be talking to a Dolgan right now!

I would come to appreciate the irony of Old Man Yeremin's last comment several months later, following several days of drinking in honour of International Women's Day, when I caught this 'Evenki' pensioner singing a Yakut song. Although he did not identify the song as Yakut, he did tell me that he learned it from his mother. This and other scattered comments regarding his parents seem to indicate that his father was an Evenki-speaking Enets from around Potapovo who had several wives. It seems that the old man was raised at some point by a Yakut-speaking woman (although he might have been born of different roots). Today his complex history is represented merely by his official registration as Evenki, a narrow identity which he passed on to his daughter. It would not be hard to imagine that had these individuals lived in a different village or a different district, they might all have been members of another 'nation'.

A similar scene was repeated in the company of a Mountain Evenki elder who was pleasantly surprised to find out that two bilingual Dolgan-Russian-speaking adolescents still registered themselves as Evenkis: 'Good for you boys: don't sell out your people [*ne prodavai svoi narod*]'. A reverse instance was encountered in the company of Khantaika Evenkis who scoffed to discover that certain Mountain youth actually 'wrote themselves' [*zapisalis'*] in the household registry as Evenkis. These examples of either sweet or angry surprise at hidden facts demonstrate that the boundaries of the nationality to which one is thought to properly belong are now extending past the restricted categories once adjudicated by the state.

More ominous than these observations on the identity that one or another individual is expected to hold are a host of small accusations over the distribution of employment positions within the state farm, or the allocation of housing amongst individuals. The occupational places [*mesta*] within the settlement which have the highest access to manipulable resources or to transport tend to be stratified along lines of nationality (Anderson 1996*a*: appendix 1). As explored above, the administrative hierarchy of this settlement was deliberately fractured by nationality in order that the 'leading peoples' of Taimyr be given the most productive places so that they might raise the level of culture of the settlement. In the whispered accusations within the crowded rooms of the settlement either Evenkis, Dolgans, or Russians are accused of helping only 'their own' [*svoim*]. Although the crumbling economy may cast these conflicts in a much harsher light, most people in the settlement felt that the nationalist bias in allocation was a recent phenomenon—a process directly related to the rate of disintegration of citizen rights generally. What makes this phenomenon representative of national inflation is the fact that both Khantaika Evenkis and the Mountain People sensed a consolidation of interests which erased liminal categories. Thus in the struggle for resources, Mountain Evenkis were accused of being equally 'brazen' [*naglie*] as Dolgans, or in fact the same as Dolgans. Similarly, some Khantaika Dolgans were called 'Evenkis' as if these terms were synonyms.

The spectre of *natsionalizm* also lurked in the background of my anthropological project. Khantaika Evenkis took great pride in the fact that a foreign ethnographer had come to study their history and their traditions. Numerous Evenki youths confessed that until my arrival they had never thought that *tongusy* had any history at all. They saw themselves as 'small people' on many scales: they were too small to have an Evenki page in the district newspaper; too small to have a cultural ensemble; to small to have radio programming in Evenki; too small to have a history. A typical statement might be 'We Evenki were just idol-worshippers and hunters without culture'. As I stayed longer in the community, there was great enthusiasm in seeking my opinion on which appliqué patterns distinguished them from Dolgans (since their sewing was thought to be 'just like Dolgan sewing') or to consult my map of place-names which showed the predominance of words of Evenki origin. My 'scientific' interest in Evenki culture coincided with a general revival of interest in nationalist histories. A stir was created when two delegates from the Khantaika were selected by the association *Arun* [rebirth] to attend the first Evenki *suglan* [assembly] held in Tura, capital of the Evenki Autonomous District, in April 1993. The Evenki language teacher later would report to me on her wonder at discovering other Evenkis 'just like us':

We were welcomed like special guests. Each of us was given a present as is Evenki custom. At first I was very shy to speak at all. I knew that I could not speak right [i.e. literary Evenki]. But when I listened closely I heard that they spoke just like us! I was really nervous before my speech to the assembly. Afterwards two old women came up to me and congratulated me saying 'You speak so well—just like we speak'. I never before realized that we had so much in common.

A similar surprising realization occurred upon the airing of a programme on provincial radio on the history of reindeer-breeding. Although I did not hear the programme myself, the reports given to me of it spoke in wonder of archaeological findings showing that the Evenkis had a history going back to the eighth century. One young student stated, 'I did not realize that we were such an old people.' It seems that this cultural revival continued after my departure. In 1996 the school opened two (separate) museums displaying artefacts of Evenki and Dolgan culture.

Dolgans were not left out of the politics of my field research nor the politics of national revival in 1992–3. Although the majority of Dolgan families proved to be very gracious hosts, I was confronted three times by young nationalists for my failure to talk to people about Dolgan culture. More typically my fascination for Evenkis was treated with humour since, as I was reminded once or twice, the ethnographers had established long ago that Dolgans were the 'aristocrats of the tundra' and thus had more culture to offer than the simple Evenkis.[5] In

---

[5] The Evenki nationalists of Taimyr will be pleased to learn that the phrase 'aristocrats of Siberia' was used by Kastren (1860: 343) to praise the manners of the Turukhansk Tunguses (in comparison to the Samoeds, who were described unfavourably). This powerful phrase is commonly misattributed to Middendorf, Popov, and Dolgikh.

November 1992 the first Congress of Dolgans was held in the Sakha (Yakutiia) Republic to tackle issues of how to preserve their nation in the new market conditions. The report in the district newspaper, entitled 'Dolgans on the Path to National Rebirth' (16 January 1993) examined the need for exclusive clan communities, clan lands, and a return to national purity [*samobytnost'*]. A local attempt to put these slogans in practice led to the departure of two families from the Khantaika to settle once again on the place where the Kamen' factory once stood in a bid to establish a 'clan community'. In the autumn of 1997 not only were these two clan communities still subsisting on a modest level, but there were numerous proposals arising out of Volochanka and Ust'-Avam to revitalize other small settlements abandoned during the great resettlements of the 1960s.

I am sure that I could be held to task by both Dolgan and Evenki nationalists for suggesting that a national rebirth [*vozrozhdenie*] is synonymous with national inflation. This is a well-known trope of North Atlantic anthropology which asserts that collective identities are 'invented' or 'imagined'. In this chapter I have borrowed from this conceptual storehouse to establish the transition from relational to authorized identities and have demonstrated the heavy hand of state ethnographers in coining nationalities. Each of these phenomena speaks strongly against the idea of a rebirth since, as this chapter and the following chapters will show, Dolgans and Evenkis recall many of the same roots in terms of languages, lifestyle, and even kin. The suggestion that a locally fuelled *natsionalizm* is out of balance, or distorting the original administrative identifiers, is not the same as arguing that they are worthless currencies. In this chapter I have suggested a link between national inflation and the generation of a belligerent sense of belonging which serves to mobilize people in struggles for places. Although the idea of nationality was forged by state ethnographers, and the strategic use of nationality was elaborated by local nationalists, the phenomenon of national inflation should not mark individuals of either group as culpable for local tragedies.

6
Sentient Ecology

THE PROPER RELATIONSHIP of people to land has always been a central concern for Evenkis when hunting, travelling, or even living the stationary lifestyle of the villagers. In times past, before the redistributive state took responsibility for providing food and shelter for the citizens within its reach, Evenkis maintained an intense and constant relationship with the land both to subsist but also to gain technical and spiritual knowledge. The provision of central state subsidies through a complex and bureaucratized division of labour has displaced most Khantaika Evenkis from a day-to-day relationship with the land, but this has not made the land any less important in their lives. Apart from receiving salaries which are in some way underwritten by activities on the territories of the state farm, most Evenkis place the land prominently in discussions over their future when the talk turns to the centrally imposed policy known as privatization [*privatizatsiia*]. With more anxiety, but with less preciseness, there is also a growing worry over the chaotic movement of wild deer herds due to the airborne pollution from Noril'sk.

While *tundroviki* and villagers now talk about the tundra when crafting nationalist arguments, in a much more profound sense discussions about the land are important to understand what it means to be Evenki. Contemporary nationalist identities are triangulated with reference to the identities of Russian newcomers and the other inflated nationalities in the village. However the identities of the older generations, or those of the *tundroviki*, are underwritten by the tundra itself, which favours certain individuals. Being a *tundrovik*, therefore, is not only a relational identity in the sense that it is a category encompassing people of multiple language groups and nationalities. It also implies an even stronger set of solidarities and obligations between people and certain places and animals. The mutual interrelation of person and place constructs a sentient ecology.[1] This complex, communicative

---

[1] Many works in ecological anthropology tend to be constructed on the premiss that nature is a passive, almost mechanical space which can be measured or observed in a more or less accurate manner by different cultures. Classic works tend to argue that non-Western peoples come to an implicit understanding of the natural world which can be reconciled with more analytic procedures (Evans-Pritchard 1958; Lévi-Strauss 1966). Recent work on 'indigenous knowledge' examines how alternate cosmologies can generate novel empirical and theoretical knowledge about nature (Cruikshank 1998; Nuttall 1998). By the term 'sentient ecology' I wish to place in the forefront of this ethnography that Evenki hunters act and move on the tundra in such a way that they are conscious that animals and the tundra itself are reacting to them. To place a more formal edge on the phrase, one might say that Evenki views of ecology stress an 'interagentivity' where animal and human persons 'attend' to each other (Ingold 1994). Evenki categories diffuse the 'ontological

understanding of a proper relationship to land is as important in evaluating the possibilities and limitations provided by the shift to nationalist politics as it is to understanding the classic riddle of how and why Evenki groups came to occupy such an immense territory.

Knowing the land

When examining the relationship of Evenkis to the land it is most appropriate to begin with the herdsmen. This does not follow from any analytical conviction that the *pastukhi* have preserved a pristine relationship to the land. In fact, as demonstrated above, the Evenki 'herdsman' is a state-created and enforced professional category which has contributed to the reification and amplification of Evenki mobile production. However, it is logical to begin with the reindeer herders since both professionals who work on the land and those who live in the extensive settlements argue that they are the ones who 'know the tundra well' [*khorosho znaiut tundru*]. Through the silent implication of this repeated phrase, all Evenki, Dolgan, or even Russian informants insisted that those who worked in the reindeer brigades had the most experience to share on this topic. Since I had declared an interest in Evenkis, it was unanimously decided that Number One Reindeer Brigade ('the only real Evenki brigade') was the best place for me to study. Most of my understandings of belonging to the land come from them.

From the outset of my apprenticeship in Number One Reindeer Brigade, I was continually baffled by what seemed to be a very loose relationship between people and the resources around them. This ranged from a seeming random criterion for selecting trees for firewood or places to gather snow or water, to an extreme confusion when trying to catch reindeer each day for harness. For the first months I displayed what must have seemed like an obsessive concern with which tree to cut down or which reindeer to chase. Whenever I asked 'Which tree should be felled?' or 'Where is it better to fetch water?' the answer was invariably 'Don't you know wood yet?' or 'It's better not to then' [*luchshe ne nado*]. Although I soon became used to these non-sequiturs as part of everyday life (and finally learned not to ask), upon reflection it now seems that the question of the relationship of the *pastukh* to the land is best understood through the category of 'knowing'.

Knowing [*znat'* 'to know'; *hade-mi* 'knowing'] is a concept which is not codified but is demonstrated by example. Rarely, elders might talk of the old man who 'could fly like a ptarmigan' or the old woman who 'knew thunder'.

---

dualism' pervasive in Western philosophy (Scott 1996). They also imply a more complex definition of personhood than that usually permitted in liberal philosophy (Hallowell 1960). These ideas are allied with Bateson's (1972: 454–71) argument for an 'ecology of Mind', which encourages would-be individual agents to recognize the links of communication which tie them to 'the environment of other social units, other races, and the brutes and the vegetable' (p. 468).

These examples of the *hamanil* [shamans; knowing-ones] are both distant in time and in relevance to everyday life in the brigade. However, the concept of knowing persists in stories of people being able to rescue themselves from impossible circumstances created by poor weather, poor luck, or bad drink. If the English word 'competence' were not so far from the actual vernacular terms it might be the best translation of this idea.[2] Another appropriate synonym might be *sobrazitel'nost'* [awareness or sharpness]; a quality which I was told was most needed in a *tundrovik*. In the following example, Liubov' Fedorovna reflects on the importance of knowing how to stitch:

> L.F. [*repairing a canvas tent*] You need to have strong seams on these tents. When the boys go up on the mountain in the summer there are often big storms. The weather pulls the tent around . . . The thunder is so loud . . . Young Natasha [Viktor's young wife] simply can't stand it. Sometimes you think the lightning is just going to run right through the tent. The way it crashes! . . . Once when it was really loud, and the men were not around, Natasha was scared. It was just the two of us. I stuck all the rubber boots up on poles—but it didn't help [it is thought that rubber on poles is a protection against lightning]. So I thought quickly. I said do this. I lay down on my back [*on the ground*] and waved my feet in the air like this [*with rubber boats on*] and shouted '*gorolo, gorolo*' ['far away, far away']. We both did it. It got quiet and Natasha was not nearly as scared . . . I don't like this canvas though—the needle doesn't go through.

This story, which might bring a smirk to the lips of an experienced *tundrovik*, illustrates with great creativity the practical manner in which knowing is performed. The narrative was striking not only for the mimed actions but for its implicit contrast of the ingenuity of the older woman to the inexperienced and frightened bride. There is much here to be admired for the syncretic combination of old beliefs in evil spirits and new ideas concerning the electrodynamics of lightning.[3] Although it is debatable whether or not rubber

---

[2] I wish to credit an anonymous reviewer for pointing out, correctly, that the proper Russian term for the type of competence displayed by *tundroviki* is *umenie* ('ability', 'skill') and not *znanie*. This is a very important distinction when trying to establish the difference between rational thought and practical ability in any epistemology (Bourdieu 1990). Unfortunately, ethnographers, unlike philosophers, are bound to use local terms faithfully. Although *tundroviki* love to quote Pushkin, they nevertheless use the Russian verb *znat'* ('to know') in a non-standard manner to describe these skills. It is my opinion that their gloss on the categories of competence and achieved knowledge is not a product of poor literacy but instead a creolization of the very important Evenki-language concept of 'knowing' [*kha-mi*, *sa-mi*]. This concept might be called a 'verb' but is almost always used in a processual rather than definitive manner. This is the same category which forms the root for the word *shaman*. In this sense, the Evenki category of knowing can be represented as an approach to knowledge which does not suffer from the marked ontological divides of Western philosophy, such as the difference between practical action and rational intentions.

[3] This is a remarkable parallel to an old belief in evil spirits that seems to be confined to the lower Yenisei valley. 'Long ago', people used to sew balloons out of the skins of dried lake cod. If they heard ominous sounds in the taiga (such as the sounds of the winged cannibals or the one-legged cannibals), they would hang the cod balloons up all over the camp on sticks to scare the creatures away. The naivety of these old-timers is smiled at now.

boots can exercise any mechanical effect on lightning, this performance of confidence and control had the desired effect of calming the young woman.

Knowing can be illustrated in a more practical manner of having the good sense to know where to find coveted commodities. The following story is typical of the type of adventure that young herders tell while escaping the droves of mosquitoes and black flies in the smoke of a campfire.

M.Ya. I was called to the army. Even three times! [*Laughter*] It was in Dudinka. This time I was in hospital because I got beat up. It was good too. *Voininkomat* [The War Commandeering Office] wouldn't take me all beaten up. When I first got to the hospital it was really quiet. I didn't know anyone. Only the second day I talked to the old guy lying next to me. It turned out he was from Potapovo and knew my sister. *Zemliak!* [Countryman] He had under his sheets a little bottle of vodka and would take shots when the nurse wasn't looking. Like this! [*Demonstration*] He gave me a shot and I felt that drink going down. Then everything took off! Across the corridor there were some friends from the Khantaika. You know, Ivan and Kesha. They sent me out to get some drink—they gave me their social security money. I went to that store . . . you know . . . with the windows.

V.N. That must be Number 3.

M.Ya. No, I think it was Number 6. Down by the 'Arktika' theatre. Yes, Number 6. Well I was standing there trying not to look drunk. Standing real straight. Like this. [*Laughter*] I had to step over this old Nenets who was passed out on the floor in his *malitsa* [Nenets parka] mumbling something in his language. I was real careful. I didn't want him to stick to me. When it was my turn I grabbed those three bottles and ran out. Real fast. You see I was 20 roubles short! [*Laughter*] I ran back to the hospital—but before I could get there I saw Sasha. He called me under to the basement. Well, that vodka didn't last long. The next thing I remember was waking up on the floor in someone's flat. I started laughing at my friends. They all had black eyes. Just black like this! So then they said 'Look at yourself!' I looked in the mirror and I was all bruised up too! [*Laughter*] So then I stole sunglasses from my friend and went out . . .

Challenges both natural and social present opportunities for a person to demonstrate his knowledge. In this case, the exotic terrain of the city provides a riveting tale of adventure and guile for those young herders who have not left the territories of the farm—and a familiar story for the few who had. The tale earns the teller respect as a person who knows the layout of the city (which is evident in his knowledge of the geography of alcohol distribution) as well as the reindeer and the lands they feed upon.

I only experienced 'knowing' a very few times during my apprenticeship. One of my proudest achievements was during a 200-kilometre journey by reindeer sled when, after stepping off my sled for a second time to untangle the leads from under the reindeers' feet, I stood up decisively to snap the reins against the lead reindeer's harness. This brought all three reindeer abruptly to attention and set them off at a great clip onto the trail, allowing me to sit calmly on the sled as it whisked accurately behind my knees (and did not trip me up as was usually the case). At this rare triumphant display our brigadier sucked his breath slightly and with a smile said that 'he knows driving' [*on znaet yekhat'*]. It was only after this incident that I was allowed to stray from the main trail on my own or would be given small tasks to do with reindeer by myself.

A competent performance of one's knowledge earns a person respect, establishes one's status, but also entitles one to enter into a relationship with the land as an independent and competent person. This idea parallels the idea of 'rights' (in this case 'rights to land') that are granted to 'individuals' in our society when they become 'mature adults'. I do not think that any of these three terms are appropriate to classify the type of relationship to land that I was shown for two reasons. First, none of the Russian equivalents for these words was ever used by my Evenki teachers when speaking of the land or of one's performed competence in using its resources. Second, each of these terms implies a certain relationship of power, sovereignty, and licence between people which is better elaborated in liberal-democratic as well as Marxist theories of society than in vernacular ideas. The relationship of power, sovereignty, and licence active here is one not exclusively between people but between people and *tundra*. Although what I will call an 'entitlement' to this relationship is achieved through people (or more exactly, through kin acting as teachers), these people do not hold the sanction of punishment or the power to exclude. Despite the fact that the entitlement to go out on the land has recently become projected in an exclusive and proprietary way in a sense closer to that of 'right', in a classic sense, knowing follows from a sense of understanding the suitability of one's experience when confronted with the challenges of a capricious natural world.

During my apprenticeship, it was pointed out that while there may not be a correct way to do things there were many wrong ways of acting which revealed that one did not 'know'. It is a particular feature of the Evenki pedagogy that a poor technical performance exposes one to verbal insult and ridicule. This is not only the case when tying knots, but also when attempting more serious projects. One of the more vivid examples was the riotous laughter generated by the case of one young herder from a neighbouring brigade who was lost for two days while en route back to the settlement. He and his wife (who was in an advanced state of pregnancy) were forced to twice spend the night in hastily made snow shelters [*kuropatchie chumy*]—an incident which for other people might produce reactions of worry or pity. Among the members of the Number One Reindeer Brigade the following comments were heard:

V.Ye. How could he lose his way? He should know the route. He has gone between *Rovda laida* and the settlement at least twice!

K.N. I've never heard of a *pastukh* who can't find the settlement! [A joke on the well-known love of the herders for alcohol.]

M.Ya He must have been dreaming of that bottle!

V.Ye. It serves them right! What are people like that doing on the tundra if they don't know the route!

A poor performance can also lead to the usurpation of one's intended task. At the outset of my training there were many times when my clumsy wood-splitting would end by having the axe in my hands vanish into the hands of another and the woodpile being quickly and efficiently split. Appropriate comments at this point might be 'you will break your leg'; 'this is my axe not yours'; 'you weren't using the axe properly'; or 'I will only have to fix the axe after you are finished with it'. Once, when returning overland to the settlement by means of reindeer caravan, a bloodied, exhausted harness reindeer belonging to a herder from Number Three Reindeer Brigade was found tied to a tree. Our brigadier stopped his sled and released the animal 'to go home'. Although not a word was said, it was clear that it was considered to be incompetent to leave such a battered reindeer tethered by itself on the tundra. The young herder, upon hearing that his reindeer was released by a more experienced herder, was angry and humiliated—but typically had no words to exchange with the older man. The usurpation of a task is shameful but it also steals away an opportunity to perform one's knowledge—hence removing a small opportunity to advertise that one is a worthy person with whom to form a partnership.

In the above three examples there is a direct link made between 'knowing' and respecting a person's actions. The withdrawal of respect can also be considered a form of sanction which enforces a sense of entitlement—although it stops short of harm or exclusion. The disciplinary effect of ridicule in a small social unit should be clear. In the case of the usurpation of a task, it must be remembered that in a crumbling redistributive economy the removal of a tool like an axe, gun, knife, or harness reindeer is a desperate circumstance since none of these items can be purchased or otherwise obtained except through the goodwill of those around you. Thus, ridicule and usurpation are two quite effective socially wielded techniques in this face-to-face community which regulate and obstruct a person's relationship to the land without forbidding access to land.

The entitlement to enter into a relationship with land goes beyond technical competence to include a sense that particular objects and tasks are suitable for specific persons. Personalized appropriation and consumption is more commonly thought of in the catering of commodities to a person's taste. The harvesting of resources from the land is also highly selective but in the more fundamental sense of being related to a person's skills, her biography, or his dreams. I would argue that what at first appeared to me to be an inconsistent preference for certain places, certain types of wood, or a team of reindeer is governed by an element of predestination. Two examples will illustrate this point.

In the selection of wood for burning, or for carving, there are a number of technical factors that must be weighed. In the winter, firewood should be absolutely dry so that it lights immediately upon the first strike of a match. It is desirable that the wood be located close to the camp so that it does not have to be carried on skis or by reindeer sled. Furthermore, the wood should be without significant twists or knots so that it can be split easily. However, beyond these criteria different people see certain types of wood as more suitable for them. For firewood, the brigadier's eldest son Viktor quickly gathered thin dry tamarack in great quantities by using a sled. Vladimir preferred thick tamarack logs which he would split from the end by using his one-sided axe as an adze. A Ukrainian veterinarian was tolerated with humour for his love for sharpening a band saw to portion the thicker logs. All young Evenkis would comment that it was 'quicker' [i.e. better] to chop whole logs with the short, forceful blows of the Evenki axe. My initial attempts to harvest spruce (as is done in Northern Canada) were regarded as the height of incompetence. In order to teach me about wood, I was sent out with an elderly connoisseur who had me press the frozen shavings of tamarack trees to my tongue to distinguish the sweet, frozen bite of sap to the powdery flavour of dry wood. Sedentary Russians on the tundra, such as the employees of the three meteorological stations, were teased for their stereotypical love of birch, which had to be meticulously split when green and then dried next to the bricks of the Russian stove before it could be burned. *Pastukhi* saw birch trees as providing good material only for sled stays or axe handles. When at night the tamarack fire would burn hot, inhaling air with a deep and even breath, Viktor would often comment that it was a joy to have good wood and a warm stove. The noisy, crackling fire of green wood is derided by the men of Number One Brigade as 'bad' in both the sense of efficiency and in the sense that such jittery flames 'speak bad news [about the future]'.

The selection of wood for carving is an even more delicate affair. The tamarack that is selected for sled runners should be without twists and knots but also should be growing on a slight incline giving it slight arc with respect to the ground. Viktor preferred thinner logs for thin runners. Vladimir preferred wider runners. Typically, when I suggested a tree for carving, Viktor would look at it and say 'That's not a runner', or with the possessive formation 'That's Vladimir's [*Vovanyi*] not mine'. In short, as the months of my apprenticeship went on, the immediate environs encircling each home camp appeared not merely as zones of supply but as complex sites of specific trees, hollows, and expanses which were more or less suited both to the people I lived with and to my own modest skills.

Plate 12. Viktor bending new sled runners over a slow fire

   Leaving the mundane realm of my direct experience—the realm of wood and water—the point of a personalized entitlement becomes clearer. The hunt of the wild deer as narrated by my companions is a fine example of the very intimate intersection of destiny and awareness in the 'taking' of resources from the land. These stories supply a catalogue of techniques but also a poetic image of young men taking reindeer trained with their own hands up into the windswept escarpments to hunt those deer's wild cousins. In condensing these stories I wish to show how the harvesting of a wild deer is only conceivable if a person holds appropriate technical skills and an awareness of the land but also a proper relationship to the land and the animals upon it.
   As with harvesting wood, there are a number of technical skills necessary in the successful hunt of the wild deer. In addition to marksmanship, there is a need for great stamina to travel for up to twenty hours without food or water while keeping a firm hold on the reins of one's harness reindeer.

Plate 13. Assembling a sled with taut ropes which are used to bend the structure into place without the use of nails

Furthermore, the hunters typically travel with only an axe, a rifle, and a knife, emphasizing a solid competence in survival skills in an environment where the weather can change suddenly and tragically. As an illustration of this hardiness, I heard one gripping story of the rescue of a hunter who, after seeking shelter under his sled from a gale-force blizzard, found himself encased in a sarcophagus of hardened, drifted snow.

While survival skills are necessary, the hunter must also have a basic understanding of the habits of the wild deer and the places where they may be found. There are certain clues which may help in this regard. Crows are thought to fly over the camp in the direction of wild deer indicating their location 'since they want to eat too' (Shirokogoroff 1933: 44; Vasilevich 1969: 188, 218). Such hints are combined with an extensive knowledge of the micro-climates that offer shallow snow, year-round water sources, or salt-licks for the wild deer. It seemed that all older Evenkis had 'their places'— such as the slopes of the dormant volcano at the headwaters of the Tehok river or the marshy shores of the Konan lake. The same connoisseur of wood, Momi Fedrovich, explained that these special places (like Tehok) 'must have a *shaitan* ["idol", "holy object"] because there are always deer there'. Altern- ately, there is an awareness of the 'bad land' [*plokhaia zemlia*] where misfortune or death plagues any person who enters its embrace. This detailed knowledge of the land and its multi-variate relationship to living things is often termed an awareness of 'landscape' by geographers and anthropologists (Basso 1984; Kwon 1993; Hirsch & O'Hanlon 1995).

The possession of survival skills and an awareness of 'landscape' does not sufficiently capture the central role of 'knowing' in having an entitlement to resources. While knowing the land's places is one of the key factors in hunting, a proper interpersonal relationship with animals is also not to be underestimated. The wild deer are reputed to have a heightened if not a supranatural sensitivity to people (Vasilevich 1969: 220). They, like the bears, can hear boastful words of a hunter and be forewarned of a hunt. The comical Ukrainian veterinarian had the misfortune of wishing Vladimir a good hunt on a morning when he declared that he was 'heading out on the mountain [*kamen'*]'. Vladimir sharply replied 'May your tongue dry up!' During a hunt those who remain in the camp are not to speculate on its success or to prepare for a feast. A hunter is not even to sharpen his knife before heading out. The ethnographers of Evenkis postulate that the respect for the deer's perception necessitates the use of a parallel language which avoids naming the creature by its proper name (Suslov 1927; Shirokogoroff 1933: 81, 90). The *pastukhi* in Number One Reindeer Brigade speak of wild deer as 'the wild ones' in both Russian and Evenki [*dikie, baiur*]. The heightened perception of deer extends to their senses of smell and sound. The *dikie* can smell a hunter from a long distance—necessitating the choice of a damping blizzardy day for a successful approach. Before setting out, the hunter will remove all metal fasteners from his reindeer sled so that the only audible sound is the staccato clicking of the reindeer's canter; a sound reminiscent of dice being thrown. In a different context, Heonik Kwon (1993: 71) quotes a senior Orok herder from Sakhalin on the subject of the *dikie*: '*Dikie* do not see. They smell. To become a *pastukh* you've got to hear the wind and smell the reindeer.'

The wild deer's perception also pierces the hunter's physical presence to examine his character. A 'greedy' man [*zhadnyi*] may find the small groups of wild deer very skittish and liable to bolt at the smallest sound. This idea is globally illustrated in comments on another's misfortunes that 'land does not take him' [*zemlia yego ne vozmet*] or more ominously 'you don't find bad people on the tundra' [*polokhie liudi na tundre ne bivaet*]. Young apprentices are advised not to be avaricious about retrieving lost or broken personal articles [*ne zhadnichit!*]. The perceptive man, and the good man, will foresee a successful hunt by dreaming of a woman (sometimes offering a gift) during the nights preceding the hunt (Vasilevich 1969: 232). The somewhat boastful Vladimir, after sharing home-made alcohol with visiting Russian meteorologists, explains how he finds the *dikie*:

V.Ye. Let me tell you this . . . listen . . . I know it's not modest—but if it is a true story modesty does not figure—right? . . . That time up on the Tengkal river it

was that night—I saw it from a dream. I knew that it would be that day. We went
up between the mountains. Just coming over the rise they were just standing there.
Two wild ones [*dikie*]. I knew they were for me [*dlia menia*]. I shot my gun. BAM!!
They both fell one by one.

The use of a possessive construction in this passage, and in the discussion of
one's 'own places' above, is quite common in Evenki hunting narratives.
Appropriation here is signalled in an imperative mood—as if this opportunity was so suitable as to be predestined. The sense of suitability is reinforced
in other stories through the maxim 'it is a sin [*grekh*, *odee*] not to take'.

It is tempting to focus in upon this possessive aspect of suitability as an
example of primal acquisitiveness—but this would be taking the moment of the
hunt out of its context of obligations and proper treatment of the harvested
prey. There are limits on the harvesting of animals, even if they are not codified
in such an explicit manner as the wildlife management agencies prefer.
Vladimir, the master of our caravan, liked to speak of the 'law of the tundra'
[*zakon tundry*] whereby the hunter never took so many animals such that lone
animals were left by themselves ('things should be in pairs'). Taking is also
regulated by certain responsibilities. This is best illustrated by the respect
shown for the meat taken from the land. In the Number One Reindeer Brigade,
as in circumpolar societies the world over, the successful hunter does not keep
wild deer meat for himself but instead displays the slain animal on his sled
before skinning and cutting the meat into portions. He may then just call out to
the eldest women, or send a child carrying a leg, head, or a heart in a bowl to the
next tent. The hunter reserves for himself some regular portion of the kill, such
as a leg, and perhaps some delicacy such as the diaphragm (which Vladimir
enjoyed frying on the door of his stove) or the liver or kidneys. The best reward
to the knowledgeable tracker, who weaves his way through rolling hills in low
visibility, and to the man who knows the habits of deer and the land's secret
places, is some of the most wholesome meat available. The fat of the wild
deer is reputed to give the hunter strength to hold his harnessed reindeer on a
straight path. The intricate tangle of cavities in the deer's intestines [*kooibgi*,
hilukta] are a delicacy valued not only for their richness but for their power of
preventing the hunter from being lost in the woods. The taking of wild meat
was always acknowledged through 'feeding the fire' or through making a gift
directly to the land [*podarok zemle*]. The bone marrow from the wild deer's
femurs was often fed to the home fire, who occasionally speaks as an authoritative witness to the hunter's future.[4] At the site of a specific kill, especially if

---

[4] Vasilevich (1969: 220–2) writes that the spirit of the home camp is an old woman [*babushka*] who
lives in the hearth. In order to have good luck she expects to be fed and not to be given rubbish or
sharp objects (like fish bones). Vasilevich also writes that the 'spirit of the fire' can foretell the future
of a hunter. The *pastukhi* of Number One Reindeer Brigade were very generous with their fire,
offering her vodka and meat, and avoiding burning the remains of fish. They did not speak of the fire
as having any presence or human attributes other than hunger or an ability to speak.

it is known that there is a *shaitan*-rock or *shaitan*-idol near by, some shells, coins, or buttons will be left on the ground or thrown out onto the land.

Gifts to the land were made in other contexts not connected with the hunt of the wild deer. If berries were collected from a rich marshy site, older women would hang a thread [*nitka, dylbiltik*] with bits of coloured cloth and tufts of the white beards from the reindeer between two vertical trees. Alekseev (1993: 35–41) interprets this particular structure as a 'gateway to the heavens'. On the Khantaika these were described simply, without elaboration, to be 'gifts' [*podarki*]. Similarly, if a foetus was extracted from a pregnant cow (wild or tame) it would be hung in a single standing tree as a gift. Any object which snapped or cracked would be placed up in a tree for the land since the fact that it broke was seen as a sign that the land demanded it.

The images of the 'giving land' or of 'animals giving themselves' are commonly quoted to identify a special moral economy of circumpolar societies and of hunting societies generally. It is an interesting detail that Khantaika Evenkis describe the hunting of animals as 'taking' and not as 'animals giving themselves'. Although reciprocity with the land was an important detail for the hunter-herders of Number One Reindeer Brigade, the possessive aspects of their stories were mediated more commonly by the emphasis on 'knowing as taking' than by the idiom of gifting. For Nikolai Savel'evich the tundra was far from a 'giving' environment. When I asked him directly on this question he laughed loudly and replied 'Oh no, she's *naglaia*' [brazen, outrageous]. The opportunism and cynicism implicit in this phrase can help to rectify the somewhat romantic portrayal of 'original ecologists' common in the circumpolar literature.[5]

Although my Evenki teachers never distinguished various types of 'taking', it may be useful to explore two contexts in which it is invoked in order to illustrate the broad usage of the term. The first is the 'taking' of knowledge. Among the many things that the old man Sergei Sergeevich mercilessly taught me was the childish refrain 'When they give—take it; when they beat you—run' [*kogda daiut—voz'mi; kogda b'iut—begi*]. For a long time it struck me as odd that this refrain was sung by him when I groaned in

---

[5] Nurit Bird-David (1990) has proposed the metaphor of the 'giving earth' as a central philosophical idea for hunter-gatherers. The images of reciprocity and hunting for circumpolar societies can be found in Feit (1994), Tanner (1979), Brightman (1993), and Henriksen (1973) for Crees; in Ridington (1990), Sharp (1988), Nelson (1983), and Osgood (1936: 155, 161) for Athapaskans; and in Fienup-Riordan (1990) and Nuttall (1992) for Inuit. Although the anthropological idea that hunter-gatherers may have an implicit conservation ethic through practices of gifting can be credited with raising the respect of northern people in the eyes of wildlife managers and biologists, it has been rightly criticized for lending an overly romantic view of the hunt, which, in the end, can be used to condemn local people when they put down their harpoons and bone tools in favour of guns and knives (Cruikshank 1998; Wenzel 1991; Fienup-Riordan 1990). It is helpful to remember, following Mauss (1969), that giving and taking must always be interrelated in complex and often opportunistic ways.

Plate 14. A *dylbiltik* thread
strung at a spot where berries
were harvested

exasperation as my sled was completely unpacked and retied before me (since
it was 'all wrong')—until I realized that in fact I was not being beaten but
being given something. If I asked to be taught to harness a reindeer I would
be presented with a lightning-fast performance of the task without any
explanation. More than once the eldest son Viktor would mutter that at
my age he just had to be shown something once for him to know it.

Another context of 'taking' is the taking of opportunities that the land
offers. This can occur when the animal signalled in a dream confronts the
hunter out on the land. It may occur when a large and coveted fish, such as a
'salmon' [*kumzhe*], is caught. When fishing, it might be said that a desirable
fish 'came to me'. Very successful fishermen are said to 'love the fish' or to be
'good men'. The proper way to treat a fish after it has been consumed is to
break the skeleton into pieces 'so that the fish come back'. Opportunity might
be evoked in contexts often thought to be controlled closely by people. I was
loudly derided when my lasso fell short of capturing a pernicious bull who
ran in a very accurate and predictable fashion between me and bluff of trees
('How can you not take him—he was coming to you!'). When the director of

the state farm opened the warehouse, the brigadier exhorted everyone to take everything they could get. I find the idea of opportunity nicely illustrated in the intense interest that hunters find in card-games like bridge or *duraki* when highly valued trump cards are triumphantly played (and the events of play are remembered and reworked to prove that someone 'did not play right' or 'did not take the right card'). In all of these contexts—contexts which might often be seen to be controlled by 'chance'—the *pastukhi* of Number One Reindeer Brigade read a sense of opportunity that is realizable only by the person who knows when and how 'to take'.

The two contexts of 'taking' represent not only moralistic stories of how one should behave, but they also stress the intersection of the land's providence with the hunter's whole memory of technique and skill which he took from others around him. The overlap of biography, awareness, and a generous landscape accounts for the drama of the hunt—as in this passage which reminds one of a professional actor in the minutes before the curtain rises. Once, during a particularly long blizzard in February, I was asked to read out an account of the hunt of the wild deer from my field notes.

D.A. Today the tasks of the camp were set aside in favour of a hunt of wild deer. In the morning Viktor said that we would catch special reindeer. I asked Vladimir what he meant by special reindeer. I was told that you need special 'alpine reindeer' with short legs in order to go up high. [*Laughter—this turns out not to be true.*] We spent several hours chasing very strong *khory* [male reindeer] and tying them to harness. There were four reindeer on each sled but Vladimir had only cows . . .

K.N. No, No, there's too many words there [*boltaesh*]. It's not like that. You should write something like this: 'You sit and drink your tea. You eat a piece of *omo* [bread, 'bannock']. [*Long pause*] You have no thoughts of the trail ahead. Drink some more tea. There's no rushing. [*Pause*] You sit and drink slowly. Then you stand up. You put on your *purta* [hunting knife] and look out through the door. Get up without rushing and . . . and then you go out.' See? That's all you need to say.

V.Ye. You should write *that* down. That's very good.

Although Evenki accounts of hunts are not nearly as wordy as my renditions, these stories—especially when they employ possessive constructions—can be best understood as claims of entitlement. Entitlement is understood here as being a more subtle and personalized relationship to land than that which is generally codified as a 'right of common access' or a 'right not to be excluded' let alone an 'individual or privately exercised right of use' (Macpherson 1978).

Instead of employing the broad language of rights, the idea of an entitlement through knowing the land can be better conceived as an element of a sentient ecology. The significant social world of the *tundrovik* is not the distant and regimented institution of the state but a perhaps stricter social

Plate 15. Momi Yelogir, Sergei Yarotskii, and Irina Yarotskaia hunting wild deer on Edyntypki

community of kinsmen and animals. By placing animals into a social context I am not implying that for the Evenki hunter they are the same as human persons. However, the competent hunter is aware of the fact that while he tries to know both the animals and the land, the animals and the land also come to know the hunter. If the language of rights stands for a set relationship between an individual and a narrowly conceived human institution, the aspect of entitlement in a sentient ecology refers to a set of understandings in the reflexive action between human persons and animal persons.

Since the establishment of the Soviet state, the sentient ecology of the lower Yenisei valley has come to be mediated by many layers of authoritative action on the part of state managers and by the new, poorly understood institution of private property in land. In these new political contexts the *pastukhi* of Number One Reindeer Brigade are coming to know the land in an increasingly possessive manner. Although the hunt of the wild deer or the harvesting of wood will no doubt continue to be understood relationally, in other contexts the aspect of belonging to the land is becoming stylized in a manner more consonant with the idea of a right. This possessive relation to

territory to many seems an appropriate political stance for a sparse population now confined within relatively isolated settlements. However, before
examining the new dynamics of nationality politics as it applies to land, it
will be useful to reflect upon how the wide territorial occupancy of Evenkis
can be seen as an effect of knowing the land.

'The old people travelled everywhere'

The person in the settlement who best remembers the days before settlements and helicopter transport is Agrafena Khristoforovna Khutukagir'. She
is by far the oldest person in the settlement, although no one is sure of her
exact age. The old women estimate her to be between 95 and 110 since the
second oldest woman (who was 93) remembers being spanked by Agrafena as
a young girl. Other woman concur that when Agrafena was widowed in 1915
she worked hard to raise her several children, who were already adolescents. I
talked to her with a trilingual translator since she knew no Russian and
alternated between Evenki and Dolgan (often within a single sentence).
Because of difficulties with her hearing and indeed difficulties in getting
her to understand what we wanted, we would ask simple questions about how
life today compared to the old days. During my last visit I asked her to
describe the places where she travelled as a child. She spoke at great length
about caravans and treacherous mountain passes. As asides, she mentioned
the trading-posts of Tura and Turukhansk, and the northern outpost of
Volochanka at the centre of the Khantanga Way. At these place-names my
translator would smile with embarrassment and apologize, 'You have to
forgive the old woman—she must be senile—it is impossible for her to
have seen those places.' As the crow flies, the distances between these three
points are measured in thousands of kilometres and are separated by the
sharp ravines of the Putoran plateau. While it is true that commuting
between these points would seem impossible to a villager dependent upon
the monopolistic and inefficient schedules of the civil aviation authority, the
old woman's stories do resonate both with the stories and practice of present-
day *tundroviki* and the archival record.[6] This section explores that aspect of
'knowing the land' which facilitates extensive land-use.

The Soviet literature on Evenkis puzzles over how a sparsely populated
nationality managed to occupy half of Asia without the use of a bureaucracy, a

---

[6] At the turn of the century P. Ostrovskikh (1904: 31) encountered 'wealthy' Evenki traders whom
he caught 'passing through' Chirinda. He distinguished ten 'clans' [including the Ukachar, Yelogir,
and Khutukagir' clans] with 'an extremely wide radius of wanderings bordered by Ekonda and the
Turu river, to Kotoi and Kureika drainages, to the banks of the Nizhnaia Tunguska'. In contemporary
terms this is practically the total contemporary territory of the taiga zones of Taimyr, Evenkiia, and
part of Yakutiia. Their wealth, Ostrovskikh notes, was not only visible in their travels but in their
silver plates, imported Chinese tea, and reserves of cereals for cooking.

regular army, or a hierarchical social structure. State ethnographers link descriptions of Evenki land-use with adjectives such as 'immense' [*ogromnaia*], 'extensive' [*ekstensivnaia*], or 'colossal' [*kolossal'naia*] but qualify them with theories which bind Evenkis to an incipient but failed social formation. In these writings Evenki land-use practices are 'uninterested in district or international boundaries', 'open . . . [or] . . . dilute', or an example of evolution from 'a commune of neighbours to a territorial group'.[7] Although state ethnographers have documented very complex instances of stratification within Evenki 'primitive-communal formations', by the admission of these scholars Evenkis tend to depart from the 'classical model' in the extent of their land use and the transitory nature of their 'territorial alliances' (Karlov 1982: 5, 42–52, 77; Nikul'shin 1939: 135–6; Dolgikh & Levin 1951: 99, 104). The difficult fit of Evenkis to orthodox Marxist models is represented in the paradoxical language of this shortened passage:

What sort of social alliances [*sviazi*] were formed and hardened within each territorial grouping . . .? In examining the economic underpinnings of the Evenki community [*obshchina*], we have established that they determine alliances for the joint exploitation of one economic region and the collective ownership of the hunting grounds [*ugod'ia*] within it. However, the conditions of life precluded solitude within the narrow boundaries of [the community's] region and the fixing of exact boundaries around it. Exiting beyond these limits was necessary. . . . One should not forget that the territory occupied by all of these linked groups was indeed enormous . . . [T]he traditional territorial system of Evenkis was not [effected] through closed [*zamknutymi*] groups but 'open' ['*otkrytymi*'] groups which permitted the mixing and reciprocal inclusion of distant grounds. . . . Because of the continuous mixing of specific groups of the Evenki population, exact and discrete boundaries between territorial systems were completely absent. These groups encompassed only the nearest limits of the living-space of genetically close exogamous clans and patronymic alliances . . . Thus all of Evenki territorial groups tended to unnoticeably and gradually blend together—one into the other (Karlov 1982: 76–9).

Although Karlov forces his own ethnographic observations and the archival record into a systems framework, his descriptions still seem to stress the indeterminate or even untidy aspect of Evenki land-use. It would seem that attributions of state ethnography ranging from Speranskii's 'wandering Tungus' to Karlov's 'blended territorial groups', are generated from an assumption that all societies must have some form of primal territoriality— an assumption which overlaps with state administrative imperatives.

In sympathy with Soviet ethnographers, it should be noted that an element of fluidity, or lack of form, in Evenki relationships to land is not contradicted

[7] The sources for these citations are Patkanov (1906: 34), Karlov (1982: 81), Dolgikh & Levin (1951: 108). It is interesting that Vasilevich (1969) avoids discussions of territoriality—although she applies the word 'wandering' [*brodiashaia*] to Evenki land use occasionally in her monograph (1969: 7, 109) and as a central idea in a prominent chapter (1972).

by Evenkis themselves. Indeed the 'lack of form' in land use was that aspect which struck me most during my first months in the brigade. The brigadier of the Number One Reindeer Brigade would answer my questions about his 'clan's original lands' with the uninterested reply that 'in the old days it was not like now—the old people travelled everywhere'. When pressed for a more specific answer about particular valleys, transportation corridors, or annual meeting places [*suglanil*] the answer stubbornly remained that Evenki lands were 'everywhere'. Moreover, although the contemporary motions of the Number One Brigade are contained within administrative boundaries, it is considered a 'sin' to set camp on the same spot or to use the exact same trail. It would be unfair to take the brigadier's words too literally. While the flexible technology of the *tundrovik* both allows and encourages Evenkis to travel 'everywhere' this does not preclude the regular return to certain named places in conjunction with the taking of entitlements from a capricious but unparcelled landscape. Knowing the land in practice is applied along discrete routes, at specific pastures in the spring and in different pastures in the autumn. However, in principle, it could be applied 'everywhere'; hence the universality implied by Nikolai Savel'evich's explanation. In order to reconcile statements of the boundless extent of Evenki lands with the knowledge-based land-use system observed in the Number One Brigade, I will present the history of Evenki extensive land-use in the lower Yenisei valley as the history of the application of extensive knowledge of the land.

Evenki land-use is indeed majestic, ranging from Taimyr to Kamchatka with large portions of Manchuria and Mongolia included. However, the list of birthplaces and the genealogies of people in the Khantaika gives an equally grand picture of the extensive travels of people before the great centralizations of the 1960s. The birthplaces of the generation of 1960 to 1969, such as *irikta, mahin, konondy amut* (toponyms with no Russian equivalents), are rendered simply as *khantaika*. Other birthplaces such as *bokh amut* or *aiakli* might be given as *sovrechenskii* or *kamen'skii*—giving the Russian-speaking listener a neat translation of toponyms into the political geography of contemporary extensive settlements. If this classification system is extrapolated, it is possible to trace the origins of the Evenki population of the Khantaika to eight 'homelands' based on birth (see Map 4):

1. *tutashie* [from here]—local
2. *kamenskie*—from the abandoned trading post Kamen'
3. *noril'skie*—from the abandoned posts Chasovnia, Valek, Kur'e
4. *potapovskie*—from the banks of the Yenisei surrounding the settlement Potapovo
5. *chirindinskie*—from the plateau above Chirinda (Evenkiia)
6. *kureiskie*—from the Kureika drainage (Igarka District & Evenkiia)
7. *iz evenkii* [*ogataduk*]—from the abandoned post Ogata (Evenkiia)

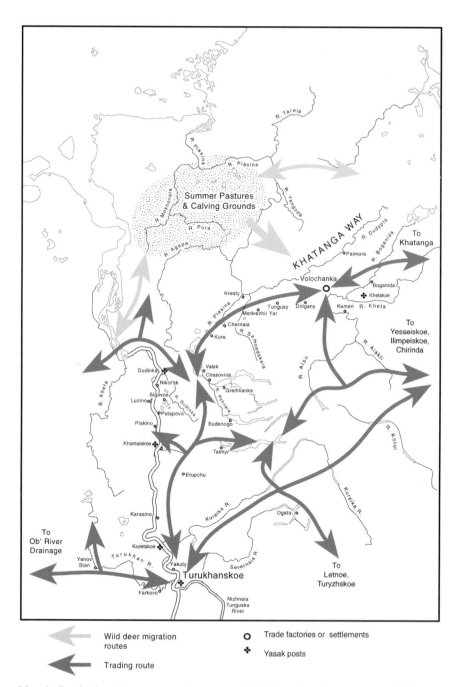

Map 4. Overland trading routes, settlements, and wild deer migration routes *circa* 1890

Legend:

Wild deer migration routes

Trading route

○ Trade factories or settlements

✤ Yasak posts

8. *sovrechenskie*—from Sovetskaia Rechka (Turukhansk District) and the
   Ob' River drainage.

If these regions are compared to Map 4, it is evident that at least all of
western Taimyr and most of northern Evenkiia and Turukhansk district are
represented within the lived experience of a single generation currently
residing within the confines of a single settlement.

   These tidy 'homelands' classed by contemporary settlements give a decep-
tive impression as to how these places were used. This matrix of birthplaces
was achieved through the daily practices of forebears acting within a landscape which was imagined differently from the bounded mosaic of post-
Soviet times. The statements of elders, as well as archival sources, suggest
several strategies of action which led to the extensive land-use patterns of
living memory: trading, taking animals for meat, taking animals for fur, and
the flight from administrative interference. In examining historical records
for these strategies I do not want to imply that they are archaic (although
their extensive character has fallen into disuse since 1968). With the collapse
of the centralized state system of intelligence and redistribution it is quite
likely that the extensive reach of these strategies may be reactivated again in
the Khantaika or in other extensive settlements. Instead, I would like to
discuss land use in an active sense in order to indicate that Evenkis' extensive
land occupancy is but a spurious consequence of a way of living which placed
more emphasis upon forming kinship alliances with human persons and
interrelating in a proper way with migratory 'wild ones' than with accumul-
ating rights in land or in objects. The product of these relationships happens
to be the result that at any particular period in time Evenkis lived 'everywhere'. By stressing the spuriousness of this product, I hope to capture the
lack of interest by which the brigadier discussed the topic. However, for
younger nationalists, the extensiveness of Evenki occupation is now becoming an important 'fact' useful in crafting arguments for the developing idiom
of aboriginal rights.

   The strategy of 'trade' will be understood broadly since in the last century
alone it carried many connotations from 'shipping', 'speculative exchange', to
'smuggling'. Trade is best understood in Taimyr through the lives of the
renowned professional *kaery* ['the transporters of goods']. Harking back to
the recent past (pre-1965) when caravans of harnessed reindeer were the
main source of transportation, the *kaery* travelled extensively along a number
of 'routes' [*doroga, khokotol*] linking disparate population points. One of the
most famous routes was the Khatanga Way, the 'reactor' which allegedly
melded the Dolgan, described here by a collectivization official in 1932:

When discussing the Khatanga *trakt* it is necessary to note that this corridor [*put'*] is
not a highway [*trakt*] in the strict meaning of the word. . . . It is no more than quite a
wide swathe of several kilometres that supports relatively constant traffic each year.

Here, in winter, people concentrate in groups of several tents [*chumi*] to form stations [*stanki*]. Between them there is the transport of passengers and the traffic of caravans [*argish, obozy*] in the employ of the high tundra co-operative trade organizations. Travel along this *trakt* is characterized by unquestionably difficult conditions which result in death to numbers of the reindeer herd. . . . Travel is especially difficult because of the need to tolerate heavy cold and, usually in winter, frequent prolonged blizzards. During the blizzards, travellers often wander from the route and are forced 'to turn circles' [*kruzhat'*] sometimes for several days on end. While doing this, it is not rare to lose parts of the transport herd since during blizzards the reindeer always try to head into the wind and thus run away. . . to be summarily consumed by wolves . . . (TsGARF A310–18–21: 83).

Kaery carried various goods for many different clients. In the 1950s caravans of up to two hundred reindeer carried food and supplies for collective farms, geological expeditions, cartographers, and various state institutions ranging from the post office to the Ministry of Education. In the 1930s, machinery and building materials were shifted from ports on the Yenisei river to the industrial forced labour camps of Igarka and Noril'sk. *Kaery* also transported the first veterinarians, doctors, ethnographers, and economists who would construct a new social order. At the turn of the century, *kaery* hauled supplies and people at the behest of less regimented institutions such as trading firms with government monopolies, tax-gathering Cossacks, or missionaries distributing the sacrament, surnames, and ritual calendars. Informally, these porters might have participated in the equally vibrant commerce in furs and fossilized mammoth ivory.

The capillary routes of the *kaery* went beyond the Khatanga Way. Extended families with large stocks of reindeer worked hunting and trading routes to the south, west, and east of Dudinka (Noril'sk (Valek)–Lake Kheta–Plakhino Factory (220 km.), Dudinka–Volochanka (400 km.), Dudinka–Igarka (190 km.)) or westwards to Igarka (Igarka–Lake Khantaika (180 km.), Igarka–Kureiskoe (160 km.)) (see Map 4). Although each route had its qualities and its adventures, for the purpose of this section the Igarka–Lake Khantaika route between 1930 and 1950 provides a good illustration of the extensive embrace of trading action in the region. The traffic along this route was organized by the Igarka fishing co-operative [*Igarskii rybkoop*], which bought smoked and salted fish from work-units in exchange for consumer goods sold at subsidized prices. Evenki *kaery*, such as Old Man Yeremin of Number One Reindeer Brigade, used their own herds to move freight on a contract basis with the co-operative.

The power of mobility brought many advantages to the *kaer*. At the same time that they transported freight they no doubt exchanged provisions and manufactured goods for furs with non-mobile Evenkis. The silent suspicion of this wealth still marks the spouses and offspring of the famous *kaery* of the Kureika and Khantaika river drainages: the Chempogirs, the western

Yarotskiis, and the Yeremins. Perhaps equally importantly for the *kaer*, the constant movement along fixed routes led to a wealth of kinship ties. The genealogies of these traders show a complicated tapestry of intermarriage with *khempo*, Enneche, Shol'kup, and Sakha surname/clan groups in addition to kin and trading relationships with Evenki clans from all of the eight regional 'homelands' (Anderson 1995*b*: appendix 2). The institution of the *posobnik* gives a good example of this intersection of kinship, mobility, and partnership.

The first Territorial Formation Officer in the lower Yenisei valley wrote the following about *posobka*:

> The [form of exploitation] that is most widely practised, most difficult to detect, and yet the most damaging [*kabal'nii*] is the lending out of reindeer for a limited time [*korta*] in exchange for labour [*otrabota*] or for the fruits of trapping. This form of exploitation is known under the name '*posobka*' and is practised as a sign of mutual aid between clans. . . . Usually the *kulak* gives a needful youth untrained reindeer. The youth trains [the reindeer] and after several months returns the reindeer fully fit for harness. For the privilege of *posobka* the poor man [*bedniak*] protects and pastures the reindeer of the *kulak*, checks his deadfall traps, assembles his caravans, and in a word, works for the *kulak* with all the power of his family (TsGARF A310–18–21: 56).

This account differs remarkably from the memories of Uliana Chempogir, who fondly remembers each *posobnik* who came to her father as an orphan or as a young adolescent asking for 'help'. Her father gave them clothing and reindeer with which to work. Uliana complained that some of them left to go back home 'but then we never heard of them—they died I guess'.[8] In Uliana's sketchy oral histories, as with the report of the Territorial Formation officer, it is difficult to distinguish actual relations between her family and their impoverished wards. Other stories on the Khantaika reveal a great variety of arrangements. The brigadier of Number One Reindeer Brigade speaks with gratitude for what he learned while he 'apprenticed' with his mother's relatives—the Yelogirs—after the death of his parents. The pensioned economist of the state farm was said to be the granddaughter of a Pankagir woman who was given as a young bride to an old man since the family had not the means to wait for a younger suitor to collect his bride-money. The Soviet literature of the 1930s viciously singles out *posobka* as the main tool of exploitation by the rich over the poor. The stigma of this label is felt today in the uncomfortable way that elders still speak of their upbringing lest they be thought of as either exploiters or as having destitute roots. It is a

---

[8] The *posobniki* of the Khantaika seem to have come from the rugged interior of the Kureika river drainage and especially the Lake Niamkanda region. A sobering account of the poverty and disease in the taiga around Lake Niamkanda is available in the diary of a Red Cross expedition of 1927 (TsGARF R3977–1–214).

great failure of the state ethnographic record that it is now impossible to distinguish between different modes of alliance and exchange, although scattered references do confirm the relationship between trade and the maintenance of an extensive social network.

Ethnographies from the previous century are even vaguer about the nature of social contract, but they often wonder at the great wealth of those who travelled extensively. The ethnographer Ostrovskikh (1902: 3) recorded the anxiously awaited arrival of the 'Ilimpeiskie' traders at the Turukhansk village market [*yarmak*]. The caravan of ten Evenki traders arrived late (10 March), setting alight rumours of illness or war out on the tundra. When these traders finally arrived they carried 'several tens of thousands of squirrel [furs], hundreds of Arctic fox [pelts], and dozens of sable furs' for exchange. The article does not record the means by which such a fortune was gathered, but it is clear from the species traded that the traders must have ventured from the Arctic tundra to the taiga, from Volochanka to the Nizhnaia Tunguska river. The geologist Cherkanovskii during his expedition of 1873 similarly recorded that Evenkis in the Nizhnaia Tunguska drainage travelled 'as far as the Arctic Ocean' in order to gather mammoth ivory and treated reindeer leather [*rovduga*] for trade. He also observed a 'clan market' on the Ilimpei river where 200 families gathered to exchange fox furs from the Arctic coast, reindeer from as far south as the Erbogachen taiga, and metalwork from as far east as Yakutiia (Cherkanovskii 1875 cited in Vasilevich 1969: 154 n.).

Two implications follow from these stories of trade. The first is that whether or not alliances and exchange were forged for purposes of bride-service, servitude, or mutual aid, it is clear that any of these arrangements were only possible through a large network of social communication. Secondly, there can be no simple delineation of stationary households with territories and 'wandering' households since individuals or even whole tent groupings could be drawn into the enterprise of extensive trading action. To paraphrase an early collectivization economist, the economy of the lower Yenisei valley of this period was one of 'mixed production uniting different combinations of hunting, fishing, herding and animal husbandry . . . [in which there is] no fundamental difference between nomadic and settled households' (Skachko 1930: 40).

The strategy of 'hunting animals' is tightly interrelated to the movements of people over the land. Although the relatively stationary 'eaters of wood' [moose, *mooti*] provided a rich and welcome supplement to the meat diet and a supply of tough leather for harnesses, the staple in the lower Yenisei valley was the meat of the migratory wild deer. The complex movements of wild deer over a territory as large as the lower Yenisei valley are even more difficult to summarize than the extensive travels of the *kaer*.

As described in the first chapter, wild migratory deer seek the security and comfort of differing ecological niches at differing times during their life cycle. The lower Yenisei valley is rich in a variety of ecological zones which are distinguished by their altitude as well as their high latitude. The vernacular animal systematics distinguish two types of deer according to their ranges: the strongly migratory *morskie* ['[Arctic] Ocean deer'] and the stationary *mestnye* ['local deer']. The latter are often further distinguished as being 'Evenki' (in this sense, from the mountainous interior of the Evenki Autonomous District). The difference between these subspecies is that while the *morskie* effect an epic migration of up to 1,500 kilometres in order to change their ecological surroundings, the *mestnye* move up and down within alpine valleys shared with their human neighbours. *Tundroviki* living out on the land also chose alpine or taiga areas in order to enjoy the security and comfort of better pastures and climate—but their movements were selected in concert with the mobile ungulates around them. Before the construction of the energy corridors with their associated urban spaces and hydroelectric reservoirs, the movement of people and wild and tame deer could be characterized as a dance where partners, conscious of each other's actions and trajectories, exchanged places with each other. Although the trading routes served settlements roughly in an east–west trajectory between the Yenisei and Lena river systems (and north–south along the Yenisei), each route was either bisected by the habitual movements of large tundra deer populations (moving north–south) or encompassed the wintering areas of local populations. Map 4 gives an indication of the intersections of wild deer and their Evenki hosts. Thus while trade continued and alliances formed, most Evenki travellers also negotiated a relationship to the wild deer around them.

It is difficult to write authoritatively on the interrelation of hunters and discrete populations of wild deer since this question is as controversial in the scientific literature as it is self-evident to the *tundroviki*. Wildlife biologists tend to write of discrete 'herds' which move in fixed 'migration routes' which reflect the land's 'carrying capacity' and the relative hunger of each herd. The orthodox models tend to deny to migratory deer any specific agency in the choices of their routes let alone any indigenous cultivation of their behaviour. *Tundroviki* on the Khantaika also affirm that groups of reindeer until recently returned along specific routes, but they imply that they did not do so out of hunger but out of respect for the humans they encounter and out of an affinity with particular places. The most significant artefacts of these migrations are the 'wild-deer routes' [*baiundyl khoktol*] trampled out over embankments or between watersheds which, twenty years later, still resemble the corridors ploughed by mechanized equipment. The stories of elder hunters also indicate that before the flooding of the Khantaika reservoir in 1976 and the construction of the polluting 'Nadezhda' smelter in 1979, there were local populations of *morskie* and *mestnye* which habitually returned to specific lichen pastures on both right and left banks of the Yenisei. The periodic returns of the overwintering deer were described as 'returnings' [*oleni prishli*] or occasionally 'returnings home' [*prishli domoi*]. The location of these 'homes' perhaps not uncoincidentally overlaps with the 'homelands' of particular surname groups. Thus the mountains above Lake Kheta [*edyn-dypki*], where the Yelogirs and Utukogirs travelled, have been (and continue to be) the home to discrete populations of both *morskie* and *mestnye* deer. The flooded lands of Lake Erupchu and the Sukharika river system, the former places of the Chempogirs and Yeremins, were once the home to migrating *morskie* wild deer. Another Yelogir brother, Bahili Yelogir, has 'his place' for *mestnye* deer in the mountains above the settlement at Lake Nerkeka.

   The formal models of wildlife biology which correlate fixed migrations to a driving hunger of herds are not unlike ethnological models which have ascribed a 'wandering' instinct to Evenki based ultimately in the fact that they were unable to control their surroundings. Recent biological research also has come to question if discrete herds are tied to habitual migration routes by mere mechanical instinct. Alaskan wildlife biologists, using radio-collars to establish the 'fidelity' of particular individuals to certain 'ranges', have established that certain lands are indeed attractive to deer but that large numbers of animals unaccountably shift their allegiances to pastures (Cameron *et al.* 1986; Valkenburg *et al.* 1983). A key Soviet biologist has even identified changing migration routes of deer as a 'pendulum mechanism' which aids the search for new forage (Syroechkovskii 1990). The interpretation of these results is difficult. It is important to note that these studies have been carried out in areas where the populations of wild deer have already been highly impacted by either industrial development, state wildlife management, or both. Thus they may not in fact represent a fine-grained study of 'herd dynamics' but instead complex case studies of regions where the relationship between people and migratory reindeer has been interrupted by resettlement and urbanization. The very few studies which have looked at the micro-relationships of deer to pastures where deer and their human stewards have not been displaced tend to identify discrete 'local' herds (Michurin & Mironenko 1964; 1966; Simard 1979; Pulliainen *et al.* 1983; Brown *et al.* 1986). It is likely that the 'unfaithful wanderings' of wild deer is a quality of those areas where the relationship between deer, their animal predators, and their human stewards has already been broken. This carries the corollary that as people become settled, civilized, and regulated, migratory deer become increasingly wild.

   If we accept the 'discrete herd hypothesis' that wild migratory deer move in some regular relationship with the tundra and the other animals and hunters on the tundra, the question then becomes how one can characterize that relationship. There has been very little holistic research on this scale. One of the more influential models postulates an enduring relation of 'herd following' between four consecutive archaeological traditions in Canada's eastern Arctic over eight millennia (Gordon 1975, 1996; Burch 1991). According to Gordon (1996), over thirteen thousand artefacts from the tree-line zone of Dene and Inuit occupancy show greater similarities within the range of discrete herds of wild migratory deer than they do between migratory routes. Most interestingly, using ethnohistorical and archaeological clues, Gordon links seasonal hunting camps to the reproductive patterns of both wild deer and indigenous peoples. According to his thesis, the repro-duction of local 'bands' was dependent on successfully 'following' migratory herds from early winter to spring.

The term 'following' is an interesting one. In an archaeological idiom it carries the implication that people passively depended upon a migratory protein source without much ability to shape or control the migration. This is very similar to how Evenki hunting is characterized by state ethno-graphers. For example, Karlov links the lack of order in Evenki territorial relationships to dependence [*bolshaia zavisimost'*, *khoziaistvennaia nuzhda*] of Evenki hunters on finding animals—the failure of which triggers desperate hunts far from their regular lands (1982: 41, 45, 52). In his view, hunger is said to drive Evenkis to 'exit' [*vyiti*] from their normal territories much the same way as hunger directs caribou migrations. It is difficult to read into the dusty archival record whether or not hunger activated the unarguably exten-sive 'exits' of Evenki hunters to follow migratory deer. While hunger is a significant tragedy of life on the tundra, one wonders if it is not better interpreted as an effect of the unravelling of the sentient ecology of a region rather than the motive which explains the behaviour of both wild deer and a stateless people.

However, the idea of 'following' can also be used in an active aspect. Gordon's work footnotes the existence of caribou surrounds and the pageantry accompanying wild deer hunts as effective technologies and rituals which are mute in the archaeological record. The ethnography presented in the pre-vious section suggests that the association of particular surname groups with discrete groups of deer and their 'homes' is best understood as one governed by forming a relationship with animals rather than the static concepts of 'instinct' or 'need'. Although it is now impossible to prove that individual deer did indeed return to individual family's places year in and year out at 'negotiated' meeting-places, it is clear that the older herders at least had a good knowledge of where the most attractive deer pastures lay. However, if we posit the hypothesis that certain households did indeed participate in a sentient relationship with discrete populations of wild deer, then the riddle of Evenki occupation becomes clearer. 'Knowing the deer' liberated people to use land extensively unencumbered with the worry of maintaining fixed lines of provision. The competent hunter could then travel for several days in a particular direction, with nothing more than his reindeer sled and his hunting weapons (as he does today), secure in his entitlement to take deer from the land. In this sense, to paraphrase Vasilevich, 'property in land was a waste of effort' (1972: 167). Regularities in the migrations of wild deer and their anticipated seasonal proximity to groups of households made the memory of homes, homelands, and hence 'territory' a spurious result of a more complex sentient relationship between people and animals. To extrapolate a general sense of territory (or lack of) to these cumulative 'going-outs' is to deny the way that memory and knowledge are used by the hunters themselves.

Since the arrival of Russian Cossack warriors and merchants, the taking of animals for fur has also set hunters out on extensive trajectories. Although requiring a great knowledge of the habits of animals, it is significant that the fur hunt has little to contribute to the symbolic affirmation of an Evenki hunter's relationship to the land. Vasilevich (1969: 69, 221, 235) observes (and my field notes affirm) that the hunt of a fur-bearer is not the source of a good story nor a matter for discussion with the omniscient fire in the hearth. Unlike the taking of ungulates, the taking of furs has less to do with reciprocity and knowledge of a sentient animal world and more to do with satisfying a very real, driving hunger of state officials for tribute, taxes, or quotas.

The exchange of fur has a long history in central Siberia, but the concrete effects on Evenki land-use came with the establishment of the *yasak* system of tribute in the seventeenth century.[9] This militarily enforced directive to deliver a fixed number of furs to specified locations is standardly credited with inducing the idea that Evenkis could share a 'territory' with neighbours who were not necessarily kinsmen (Dolgikh & Levin 1951). Although this model suggests a pre-Soviet analogue to territorial formation and collectivization, there were some significant exceptions. Karlov (1982) indicates that the number of recorded cases of *yasak* providers appearing 'outside' of their expected administrative units in the eighteenth century was quite great (pp. 41–61). Rather than enforcing an unambiguous mechanism of sedentariza-tion, the historical evidence indicates that at least for many households the coerced exchange of furs *expanded* the use of space.

In the lower Yenisei valley, the technology of fur trapping revolved around the maintenance of networks of wooden deadfall traps [*pasti, langil*] until the late 1960s. These traps were constructed out of logs on exposed hummocks in between the line of forest and either arctic or alpine tundras. The placing of *langil* required an awareness not only of which areas the arctic fox, wolverine, or sable preferred, but also of terrains which would be kept clear of snow by the strong blizzards between December and March. Although

---

[9] For accounts of the Evenki fur trade with China see Kiuner 1961 and Karlov 1982 (pp. 20–1). The workings of the *yasak* tribute system in Mangazeia *uezd* [county] is best described in Bakhrushin 1955, Dolgikh 1960, and Karlov 1982 (ch. 2). An English account is available in Forsyth 1992 (38–42, 57–69).

Vasilevich (1969: 181) records the private ownership of deadfall traps by mercantile Yakuts, on the Khantaika the materials and locations of deadfalls were circulated between kin groups. At least in this region it is not surprising that locations and materials would be recycled. The appropriateness of collective labour is suggested by both the great effort involved in hauling three-metre-long logs by reindeer sledge from valley bottoms to high, wind-swept locations up to twenty kilometres distant, as well as the limit on the number of suitable places. Following from the technical and ecological limits on building traps, the deadfalls would typically be built along habitual travel routes. While travelling to fish, hunt wild deer, or to tend reindeer, Evenki men would build or repair the deadfalls in December and check them intensively between February and April.

Although deadfall traps were set in a discrete number of places, it does not necessarily follow that their architects remained tied to them as the literature suggests. Present-day hunters in the Khantaiskii state farm distinguish between the person who built a deadfall trap and the person who used it. Similarly, Evenkis of the archival records may only have set traps in the region where they chose to overwinter [*zimovat'*]. It also seems likely that only certain households were forced to remain stationary near their fishing spots and a small number of deadfall traps for lack of reindeer while wealthier kinsmen operated extensive trading networks around them. The ecology of fur-trapping makes it unlikely that families poor in reindeer were extensive fur trappers. In order to gather pelts in their thickest and most colourful condition, the trapping activity must be effected between December and March. A trapper with 200 deadfalls would have to cover a territory of up to half a million hectares on skis or a limited complement of reindeer while simultaneously serving the needs of his stationary kinsfolk. Although most Soviet accounts emphasize the link between fur harvesting and narrow territoriality, they paradoxically also stress the importance of richer herders who gathered fur from sedentary fishing families in exchange for provisions (Rychkov 1917–23; Vasilevich 1969: 52, 79 n., 181; Karlov 1982: 118–22). The successful trapper must have been a highly mobile entrepreneur with herds of reindeer numbering over 500 head. With such lucrative mobility, it seems unlikely that such a family would confine itself to a narrow territory, as post-1969 trappers have tended to do, since they could also maximize other opportunities of marriage, trade, and alliance.[10] It seems much more reasonable to consider fur trapping as a very complex economy which amplified

---

[10] There are several historical snapshots of hunters with Khantaika surnames engaged in extensive fur-trapping. Khein (1909) quotes a transaction with a Khukochar steward of 1,000 reindeer on the Kureika river who sold several sable furs from the Viliui river drainage some 600 km. distant (cf. Karlov 1982: 118). Middendorf (1869: 700) recounts an encounter with a Yelogir (Yalegirin) on the Avam river who regularly travelled between the Avam and Khatanga rivers as well as to the south of Lake Yessei.

mobility or, at most, stratified Evenki producers into highly mobile and strictly sedentary segments. Similar conclusions have also been observed in other areas of the circumpolar Arctic (Burch 1975: 31; Milloy 1988).

While 'knowing the land' put Evenki households in a position to benefit materially and socially from extensive travel across the larch-fringed taiga of eastern Siberia, this knowledge could also be used to loosen the ties of dependence on the Russian state. Although I do not want to invoke the romantic rhetoric of the nomad as the free-spirited adventurer of the Asian steppes, written records and the statements of informants do suggest a cagey resistance to the accounting projects radiating from the intensive settlements of the Russian state. One of the easiest ways to subvert unequal exchange and regulative state action is to create uncertainty about the amount of production, number of people, and total days spent within an authorized space.

Extensive travel as a strategy of resistance can be encountered today within the boundaries of contemporary state farms. On the Khantaika, Number Three Reindeer Brigade, in addition to being 'wild Tunguses', had the reputation of being 'partisans' [*partizany*]—an appellation which is drawn from the heroic genre of Soviet war-time literature to indicate wildly auton- omous (yet loyal) activity within a territory overrun by foreign forces. The *partizany* stubbornly refused to recharge the batteries for their radio- transmitter, frustrating the director from co-ordinating helicopter flights to gather production or to effect an account of reindeer. More pernicious was their preference for heavily wooded locations which would make them invisible from the air, a habit which also earned them the title of being 'wild Tunguses'. Reputedly, individual members of the brigade would make unauthorized trips into the settlement by reindeer while being paid for the days they spent on the tundra. The *partizanskii* type of action was common to all brigades. The men of Number One Reindeer Brigade would make long trips into the mountains to hunt deer, or, more seriously, to the meteorological station or even to the hydroelectric settlement of Snezhnogorsk for a drink. Famous in the lore of the tundra is the Nenets practice of keeping substantial herds of reindeer in distant places out of view of the state in order to avoid the biannual census of herd size. Although the herders in the Khantaiskii state farm preferred to tell tales of Nenets exploits as if they were innocent of these practices, there were also occasional circumscribed hints of their own private reindeer ownership. Both extensive travel and private appropriation seems to have been possible if a mobile production regime was used to keep property and people in the blind-spots of the redistributive state.

There is evidence to suggest that there is a long history of avoiding the enclosing pressures of Russian administration in Taimyr. Two of the most independent groups in the lower Yenisei valley of the 1930s are both closely connected with the contemporary settlement of the Khantaika: the 'wild work-unit' [*dikii artel'*] and the Mountain Yakuts.

The *dikii artel'* is recorded only in the preface and footnotes of the first and only monograph on Dolgan grammar (Ubriatova 1985) and a few scattered archival references.[11] In the period between the formation of authorized territories (1932) and the strict enforcement of collective farm boundaries (1937–9), this group of Evenki- and Yakut-speaking natives represented themselves to officials as the *artel' Budennogo*. It is unclear whether or not the *artel'* was formally approved or if early collectivization officials just tolerated their claim. The sketchy accounts suggest that between twenty and forty families travelled in an arc in between the frontiers of the collective farms in Noril'sk, Potapovo, the Khantaika, and Volochanka (Mount Baerak–Lake Kheta–Lake Lama–Mikchanga river–Aiakli river) trading into a variety of factories, maintaining their separate cemetery, and developing a local creole language. The mobile economy of the *dikii artel'* allowed it to weave in between the authorized territories being constructed around the *kolkhoz RKKa* (Chasovnia), *kolkhoz* Truzhenik (Potapovo), and the work-unit 'Red Trapper' (the Khantaika). The fate of the members of the *dikii artel'*, and their strategy of extensive travel, was sealed by the establishment of increasingly complicated institutions for monitoring production and exchange. Following the 1938 meeting, the Evenkis, Dolgans, and Enneches of the *dikii artel'* became incorporated with the Noril'sk farm.

The Mountain Yakuts do not seem to have presented themselves as a distinct group in the 1930s, but all evidence suggests that they also used their very powerful mobile resources to move in between the first boundaries established by the Soviet state. The administration came to know very late of the existence of herders with stocks of over one thousand head living at the headwaters of the Aiakli river. Although it is possible that the gaze of the state simply missed the existence of wealthy herders in this remote, mountainous location, it seems an interesting coincidence that a number of wealthy herders with the same surnames were exhorted to pay a 'civilizing

---

[11] The direct evidence of the *dikii artel'* in the archives is sparse (GATAO 2–1–3: 2–11; 2–1–4: 1–52; 2–1–12: 44; KTsKhIDNI 28–1–26; AMAE K2–1–129: 17; K2–1–128: 77; 14–1–134). The indirect evidence is suggestive. When in 1937 the Lantaiskii-Evenkiiskii clan council near Potapovo was liquidated some of its members reappear on the registers of farms in Noril'sk and Potapovo and possibly in the registers for Budennogo. Similarly, the 1931 liquidation of the Piasino-Dolganskii clan council (to the north of the Noril'sk collective farm) seems to have precipitated a similar dispersion of personnel into Budennogo (TsGARF A310–18–37: 361–94). Some of the registered names in Budennogo correspond with those activists in the Volochanka rebellion of 1932. If one proceeds from the point of view of today's authorized nationality structure, the surnames of the group's members tantalizingly suggest that this was an 'intra-national' collective of individuals recruited from the Enneches, the Evenkis, and the Sakhas. In person, I imagine these individuals to have been like the Old Man Yeremin of Number One Reindeer Brigade with a heredity and linguistic scope that defies classification. The interstitial nature of this group—living in-between spatial and nationality categories—seems to have contributed to their invisibility in historical documents.

tax' [*kul'tsbor*] in roubles at Lake Yessei in the previous year (GAKK R2275–1–83: 4–6). Although by 1930 some poorer Yakuts and interrelated Evenkis agreed to work within the framework of the 'Aian Nomadic Soviet', state managers discovered a decade later that three wealthy families were holding a herd of over four thousand reindeer in the interior of the Putoran plateau (AMAE K2–1–118: 3; K2–1–128: 43, 100, 261). In the intervening period the Kamen' region was infamous in government literature for being a haven of tax-evaders, Yakut nationalists, and various counter-revolutionary bands (GAKK R2275–1–144). The voices of these 'wandering' Tunguses would only appear in the documents analysing the causes of the Volochanka rebellion. The rebels directly asked Party officials, 'Why should we pay such high taxes and denounce our relatives. Who is a *kulak* anyway?' (Troshev 1993; 1998). Although the paper record suggests that Mountain Yakuts and Evenkis were integrated into the collective farm system by 1935, the odd *tundrovik* on the Khantaika speaks of the 'route to Yessei' with details that suggest that it has not been long since he was travelling it. A photograph in the album of an elderly woman shows a meeting out on the tundras of the Aiakli watershed between Lake Yessei and *kamenskie* Yakuts in 1978 (Plate 16). As these examples show, mobility for this group of free-ranging hunters has for many generations been connected with resistance to the state.

Isolated archival documents suggest that Yakuts and Evenkis travelling in the Putoran mountains used their mobility to escape the tax-collecting Cossacks of the Imperial state. The distances between the seventeenth-century *yasak* collecting posts of the lower Yenisei valley were between 400 and 700 kilometres—distances which gave great scope for the know-ledgeable hunter to escape the attention of the authorities (Map 4). As an example of the administrative chaos which this created, Karlov (1982: 55) cites confrontations between Evenkis and Cossacks in the eighteenth century when the latter attempted unknowingly to extract tribute from the same person in different places. Foreshadowing the administrative instruments of the Soviet era, receipts [*otpisi*] were issued to create greater clarity on who had paid the *yasak* in a different place and who was feigning payment. Ironically, these written receipts would become part of the arsenal used by state ethnographers to assign nationalities to particular spaces.

Once again, it is difficult to estimate the proportion of Evenki producers who travelled the lower Yenisei valley, and perhaps the rest of eastern Siberia, with a keen awareness of how best to avoid the gaze of the state. The historical record also captures instances of settled Evenki fishing families who fell fully within the Tsarist tribute apparatus through intergenerational debts owed to both trading organizations and the government bread ware-houses (Tugarinov 1919; Isachenko 1913; GAKK R1845–1–210: 26). Clearly, only the most wealthy herding families—families with between 200 and 2,000

Plate 16. A memorable meeting between members of the Number Two Reindeer Brigade at Lake Yessei and their Mountain cousins on the tundras above Lake Khantaika in August 1978

head of reindeer—had both the strongest interest and the capacity to weave their way around the administrators who collected taxes and tribute.

A competent *tundrovik* who could effect a proper relationship within the sentient ecology of the lower Yenisei valley would have the knowledge and indeed the entitlement to travel extensively. The taking of animals for fur or meat, as well as the taking of opportunities for trade as well as for autonomy, can be considered not so much as a chance possibility but as an imperative. Rather than interpreting an extensive land-use system as the result of a vulnerability to hunger and poverty, it is better to understand Evenki movements as being the product of a multiplicity of strategies each meaningful in its own right. Both statements from *tundroviki* as well as historical sources indicate that the old people did travel everywhere—but it is important to understand this movement not as chaos or frenzied movement. Knowing the land and its human and animal persons provided both the mechanism and the demand to travel without recourse to an agenda of property or territoriality. Although the enforced taxation system of the Tsarist period may have impoverished some families while amplifying the mobility of others, the licensing of movement by the Soviet state has led to a more particular notion of territory. The idea of belonging both to an exclusive territory and a nationality is now fuelling the nationalist sentiment on the Khantaika.

7
Exclusive Territories

THE FOUNDATION OF Soviet power, with its characteristic centralization of economic, political, and cultural activity in the hands of carefully recruited managers, is often thought to begin with the policy of collectivization [*kollektivizatsiia*]. The second, successful attempt at nationalizing the tundras of the native peoples of Taimyr in 1938 did indeed discipline people to work within a rationalized system of accounting and spatial control. However, this was achieved only after land had already been parcelled into territories. The distinctive segmenting of administrative power into councils, districts, and republics, stratified by nationality, owes its origins to an early series of campaigns to carve out the 'territorial formations' thought to be congruent with a socialist society. While the internal dynamics of collective institutions are important for understanding post-Soviet society, the 'territories' in which work-units were inscribed were both a necessary first step in building a new order and proved to be a more poignant legacy than the institutions themselves. This chapter explores the manner in which a different type of 'knowing'—termed here 'intelligence'—was used to construct boundaries which came to be meaningful to managers and producers alike as territories were linked to nationalities.

Territorial formations

With the term 'territory' I capture those connotations of the Russian word *territoriia* conveying, not merely a sense of bounded space, but one on which all action is authorized by an appropriate state or civil institution. 'Territorial formation' refers to two early campaigns of Soviet state-building in Siberia: *zemleustroistvo* and *raionirovaniia*. Both of these campaigns, occurring between 1927 and 1932, were concerned with the appropriate allocation of territory to early native councils or to state-controlled enterprises. *Raionirovaniia* (from *raion* 'county') refers to the establishment of the territorial limits of particular county and provincial state agencies. *Zemleustroistvo* (from *zemlia* 'land' and *stroit'* 'to build') can be variously translated as the 'arrangement', 'organization', or 'allocation' of lands to producers. This compound word implies both that space should be ordered but also that authorized territories are part of an ordered society. To capture this latter aspect, the somewhat militaristic word of 'formation' will be used to create a link to the project of civilizing the frontier. It is tempting to use words like 'land claim', 'land reservation', or 'land enclosure', invoking similar processes in North America in both the 1880s and the 1980s, or in England in the seventeenth century. Although the theme in each case is similar in so far as space became regulated by external social institutions, territorial formation in the Soviet context is special in that it created a highly localized sense of belonging to specific places while recentring control over how land was used in a distant authority structure. This new dimension to the history of common property deserves a distinct term.

The campaign for territorial formation was designed and effected by the populist state institution known as the Committee of the North—an inter-departmental federal institution literally designed to 'provide assistance' through the tailoring of policy to the sparse peoples of the northern frontier (Slezkine 1994; Vakhtin 1994; Forsyth 1992; Grant 1993). The issue of territoriality arose in 1924 with the first resolution of the Committee calling for 'reservations [*reservatsii*] of territory necessary for the sparse peoples of the North' (Skachko 1930: 21). The choice of this word was deliberate since many of the Committee's founders were inspired by the idea of land reservations in North America as a means of strengthening the cultures of Northern peoples (Bogoraz-Tan 1923; Slezkine 1994: 148–9) while simultaneously clarifying which lands would be left for Russians to colonize (Skachko 1923). As with North American policy for native peoples, the Committee of the North was also concerned with 'protecting' the sparse peoples. However, this Committee distinguished itself with a passion for 'raising' people to a higher social state through making their activities on the land regularized and 'efficient'. Contemporary historians of Siberian policy tend to distinguish the leaders of the Committee as being either conservatives or protectionists (Vakhtin 1994: 40–2; Slezkine 1994: ch. 5) in terms of their preference for the tempo of change. However, both con-servatives and protectionists were allied in their conviction that evolution to an industrial order was inevitable (although some embraced change while others feared it). The most isolationist idea of protection quickly became an intrusive instrument when the people in question were seen as needing the protection of their territory from outsiders, the protection from the economic exploitation of their relatives, or the protection from the un-certainties of nature through housing and better technology. All three of these elements can be found in the resolution passed in 1928 at the Fifth Plenary Session of the Committee of the North on 'The First Stages of Land and Water Formation' (Skachko 1930: 22–3).[1] Just as the state ethnographers strengthened the identity of the sparse people by giving them nationalities,

---

[1] Northern administration until 1926 was determined by Speranskii's 'Code of Native People' (passed in 1822 and amended in 1892). In 1926 the 'Temporary Declaration of the Administration of Northern Tribes on the Northern Frontier' replaced Tsarist law. It made provision for 'clan councils' and 'regional native congresses' based on a meeting of clansmen at a 'clan gathering' (Vserossiiskii 1927; Vakhtin 1994). In 1928 the resolution on land and water formulation affixed specific territories to recognized clan councils.

the provision of territory was seen as filling the need of the sparse peoples for a fixed homeland.

Both rhetorically and in terms of political impetus, the protection of native lands was seen as the primary objective behind this resolution. In his support for the resolution, the first Chairman of the Committee of the North spoke of the importance of territorial registration [*zakreplenie*] before any subsidiary objectives could be achieved:

Only such registration creates the conditions for the awakening of the voluntarism and action of each member of the native population; for the inclusion of him in the work of local councils and executive committees, and the use of his primal communistic traditions in planned collective work. Only such a registration creates the conditions for the rationalization and all-sided development of the native household and the provision for his future existence both to more fully use the natural wealth of the northern frontier and for the interests of the native population and all of the Soviet Union (P. D. Smidovich, GAKK R2275–1–144: 257).

The need for an authorized registration of native lands seems to have been a pressing one. It is a tragic irony of the early stages of Soviet development that the annulment of Tsarist land regulations under the slogan 'all land belongs to the people' led to a land rush by Russian peasants and would-be trappers eager to present themselves as a people more deserving to be tenants than the sparse people they were displacing (Skachko 1930: 15–17; Berezovskii 1930: 74, 77).

Early documents arguing the case for territorial formation were designed to dispel the illusion that sparse peoples simply 'wandered' and thus had no fixed affiliation to land. Both Skachko and Berezovskii interpret the explosion of Russian trappers as yet another sign foretelling the 'dying-out' of native peoples. Berezovskii (1930: 78–9) makes the exaggerated claim that there were absolutely no Russian trappers in Turukhansk district until the start of the 1920s (this is empirically contradicted by Pavlov (1964)). Skachko, in a widely distributed handbook for Territorial Formation Officers, employed a fine summary of concrete land-tenure institutions from the Kola peninsula to Sakhalin Island (1930: 10–14) to fight what must have been a prevailing opinion that northern lands belonged to 'no one' [*nich'ia*] (pp. 8, 10). These are both early examples of that tendency in Soviet ethnography which reads politically expedient ideas backwards through the ethnographic record.

Territorial registration quickly came to include broader tasks than the stemming of the flood of Russian immigrants. In his handbook, Anatolii Skachko (1930) clearly outlined three main dimensions of *territoriia* as it later came to be institutionalized. The first was a conviction that it was not sufficient to 'juridically' organize land but that the state must also establish a 'system of socio-economic and technical measures directed to the restructuring of rural production' (pp. 21, 25). The second was the imperative that territorial formation be effected quickly and strongly institutionalized to protect both the environment and the sparse peoples from the exploitative characters of Russian newcomers and indigenous *kulaki* (pp. 15–17). The third element, which is often repeated in the literature, is that 'aside from the organization of production, the territorial formation of the sparse peoples of the North also pursues the goal of organizing these same peoples; of collecting them into one whole [*odno tseloe*] on discrete territories and united into one whole by a single national self-administration' (p. 20). In all three of these propositions the common justifications for state action are the imputed 'needs' of the sparse peoples which the state sees as its duty to fill.

The easy slippage from 'protection' of territory to an enumeration of 'needs' can be seen in the practice of regional managers administering the Territorial Formation Programme. The instructions given to the District Administrations of the Siberian Territory ordered local workers to effect water and land formulation but 'at the same time' to clarify issues relating to 'administrative *raionirovaniia*'. This forward-looking list asked officers to gather complex demographic and economic data, and to make informed recommendations on which were the best sites from which to provision sparse peoples and what practices might be exploited to encourage nomadic families to settle (GANO R354–1–238: 12–14) (Table 12). Between 1928 and 1934 numerous expeditions of scholars from the People's Commissariat of Land Use were sent to study the habitual patterns of land and water use amongst specific clan councils.[2] The results of their work were maps purporting to show the boundaries within which native households moved, the establishment of the first household registries, and the affiliation of each clan council to specific state agencies providing trade, transport, education, and medical services. Characteristically, the officers saw their task as a purely technical one since clan membership, economic profiles, and movements were thought to be transparent and readily recordable by trained map-makers and economists. The reports of the Territorial Formation Commissions provided a remarkably standardized sketch of the demography, distribution of visible wealth, and main economic indicators in each clan council of Siberia, filling a lacuna of basic intelligence on the activities of people. These data would later be used in setting district budgets, establishing collective farms, and targeting specific households for expropriation. The type of intelligence gathered is striking when compared to the principle of 'knowing'

---

[2] The Territorial Formation Programme started in 1928 in Krasnoiarsk, Tomsk, and Kirensk Districts (GANO R354–1–238: 12). It reached Dudinka County in the lower Yenisei valley in 1932 and Avam County in 1934 (TsGARF A310–18–21; AMEA K2–1–124–133 & 14–1–42). The Nenets households at the outer reaches of Ust-Yenisei County were never contacted by the Programme. Territorial Formation was barely completed in Avam County (TsGARF A310–18–20) before collectivization began in the southern reaches of the lower Yenisei valley in 1937.

TABLE 12. Sample schedule of clarificatory questions concerning preparations for the national *raionirovaniia* of the native population of the Northern frontier

1. The tribal composition of an administrative unit (clan or village soviet).
2. A statistical breakdown of each sparse people by clan for the given administrative unit.
3. Does the given administrative unit unite one or several groups of natives which might present themselves as 'discrete wholes' in tribal interrelationships, in language, a common clan forebear, lifestyle, religion, etc.?
4. The dispersion, compactness of the native population of each group; the level of compactness [*splochennosti*], organization, level of mobility (over what distance and for what reason do natives leave the main region or point of their habitation), tendencies to a stationary lifestyle.
5. The level of Russification. The influence of mixed [*smezhnikh*] peoples on the language, material culture of the given group. The interrelationship of each native group located within the given administrative unit with other [*smezhnikh*] groups (with whom they consider themselves to be related, with whom they are at what level of animosity).
6. The place and date of tribal meetings [*suglan*]. The number of households at each meeting. The period during which they arrive at the meeting. The reason for the choice of place of the meeting.
7. The appearance of land and water territories in actual use of each native group located within the composition of the given administrative unit at the present time; with the names of rivers, lakes, mountains, places [*urochishch*] which are the given group's hunting territory, pasture, wintering place, summering place, nomadic route, etc.

   In addition, it is necessary to clarify if the borders of the above territories have lessened in the sense of their shortening or widening [*sic*]; since when and why was it undertaken to maintain territories; have the above groups been exclusive users for a long time?
8. The appearance of a natural point of economic gravitation of the given group of native people. The explanation of how the given point overlaps with existing administrative, economic, and cultural centres of the given administrative unit with respect to the choice of routes of travel; in other words, are the locations of trading posts, schools, nursing stations, the District Executive Committee, the Settlement Administration, in a true overlap with the nomadic centre of the given group?
9. The appearance of arguments and misunderstandings on the subject of water and land formulation between different native groups (of one or another tribe) or between natives and Russians (inclusive of long-time dwellers, exiles, and run-aways [*samovol'shchiki*]), or between hunting organizations. The existence of territories of common use for the native groups of the given administrative unit.

Source: GANO R354–1–238: 13. Attached to a memorandum sent to all local Committees of the North from the Secretary of the Committee of the North of Siberian Territory Dobrova. Dated 29 May 1928 in Novosibirsk.

the tundra. Whereas the latter was directed to a proper and personalized relationship of a person to the land and its animals, the former quite clearly concentrated on those parameters which could be used to manage and intensify the movements and activities of people within an arbitrarily defined area.

The primary criterion for the inscription of boundaries was the principle of the ease of access to the channels of economic and political power, or as it is called in the literature, 'economic gravitation' [*ekonomicheskoe tiagotanie*]. The administrative restructuring of Siberia did not take place in a social vacuum. For many centuries native producers carried on extensive commerce with a number of trading posts [*faktorii*], markets [*yarmarki*], grain-warehouses [*khlebo–zapasnie magazini*], as well as with mobile caravan operators and sedentary fur trappers. Since subsistence economic activity was thought to be chaotic and irregular, gravitation was defined by sustained contacts with stationary trading points where transactions for manufactured goods could be counted. With such a narrow definition of 'economy', the task of inscribing boundaries amounted to making decisions as to which territories would be the best transportation portholes for the boats and caravans of administrators. On the maps of the Territorial Formation Officers the Evenki routes linking the places where hunters encountered animals are conspicuously absent while seasonal trap lines and fishing sites were solidly demarcated with 'gravitational' vectors showing their proximity to collection points. The 'boundaries' then sketched in the interstices between these star-shaped clusters did not at first represent allegiances to a discrete two-dimensional space but instead the horizons beyond which early Soviet surveillance instruments would no longer be reliable. However, by the mid-1950s even the most independently minded *tundrovik* would have difficulty escaping the pull of various administrative centres, in effect making the hastily drawn borders between regions watersheds of human activity.

Given the thin distribution of trading posts at the time, the obsession of Territorial Formation Officers with trade must have struck native peoples as odd. In all of Taimyr in 1931 there were only eighteen trading posts belonging to two trading monopolies (TsGARF A310–18–21: 73). The ethnographer Dobrova-Yadrintseva, at the start of the campaign, argued against the registration of territories to trading posts since they 'served an area much too wide in which land was used not only by different clans but different tribal groups' (GANO R354–1–118: 22). Furthermore, within concrete regions, the attention devoted to trade in written reports could only be achieved by ignoring local economic patterns. For example, the 'classic' case study of subsistence economics in the lower Yenisei valley by Berezovskii (1930: 76) dismisses the Evenki wild deer hunt as 'sport'. The Territorial Formation report for the Khantaiskii-Evenkiiskii Native Soviet identified fishing as the 'primary industry' despite both statements by informants and an analysis of 'potential' [*valovaia*] income which stressed the centrality of the hunt of wild deer (AMAE K2–1–127: 7–8). Inconsistencies such as these can be explained by the fact that the Territorial Formation Officers had a different agenda from sketching an emic account of how people lived. The identification of points of gravitation was central to building a different principle of social power, as an early document on *raionirovaniia* argues:

The former *volosti* [Tsarist provinces] were too impotent [both] in population and territory. This was acutely felt from the moment of designing a budget in each *volost'* as a first step in the cultural and productive activity of Soviet organs in the concentrating of the peasant masses . . . Soviet *raionirovaniia* strengthens the potency [of *volosti*], expands their resources, and provides the possibility of a greater economy with the fulfilment of cultural and productive needs (Boldyrev & Girinovich 1926).

While it should be clear that technicians of 'economic gravitation' carefully selected data when they imputed boundaries between regions, it is important to remember that these boundaries then became real. The gravitation vectors through which people travelled to trading posts soon became the exclusive corridors for the trade of commodities, the supply of civic services, and the exchange of administrative intelligence on the nature of productive activity.

The principles by which economic gravitation were established led easily into issues of national gravitation. Instructions given to fieldworkers clearly underscored that incipient nationalities were not to be arbitrarily severed from their kinsmen (GANO R354–1–118: 24; GAKK R2275–1–144: 256). The governing assumption of these documents was that identity and territory must naturally coincide. In the field reports, this was reflected in a sensitivity to classifying people by their authorized identities, deducing the neighbouring nomadic councils to which producers felt an allegiance, and selecting an appropriate hyphenated title for the council expressing both territory and nationality.

Although the act of *raionirovaniia* was interpreted as a technical task, the reports for both Dudinka and Avam districts wrote of problems with matching economic boundaries with the gravitation of nationalities. Evenkis, Dolgans, and Nenetses alike displayed a disturbing tendency to wander into each other's territories. When encountering such anomalies, Dobrova-Yadrintseva, the head of the Siberian section of the Committee of the North, encouraged fieldworkers to try to imagine how provincial and county borders might reinforce a deep feeling of belonging amongst a migratory population. She directed their attention to how a 'group's coherence and uniqueness [*samobytnost'*]' was reflected in 'economic and territorial instances' (GANO R354–1–118: 18–19). If a 'veneer' of national homogeneity was not confirmed by common economic interests in a given territory, she prescribed that either the protective powers of the state be invested in establishing 'national native regions' for the weaker groups in which 'administrative, economic, territorial and national elements tightly interweave between each other', or that small compact groups be encouraged to merge with the 'culture of a stronger diminutive people' (p. 25). She saw this situation to be particularly relevant in the northern portions of Turukhansk district between Dolgans, Yakuts, and Tunguses. At the early date when her paper was presented (*c.* 1928), Dobrova left the choice between these two options open. However, her tightly argued alternatives showed the intent and capacity of the state to use all administrative tools at its disposal to shape the evolution of national groups. It might be said that intense molecular pressure generated by economic gravitation at the local level created the 'reaction' which melded national identities.

An example which illustrates the difficulty of engineering an optimal distribution of people to territories is that of the *raionirovaniia* of the borderlands between the Yakut Autonomous Republic (established 1922) and the districts of Siberian Territory which would become the Taimyr (Dolgano-Nenets) National District and Evenki National District (both established in 1930). The highly mobile hunting and herding population living at the divides of the Lena and Yenisei river systems tested the limits of administrative tools designed to measure 'national gravitation'. While the classic examples of *raionirovaniia* and 'gravitation' were designed with compact, semi-sedentary communities in mind (Berezovskii 1930), the Yakut- and Evenki-speaking *tundroviki* interwove extensive modes of alliance and hunting with trade at factories provisioned both by Turukhansk and by Yakutsk. To resolve the dilemma of discerning 'gravitation' where centrifugal economic action seemed to be pervasive, a special territorial formation commission was established to study the question of the national 'allegiance' [*prinadlezhnost'*] of the native peoples of the Anabar river basin and the region around Lake Yessei. Moscow eventually awarded the region to the west of the Anabar river to Turukhansk County in July 1930 and affirmed Turukhansk's claim on the Lake Yessei region.[3] This move to curtail Yakutsk's territorial claims was quickly followed by the legislation in December 1930 to create the Taimyr (Dolgano-Nenets) National District and the Evenki National District. In Chapter 4, I examined the process whereby a relationally defined group called *dolgany* became a nation displayed conspicuously in the authorized title of a new district. Here I will confine myself to demonstrating that in drawing boundaries, the state successfully introduced the centripetal principle of *territoriia* as a necessary and a meaningful part of everyday life. This principle became that much more powerful with the selection of one or another nationality to be a 'leading people' within a territory.

The substantive case behind securing the Anabar and Yessei territories for Turukhansk district revolved around the proven capacity of Turukhansk to provision these outlying districts with trade goods, medical assistance, and with schools. Documents assembled by Novosibirsk managers in 1928 demonstrated to their Muscovite superiors that prices on heating oil, sugar, and pork [!] were between 120 per cent and 252 per cent more expensive if provisioned out of the Viliui division of YakNarKomTorg (GAKK R1845–1–210: 13). Turukhansk

---

[3] The expedition was dispatched from Krasnoiarsk in Nov. 1929 and returned to Novosibirsk in Aug. 1930—two months after Siberian Territory was divided into East Siberian Territory [capital Irkutsk] and West Siberian Territory [capital Novosibirsk] and one month after the decision of the Administrative Commission of the Central Executive Committee in Moscow. Some documents indicate that, in evident anticipation of the results of the commission, Moscow 'informally' [*uslovno*] transferred the Anabar region to Turukhansk on 12 Aug. 1929 (GAIO R538–1–196: 22; GANO R47–1–1089: 352). The documents of the commission are today randomly distributed between Novosibirsk, Krasnoiarsk, and Irkutsk. The preliminary results of the commission with respect to economic gravitation and ethnonyms are in GAKK (R2275–1–143). The formal report on the boundary between Yakutiia and Taimyr is in GAIO (R538–1–196).

also carefully presented the steps which it was taking to open a nursing station, school, and bread warehouse at Lake Chirinda (GAKK R1845–1–5: 46). In an escalation of rhetoric, Turukhansk exposed Yakutsk for not only refusing to provision disputed territory with trade goods but also for exporting 'wine, maps, and Russian priests' to win over the population. Perhaps more startling were the attempts by Yakutsk to arrest Turukhansk officials as they tried to 'straighten out' affairs (GANO R47–1–1089: 352). Whether or not these accusations were true, the central principle in these documents is that a single population could not be served by multiple trade or cultural organizations. The impossibility of working under 'conditions of dual-power [*dvoevlastiia*]' was specifically cited in the representation by the trading organizations (GAKK R1845–1–210: 13). After the settlement of the dispute in favour of Turukhansk, not only were native people in each bounded region served by a single trading organization but the nationalization of trading posts in 1936 affixed the planned consumption of people to single points of provision (GATAO 85–1–2: 1–3). For the self-reliant *tundrovik*, the availability or dearth of trade goods did not necessarily prevent extensive movement on the land. However, these administrative changes were bound to concentrate travel in orbits around a single authorized point from where consumption goods could be obtained.

What troubled state managers more than indeterminacy in trade was the prospect that the Yessei-Anabar region was torn by sharp differences in wealth and perhaps expansionist territorial ambitions emanating from the Yakut side of the border. In the region around Lake Yessei it was argued that powerful Yakuts were 'crowding' out Tunguses:

At the present time at Lake Yessei, Yakut traders arrive and shamelessly conduct a trade of buying furs and exploiting the poorest people who are [for the most part] Tungus. If Lake Yessei becomes part of the Yakut Republic fighting this important problem will be extremely difficult. [Furthermore] the unhealthy effects of this trade also extend to the neighbouring regions inhabited by the Ilimpei Tungus of Turukhansk District. The wealthiest strata of the native people of Lake Yessei— rich Yakut reindeer herders—quite possibly wish to leave for the Yakut Republic counting on the fact that their distance from the administrative centres of Yakutiia will allow them to preserve their independence. For Tunguses and the poorer strata of the Yessei Yakuts such a change in the boundaries will be economically disastrous (GAKK R1845–1–5: 46).

In this passage there is a clear recognition of the disciplinary aspect to boundaries which would allow authorities to police territory for irregular trade and accumulation practices. Most interesting in light of the previous chapter is the consciousness that both distance and extensive movement add to the independence of herders from the state. In addition to the imputed need to protect a poorer and weaker people, other reports wrote of the need for a rational *raionirovaniia* which would not break up the clan affiliations important to the raising of native consciousness (GAKK R1845–1–5: 5, 7). Perhaps most worrying to the Moscow officials was evidence of threats and political pressure from expansionist Yakut 'bands'. In 1925 the Zatundra-Dolgan clan council was told in no uncertain terms that by 1926 all of the territory as far as Dudinka would be in the control of Yakutsk (and that those who did not join them would regret it) (GAKK R1845–1–5: 10). With a style reminiscent of a political thriller, the report of the commission charged with drawing a boundary around the disputed territory wrote of how their meetings were disrupted by 'counter-revolutionary bands' inciting the people against 'agents of the Russian dictators' (GAKK R2275–1–144: 223). These incidents of civil unrest suggest that the state may indeed have been worried about Yakut imperialism when they deliberated excluding the ethnonym of demographically more populous *sakhalar* from the title of the new Taimyr (Dolgano-Nenets) Autonomous District. Subsequent events in Taimyr from a variety of sources seem to confirm the fear of a civil rebellion in the Yenisei-Lena watershed. In 1929 State Political Police [OGPU] agents chased a 'band' of nationalists across the Anabar tundra in a series of battles which killed twenty people and wounded twenty-one. The escaping bandits were said to have run off to join the 'wandering' Tunguses at the headwaters of the Kotoi river [the region of the Kamen' trading post] (GAKK R2275–1–144: 245). In 1932 the state dispersed the Volochanka rebellion, which, according to elders on the Khantaika, was organized by a Yakut agent provocateur. While the creation of nationally homogeneous districts would eventually lend greater currency to nationalist rhetoric, in terms of the organization of travel, trade, and human relationships, centripetal boundaries were seen as a founding condition for Soviet power.

The creation of state economic enterprises strengthened the melding 'reaction' creating a sense of belonging to a territory. Two examples drawn from the history of the collective farm 'Red Army of the Workers and Peasants' [*kolkhoz im. RKKa*] will demonstrate how authorized state economic institutions locked producers into fixed spaces.

The *kolkhoz RKKa* (established 1930) was one of the only local institutions to become a proper collective farm amongst the loose collection of clan councils and work-units in the lower Yenisei valley. It was designed to be a transport and provisioning enterprise for the growing metal works at Noril'sk, while at the same time being a model farm which would encourage the collectivization of the whole valley. The consolidation of the farm did not occur until 1938 due to many difficulties encouraging producers to ally themselves with only one production point. The manner in which this consolidation was conducted helps lend a more active mood to the phenomenon of 'gravitation'. Rather than exploiting natural sinks in the economic geography of the land, the leaders of the *kolkhoz RKKa* actively pulled producers into its orbit.[4]

From the date of its formation, officials at the collective farm claimed that the lack of enforceable boundaries compromised the farm's productivity. The Territorial Formation Officer Kopylov complained that the resources of the farm were being drained by independent Evenkis and Dolgans associated with the Khantaiskii–Evenkiiskii clan council (to the south) and the Piasinskii–Dolganskii clan council (to the north). Specifically, territories set aside for the pasturing of state reindeer and the building of government deadfall traps would be used casually by natives 'foreign' to the collective farm. The furs they harvested would then be exchanged privately in the yet unnationalized trading system (TsGARF A310–18–37: 333–8). To solve the dilemma, the gravitational pull of this key collective farm was directed northwards and then southwards by moving the points of provisioning more unambiguously within the boundaries of the *kolkhoz RKKa*. At the 1931 congress of native deputies, officials from the Territorial Formation Office encouraged the officials of the Piasinskii clan council (who were presumably Russian) to affiliate with a trading post relocated deep within the territory of the Noril'sk-based farm. A written protest from *sakha* herders in the threatened council records the impact of this move:

We were born on this land. We want to be with land longer. We ask that the Piasinskii clan council not chase us from this land. We do not want to merge with the Piasinskii division of the [trading organization] because it is too far to travel with our reindeer and there are no places to keep them. If the [post] was put on the Ikon [river] then we would travel [to trade] with the Piasinskii [division] (TsGARF A310–18–37: 372).

Notwithstanding the dissatisfaction over this adjusted gravitation, the Territorial Formation Officer assigned to the case, B. O. Dolgikh, justified the unification on the grounds of the common language and culture of the groups concerned.

It is telling that the concern with boundaries did not end with this early 1931 meeting. Throughout the 1930s 'indistinct or absent boundaries' continued to plague the enterprise. In 1938 another meeting was held in Dudinka to 'create exact boundaries' for the 'proper assignments of territory for rational use'. The territories of concern seven years later were the southern pastures in between the work-unit 'Red Trapper' on Lake Khantaika and the *kolkhoz RKKa*. This interstitial territory was being exploited by the Wild Work-Unit [*dikii artel'*] which, although duly registered by this date, managed to subsist without any authorized territory. At this second encounter

---

[4] These offices of the farm were located at Chasovnia—the site of an early Orthodox chapel—at the confluence of the Rybnaia and Noril'sk rivers. The farm's territories extended as far south as the southern banks of Lake Keta overlapping with the territories of the work-unit 'Red-Trapper' based at the Khantaika. The site of Chasovnia is now within the city boundaries of Noril'sk.

with a familiar foe, the leader of the *dikii artel'* Konstantin Naumovich Suslov made a similar complaint:

Our *artel'* was organized [i.e. officially authorized] in 1937. All members of the *artel'* grew up in this region and on this territory that is now going off to the *kolkhoz RKKa*. We have hunted for a century on this territory and these trap-lines. The question arises: where will the members of our *artel'* hunt? For fishing spots we have only Lake Kheta. Yes and even only a part of it. Our deadfalls are placed on that territory that is now going to the *RKKa*. And that collective farm is requesting that we remove our deadfalls and stop fishing. Our *artel'* has nowhere to go (AMAE K2–1–128: 77).

The fate of the members of the Wild Work-Unit was set by the establishment of increasingly complicated institutions of monitoring production and exchange. Following the 1938 meeting, the Evenkis, Dolgans, and Enetses of the *dikii artel'* became incorporated with the *kolkhoz RKKa*. Within two years, the entire territory of the *RKKa* in turn was swallowed by the Noril'sk Factory (then under the administration of the People's Commissariat of Internal Affairs—*NKVD*). The composite membership of the enlarged *kolkhoz RKKa* was then relocated east to Levinskii Peski, south to Lake Khantaika, and north to Kur'e to a site which, ironically, was very close to the point from which the Piasina members were removed in the first place (GATAO 2–1–11: 40 ff.).

The rationalizing intent of the early architects of Soviet land reform in these examples stands in bold contrast to the more flexible mode of knowing the land as a *tundrovik*. The purpose behind territorial formation was not so much to represent the multi-stranded relationship between people and land but to introduce a pattern of directed land use on encapsulated spaces. The argument that territorial allegiance originated with the Soviet state displaces models of Russian state ethnography which suggest that primal territoriality is incipient in all societies. I have shown that regularities in land use which follow from the imperative of taking animals in a sentient ecology were methodically displaced by the intelligence agents of an administrative economy intent instead on elaborating the social links between hunters and the state. By placing Soviet rural reforms within a deeper historical context it is possible to understand the later stages of collectivization as campaigns which, among other things, gave meaning to the boundaries inscribed on the extensive lands of eastern Siberia. From the start of collectivization in 1938 to its completion with the establishment of state farms in 1968, the native people of the lower Yenisei valley would be forced to assimilate new kind of extensive knowledge of their landscape. The members of contemporary state farms now have a memory of experiences within a large number of discrete territories and farms from which they were forcibly resettled during a number of successive rationalizing campaigns. The fact that the gravitation of farms is understood to be a necessary and yet fickle force lends a subtle tone of anxiety to thoughts about territory as the state managers turn towards a project of privatization. Older producers within the state farm Khantaiskii remember the alternating consolidation and break-up of the *dikii artel'* or the *kolkhoz RKKa* as much as a younger generation remembers the sudden liquidation of the Kamen' settlement. The effect of injecting an idea of *territoriia* did not so much negate Evenki knowledge of extensive travel as make a productive life on the *tundra* conditional upon a secure base within an exclusive territory controlled by trustworthy kin, partners, and *zemliaki* [country-men].

The puzzle of privatization

In the autumn of 1992 the Ministry of Agriculture of the Taimyr Autonomous District, in accordance with republican and territorial legislation, officially relinquished its control over the state farms of Taimyr. Despite this sudden policy shift, the territories and structures of all state farms in the district remained frozen in place as if no change had occurred. According to republican laws, all state farms were to be parcelled into various forms of private tenure by January 1993. During the summer of 1993, almost all of the state farms of the neighbouring Evenki Autonomous District were broken into 'clan communities' [*rodovye obshchiny*] (Popkov 1994). In Taimyr, by the end of 1993, all centrally supported purchase prices and subsidies had been stopped (to be replaced with high-interest loans) yet only the smallest fractures were evident within the seamless expanse of state farm territories.[5] The sense of inevitability implicit in the rhetoric on privatization indicates that on one much-anticipated morning the collectivized institutions of Taimyr should suddenly shatter with the tumultuous thunder of a northern spring. However, correspondence from the Khantaika from 1993 to April 1998 indicates that the state farm Khantaiskii still persists intact as a single territorial unit albeit with little control over the economic forces which determine its welfare. Among the many factors which have contributed to the late spring of privatization in Taimyr, the nationalist attachment to bounded territories seems to be the strongest.

The common-sense interpretation of the 'failure' of decollectivization among Russian newcomers at the Khantaika is that Taimyr bureaucrats are inherently conservative. A young Russian hunter-fisherman from Tomsk declared that 'Taimyr is a [nature] reserve [*zapovedenik*] for Communists'

---

[5] In Aug. 1993 there were approximately twenty *fermerskye* and 'clan' enterprises registered with the Territorial Formation Office of the Dudinka Department of Agriculture. Most of the new farmers were Russians in the immediate vicinity of Dudinka. There were two significant Dolgan operations: one on Lake Sobachye and one at the site of the former settlement Kamen'. Surprisingly, there were three registered 'clan communities' (2 Russian and 1 Dolgan) within the territory of the Khantaiskii state farm—although there was absolutely no sign that these lands were being used.

as he explained to me how he had failed in an early bid (February 1992) to win private ownership over his trap line within the territory of the state farm. There is some evidence for these claims. History has shown that all centrally launched initiatives from territorial formation to collectivization have taken many years— if not decades—to inscribe on this Arctic district. Although state managers, such as the director of the state farm Khantaiskii, do have real economic interests in remaining in their positions as co-ordinators of an expansive capital resource, I argue that this fisherman is dismissing another important factor: a deeply felt conviction among native producers that a consolidated territory is now necessary for their future as a nation. If there is any truth to the charge of conservatism on the part of government officials it would be in a fear of disrupting a brittle social order. Aside from the fact that most Territorial Formation Officers and indeed senior administrators were Dolgan or Nenets cadres, my interviews revealed that many shared the old convictions of Siberian administrators that their jobs were to 'protect' their native cousins from a land-grab by Russian speculators. Perhaps the more haunting worry was that should Russian newcomers be granted exclusive access to particular parcels of land the tundras would erupt again in gunfire as in 1932. While this seeming support for the boundaries and institutions 'gravitated' together in the Soviet period may seem to be conservative, it will be shown to represent a radical rejection of the exclusive type of individual tenure exercised by newcomer hunter and fisher-men within the state farms of the Soviet era. However, if the native peoples of Taimyr are being protected by the patron kinsfolk, why has there not been a rush to institute clan communities such as in the Evenki Autonomous District? The answer seems to lie in the attractiveness of a different type of exclusive tenure. Several generations of experience with the Soviet state has proved that the overlap of a bounded nation to a bounded territory carried distinct political advantages. In 1993 this was the ideal that many Evenkis wished to achieve in their nationally divided settlement.

Before discussing Evenki views on the future of the *sovkhoz* territories, it is first necessary to describe the constellation of land tenure engagements existing at the outset of privatization. Under the laws of the Soviet state, all land belonged to the state and, in the area of the Khantaika, the state farm was the sole state institution which had the right to control the exploitation of the animals and fish within its territory.[6] Nevertheless some people

---

[6] Other state agencies had rights which overlapped with the jurisdiction of the state farm. The Territorial Department of Forestry [*goslesfond*] charged the state farm with a yearly tax for the harvesting of firewood for local needs. Military helicopter pilots regularly flew past, landed, and evidently hunted at some spots at the end of Lake Khantaika. Employees of the Snezhnogorsk hydroelectric facility and its associated weather and hydrological stations gained hunting and fishing rights on the territory of the state farm as a fringe benefit to their contracts. Various mining interests, which in 1992 were taken over by the Noril'sk Factory, had rights to establish camps on the territory of the farm in order to search for subsurface minerals. In 1992 and 1993 there were two expeditions provisioned out of Igarka working on the territory of the farm.

authorized to work under one of the forty-three professional categories of the
farm exploited specific parcels of land for long periods of time in ways which
emulated forms of exclusive access to land. It is this experience with exclusive access which serves as a model both for newcomers who would like to
become farmers [*fermery*] and for Evenki producers who envisage a regener-
ated national community built on Evenki lands.

The clearest example of exclusive access within the state farm was the
institution of the *tochka* [production point]. This was quite literally a point
on a map with a self-built cabin and a numbered two-way radio station from
which lone or paired employees would be authorized to exclusively harvest
fish and fur on the lands radiating out from that point to formally affixed
boundaries (see Map 5). The phenomenon of exclusive access to hunting
territories, which was common throughout Siberia, was calculated as a
regulatory tool to facilitate the gathering of intelligence about the numbers
of animals harvested from the land and to prevent any individual from
harvesting animals without entering into a contract with the state. As one
might anticipate in a two-million-hectare farm which is buffeted by gale-
force winds for most of the winter, there were large oversights in enforcement which allowed individuals to harvest furs and to trade them informally
for goods or for cash without much difficulty. Thus when seen from the point
of view of the producer, the *tochka* with its scrap-lumber walls and log steam
bath was a secret 'black hole' within which one could enjoy both autonomy
and profit from the lack of capacity of the state to police its territories
(Shmelev & Popov 1990).

The vast majority of the sixteen *tochki* of the Khantaiskii state farm had
been occupied solely by Russian or Ukrainian newcomers until the collapse
of the collective farm system. Since 1992 the out-migration of newcomers to
the Russian heartland has given a small number of Evenkis and Dolgans an
opportunity to taste the entrepreneurial benefits of this exclusive territory for
the first time.[7] There are several cultural factors which have determined
this national division of labour. The least salient are 'love of the reindeer',
the general non-productiveness [*nekhoziaistvennost'*], or the drunkenness
attributed to the 'ethnics' by Russians. The most powerful forces determining the allocation of these places are personal contacts between the hunters or
fishermen and the newcomer director, or the fact that newcomers generally
hunt and fish with such a passion that they can both fill their quotas and
accumulate enough fur on the side to make their frenzied activity worth
while.

The engagement of a newcomer to an authorized 'point' is arguably one of
the most exclusive forms of territoriality devised by the Soviet state. The

---

[7] In 1993 there were four Dolgan and Mountain Evenki *tochka* holders. By 1998, with increasing
out-migration, three Khantaika Evenkis had joined their ranks.

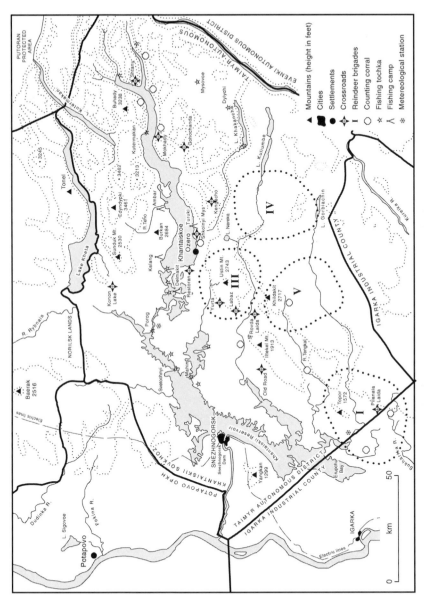

Map 5. The exclusive territories of the state farm 'Khantaiskii', 1993

Plate 17. The Russian fishing *tochka* Mahin featuring a log house and steam bath

immigrant producer is both ignorant of sentient ecology of the area and, according to Soviet norms, is not strongly charged to respect the letter of the environmental laws in the absence of real enforcement. The ideology of a *tochka* fisherman is illustrated by the ringing phrases of the 1992 Manifesto of the Union of Hunters of the Khantaika (see Table 13), where the highest callings are the glorification of private property and a conspiratorial silence as to the unauthorized activities of other members of the Union.

The exclusivity inherent in the territorial engagement of other authorized producers is not as clear as with the *tochka* fishermen. More traditionally collectivist forms of labour organization mediate the relationship of hunter-fishermen, contract hunters [*liubiteli*], and reindeer herders to their territories. In the summers, the hunter-fishermen and contract hunters come together to fish at the same fishing camps where in the 1960s and 1970s fishing brigades were organized (see Map 5 and Plate 18). These *kollektivy* have developed a strong sense of symbolic attachment between themselves and their camps on the land. These sentiments of belonging ripple out across the lake to include the villagers for whom the summer fish camp is one of the few points of contact with the extensive territories around them. Generally at any fish camp, like Ambar, one will find one or two elderly couples who regularly set nets for 'red' fish like salmon or grayling. They entertain visiting boatloads of nieces, nephews, and grand-children who come to run about the conical tents and to taste smoked dry-

TABLE 13. Manifesto of the Union of Hunters of the Khantaika

Those individuals who want to preserve their humanity [*chelovecheskie dostoinstvo*] and to be masters on their trapline [*uchastok*] have entered into the Union of Hunters with full responsibility for their actions before their good sense [*zdorovaia smysl'*] and these laws:

1. Live and work in such a manner as if you will be here forever. The economic success of our work is directly related to an ecologically exploited trapline.
2. Having been asked for help . . . help out! Each of us could wind up in a tight spot.
3. Ownership is inviolable [*neprikasnovenna*]. The first task is to remain within the trapline and the natural resources spread out within its boundaries.
4. Be able to keep a secret. You may speak with whomever you choose, but do not compromise the interests of the members of the Union of Hunters.
5. The programme of privatization of traplines is the necessary foundation for the preservation of the interests of the members of the Union of Hunters. Private property in land is the path to freedom!

---

fish [*yukolo*] or sample rendered fish fat. When it comes to discussing tenure, the hunter–fishermen and contract hunters usually choose possessive idioms drawn from the language of the *tundroviki*. Old-time Evenkis are gracious hosts who articulate a distinctively noble attitude that they would 'not begrudge [*ne zhalko*]' sharing their places with Dolgans or newcomers. Despite these welcoming words, the absence of both Russian and Dolgan fishermen at each site is conspicuous. Perhaps it is best to judge this national division within the frame of the personalized entitlement advocated by *tundroviki*. The productive potential of each fishing camp is paltry when compared to the lucrative *tochki* on the reservoir or the Khantaika rapids [*porog*]. A state fisherman or would-be farmer would have little interest in occupying these sites since he or she could accrue only a modest personal profit, and in the process would rapidly deplete the local stocks of salmon and arctic char. Thus, while the Evenki fisherman may not use exclusive language, these sites are treated by farm managers and other *tochka* fishermen as if they were exclusive production points for 'ethnics' in the sense that they are spots reserved for low-intensity production. It would not be hard to imagine that a more aggressive form of belonging would develop should a misinformed newcomer attempt to practise high-intensity fishing methods on sites that have been set aside for a very different relationship between people and the land.

Exclusive territories can be identified with some ambiguity within the tenure of the four reindeer brigades of the state farm 'Khantaiskii'. In comparison to the territorial horizons of a *tochka* hunter, the pastures of a reindeer brigade seem amorphous and massive. As one hunter confessed during a contract hunt of wolves for Number One Reindeer Brigade, 'I don't listen to a *pastukh* when he gives directions. For him "a little way" [*nedaleko*] means a five-hour trip on a snowmobile.' Without much exaggeration one could say that if the *tochka* hunter knows a one-hundred-square-kilometre territory around his cabin and a few routes back to the settlement, an older

Plate 18. The Chempogir family at their fishing camp Peski

Khantaika reindeer brigadier would know most of the two-thousand-square-kilometre territory of the state farm and perhaps a few routes to other settlements. Nevertheless, this unarguably extensive knowledge is much more confined than that of the old people who 'travelled everywhere'. Unlike the *tundroviki* of the 1950s and 1960s who might have visited several regions through the course of the year, the contemporary *pastukhi* keep their enlarged herds divided between two authorized summer and winter pastures. Dotting the landscape between these pastures are a number of built storage sites [*labazy, nekul*], counting corrals, and a base [*baza*] where in the summer months *balki* are mended and the women bake bread [*omo*] for the roving young men tending the herd. The establishment of fixed structures and fixed sites has for a long time been a strategy of reindeer pastoralists in this area.[8] However, the importance of fixed sites in everyday life has increased due to the facts that production since the 1960s has been surrendered [*sdana*] through central production portholes (like counting corrals) and that trade

---

[8] The construction of exclusive territories for reindeer herders was much clearer in the late 1970s and early 1980s. During this period much money was spent on building fences [*izgorody*] for various brigades so that both brigade territories and summer and winter pastures could be accurately identified. The remains of these fences can be found around the Kuliumbe lakes and between the steep fjords of the eastern branches of Lake Khantaiskii. Whether due to poor budgets for maintenance or to the extreme weather of this region, the fences quickly fell into disrepair. The state farm from 1985 onwards reverted to the time-tested techniques of open pasturage of herds interrupted by vast expanses of land between brigades. The number of brigades was reduced from six to four.

goods have been unpredictably thrown [*brosany*] to the herders by helicopter or all-terrain vehicles. In the course of three months along the plateau above the Gorbiachin river, we had cause to visit six *labazy*, two corral sites, and two 'old' bases within 360 square kilometres in order to retrieve either flour, skins, sewing kits, radio parts, or traps that were stashed where a helicopter happened to land. The dispersion of goods was the cause of some irritation to Konstantin, who could not remember where he had left his rubber boots. Older *pastukhi* reflected with some embarrassment at this 'disorder' but indicated that there was little that they could do about it working under the 'crazy' plans of the state farm administration. While in the past old Evenkis might have known certain places where the wild deer returned home, it seems that contemporary *pastukhi* are used to moving across the surface of an extremely wide target from which they retrieve the goods aimed at them by short-sighted archer-administrators. In this broad sense the plateau of the Gorbiachin river, like that of the Kuliube lakes some years previously, is the exclusive territory of Number One Reindeer Brigade. It is the territory upon which the herders 'feed the settlement'. When the spring *argish* arrives at the base camp, Evenki young and old speak with relief at arriving 'home'.

While the intensity of the engagement with exclusive territories differed between the *tochka* hunter or fisherman, the hunter-fisherman, and the reindeer brigade, all three occupational categories were subject to the same administrative limits on their tenure. In all three cases, a producer could be dismissed [*uvolen*] or reassigned [*pereustroen*] from their authorized allotment by a decision [*ukaz*] of the state farm director. This power was used rarely, since producers and state managers negotiated an uneasy alliance between the former's desire for individual privileges and the latter's anxiety over the shortage of loyal and motivated workers. Yet the arbitrary nature of an administratively organized hunting enterprise hung heavy on the minds of Evenkis, who had been collectively excluded from reindeer herding completely in the early 1970s, and amongst newcomer hunters who chafe against the restrictions on their private accumulation. This statement by a Russian *tochka* hunter, made two years before he abandoned his cabin for his home in central Russia, expresses the strong resentment against the surveillance economy.

T.K. I am a man without rights. I live in complete dependence on the state. You see I built this whole house with my own hands but I can be evicted upon a whim of the director. They don't pay me. But if I so much as sell one fur on the side [*na levo*] I will be gone and a *natsional'* will be sitting here.

D.A. Maybe it's because of Rovda. He sold [illegally] all the time.

S.L. Well Rovda is a special case. He didn't give a single fur to the state. He sold too much. Tumentsev too. [Both had left the farm voluntarily by the end of 1993.]

T.K. They wouldn't have done that if we had rights to the land [*sobstvennost'*]. Now
   it just gives us a bad name.

Although Evenkis, Russians (and to a lesser extent, Dolgans) alike were
dissatisfied with administrative controls on production and land tenure,
when this system legally dissipated in 1992 each community took radically
different stands on how the territory should be used. Khantaika Evenkis
wished to maintain the territory of 'their farm' in one unfractured whole.
Newcomers petitioned for private tenure of their *tochki*. Some Dolgans and
Mountain Evenkis experimented with the idea of group tenure of 'open-term
leases of land' [*perevod zemlii na bezsrochnoe polzovanie*]. The one proposal
that was missing from this list was one that advocated an open and
unbounded use of all tundra lands. Whether or not the best future was
envisioned through exclusive individual tenure or with nationality-bounded
territories, the metaphor of an exclusive territory so carefully cultivated since
1932 by the Soviet government remained a common point of departure for
all claimants. Having looked briefly at newcomer demands for individual
tenure at the start of this section, I will focus now upon demands for
exclusive territories from the native community.

Between 1992 and 1998 there still have not been many claims to exclusive
individual territories amongst Evenkis and Dolgans within the Khantaiskii
state farm. A few months after the new regulations on privatization, two
Dolgan households left the settlement and the farm altogether in order to
establish 'clan communities' within the Noril'sk Industrial District and within
the territories of the Volochanka state farm. Another Dolgan household and
one Mountain Evenki had laid claim to fishing lakes (Lake Gorbiachin and
Lake Sigovoe) within authorized reindeer pastures which had been set aside
for lichen recovery. By August 1993 another three Dolgan households
boasted privately of their plans to claim clan territories but had not taken
any concrete action. In an interesting development, one Russian newcomer
and his Khantaika Evenki wife in 1996 laid claim to the *tochka* 'Svetochnyi' as
aboriginal 'trappers'. When asked why Mountain households were starting
the claim process the answers from members of each of these households
referred to the acumen [*khoziaistevnnost'*] of people from Kamen' or the
laziness of the *tongustar*. The equally polarized reaction of Khantaika households can be summarized by this outburst of our usually silent brigadier:

N.S. The talk about privatization is just greed. Already I heard on the radio that those
   Ukrainians were shooting down on [Lake] *delamakit*. Shooting on the tundra! . . .
   But it's wrong too that the *kamentsy* are asking for land. This is our land. I have
   travelled all over this land. If they try to take it from us I will fight for it.

Fortunately, extreme rhetoric such as this remained only words. However,
words of this type no doubt had their effect by dissuading at least two
Mountain households and several newcomers from claiming their allotments.

The hearsay censure on private claims was sharpened by the actions of the director, who pledged not to give the entrepreneurs any ammunition, kerosene for light, overland transport, or helicopter support. The director performed a dual political role: he was both enforcing a popular policy and solidifying his position as the sole gatekeeper to the mysterious market forces turning outside the boundaries of the farm.

The rhetorical resistance to attempts by Mountain households to gain private lands can perhaps be dismissed as instances of jealousy. The outbursts referred to above bear much in common with the suspicion shown to other native groups such as the Potapovo Evenkis and the Gydan peninsula Nenetses who had never surrendered their reindeer for collective ownership or had covertly maintained private stocks of their own. The eldest generation may also have been troubled by near-forgotten memories of poverty when they depended upon rich Yakut families. However, I interpret exclusive statements of this type as a different kind of rhetoric which points to a consciousness of the benefits of belonging to a territory. First, in a community where not much is said generally, such threats tend to ring out more loudly than simple murmurs of distrust. Second, in statements such as the one by the brigadier above, there is the first appearance of a concept that might be identified as a claim of 'aboriginal right': the right to a territory deriving not from a personalized entitlement but from a life spent within a certain space. Third, in defence of 'our *sovkhoz*' there is a feeling of a civic sense of belonging that is felt most intently on specific exclusive territories in the farm and dissipates rapidly beyond the collectivized boundaries of the institution.

To these three elements one can add practical and technical considerations which serve to make a defence of an integrated territory necessary—although none of these aspects were spelled out explicitly to me. In the case of the proposed privatization of Lake Gorbiachin, the ire of the reindeer herders was no doubt raised by the memory that they had taken their herds across that land along the route between the settlement and the Kureika drainage— and would presumably want to do so again. Access rights over allocated territories were easily negotiated within a state farm which, despite its administrative distortions, nevertheless represented a common community of interest. Such access agreements would be more difficult to arrange with freehold farmers, who would be jealous of their territories. Furthermore, all actors in the Khantaiskii *sovkhoz* were no doubt aware of the amount of land which had been rendered unusable by heavy-metal pollution from Noril'sk. This issue raised the odd prospect that in a two-million-hectare farm there may not be enough land for extensively oriented Evenki herders, Mountain settlers, not to mention intensive Russian fishermen. As a direct result of pollution, Number One Reindeer Brigade had already moved its winter pastures outside of the territory of the farm and indeed across the boundary into the Igarka Industrial District onto lands for which they would not be legally allowed to claim ownership. The prospect of a land shortage threatened to place Khantaika Evenkis in a similar position to their forebears in the *dikii artel'* who in an earlier state-sponsored reorganization of territory had been drawn away from their habitual places.

Although most producers within the state farm Khantaiskii have many reasons to be dissatisfied with the administrative controls placed on their activities and their movements, it would be fair to conclude that the prospect of dismantling the state farm along with its juridically demarcated territories is perceived as a greater threat. In an abstract sense, this sluggish support for collectivized territories can be interpreted as a form of conservatism. It would seem that the passions that exclusive territories evoke are better understood as a form of patriotism invigorated by rational concerns over the difficulty of parcelling out a diminishing amount of unpolluted territory. When viewed historically, it is possible to establish a shift in emphasis among Evenkis from a relationship to land based on a personalized entitlement to a growing consciousness of territory and the incumbent notion of rights. The latter development has taken its inspiration from several rationalizing campaigns of the Soviet and Russian states. In the next chapter it will be shown how discrete *kollektivy*, allied to specific territories, use their occupational and territorial positions to make claims on the citizenship regime established by the Soviet state. When territory is considered in this light, it can be understood to resonate as a useful political instrument with which to negotiate with unknown state managers in Dudinka and beyond in the Russian heartlands.

8
Divergent Trajectories

FOLLOWING HIS ARRIVAL back in Dudinka, the retired brigadier and new member of the Prezidium of the First All-Evenki *suglan* was questioned by a journalist from the district newspaper about the history and future of Evenkis in Taimyr (*Sovetskii Taimyr*, 25 Apr. 1993). 'So, is it true that there are old Evenki clans on the Khantaika? Will you now seek to form clan communities?' asked the reporter with pointed curiosity. True to the idiom of a *tundrovik*, Momi Fedorovich replied with sparing words, 'Of course there are clans! The Yelogirs, Ukochers, Utukogirs, Kilmagirs, Pankagirs. Clan communities? Well, there's an idea . . .' In the space of the half-page article, the reporter thrice emphasized the staid replies of his informant in an apparent attempt to leave the reader with an image of a wise and simple man. The passion in the article lay instead in the logic of the reporter's questions: if a people had clans in the pre-Soviet past then its post-Soviet future must lie with returning to those same clans. The young reporter could not know that Momi Fedorovich twenty years earlier was interviewed for the same newspaper on how he saw his newly awarded Order of Labour reflecting a lifetime of collectivized reindeer herding. At that time this distinguished communist, and son of the rich Yelogir herder who donated his herd to the collective farm 'Red Trapper', replied with the same clipped enthusiasm to similarly leading questions about a very different future. To a man who spent his life living with kin and reindeer within an extensive landscape, the narrow ideas of 'clan community' and 'state farm' set before him in different decades must have seemed equally abstract.

In the Russian ethnographic literature, as with the new political reflections on the 'clan community', the *rod* [clan] is formally described as a tightly organized, exogamous, unit of interrelated kin. This technical definition usually carries the implication that clan solidarity is a primal force which can persist for generations even under conditions in which local control of estates is denied. Although many managers and state ethnographers alike now expect the timeless patriclan to re-emerge from the rubble of state farms, the stories which are told on the Khantaika reveal a different pattern. The kinship idiom today is used to link well-positioned matrilateral as well as agnatic kin in relationships of 'travelling together', 'teaching', or 'help'. Rather than a re-emergence of several hegemonic patrilineal clans the most common kinship story is that 'all Evenkis are related'. A strict application of what Bourdieu (1976) describes as 'legalistic thinking' to the Evenki clan in this settlement only yields the conclusion that kinship has been lost or

forgotten, or the odder conclusion that in this stressful economic transition
Evenkis are reverting to matrilineal modes of social organization.

In this chapter I critically examine past and present understandings of
'clan' in the lower Yenisei valley with a view to demonstrating that it has no
privileged future. Instead I argue that 'communities of producers' united by
their common experiences and by their places in a hierarchical occupational
ladder provide a focus for mutual aid and for nationalist strategy. I do not
want to imply that Soviet power fragmented and atomized all pre-existing
solidarities (and prevented new ones from forming). Indeed kin-based
solidarity still is the preferred tool for extending and reproducing one's
knowledge of the tundra today as it was in the past. Rather, I wish to consider
the fact that while the state invested much energy in prescribing solidarity to
a *sovkhoz* and to a brotherhood of nations, Evenki producers found a
particularist notion of *kollektiv* to be more useful. Both the kinship idiom,
and the idiom of *kollektiv*, are not mutually exclusive. The best strategists in
the village have tried to employ a policy of 'national endogamy' in order to
strengthen the position of both families and collectives through marriage.
This strategy had a bitter-sweet success. While the elaboration of bilateral kin
linkages across different occupational rungs but within the bounds of nationality gave Evenkis a measure of security in an unpredictable administrative
economy, the rights and obligations assigned to discrete positions also set the
life course of young people on divergent trajectories such that many speak of
a 'kinship crisis' which is seen as fundamentally eroding the Evenki 'nation'.

Clans, surnames, and the eclipse of extensive kinship

Although most state ethnographers have started from the assumption that
Evenki land tenure was unstructured, they have typically associated Evenki
society with a rigid clan structure. Seventeenth-century Cossack tribute
takers craftily studied the social relationships between native peoples so
that upon the taking of hostages they could be guaranteed a lucrative ransom
in furs [*dobryi amanat*] (Karlov 1982: ch. 2). The rational reorganization of
Imperial Russian administration by Count Speranskii in the eighteenth
century was founded upon the presumed existence of both clans and clan
princes [*kniazi*] ,who were duly registered in periodic censuses. At the end of
the nineteenth century, the Russian ethnographer Lev Shternberg (1933)
influenced European debates on social evolution through his correspondence
with Frederick Engels on 'group marriage' among Nivkhs and Oroks (Grant
1995). At the start of the Soviet period, Anisimov's (1936) founding work of
Soviet Evenki ethnology, *The Clan Society of the Evenkis*, corroborated
Engels' argument on the transition from group marriage to the patriarchal
family and eventually to the socialist family. The correct interpretation of
clan allegiance underwrote the ambitious ethnogenetic project of B. O.

Dolgikh (1963) to authorize the origin of the Dolgan and to affix the boundaries of neighbouring peoples. At the end of this century, political reforms in Siberia focus on the formation of independent 'clan communities' (Vitebsky 1992; Popkov 1994); a development which is spawning a renewed interest in old ethnographies in order to untangle what is assumed to be the pristine and primordial tie of clans to particular territories.

Despite three centuries invested in the study of Evenki clans, there has been very little written on kinship as strategy and indeed on specifying how kinship is used by Evenkis to build relationships. Part of this oversight is due to a terminological ambiguity in the language of administrative records which has led contemporary ethnographers to assume that Tsarist 'administrative clans' exactly mirrored actual relationships.[1] Part is due to a theoretical conviction amongst many generations of ethnographers that all clan phenomena were by definition archaic survivals just on the verge of being irretrievably lost. Both aspects are intrinsically linked to the state ethnographic project of identifying bounded and discrete social units and ranking them on an evolutionary scale.

The conviction among Russian ethnographers that clan practices are disappearing follows from a vision of social evolution originating with Morgan (1878). Many generations of Russian ethnographers identify this founder as their authority on matters of kinship (Shternberg 1933; Shirokogoroff 1933; Dolgikh 1960; Simchenko 1976; Afanas'eva 1990). Amongst Evenkis, the disappearance of clan was reported first by Rychkov (1923: 134), who noted that in 1906 Evenkis 'knew no kind of kinship and had total freedom in sexual relationships . . . they behave like reindeer'. Anisimov (1936: 22) writes in the past tense about clan organization, noting that 'at the present time [1929] the institution of reciprocal matrimonial exchange has been seriously broken; now Evenki men are allowed to take wives from any clan'. Even the most sensitive and evocative work on kinship and marriage strategy by Shirokogoroff records the waning and imminent disappearance of the clan principle (1933: 124–5, 188, 357). The same claims are made by recent Soviet ethnographers working in the lower Yenisei valley (Afanas'eva 1990: 359; Karlov 1982: 145–7; Tugolukov 1963: 27–8).[2] The

---

[1] It is doubtful if the administrative clans used for tax collection had any direct relationship to the vernacular kinship units among any Siberian people—although many Russian ethnographers disagree. There are three main arguments for the identity of 'blood' kinship [*krovnoe rodstvo*] and administrative clans. Patkanov (1906) argues for a simple congruency of the census units of the 1897 census and vernacular clans. Dolgikh (1960) recognizes book-keeping errors but at a higher level of analysis argued the congruence of administrative clans to the territorial group or 'tribe'. He also makes the case that in the distant past administrative units matched local clans exactly. Afanas'eva (1990), in what is arguably the most detailed examination of archival records for the lower Yenisei valley from 1628 to 1978, argued that the early records accurately identified 'extended families' and that the later records identified patriclans.

[2] Vasilevich (1969: 151; 1970) is a vociferous exception to those who bury clan organization. Bending the argument in the other direction, she asserts a coherence in clan organization among Evenkis persisting for several centuries.

unanimity on the decline of clan organization would be tragic if it were not such a melodramatically prolonged 'death'. What is most striking in these proclamations is the assumption that the move away from a perhaps overly formal model of marriage strategy is coupled to the implication that Evenkis have absolutely no patterned way of regulating relationships. Although from various vantage points over the last century a single, monolithic marriage system seems to be disappearing, the fact remains that Evenkis have persisted by reproducing themselves using one of several consistent marriage strategies. Contemporary Evenkis may complain of different problems in making good matches, but they all concur that they 'never marry their own relatives'. Rather than presuming the extinction of structured kinship relationships, I argue that vernacular kinship ideologies in the lower Yenisei valley have been adapted to manage the unpredictable fortunes of an administrative economy (Humphrey 1983). One distinctive shift in strategy is a change from a practice of making marriage alliances across a wide area to an experiment with 'nationally pure' marriages within a narrow territory. A second import-ant element is the use of a bilateral marriage strategy which maximizes the returns from a redistributive network which favours households structured around a single 'household head' and a single surname. Thus, a century-and-a-half tradition of recorded changes to the Evenki clan system are better understood not as the erosion of a once pure system but as the artefact of a people keen to experiment with various kinship strategies. This creative aspect is nicely captured in Shirokogoroff (1933: 124):

When a Tungus is asked in Russian as to his clan [*rod*] he replies without any hesitation something like this: 'Before the Russians came we lived like wild people, and did not know anything about the clan [*rod*] organisation.' But if one asks him in Tungus (*omok* or *kala* [these are Yakut and Manchu words!—D.A.]), the reply is entirely different, something like this, 'We always had our clans and we lived by clans, but nowadays clan organisation is declining.'

In this passage, Shirokogoroff emphasizes the artificiality of Russian clan constructions and expresses a scholarly nostalgia for the disappearance of the old ways. However, the same passage can also be read as a literal account of the rise and fall of clan ideologies as if Yakut [*omok*] clan organization was once fashionable but that then administrative *rod* became the rage. The history of kinship in the lower Yenisei valley can be understood as a series of strategies designed to work within progressively more refined state categories ranging from 'tribe', to 'administrative clan' to 'surname'.[3]

---

[3] A similar argument has been applied to Mongolia. Bulag (1993) records the attempt of Soviet planners to replace Mongolian clan identities of *obog* with a Russian notion of surnames [*familiia*] (pp. 61 ff.). There was also an attempt to translate Russian notions of clan [*rod*], tribe [*plemia*], and diminutive people [*narodnost'*] into Mongolian terms (p. 31). Bulag argues that in conjuncture with a centralized administrative system these ways of classifying people resulted in an endogamous 'localism' which is similar to nationalism (pp. 75 ff.).

Discussing kinship on the Khantaika is a difficult experience. Any particular individual can have a variety of reasons to want to avoid discussing his or her ancestry. If one sets aside the problem of building trust as a Russian-looking outsider, there is the challenge of encouraging people to talk about a subject that is known implicitly and is considered unsuitable for words. Recently deceased ancestors are often referred to but very rarely *named*. This seems to be a common problem for ethnographers in the lower Yenisei valley, as Afanas'eva (1990: 259) recounts:

It is necessary to note several distinctions in the conceptions that Nganasans have of their forebears and their kin links to them. As a rule, informants named very distant forebears, although they often confused [*putali*] the degree of distance, the level of kinship of different forebears, and were not able to give a date of birth. There were cases of recalling anonymous kin; that is, they were not able to give their names but were accurately able to recall the situation: the degree of distance between different lineages, the number of descendants of one or the other forebear, and were able to imagine clearly the relationship with the forebear and the informant himself.

Rather than imputing a weak memory to informants, it seems that the circumspect silence concerning the dead is a sign of respect. The informant who protests, 'Why do you keep asking for names? He is dead!', may also be referring to the belief that naming the dead can have the unwanted effect of hailing them (Shirokogoroff 1935: 139–42, 203, 209; Humphrey 1993). In regions with a violent history such as the lower Yenisei valley it may also be considered advisable to forget certain relations altogether. However, in sympathy with Afanas'eva, it is very frustrating to try to interpret statements which are couched in an implicit relational language, as these statements from my field notes illustrate:

Neru's oldest aunt—[is this Agrafena?]—told him that the Utukogirs are related to her father in Chirinda [Is the common ancestor her father's brother or her father's uncle?].

Devgonche's Russian name is Pavel Pankagar— *baekon aminin* [Baekon's father]. Is *aminin* being used figuratively or literally?

The Kuropatovs are the same as the Sapozhnikovs. [But Vasiliev writes that Kurupatovs are Pankagirs!] Proskopii is the eldest [Is he a Sapozhnikov or Kurupatov —or both?]

Apart from a reticence about naming people, the relational portrait of kinship is complicated by a multiple number of 'Evenki names' [*evendyl gerbil*] for people from the turn of the century and before. This already complicated web becomes more intricate when one considers that the high mortality rate of males resulted in a large number of adoptions and remarriages. Consistent with Shirokogoroff (1933: 248), adopted children on the Khantaika gain ties to both their native clan and their adopted clan. Similarly, women retain their membership, obligations, and prohibitions of the clan of their birth (1933: 203–4, 214, 223). Finally, to make matters more difficult, there are certain ambiguities implicit in terms for relationships which complicate the task of the ethnographer or census official who wishes to slot people into a rigid framework. For example, the Evenki word for 'father' *amin* often meant any older male in direct ascendance: father, older paternal uncle, older paternal cousin.[4] The Russian word *brat* [brother] could often be used ambiguously for first or second cousin on either the maternal or paternal side (cf. Vasilevich 1969: 145).

Just as with the Evenki pedagogy on knowing the land, the sign of my success in understanding kinship was either silence or a mundane lack of interest when I made an acceptable statement about a relationship. The slightest contradiction in my statements would provoke hearty laughter but rarely any helpful elucidation. Through successfully minimizing the entertainment of several young families and four old women (and with the help of archived household registries), I derived sixteen composite genealogical accounts which consistently record clusters of the ascendant generation as well as consistently omit certain relationships between these clusters for Evenkis, Dolgans, and Yakuts. For this discussion, I have selected four Evenki charts representing both Khantaika and Mountain groups to represent the shift from extensive kinship to the use of registered surnames nested within producing communities defined by nationality (see Charts 1 to 4). I will be closely analysing two 'different' sets of lineages: the Khantaika Utukogirs and Khantaika Yelogirs; and the Mountain Khutukagir's and Mountain Yelogir's (Chart 3). These surname groups are today distinguished by nationality and by small differences in orthography.[5] The formal charts rather poorly represent the intuitive way that people feel their relatedness to their neighbours, but they are helpful in illustrating changes in extensive linkages, land use, and kinship ideology through the growing division between these lineages over the last seventy years.

Khantaika Evenki genealogies displayed a patrilineal ideology. The most complete accounts traced descent to a single male ancestor three generations back. Many accounts were even shallower.[6] Women in the third or fourth

---

[4] These ambiguities are exactly the same as those noted by Shirokogoroff at the turn of the century in the Lake Baikal region (1933: 174). Shirokogoroff interprets this ambiguity as signifying the lack of any need to distinguish members within the clan beyond the immediate family (which is interpreted by Shirokogoroff as a remnant of a primeval matriarchy (pp. 181, 242–5)).

[5] The different spellings of Khutukagir'/Utukogir and Yelogir'/Yelogir is the legacy of a nameless clerk who in the late 1950s registered these Mountain surnames with a different (and archaic) orthography from that used in the Khantaiskii-Evenkiiskii Nomadic Soviet. This authorized difference has now been accepted as a real difference.

[6] Shirokogoroff (1933) records Evenki kinship terminology for only two ascending generations (pp. 171–3, 183–4) and notes that words for generations beyond that are either borrowed from other languages or compounded (pp. 176, 182, 185). Popov (1934a: 131) records exogamy to the fourth

ascendant generation might be named but would rarely have their Christian names or even their clan affiliation remembered. None of the informants spoke of clan exogamy or even of clans. The Russian term *rod* [clan] was understandable to the generation 40 years of age and under who tended to use the word as if it were interchangeable with 'surname'. Older people would respond with a genealogical account upon the question of 'who are your people?' or 'who were your parents (and parents' parents)?' Young and old Evenkis alike insisted that they 'knew their relatives'. By contrast, some Evenkis insinuated that Dolgans (including Mountain Evenkis) 'did not marry right'. Although the older generations were particularly clear on how they were related to their neighbours, no one was able to present an example of not 'marrying right' or of 'how one should marry'. The only mysterious clue to a problem in matching descent to an acceptable marriage strategy were the dismissive comments of the young that 'they were related to everyone' or that particular young women 'had no one to marry'.

According to the ethnographic literature, exogamous Evenki clan members carried out restricted exchanges of marriage partners between an allied pair of clans or a quartet of clans (Anisimov 1936: 22–3; Shirokogoroff 1933: 182, 188, 213, 367; Vasilevich 1969: 154, 156–7; 1970: 464–6). Some isolated Evenkis are said to have effected cross-cousin marriages within a single residential group (Shirokogoroff 1933: 367; Suslov 1928). The literature gives the impression that marriages were concluded within a compact area. Within the Khantaika genealogies there is some evidence in the older generations of repeated marriage between two clan/surname lineages. The clearest example is between the Yelogirs and the Utukogirs (Chart 1).[7] Thus, from the fourth generation and before, the kinship ideology of Khantaika Evenkis can be made to fit the classic type of patrilineal descent and cross-cousin marriage between

---

generation for the Dolgans of the nearby Noril'sk lakes (or to the third generation if there was a history of matrilateral marriage between two clans). Karlov (1982: 133), during his 1968 field research in the region of the Podkamennaia Tunguska river, records the splitting of the clan Khorbol' into three lineages after the third generation (yet these Evenki remembered their descent beyond three generations). Afanas'eva (1990) records a traditional restriction on marriage up to three generations for Taimyr Nias and Enneches. The only accounts of descent going beyond the fourth generation among neighbouring people are Reindeer Yakuts [7] (Gurvich 1977: 123), Central Yakuts [9] (Seroshevskii 1993: 419–20), Buriats [4–5] (Humphrey 1983: 340), and Mongols [9] (Bulag 1993). Vasilevich (1969: 152–3), on the basis of her extensive field research, writes of restrictions on marriage from the seventh to tenth generation for Evenki couples. In light of the evidence, this claim seems to be idealized, although it may hold for Evenki groups neighbouring the central Yakuts, or Mongols.

[7] Of 42 recorded marriages in the Utukogir and Yelogir clans (roughly between 1910 and 1990) there were five cases of intermarriage between members of these two clans. Two of these cases were marriages between Mother's Brother's Daughter and Father's Sister's Son. There was no case of a bride being the Father's Brother's Daughter. It is possible that three more cross-cousin marriages could have been confirmed if it had proved possible to build these genealogies past the fourth ascendant generation. To do so would have been to affirm a genetic link between the Mountain Evenkis and the Khantaika Evenkis which would have contradicted the policy of national endogamy.

paired sets of exogamous clans but, as I shall demonstrate below, not the presumed compactness of marriage alliances.

On the Khantaika today, patrilineal kin are marked with a registered surname [*familiia*] taken from the man to whom one's biological mother is married. The majority of the surnames of both Mountain and Khantaika Evenkis are inflected with the ending -*gir*; which may be the closest linguistic approximation of 'clan' in Evenki (Shirokogoroff 1933: 122, 355–6; Vasilevich 1969: 148, 152). In both vernacular understandings of kinship and in the Russian system, the surname marks the lineage of the husband and male parent (regardless of identity of the biological father). In both systems, the children who are brought by their mother into a new marriage commonly take the surname, but not the patronymic, of the new husband. Despite these formal similarities, there does not seem to be a complete overlap between the Russian model of registered surnames and the Evenki kinship ideology. Unlike in the Russian system, there are often significant matrilineal exceptions amongst Khantaika Evenkis. It is not unusual for a girl to keep her mother's surname (either maiden or married surname) if she marries a newcomer, or when she divorces a local man. In Liubov' Fedorovna's case, she kept her grandmother's maiden name until her last marriage (Chart 2). On the Khantaika, the formal rules of the Russian surname system are respected unless there is a desire on the part of a woman to emphasize the maternity of her children or to remember the line of a deceased spouse.

Afanas'eva (1990: ch. 4) makes a strong argument that the official registering of Nia surnames effected a change in kinship practice such that the memory of the father's lineage has become 'infinite' [*bezkonechnoi*]. While it is difficult to agree with her that this contribution of Russian culture has had the positive effect of stabilizing and reducing the 'inbreeding coefficient' of Nias by teaching them how to remember kin, it is true that it is now possible to use written records to imagine a continuity between specific surnames for Evenkis as well as Nias beyond four generations. Thus, the surname 'Yelogir', which is common today in the Khantaika, can be discovered in the lower Yenisei valley in the nineteenth century (Middendorf 1869: 692), travelling the taigas of south-central Siberia in the seventeenth century (Dolgikh 1960: 156–7), or populating a number of villages from Ust'-Avam in Taimyr to Ekonda in the Evenki Autonomous District. Afanas'eva's exhaustive analysis of 945 Nia marriages from 1628 to 1978 correlates the steady decline in marriages between bearers of the same patrilineal appellation to the novel recognition of patrilineal kin for seven generations (instead of three).[8] Again, it is difficult to agree with her that the Nia kinship system

---

[8] Afanas'eva's argument on the meaning of names is ambiguous. Nia persons in the 18th cent. possessed many names but not surnames. However, Russian Cossack scribes made an attempt to give patrilineal surnames on the basis of vernacular appellations. She assumes that in the 17th and 18th cent. these appellations accurately recorded extended families.

has changed, since her conclusions are not based on fieldwork with people but rather with household registries. Nevertheless, she raises an interesting hypothesis about the effects of 'infinite' registered surnames. As with the case of authorized nationalities in Chapter 5, there is some evidence on the Khantaika that younger generations now find themselves 'captured' by their surnames. Thus, when recounting the marriage of two persons who both carried the surname Ukocher, three informants hastened to add that these are 'different people'. People with the Yarotskii surname pointed out that 'Yarotskiis are everywhere' ['we are not all kin']. In both cases the informants pointed out that local notions of kinship are different from the surname system, yet the fact that this information was so quickly volunteered also demonstrates that the independence of the surname system from kinship system is no longer obvious. Although I did not find a situation where two young people of the same surname were contemplating marriage, when discussing the differences such as between the Mountain Yelogir's and the Khantaika Yelogirs all young informants thought that people with these surnames 'must be related somehow'. In a clearer case, I was twice cautioned to make sure I spelled 'Utukogir' correctly (one journalist had recently printed the surname as 'Khutukagir') in order to make a sharp distinction between two surnames which might otherwise appear to be one. Although one must be cautious with interpreting Afanas'eva's genetic arguments, her findings do seem to suggest a tendency for authorized terms such as registered surnames to become stable markers of identity. This may also contribute to the 'kinship crisis' indicated when young people claim that they can find no one to marry.

Although the classic ethnographic accounts of Evenkis teach us to expect localized cases of marriage and descent, the genealogical accounts on the Khantaika suggest a more prominent pattern of extensive kinship over great distances and diverse language groups. Once one delves into the histories of couples older than 50 years of age, one discovers ascent extending back to individuals from multiple 'homelands' and who would be now classified by state ethnographers as belonging to different nationalities. It is unclear whether extensively negotiated marriages are a feature peculiar to the lower Yenisei valley or a poorly documented practice of Evenkis in general. The orthodox ethnographic argument is that Evenkis kept a strict exogamy from neighbouring peoples (Shirokogoroff 1933: 367). However, both Karlov (1982: 77–9) and Vasilevich (1969: 149–54, 159) occasionally remark upon the expansive range of Evenki kinship (with the former writing of the 'washed-out' [*razmytaia*] quality of exogamic divisions). The memories of Khantaika elders confirm that Karlov's 'extended genealogical clan' extended well beyond the boundaries of the Evenki nationality as it is currently defined. Among the more cosmopolitan genealogical accounts are those of the Kashkarevs and Sapozhnikovs (Charts 2 and 4). If for the moment one

ignores the matrilateral moments in these genealogies, their most distinctive
feature is a record of intermarriage between Evenkis, Dolgans, Sakhas, Nias,
Enneches, Tundra peasants, and Russians within a territory ranging from
Potapovo on the Yenisei river to Chirinda near the Yakut border. When these
two accounts were given, what is today recognized as nationality was usually
expressed with non-authorized identities such as *khempo* [Ennecho-Evenki],
ostiak [Ennecho-Nenets], *evenko-dolgan*, or *samoed vospitan dolganom* [a
Samoed-raised-as-a-Dolgan].

Contemporary genealogical memories are also heavy inflected with the skill
of reproducing that knowledge of extensive territoriality which is a product
of collectivization. The cosmopolitan Kashkarev genealogy records the effort
of people trying to weave families together as they were repeatedly resettled,
along with other producers of the ill-fated *kolkhoz RKKa*, from Chasovnia
(Noril'sk), to Kur'e, to Levinskii Peski, to Dudinka, and finally to the
Khantaika. The 'forgotten' history of the Khantaika Utukogirs and Yelogirs
also speaks of the private tragedies associated with the nationalization of
reindeer herds. Officially no Yelogir or Utukogir on the Khantaika today can
remember why it was that 'the old ones ran away', to use the words of my
balok-mate Vladimir Yermolaevich. However, other kinsmen in the village of
Ekonda, 750 kilometres to the east make an exciting and moralistic tale of the
events that led these families to split.[9] According to Ivan Nikolaevich
Khutukogir, a former brigadier and holder of an 'Order of Labour', the
entire family originally lived at Chirinda and enjoyed a prosperous life with a
large (but typically unspecified) number of reindeer. In the 1920s, presumably while evading the first agents of the Soviet state, the family hit a 'bad
place' where there was little feed for the reindeer and little fish or wild deer
for the people. The various kinsmen of the rich 'prince' Kohon proposed
splitting the herd in the various cardinal directions in a search for food. The
'greedy' rich man refused, triggering hunger and then starvation. Three
cousins took events into their hands by dividing the herd and accompanying
their respective parts in opposite directions: Terafim and my friend's father
Yermolai went westwards towards the Khantaika, Bahilii went in the opposite
direction to Ekonda. These fragments of a large family became rich and
successful Soviet herders in two locations (which is how Ivan Nikolaevich
remembers his distant kin on the Khantaika). The greedy prince was
imprisoned by the state police and never returned.

There are too few examples here to speak authoritatively of a model of

---

[9] Within both the villages of Chirinda and Ekonda of the Evenki Autonomous District the Yalogir
and Khutukogir surnames are prominent and associated with great private wealth as well as with a
loyalty to the former state farms of the region. As with Mountain surnames, there are slight but
important changes in orthography here as well. Here Khutukogirs are spelled without the archaic
soft-sign and with an 'o' instead of an 'a'. The Yalogirs are represented with an entirely different
iotized vowel at the beginning of the surname.

extensive kinship for Evenkis in general. However, when examples of extensive intermarriage are considered in the light of the legacy of extensive travel
it would seem that extensive marriage alliances were a common practice of a
people who 'travelled everywhere'. Several interesting footnotes in
Afanas'eva's (1990: 184, 296, 322–4) epic three-volume genealogy of the
Nias demonstrate this point nicely. Among this infamously insular people,
40 per cent of their marriages were to non-Nias (including Evenkis) from the
eighteenth century to the twentieth century. The most evocative case of
territorially diverse marriage from the Khantaika comes from the Chempogir
family (Plate 19). Here, older matrons identified marriages of 26 couples
between 1820 and 1990 embracing a territory from Lake Makovskoe
(Turukhansk County) to Dudinka and Volochanka—or the entire territory
of the lower Yenisei valley. Comparative material from Inner Asia suggests
that the ideology of extensive kinship is not unusual in a region with a regime
of extensive land use. As Caroline Humphrey (1979) demonstrated amongst
the Western and Eastern Buriats, the deep memory of lineages is found only
in areas where producers and their families were confined to one narrow
valley for a long period in time. In areas where travel was unrestricted as in
eastern Buriatiia, or practically boundless as in Mongolia, the most appropriate strategy was to weave a 'network of social obligation' between
economic units, lineages, and kin (Sneath 1993). To use A. A. Popov's
analogy, the people of the lower Yenisei valley as late as the early twentieth
century presented themselves as a 'wondrous mosaic' of intermarried and
cosmopolitan voyageurs who were difficult to classify into discrete nationalities and 'infinite' registered surnames.

The conditions with an extensive type of kinship were eliminated by the
administrative reforms of the Soviet state. In the lower Yenisei valley, territorial formation and collectivization decisively anchored both producers and
suitors to specific clan councils and state farms which limited access to the
land to individuals belonging to duly registered *kollektivy*. Instead of representing deep exogamous clans comfortably in control of specific *kollektivy*, or
belligerent *kollektivy* which might be said to emulate the patrilineal *rod*, the
dominant kinship ideology on the Khantaika is not concerned with clans at
all but with what can be identified as a policy of national endogamy.

National endogamy

The most controversial legacy of extensive kinship on the Khantaika is the
genetic link between nationalities which are now understood to be the most
different. As I recorded an account of a marriage between an Enneche trade
union official and his respected Khantaika Evenki wife (see Chart 4),
(Plate 20) Tat'iana Bolina laughed at the memory of how she and her fiancé
had to approach their grandparents with embarrassment to see if they were

Plate 19. Three generations of Chempogirs in front of their house in the village

not already related through other Evenki–Enneche marriages in the ascendant generations. The humour in the story lies in the fact that today 'everybody knows' that these two families are now thought to be so distant as to
constitute discrete nationalities and not close cousins. The living legacy of
khempo intermarriage between Evenkis and Enneches, like the discovery that
some elderly Dolgans also speak Evenki, comes as an unexpected surprise to
the younger generation. Surprises of this sort are not always pleasant. On the
Khantaika the most distinct 'peoples' today are Evenkis and Dolgans despite
the fact that in every one of the sixteen genealogical accounts gathered there
were prominent partners drawn from both these now separated peoples in
the fourth and third ascending generations. 'Forgotten' links of these types
contradict a recent tendency for people to try to marry representatives of
their own nationality.

The ideology of national endogamy on the Khantaika seems to use some of
the techniques of extensive kinship ideology of the past. In genealogical
accounts, elders make long mental journeys to link together people by means
of affines or even adopted kin. Representations of descent often do not go
deeper than two or three generations. Indeed, to remember relationships
greater than this depth would necessitate a very different story. Instead
genealogical accounts spread laterally with a vigour which spills over the
edges of notebooks creating a large catalogue from which one could easily
'find a relative'. The marked feature of these mental webs is that they wove

Plate 20. Petr and Tat'iana Bolina with Irina Yarotskaia at a 'musical café' organized in the village house of culture

ties between patrilateral *and* matrilateral kin of one nationality while making extensive diplomatic detours around 'other kin', who might at one time have been closer, but now belong to different nationalities.

This phenomenon is especially conspicuous in the intertwined history of the Utukogir/Khutukagir' and Yelogir/Yelogir' surname groups. These two groups of kinsmen would in other circumstances be the best model of a classically paired Evenki clan system. I have chosen controversially to represent both on the same chart (Chart 3) even though representatives from either family would not establish (and some might deny) any common link. In Chart 3, the eldest generations show evidence of a history of paired alliance between all four Mountain and Khantaika lineages of Utukogir, Yelogir, Khutukagir', and Yelogir'. The younger generations of the Mountain sub-group are the only ones actively maintaining an old tradition of intermarriage between Yakut-speakers and Evenki-speakers as evidenced by two fraught marriages. The single Mountain Evenki who was a member of Number One Brigade—Misha Yelogir'—was linked to the Khantaika Yelogir family through either his father or grandfather. More globally, the Khutukagir' family (which is intermarried to many Dolgan families in the settlement) and the Utukogir family ('the most Evenki family') seem to be related to a common ancestor who was either one or two generations ascending from the two eldest representatives of these two lineages. What is most significant in both of these cases where I am imputing common descent is that no one was able or willing to remember the exact link. Although Evenkis in this area usually recall a minimum of three ascending generations, for many informants of these lineages the line of ascent stopped after two (or even one!) as if it had been wilfully cut. In this example, the different spellings of these registered surnames is used by some as handy authoritative proof of their separateness rather than an artefact of common descent.

It would seem plausible that the growing division between Khantaika Yelogirs and Utukogirs from Mountain Yelogir's and Khutukagir's might represent a case of clan fission. Instances of clan fission purportedly are common to Evenki clans (Shirokogoroff 1933: 212–14, 368–70; Vasilevich 1969: 153, 157). In these cases the division of clans is initiated when there is a male founder with a large number of sons and some consensus between clan elders about the need to expand the number of lineages which are allowed to intermarry. There are cases of such fissioning within both surname groups, such as the tragic story of the splitting of the family at Chirinda to avoid certain starvation. However, the fracture between the Khutukagir's/Utukogirs and the Yelogir's/Yelogirs is of a different order. In terms of process, the physical separation of these intermarrying lineages was a result of the Soviet policies of territorial formation and settlement and not of consensus. The soft-signed Khutukagir's and Yelogir's became Mountain people for it was at Kamen' in 1932 that the net was dropped which restricted them to one settlement, the spelling of one clerk, and one set of boundaries. The Utukogirs and Yelogirs became linked to the Khantaika due to the fact that their extensive travels were stopped around lakes Kheta and Khantaika. However, the fact that events transpired to make these two fractions grow apart would imply that after four generations (generation V in Chart 3) there should be instances of intermarriage all things being equal. In all four of these lineages there are no examples of contemporary intermarriages in generations III, IV, and V and indeed there is only one example of a marriage between a Khantaika and Mountain person. It is possible that parents do not think that these clans are yet sufficiently distinct to allow intermarriage—but in this case one would expect a clear memory of their common ancestors and where they fit in terms of generations. Finally, two events in the biographies of informants correlate with the resettlement of the Mountain people and the cut in accounts of common descent between the groups: the change of Liubov' Fedorovna's nationality from Dolgan to *evenka*; and the genealogical amnesia of the Utukogir and Yelogir elders who were alive in 1969 when the Mountain People arrived on the Khantaika. Instead of clan fission, I would postulate the development of a deliberate policy of endogamy within these groups which, although not flawless, prescribes marriage of Khantaika Evenkis to Khantaika Evenkis. In this case the endogamy practised is not effected using the vocabulary of clan but the vocabulary of nationality.

The policy of national endogamy in this settlement would seem to be parochial if it were not so pervasive across Siberia. In the popular press as well as in the speeches of native leaders one hears much discussion of the loss of the *genofond* of the sparse peoples of Siberia as they 'assimilate' with the other nationalities of the former Soviet Union. Heonik Kwon (1993) found much worry among Orochons about their 'mixed households' and the consequent troubled future for their nation. The same anxiety troubles Khantaika Evenkis, who see themselves as a people about to disappear. This leads seemlessly into the elaboration of a distinct set of marriage strategies consonant with the political and economic conditions of a re-distributive economy. As Caroline Humphrey (1983) observed in two Buriat collective farms, there was a vibrantly articulated 'women's own kinship' (pp. 289, 297) in which matrilateral linkages were used in order to 'choose kin ties' across the collective farm hierarchy (pp. 340–1). This bilateral strategy was vigorously elaborated despite the fact that one would expect a strong patrilineal clan ideology in a Mongol region. The design of flexible, bilateral strategies of making a wide network of alliances between people can be understood to be a common strategy across Siberia. The strategy of national endogamy, while exclusive, is nevertheless embracing in its hunger for identifying kin from permissible groups. The division of the kinship pool into controversial mates of suspect nationality and 'close' allies of permitted nationality within small Siberian enclaves understandably creates problems for younger people trying to design families. This latent biproduct of resettlement and consolidation underscores the debate on the future of national communities all over Siberia.

What is particularly tragic about the anxiety created by national endogamy is the close link between this local ideology and the system of authorized nationalities devised by state ethnographers. Soviet ethnographers not only 'discovered' national endogamy in the late 1960s but subtly marked it as a possible lever for political power. In 1969, as the outlying trading posts of Siberia were being forcibly consolidated into dense settlements, the head of the Institute of Ethnography wrote a theoretical article on '*etnos* and endogamy' wherein the 'objective and unconscious link' between an *etnos* and a 90 per cent rate of endogamy within tribal groups in his view proved that the 'tribe' and not the 'primitive clan' is the 'fundamental ethnic unit' (Bromlei 1969: 84, 91). As explored above, in an administrative system where nationalities are provisioned according to their place on a ladder of culture, there are great material advantages to inflating the status of one's group of belonging. In a political context where administrators and ethnographers are hired to identify endogamous groups and declare them to be proper *etnosy* or proto-nations, older strategies of making linkages which do not fit on the pages of the ethnographer's notebook also run the risk of pushing the group off this cultural ladder. By uniting Evenkis together through marriage, as well as across *kollektivy*, it is possible both to gather together multiple strands of mutual aid as well as to broadcast one's group as a discrete nation deserving of special executive attention in the corridors of power. The prospect of dying out as a people, on the other hand, not only offends one's pride but restricts still further the possibility of travelling the land or build-ing a future within a nationally mixed state-farm.

The policy of national endogamy within authorized nationalities is far from perfect. Two anomalies suggest that it is an improvised strategy. First, the most obvious marriage pattern for young women is with newcomers (i.e. Russians and Ukrainians), thus skirting the restrictions imposed by the policy of national endogamy. Second, while there is clearly a rift between Mountain and Khantaika Evenkis, the discrimination between Evenkis according to their 'homeland' is not the same as discriminating on the basis of the official identity inscribed in one's passport. It should be remembered that among the young generation of the Khantaika group (as among state ethnographers) there is little awareness that Yakut-speaking Evenkis from Kamen' are in fact registered as Evenkis. They are locally classified with a proud inflationary logic as if they were (already) Dolgan.

The anomalous fact that people who are registered as Evenki are now taken as Dolgan is particularly suggestive of a change in corporate organiza-tion and in marriage strategy in this settlement in the final decade of the Soviet period. Older generations seem to have accepted that marriage with partners from diverse environments was desirable. The younger generation use national differences as the rationale for avoiding certain marriages or making overtures for mutual aid based on kinship. Although the clan may at one time have been a central institution in the organization of land use and access to reindeer, it would seem that access to lucrative places now depends upon an affiliation to a different institution. The next section shows how *kollektivy* can be identified as discrete and stable corporate groups which are ranked by nationality. The fact that many Mountain Evenkis have a per-nicious 'Dolganness' has more to do with their success in using a Dolgan ladder to climb the state farm hierarchy. If this is the case, then a policy of national endogamy on the part of Khantaika Evenkis represents a form of resistance where the 'real Evenkis' are prepared to 'get by on their own'. Although kinship still plays an important role in how people work together and negotiate mutual assistance in this community, the kinship net ties together people who are primarily stratified by nationality and not by the classic paired Evenki clans of the ethnographic literature. The eclipse of clan in this case is not so much a product of social evolution as a tactical necessity in an administrative context where extensive linkage between clans is perceived as a national weakness and not as a national strength. As the administrative regime crumbles, proposals for revolutionizing the tundra with market reform focus ironically upon clans. This conflicts with the experience of producers in this state farm who see nationally stratified *kollektivy* to be the most stable units of mutual aid and for building a future.

Belonging to a kollektiv

The areas of social life where kin and national solidarity are most strongly experienced are in the 'places' [*mesta*] established by the administrative division of labour. In the redistributive economy, the place that one was 'set into' [*ustroen*] directly determined the goods that one had access to and quality of housing, leisure, and security that one enjoyed. It was a peculiarity of state socialist economies that these places were not allocated individually but to specific social groups. Thus the *kollektiv* that one belonged to was intricately bound up with the statuses and rights which were linked to one's nationality thus emulating an idea of citizenship rather than ethnicity.

The Russian word *kollektiv* translates awkwardly because of the relative poverty of English for corporate terms. *Kollektivy* tend to be more localized than 'professions' or 'trades'; and at the same time more collegial than a 'staff'. Most importantly, its similarity to the English word 'collective' leads the reader to think that a *kollektiv* is composed of 'members' of some multi-tiered institution like a 'collective farm' (the correct term for this idea is *kadry*). As outlined above, one institution, like the state farm 'Khantaiskii', can have many different 'communities of producers' each of which have very different statuses associated with them. These *kollektivy* are often symbolic-ally demarcated during statutory feast-days like 'day of the reindeer herder', 'day of the fisherman', or 'day of the teacher'. The professional bond that a *kollektiv* induces in its members also runs deep into their life histories. All professionals, from reindeer herders to teachers, have participated in some form of pedagogy or formal training (often financed by their home institu-tion) in the company of other colleagues with whom they will continue working for many years if not a lifetime. The strong overlap between a person's life history and state-run institutions of health, education, and employment was identified by Borneman (1992) as the sense of 'belonging' which distinguished East and West Berliners; people who were otherwise indistinguishable by physical features, language, or deep cultural markers. The important subtlety invoked here of sharing a sense of being with specific individuals with whom one has a localized shared biography expresses well the ardent sentiments that Dolgans and Evenkis have for their 'own' kind despite marked similarities in history, practice, and language.

As with the language of kinship, in vernacular discourse, *kollektivy* were seldom marked with this abstract structural category. Instead, they were referred to by their proper titles (*pastukhi* [herdsmen], *uchitelia* [teachers], *rybaki* [fishermen]) in contexts which evoked their structural significance. If there was any attempt to speak about collectives in aggregates it would be in the difference between *tundroviki* and villagers, or the more abrasive distinction between Khantaika people and Mountain people. Most often, these titles and aggregate categories were employed in contexts where they were distinguishing themselves from others within the 'status ladder of hierarchy' of the farm (Humphrey 1983: 433). It is important to note that differences between these corporate groups are not cultural or innate but are the product of the status hierarchy which was established and invigorated by the bureaucracy. This point might seem self-evident in cases where one distinguishes the state farm administrators [*apparatchiki*] and common, unskilled workers [*raznorabochie*], but it is not always granted when distinguishing reindeer herders [*pastukhi*] from meteorologists. *Kollektivy* are weighted and graded most objectively in the large ledger books written by mysterious employees of the Ministries of Agriculture and of Labour which give the coefficients establishing differential salaries and privileges. In everyday discussion, the criterion that is most intuitively understood is a hierarchical notion of *kul'tura* which sets the rungs upon which one *kollektiv* is placed above another.

The alliterative twin to *kollektiv*—*kul'tura*—is no less difficult to translate into English. *Kul'tura* is usually translated by the word 'culture' but in practice it tends to be used more like the English word 'civilization'. The classic examples of *kul'tura* are courtly institutions such as the ballet, symphony, or opera; Russian institutions which are world renowned for their level of refinement. There is also a direct connection between *kul'tura* and being 'scientific' (Humphrey 1983: 364). However, the term clearly has a wider meaning than 'high culture', embracing the everyday civic services which are supplied as a social right. On many occasions before exiting from Krasnoiarsk to Dudinka, or from Dudinka to the Khantaika, and then again from the Khantaika to the Number One Reindeer Brigade I was repeatedly warned away from the 'low level' or even 'complete absence' of *kul'tura* awaiting me at my destination. Highest on the list of concerns of my well-wishers was not so much my boredom at not being able to discuss critical philosophy but the physical condition of the built surroundings. For all of its short-comings (such as the lack of a public sauna) the Khantaika was lauded over other settlements in the valley for its 'culture' in the form of a bread bakery and electrical plant which continued to function in a climate of economic chaos. It is important to emphasize that for the Russian newcomers, the state authorities, and sometimes the native intelligentsia, the word *kul'tura* embraces both a certain collection of mundane social services and 'high culture' without diluting a judgemental and somewhat imperial scale of values.

On the Khantaika (and indeed any rural settlement in the Russian Federation) *kul'tura* is unevenly associated across positions of employment. Until very recently there was no category for the unemployed in the state-run economy. Thus, just as the web of employment and administration was universal, so was the ranking of positions with respect to the overriding priorities of social and civic development. At the top of the hierarchy, not surprisingly, were the teachers, administrators, Party or state farm leaders. Towards the bottom were the settlement labourers and the hunters, herders, and fishermen on the land. To the modest extent that the Party-controlled bureaucracy was successful in building a meritocracy, the rule of entrance to one level or another was the state-set recruitment requirements of formal education. Yuri Slezkine (1994: ch. 10) documents many of the privileges which were granted to members of the sparse peoples with a view to aiding their assimilation of *kul'tura*. These rights ranged from special boarding schools, subsidies on milk and children's clothing, special provisions for maternity leave, and quotas ensuring guaranteed employment in targeted sectors. However, to understand national rivalry in this settlement it is important also to distinguish the allocation of *kul'tura* between nationalities. Thus, while the newcomers were 'raising the level of *kul'tura*' of the ethnics, the resettlement of the *kamentsy* was engineered to 'raise the level of *kul'tura* of Evenkis'. Although this particular experiment in nationality-directed economic intensification ended in 1974, to this day Khantaika Evenkis and Mountain Dolgans and Evenkis still occupy different occupational groupings and engage with the land at different fish camps and in different brigades (Anderson 1996*a*: appendix 1).

Ironically, the naive attempts to rationalize the rural production created 'positions' quite obviously devoid of the other markers of *kul'tura* such as a comfortable dwelling, desirable commodities, and, to paraphrase Marx, a community with whom one could 'criticize after dinner'. Within the ranks of the *tundroviki* the attempt to build civilized spaces in the settlement has resulted in the construction of a 'wild' fragment of unsettled bachelors who move in nomadic orbits around the farm. Thus, just as industrialization of domestic reindeer-breeding created a wild ecology, the sedentarization of domestic space creates wild enclaves of people on career trajectories which do not overlap temporally or spatially with that of the rest of their kin. The self-reliant *pastukh* who participates in the sentient ecology of the land is as distant from *kul'tura* as he is a product of it.

Where do the other *tundroviki*, such as the fishermen, the trapper-fishermen, and the hunters, fit on the status ladder? Each of these state-inscribed positions is seen to be more conducive to conferring *kul'tura* than the strongly mobile position of reindeer herder. Aside from potential opportunities for informal exchange these positions have better access to mechanical goods, consumer items, and to a flexible pattern of work. These are the benefits that can be seen to contribute to making these other positions more 'cultured', and perhaps not uncoincidentally more appropriate for a Dolgan or a Russian person.

The position of the fishermen [*rybaki*] is thought to be the most lucrative. This is visible in their dwellings, which are constructed out of cut lumber, have garages with a bewildering mixture of tools and spare parts, and true to the Leninist vision of socialism have a selection of portable electrical generators in varying models and voltages. While the *tochka* appears to be a smaller frontier homestead cleaved off from the larger mainland settlement, the work of the fisherman can be distinguished by its concentrated and hence easily measured quality. On the lake and reservoir of the Khantaika river system, the biannual fish runs create two fishing seasons: June and September. During these two months, as the brigadier of Number One Reindeer Brigade observes 'the fishermen appear like flies'. Between these months there is much time to be spent in the settlement preparing nets, drinking, watching Mexican soap-operas, or hunting as one sees fit.

The same qualities can be found in the other two professions, the state hunter [*okhotnik-promyslovik*] and the hunter-fisherman [*okhotnik-rybak*]. A reverse rhythm of work to the fishermen tends to apply to the hunters, who spend much time checking and setting traps in the fall and spring and have many openings for leisure in midsummer and midwinter. Although both the fishermen and the hunters deal in a commodity that is readily tradable, the fisherman achieves a higher income and greater access to state goods by producing large, tangible quantities of fish. The hunter is also encouraged and indeed closely monitored to surrender large quantities of fur, but nevertheless such small and valuable items can be more easily hidden and traded. Thus the fortunes of the fishermen tend to be tied more closely to the state farm and to the contract that the farm signs with the Noril'sk fish factory while the fortunes of the hunter tend to be dependent purely upon exclusive access to a trapline. The fisherman, correspondingly, tends to have more machinery, better radios, better access to parts and other material symbols of *kul'tura* than the hunter. The hunter-fisherman has a more balanced work regime of setting traps or hunting wild deer in the winter and fishing modest amounts of high-quality 'red' fish in the summer. This mixed economy attracts young Evenkis and Dolgans who, upon mastering the transport machines of the Soviet era, are able to travel widely, learn about the land, and yet maintain a comfortable home in the settlement. While it is not entirely accurate to classify the hunter-fisherman as a median category, this position does seem to allow the most opportunities for negotiation as to the work regime and access to consumer goods while avoiding the regulative excesses of the state.

What unites all three of these positions is the fact that the exits of the men out onto the tundra are not sustained but abbreviated. While reindeer herders live in either mature family units or in groups of bachelors, the other *tundroviki* can more successfully maintain bifurcated family wherein the residential and consumptive elements of *kul'tura* are developed by women and children in the settlement while the productivist elements of *kul'tura* are realized by groups of men either sitting on *tochki* or travelling extensively over the land. The same gendered division of domestic space is observed by Heonik Kwon (1993: 160) with the Sakhalin Orochons, who say the house is 'where the women live'. One hunter-fisherman, whose father was a well-known herder, went as far as explaining to me that he chose this position over that of a herder in order to get married: 'The women aren't any good any more—they don't want to live on the tundra. If you are a hunter you can stay in the settlement.'

When examining the daily regimes of the four 'most traditional' occupations (reindeer herder, fisherman, hunter, fisher-hunter) it should not be surprising that they are not inflected by clan practices—or if they are, only in a very abstract manner. Although kinship still determines with whom young boys will be apprenticed, the transfer of small numbers of reindeer, or the circulation of handmade clothes or products from the hunt, the more vibrant kinship net is that imagined by women in the settlement. The *tundrovik* appears in genealogies as an important appendage in very extensive bilateral networks which include members of many other *kollektivy*. While the herders provide fur and meat, the genealogies also remember people on lucrative social security payments, people placed in Dudinka, or in the farm *apparat*. If there is a 'clan society of the Evenkis' in this settlement, the *tundroviki*, relegated to a regime of state transhumance, are but a part of it and not at its centre.

While it would be inappropriate to locate each of the above tundra positions in a strict order against one another, it should be evident that each of these positions falls under a differing regulatory matrix and boasts differing remuneration in terms of wages, housing, tempo of work, access to consumable goods, and access to a community of friends and kin. A similar phenomenon occurs with the forty positions which are available to the villagers. It is beyond the scope of this chapter to examine each one of these professions (many of which are held by only one individual). Suffice it to say that the resources available for ranking within the settlement positions are expanded through the differential quality of housing, opportunities for state-paid travel, access to commodities, or the reliability of receiving one's pay. To access each of these dimensions of stratification one must achieve a certain level of formal education or satisfy the recruitment norms of the state farm. The consciousness of position is illustrated by the following discussion on the career plans of one young teacher:

I.A. I am thinking of changing my profession. It might be better to be an accountant.
I heard on the radio that with privatization they will be needing accountants. Or if
I worked with *Zapolarii* [the kindergarten run by the Noril'sk factory] I would get
a trip to Sochi.

S.G. You should stay as a teacher! Don't you know that *GorONO* [the City Department of Education] has the best budget? Besides, you get to take a trip every now
and again [*komandirovka*].

I.A. That's true. I was thinking of applying to study in Leningrad [at the Hertzen
Pedagogical Institute]. At least I could get new eyeglasses then.

L.I If you take an upgrading certificate you would be able to teach a higher course
and get a higher seniority [*stavka*].

I.A. But I'm bored with teaching! I don't know how the older ones [*stariki*] can stay
in the same profession all of that time. I can't do that.

The villagers live in a social world at least as intricate as the sentient lands of
the *tundroviki* peopled with perceptive animals, masters (dead and alive), and
the memories of routes. However, the difference between villagers and the
tundrovik is maintained not so much from the character of the individual in
question as by the regulatory nature of the administrative status hierarchy.

While members of a *kollektiv* might share many things such as a particular
subsidy coefficient in their pay-cheques, access to housing, rights to travel or
for education, the distinctive effect of the Soviet era is a shared life history.
Alexia Bloch (1996), in her ethnographic analysis of the boarding school in
Tura, examines how the curriculum, daily regime, and even architecture of
the boarding school 'incubates' and 'medicalizes' a distinct Evenki self-
identity with a distinct investment in an idealized past. All members of
various collectives had experienced a similar incubation, starting in the
Khantaika boarding school. The young Evenki teachers of the Khantaika
school had their identities further formed by collective study in the Dudinka
boarding school, and finally in the Igarka Pedagogical School or in the
Faculty of Northern Peoples in Leningrad. Specialists within the state
farm *apparat* have a common history in agricultural institutes in Noril'sk
and Krasnoiarsk. Party members attended the same Party schools and congresses. Even reindeer herders, who otherwise had little formal education,
would be selected to go to the reindeer herder congresses held biannually in
Dudinka. Unlike extensive kinship, the *kollektiv* builds vertical solidarity
between professionals (who may happen to be kinsmen) through an array
of positions which are authorized by the state.

Although *kollektivy* might be constructed by arbitrary shifts in policy, they
were nevertheless meaningful and stable. In a comparative study of social
obligation between rural producers in post-socialist Mongolia, David Sneath
(1993) found that alliances with schoolmates, military comrades, as well as
within collectivized institutions formed some of the most stable relationships
around which to meet the new challenges of the market reforms. For the

tundrovik, who places great import on negotiating the sentient ecology of the land, the *kollektiv* is a flexible forum within which to live with kinsmen and to sate the bureaucratic appetites of the farm administration. The fact that a *kollektiv* has its own substantive ethos explains why some young men do in fact want to become reindeer herders in spite of the arduous conditions of work. When I learned that the brigadier of Number One Reindeer Brigade had spent many years fishing, I asked him why he went back to a less lucrative profession. His simple but complete answer was 'Who else would work with reindeer?'

With this vocabulary, it is possible to explore from a different angle that element of *natsionalizm* which implies that certain fragments of the state farm enjoy differential citizenship entitlements. The central role of *kul'tura* in the legacy of social provisioning of the Siberian frontier with the creation of state farms established a close link between nationality and lucrative positions within state institutions. Positions could be lucrative in more than a mere monetary sense, embracing moments from the quality of housing to the type of social community in which one lives. The strength of this ethos of a shared life approaches the idea of a 'domestic mode of production' (Humphrey 1998).

Nationalist rivalry on the Khantaika often draws on the substantive idioms associated with the history of *kollektivy*. When making claims for exclusive territories, Evenkis will often cite a lifetime spent at a particular fishing spot or a registered reindeer territory in the company of brigade members (who are also extended kin). The worthiness of some *kollektivy* was supported historically by arguing that Evenkis were 'communist' and thus civil while Dolgans were 'rebels' and or 'wild'. One occasionally hears among *tundroviki* that 'Evenkis are better *pastukhi*' or that the 'farm should work for Evenkis'. In cases such as these, a nationalist claim for 'our land' works on many levels. It captures the personal entitlement of a *tundrovik*, the claim of a brigade to an authorized territory, and a claim on behalf of the Evenkis as a nationality. There is evidence that the multivocal nationalist claim for local resources nested within a hierarchical administrative structure may be common across the post-Soviet space. A recent ethnography of Mongolia reveals a very similar phenomenon:

The interesting fact about socialism is that it has created identities through its command principle, which redistributes goods to defined groups, supplemented by its other major principles based on class and evolution. Territorial-administrative units were set up to accommodate the government's understanding of the relative status between these groups. The result is an inward-looking localism which is closely related to the 'excluding others' type of nationalism (Bulag 1993: 19).

The *natsionalizm* evident on the Khantaika is not simply a strategy to exclude others in a zero-sum struggle over resources. Instead, in a social universe where one's *kollekiv* is linked to privileges, remuneration, and ultimately *kul'tura*, nationalist rivalry serves to make the constitutional claim that people 'deserve' to live better *because* they are Evenki or *because* they are Dolgan.

It would be misleading to brand the *kollektiv* as either an alienating or consolidating institution. It is sufficient to note that this corporate institution is much more visible than the patrilineal clan as a rubric under which people reside together, collect their remuneration, and build relationships (Humphrey 1983: 300, 342). *Kollektivy*, formally defined by career posts and strengthened by the institutional direction of the life course, are a locus of social life with multifaceted social rights which may in fact be closer to a concept of citizenship than to a concept of status. The position into which one was 'set' included more than rights to a salary but also included rights of *kul'tura* defined by access to housing, consumable goods, transport, and 'communal services' (heat, water, bread, milk, light).

Finding relatives

In the preceding two sections, it was shown how *kollektivy* and marriage strategies have been used to support a nationalist agenda on the Khantaika. The sense of nationality shown to be embedded in civic and kin practices stands in marked contrast to the subtle patterns of extensive kinship existing previously in the lower Yenisei valley. In both sections I have portrayed the twin strategies of building national endogamy or taking culturally stratified positions as flexible attempts to adopt social models imported from outside. This lends a sense of continuity between past practices and people and present-day Evenkis. However, such a tone would betray the anxiety with which many Evenkis on the Khantaika, and elsewhere, look to their future. It is important to convey the element of sadness and sometimes anger evident in narratives at the increasing tendencies of personal and communal ambitions to fly apart. While Soviet administrative tools themselves prescribe nationalist mobilization in professional and kinship spheres as practical strategies with which to negotiate the ladder of culture, a serious engagement with the nationalist agenda sends individuals off on diverging trajectories bringing the reproduction of the community into question. This section will examine the strategies of the younger generation trying to direct their lives as Evenkis in a changing constitutional framework.

The clearest tale told by genealogical accounts is one of bilateral linkages between clan/surname groups. In Charts 2 and 4 there is such a heavy use of affinal kin in the accounting of kinship that one might suspect the development of an incipient matrilineal kin system. While older women tend to spin these stories of common descent with a certain joy, younger people tend to speak dismissively or even sarcastically about kinship. Once, when asking a young member of the Number One Reindeer Brigade how a Mountain Evenki with a snow machine was counted as kin, I was told with a smile, 'If you want, everyone in this settlement can be your kin.' Young unmarried women can often be heard to speak in disparaging terms about the wide kinship net woven by their elders: 'There is no one for me to marry here—everyone is my relative.' In general, both young and old can be heard to express the sentiment that 'Evenkis are disappearing; every year *real* Evenkis are fewer and fewer.' The net of wide bilateral linkages so carefully tended by the older generation seems to work equally well at entrapping their nieces, nephews, and grandchildren. Before examining the implications of the 'kinship crisis' on the Khantaika, I will first present the benefits of the bilateral network built by the senior generation.

The linking of bilateral kin seems to be a common strategy in Siberia if not in the former Soviet Union as a whole. In the Buriat collective farms which are the subject of Caroline Humphrey's research, one finds both an expanding circle of exogamy and the sensitivity to bilateral kin starting with the Soviet period (1983: 296–8, 340, 395–8). I am in full agreement with her that this strategic change enables families to 'choose which kin ties they wish to emphasise' in order to introduce an element of control into an otherwise rigid and unpredictable bureaucratic structure (pp. 340–1). In the example of Chart 4 two Enneche-Evenki sisters managed to capture through adoption and serial marriages a representative of nearly every Khantaika Evenki patriclan. Each of the descendants of these sisters, now occupying positions of prestige in the settlement administration, the school, and the state farm, feel their kinship through the fact that they lived together in the same household and grew up together. Despite changing her nationality, Liubov' Fedorovna in the Number One Reindeer Brigade occasionally activated her affinal links amongst Dolgans (Chart 2), often embarrassing her family by her careless crossing of lines. There is evidence that market reforms intensify the need to use directed kin relationships to build reliable alliances. Alexia Bloch (1996: 144) notes that certain Tura Evenki households are specifically designed to 'funnel' resources. If the political climate of a settlement is such that a policy of national endogamy is encouraged, the reliance on affinal kin can compensate for losing certain opportunities to imagine kinship links within the settlement.

The dense networks of affinal kin seem to have been crucial in reproducing the Evenki pedagogy and in introducing young people to the sentient ecology of the region. After fifty years of attempting to displace local 'uncultured' methods of knowing the land or raising reindeer, the best *tundroviki* learn about the land from their fathers or from their uncles and not from textbooks. Of three young teenagers clearly participating in some form of apprenticeship in 1992–3, two were working with uncles on their mother's side. One village woman straightforwardly explained to me that 'you cannot go onto the *tundra* without relatives'.

Affinal linkages not only help to reproduce knowledge of the land within *kollektivy*; they also reinforce the nationalist sentiment within these corporate bodies. Affinal kin not only live and work together in the same community of producers, but they support each other in reproducing Evenki cultural traits. It is in this sense that I understand the statement that the Number One Reindeer Brigade is 'the most Evenki brigade'. This is not so much a factual (as Chart 1 shows) as imperative statement that by 'feeding the settlement' as *pastukhi*, Evenkis, and kin they are also making their biggest contribution to making the land and the state farm Evenki.

Bilateral linkages are also needed to make Evenkis on another level. The project closest to the core of reproducing Evenki identities is the matter of marriage and child-rearing. In achieving this future aim the network of extensive linkages, forged by the generation born of the age of extensive travel, seems to confine the younger generation raised in the age of schools, settlements, and professions. The complex sentiment among younger women that 'there is no one to marry' can be broken down into several aspects. First and foremost a mate must be considered desirable. This usually implies that a man should not be alcoholic, violent, and should be 'cultured' [*kul'turnyi*]. Many Evenki women underscored that their men should be 'higher [*vyshe*] somehow'. Second, the potential partner should not be considered to be a relative 'since Evenkis never marry their own relatives'. The policies of national endogamy and affinal linkages make these two criteria difficult to meet. A case in point is the dilemma of Roza in Chart 4. This tall, 16-year-old girl was just completing her studies at the Igarka Pedagogical School to become a teacher. In the summer of 1993 Roza returned to the settlement with her new wardrobe of elegant clothes and advertising her knowledge of the most recent modern music from Moscow and from the West. The question of who she would marry was often discussed amongst young married women in the settlement. Although Roza was conceptually a *metizka* (whose father was never identified), she was generally taken as an Evenki girl. Most observers of her dilemma did not even consider matching her to a Dolgan man. Chart 4 indicates potential suitors in the bottom row as generation V. Of the certain eligible Evenki men many were eliminated due to a kind of matrilateral 'rule' of exogamy stemming from the affinal linkages of her mother and grandmother. Setting aside the issue of whether or not Roza wanted to marry one of these boys, every candidate was considered ineligible since they were direct descendants of one of the marriage partners of Roza's grandmother or grandfather, or they were the descendants of her great-aunt. Complicating the picture even further was the need to find a *kul'turnyi* man:

I.A. There is no one for her here. She needs a good man. Most of the villagers are always drinking. Then there is her height.

D.A. What about Vitalii?

I.A. He is a relative somehow—I don't know how. Besides, what would she do with a *tundrovik*? She needs someone to talk to—to take her out. She likes to dance. Masha has a wider choice. She can go either way—either live on the *tundra* or in the settlement. It will be easier for her. But Roza—she will have to go to Dudinka I guess.

There are several aspects of Roza's case which point to stresses in the accumulated history of many different types of alliances. As Afanas'eva hypothesized with Nias, Roza's dilemma hints at the extension of exogamy through both the mother's and the father's lines. In addition, her biography shows a strong trajectory tied to formal education and urban *kul'tura* which make some marriage strategies inappropriate for her. These qualities send her on a trajectory far from the networks in the village. In the end, Roza did marry a Russian man in 1997 whom she had met during her studies at the Dudinka boarding school.

The history of 'finding relatives' among one's bilateral kin is also reflected in another common 'marriage' strategy: the strategy of 'finding children'. One Evenki grandmother who was approaching pension age complained openly one day in the farm office that 'before parents used to marry their children, now you just hear from someone that your daughter is staying with someone [*zhenit'sia*]'. Another pensioner, remaining at home to tend a one-year-old infant muttered, 'I don't even know where she found this child'. It was unclear to me if these old women were more unhappy about their loss of power in shaping the lives of their daughters or about their fate of taking responsibility for children while their daughters worked in one of the settlement offices. Young women, in contrast to the sour feelings of their mothers, tended to take pride in 'finding' children. It was not uncommon for women to boast about the mixed origins of their children, which represent to them their successes in managing short-term affairs. To one middle-aged mother, her three children from different fathers reminded her of her various suitors and 'the days when I was young'. Other women spoke with some admiration of a woman in Potapovo who had children of eight differing nationalities. Some women claim that they would rather have children out of an affair than a long-term spouse. This radical stance is due to the fact that men have a particularly bad reputation amongst the women of the Khantaika. They are reputed to be drunk, violent, uncultured [*nekul'turnii*], and a drain on the emotional and financial resources of the family. Single motherhood is a much more attractive prospect since the new social welfare state seems intent upon subsidizing large families, single-parent families, and accommodation for single mothers. In 1992–3 single mothers were among the highest-earning individuals in the village. Unlike in Eastern Europe where some authors argue the collapse of the redistributive state has led to the marginalization of women in the domestic sphere, women in this Arctic village seem to be taking advantage of social welfare to consolidate their positions as heads of house-holds (Einhorn 1993).

In a sense, these examples of contemporary 'marriages' were more exten-sive than those of the older generation both in terms of contact with other nationalities and their territorial compass. The marriage between Evenki women and newcomers yields the potential of moving across Russia and even beyond its borders to Kiev, Tashkent, or Baku. Although women occasionally take advantage of such links to visit these foreign capitals, most of the young women of the Khantaika entering into relationships with newcomers eventually either marry local men or tend the offspring of the newcomers within the settlement of their birth giving them their own surnames. Their children eventually grow up to be Evenki or Dolgan.

The strategy of 'finding children' has double-edged implications for women. As Kwon (1993: 180) observed with settlement Orochons in Val, Sakhalin, to be able to feed your children without the help of a man is a matter of great pride. However, there is also the stigma of not marrying 'our own people' or of giving birth to 'mixed children' [*metisy*]. The Sakhalin reindeer herders spoke of their women 'going wild' as if they had been abducted by droves of chaotically migrating deer. On the Khantaika, objec-tions to the production of *metisy* were more ambivalent. On the one hand, *metisy* are thought to be more beautiful than 'pure [*chistyi*] Evenkis'. As an example of the Evenki word 'beautiful' I was given the image of wide [Russian] eyes. On the other hand, 'pure' Evenkis take the opportunity to tease either the parents of mixed children, or fellow members of their own age cohort for light-coloured hair or light skin.

The most controversial relationships in this regard were those between Azerbaijani newcomers and Mountain Dolgan women. There were some cultural commonalities mediating these relationships. The Azerbaijani men claimed that they could understand Dolgan (which like Azerbaijani is a Turkic language). On the other hand, some Khantaika Evenki women openly derided the patriarchal structure of the Azerbaijani households, where the women were prevented from inviting their friends to their homes as guests. While the Azerbaijani men were unfavourably compared to dark lake cod, their children were sometimes looked down upon for being 'dark' but obviously with not the same degree as their fathers.

I do not want to overemphasize the vehemence with which women were encouraged to marry 'their own'. On the whole all children were treated with great fondness in this settlement. Even the grandmother who complained dourly about having to tend to yet another infant on a different day observed that 'children appear, they grow up, and then they walk around . . . Isn't that good?' Another woman with a firm upbringing on the tundra shrugged her shoulders with a smile on the subject of adopting young children: 'People are just the same as reindeer, they also leave their children for others [to take care of]'. Nevertheless liaisons which slip away from the policy of national endogamy are still seen to lead to the 'disappearance of Evenkis'.

The most radical exponents of national endogamy are the reindeer herders, who as transhumant state employees have been set on a trajectory which demands much solidarity amongst themselves but does not elicit much support from the settlement. In Number One Reindeer Brigade, the young bachelors occasionally derided women as 'prostitutes' or 'bitches', sometimes directly, or often metaphorically while trying to lasso cows during the daily round-up of the herd (cf. Kwon 1993: 180). However, the bitterness of the reindeer herders is not simple disappointment with being sent on a professional trajectory which is diverging from those of the *kul' turnye* women. The rhetoric of the herders is allied with that of many of the Russian newcomers who look at the children of single mothers as a sure sign that the *kul' tura* of Evenkis is decaying. The Azerbaijani technicians and engineers were the most boastful on this count when they remarked that Evenkis show a lack of pride in their homes and in their families. Although both the celibate reindeer herders and the single mothers of the settlement consent to living within the professional trajectories set by culturally fractured *kollektivy*, the nationalist overtones which overlay these decisions to a certain degree reflect wider models of culture and civilization as articulated by the state.

The link between the institutions of Russian civilization and the issue of how to use national endogamy to build a great nation was presented to me by one of the discontented grandmothers of the settlement:

You have been sitting here for months writing things—working with the household registries. Well, what future is there for us? You're an ethnographer. You *must* know these things. Why are you silent? In twenty years will there be Evenkis or not?

If one understands that both nationality and the status associated with it is administratively set, then it is entirely appropriate to ask a technician of culture (an anthropologist) to lend a professional opinion on how the 'kinship crisis' of Evenkis is to be solved. There is of course no step-by-step model which can supplement or displace the accumulated marriage strategies of several generations which have given rise to a situation where the opportunities for expanding their numbers and their linkages are now limited. The first steps towards answering this challenge are to understand how national identity, the nationalist sentiment, and the 'kinship crisis' have been created by ethnographers, administrators, and matchmakers. Such a culturally created knot can also be unravelled and bound together into a different tapestry where Khantaika comes to mean 'all of those living on the Khantaika', or *tundroviki* retains or expands its meaning as 'all of those who work out on the land'. This vision of a more flexible and extensive social community which I have read into the statements of older informants and in ethnographic anomalies is unlikely to be met by carving up a unified 'ethnic' territory into smaller, exclusive clan communities. In a settlement where first territory, then nationality, and finally lineages came to be registered by the Russian citizenship regime, the reification of bilateral kinship linkages into tightly defined *rody* could only heighten the fragmentation of this over-classified people.

9

Three Senses of Belonging on the Khantaika

THE MOST CONSPICUOUS result of the reforms to Soviet state socialism has been the eruption of claims to self-determination and territorial autonomy, and in the end, the crumbling of the union altogether. The strength of social movements organized around nationality in this former socialist state are paradoxical along several dimensions. First, such groundswells of political activity contradicted with resounding emphasis the reigning models of state and society which portrayed the Soviet Union as a seamless, although atomized, whole. Second, the success of national identity as a political discourse directly contradicted official communist ideology which proclaimed the unity of peoples along class dimensions and not dimensions of nationality. Third, although modernist theories predict nationalism in societies organized by strong states promoting standard literacy through a mass media, they cannot account for the development of multiple national identities within a single modern state let alone within specific local segments of a state. This ethnography of belonging to a nationality, a territory, and a *kollektiv* in a relatively isolated Arctic state farm allows us to understand the diverging tendencies within Soviet state-building which continue to contribute to its unravelling.

In terms of state theory, this case study of identity is an extreme example. The processes of territorial formation, collectivization, consolidation, and ultimately privatization on the Khantaika illustrate the capacity of a state to reorganize the lives of a people difficult to engage in terms of distance, population density, economy, mobility, language, and fiscal cost. Although public administration on the Khantaika may not be the most flawless or most representative example of state policy, the fact that the state was at all able to rationalize identities, control the movement of people, and finally inflect the life course of people, presents itself as a limiting case of the power of this administrative apparatus. Instances of national inflation and indeed the invocation of authorized identities as a cause speak to the success of this social order in transforming practice even in a place as difficult to reach as the Khantaika. In terms of the debate on national identity, this is a clear and detailed illustration of how Soviet nationality policy did not suppress, contain, or assimilate national identities but instead made them one of the most central distinctions of civic life. The Soviet state introduced the principle of nationality to people who, upon the collapse of the redistributive civic order, inflated this idiom in an effort to better their positions. Finally, this study is a testimony to the creativity of local producers in manipulating the symbols of nationality, territory, and *kollektiv* to make the best of a worsening situation.

Although the exposition of politics on the Khantaika may contribute to an understanding of why nationalism might be one answer to the choking of civic entitlements within post-Soviet society, it does raise one additional paradox. In terms of the substantive history of the lower Yenisei valley, and the circumpolar North in general, the choice *least* expected would be the cultivating of an exclusive nationalist idiom amongst all other possible axes of identity. Within the space of one or two generations, Evenki and Dolgan strategists have moved away from a tradition of complex, relational understandings between themselves and the land, and between themselves and their neighbours to build a social landscape that is remarkably stark. Missing or inchoate are other idioms which one might expect such as the idea of 'aboriginality' or experiments with Metis/mestizo identities which so characterize other rural, aboriginal contexts worldwide. It is my hope that this is a transitory phenomenon. However, since my last visit to Taimyr in the autumn of 1997, national rivalry remains a simmering fact in settlements now starved not only of cash but of electricity, medical care, and in some cases schooling. The lack of respect to the investment made by local Evenkis and Dolgans in state socialism must be framed by the fact that on radio and on television people learn of the daily dramas surrounding the privatization of the Factory in Noril'sk; an entity which despite the pollution of hundreds of square kilometres of tundra manages to attract trillions of roubles in monetary investment. To use Nikolai Savel'evich's words, if gifts to the tundra are given to appease a 'capricious' landscape, the effort invested for so many generations in feeding the Soviet legal landscape resulted in a much more 'outrageous' reply. The fact that national rivalry has not faded lends support to the central argument of this work that it was not a position taken of convenience but instead a complex commentary on the entire set of relationships between people, land, and the state.

National identity and belonging

Like an Evenki fisherman in a bark canoe who prudently keeps close to the shore, I have chosen to represent the nationalist sentiment in this troubled community with categories close to the vernacular originals. The most obvious categories in circulation are those representing the complex notion of *natsional'nost'* [nationality], which blends a notion of authorized identity with the expectation of certain civic entitlements. I have made a direct link between the attack on the citizen rights associated with the recent campaign of privatization and the growth of what is known locally as *natsionalizm*; the inflated, unbalanced support for members of one's own nationality. In this light, the assertion of national identity does not so much appear as the recovery of cultural attributes as an active defence of a stable and secure position in a constitutional structure which is under attack.

These vernacular ideas, however, do imply other, prouder categories which have been rigged to venture out on to the deep seas of social theory: terms such as 'nation', 'nationalism', and 'ethnicity'. My wariness of these terms is based upon a lingering suspicion that the distinction between nationalist and ethnic phenomena represents a covert distinction between modern and pre-modern types of people, and that ethnic groups are in some way 'survivals' of what nations once were (Kuper 1988: ch. 1). This evolutionary division is perhaps most clearly seen when conducting a cross-disciplinary survey of literature on one particular region. In analyses of Russia, 'nationalism' tends to apply to peoples whom the Soviet state had classified as nations (titular nations) while other social movements are described as 'ethnonationalism' (Smith 1992; Verdery 1993), 'ethnic mobilization' (Zaslavsky 1991), or even 'subgroupism' (Taras 1993). Some students of the former Soviet Union also use the term 'nationality' in their analyses (Hajda & Beissinger 1990; Zaslavsky 1991; Horowitz 1992; Armstrong 1992; Bremmer 1993; Suny 1993), although in each of these cases their usage suggests that nationalities are a diminutive form of proper nations. It is an interesting exercise in works of this type to examine how the category of Russian nationality is handled. More often than not, Russians are not seen to present a 'nationality problem'. In analyses of China, similar terms come to the fore when the discussion turns to identities other than Han Chinese: 'cultural nationalism' (Harumi 1993), 'minority nationalism' (Watson 1990), 'cultural identity' (Siu 1993). The analysis of the social movements of circumpolar peoples displays the widest range, with some authors finding manifestations of 'ethnicity' (Balzer 1983; Paine 1977), 'ethnic autonomy' (Dorris 1979), 'ethnonationalism' (Asch 1984; Levin 1993), or 'ethnopolitics' (Tanner 1983*a*); and others detecting the presence of distinct 'nations' (Watkins 1977; Little Bear *et al.* 1984) and of 'nationalism' (Nuttall 1992: 177–82; Fondahl 1993; Alfred 1995). In other contexts, one finds minority political movements in Europe termed 'neonationalisms' (Nairn 1977), which, according to one theorist, may draw upon a symbolic reservoir contained in a 'pre-modern' *ethnie* (Smith 1986; 1992: 48). While this list of hybrid terms is not comprehensive, it does show a tendency to classify national rivalry in places peripheral to Europe at a subordinate level of analysis.

The most convincing argument for a bifurcation in studies of national identity is that the dynamics of social organization differ qualitatively with the scale of a society. Face-to-face communities are thought to support either a 'simpler' or a 'richer' form of social interaction which has no need for the abstract generalizations of nationalist ideology but instead negotiates ethnic boundaries at the level of the individual (Cohen 1985: ch. 1; Gluckman 1965; Barth 1969; Eriksen 1993: 99–101). There is no question that the regulated pattern of social life within powerful states represents a different type of social organization from a locally invigorated model of extensive travel, relational identity, and extensive kinship. However, one must pose the question for *whom* is this a difference of scale? As Gellner (1978: 137–41; 1983: 29–38) often stresses, the experience of social life on a grand scale is only truly accessible to a class of people, such as intellectuals, teachers, or clerks, which has been trained in the iron rules of state order; in short, people most similar to those who write about ethnicity or nationalism. However, there are many other categories of people in a society. Many of these find themselves in the 'grey zone' of being categorized sometimes as an ethnic group or sometimes as a nation, depending upon the boundaries within which they happen to live, the official labour policy of the state, or their own political opinions (Eriksen 1993: 119, 156). This ambiguity of scale is further clouded by what many analysts see as the end of the nation-state form altogether whether through the loss of its monopoly on violence (Tilly 1990), through the rising influence of transnational corporations (Harvey 1989), or through competing axes of local 'loyalties' ranging from gender to 'fourth world' demands for stateless autonomy (Eriksen 1993: ch. 8).

The difficulty of distinguishing between ethnic and national phenomena is particularly acute in the lower Yenisei valley. Russian ethnography, not to mention North Atlantic Sovietology, teaches us to categorize Sakhas [Yakuts] and Russians as 'nations' while Dolgans and Evenkis are thought to reproduce themselves in some other diminutive form. However, a sensitivity to the perspective of those who are not members of elite institutions quickly produces irreconcilable paradoxes. Russian fishermen more often refer to themselves with the exclusive labels of *sibiriaki* [Siberians] or *sudiaki* [locals] than with reference to their 'nation'. Dolgan activists, on the other hand, often advertise their close identity with the Sakha Republic to the extent that some will call themselves *yakuty*. An empirical analysis of identity in the lower Yenisei valley, therefore, could lead to the interesting conclusion that the Dolgan ethnic group is rising to become a nation while local Russians are devolving into an ethnic group.[1] If strict technical criteria are applied, such as the will or capacity to actually form a successful nation-state, this paradoxical situation does not improve. Members of the Dolgan 'ethnic group' presently do not make demands for the formation of their own state with a corresponding flag, currency, and customs establishment. However, their exclusive and aggressive sense of belonging is difficult to distinguish from that of their diamond-rich Sakha cousins who the Russian Federation fears would be well capable of instituting each of these three conditions. In order to place the

---

[1] Ironically, this argument has been made by several scholars. Lev Gumilev (1990; 1993) is a strong proponent of assigning essentialist and 'energetic' destinies to nations. In his view, Turkic peoples are 'rising' while older nations, such as Russians, are 'declining'. His somewhat racialist conclusions echo older literature from the turn of the century which worried over the 'degradation' of Russian settlers into a mixed, creole category which was neither Russian nor native (Tugarinov 1919).

sentiments of Dolgans within a typology of being either disgruntled ethnic activists or shrewd national strategists, one must either have a sixth sense to foretell the fortunes of nations, or perhaps more honestly, implicitly assume what Hobsbawm (1990) calls 'the government perspective'.

The difficulties of distinguishing between ethnic groups and nations may be particularly difficult in the circumpolar region generally. Within the Canadian Arctic, one can find an inverse situation to Taimyr, where communities of 'aboriginal' hunters and trappers have been distinguished by settlers, anthropologists, and historians alike as being 'nations' while English, German, Ukrainian, and French newcomers are treated as ethnic groups or 'Euro-Canadians'. The political organizations of Canadian native peoples take advantage of this historic distinction by referring to themselves as the 'First Nations' (Opekokew 1982).[2] The use of the word nation in this context blends exclusive identity with an idea of 'aboriginality' or 'indigenous-ness'. While in many states, like Canada or the United States, distinctions of blood may define membership of aboriginal categories, the political useful-ness of these terms lies in the assertion that these communities are the only ones with a legitimate claim to a common cultural unit and a reserved territory. The fact that contemporary land settlements with North American native groups, like Inuit or Gwich'ins, are linked to surface, subsurface, and zoning rights on territories larger than many European states, and the fact that access to these areas is governed by complex membership regulations, makes First Nations' identity at times seem like a purer form of instrumental nationalism than what one might find in the Old World.

If one rejects the enthusiasm of state managers and macro-sociologists for absolute distinctions of scale between ethnic groups and nations, then there is little to distinguish the ethnic sentiment from the nationalist sentiment. The analyst is best advised to choose one or the other category, but not to imply a development from one to the other. To underscore the point that the sentiments of Evenki and Dolgan actors are neither anachronistic nor limited to interpersonal negotiations of identity, I have favoured the adjective 'nationalist' for types of belonging presented here rather than the word 'ethnic'. Apart from being ethnographically appropriate to Taimyr and to the circumpolar North, this word has the double advantage of drawing attention to the multitude of political/institutional segments to which one can wed an identity (Gellner 1978). As this book has demonstrated, the

---

[2] By far the most common collective terms for the aborigines of North America are 'peoples' or 'societies', or in an older idiom, 'bands' or 'tribes'. However, the term 'nation' is conspicuous in a number of contexts. In legal writing it can be found in Snow (1921) and Davies (1985). Contemporary historians and anthropologists use the word nation to denote a people with an established territory, language, and distinctive identity (Osgood 1936: 13, *passim*; Abel 1993: 18, *passim*; Tanner 1983*b*; Champagne 1989). The term is widespread in the history and anthropology of Metis societies (Slobodin 1966: 7, 152–4; Brown 1980).

catalogue of possible political units in a relatively isolated region of Siberia is astonishingly large and not limited to a choice between a sovereign state or a political/territorial vacuum. What makes Evenki and Dolgan sentiments interesting is not a lofty goal of absolute sovereignty but their conviction that their lives would be better if only they could reorganize within nationally bounded units which would be larger than the *kollektivy*, settlements, or districts to which they already belong.

In the past few years there has been a growing theoretical literature which has tried to engage the differing connotations of 'ethnicity' and 'nationalism' (Tonkin *et al.* 1989; Eriksen 1993; Banks 1996). Apart from ongoing terminological disagreement on which term is the master category, the debate tends to centre upon where (or rather within whom) chauvinistic identities can be rooted.[3] The now classic division between 'primordialist' and 'modernist' interpretations of identity (Cohen 1986), which alternately buries national/ethnic sentiments deep in the human condition or simplifies them to the instrumental needs of complex organizations, has not captured the richness of the phenomena. On the one hand, as Marcus Banks (1996) cleverly notes, those authors who most stridently assume a modernist or instrumentalist standpoint (such as Glazer & Moynihan 1963, Bromlei 1983, or even Gellner 1983 and Barth 1969) can be caught leaning on primordialist images or examples to make their argument convincing. On the other hand, as testified to by recent political phenomena such as 'ethnic cleansing' (Banks 1996; Moynihan 1993), or by the cross-examination of the category of 'people' at the UN Working Group on Indigenous Populations (Gray 1997), categories of ethnicity or nationness are now being reproduced widely among so many 'non-state' groups that it has become difficult to distinguish when the phenomenon is being felt as an affective tie or being wielded for instrumental ends. In the majority of cases today, if not in the past, it is probably best to assume that both tendencies are present simultaneously. If the categories wielded by nationalists originate neither unambiguously 'in the people' or 'in the state', where do they in the end rest? In step with the reflexive turn in anthropology, the not unreasonable consensus seems to be that they can be located in the imagination of the analyst, who is usually a member of the same elite group which traditionally serves the state. Benedict

---

[3] There seems to be no consensus on categorical clarity of one term over another. In terms of pedigree, 'ethnicity' is generally noted to be the junior term, appearing in the middle of the 20th cent. either to replace more unpalatable terms such as 'tribe' or 'race' or to capture a qualitatively new phenomenon (Moynihan 1993). In terms of explanatory power, analysts seem to be divided. Those who take their cue from Barth (1969) see ethnicity to be the more general term. Nationalist phenomena are represented as either a special case of successful ethnic mobilization (Moynihan 1993) or are seen as a particularly reified example of the human propensity to classify (Banks 1996; Eriksen 1993). Those who privilege the act or intention of building a nation-state tend to subsume ethnic phenomena as one of the preconditions to successful nationalist mobilizations (Cohen 1985; Gellner 1983).

Anderson (1991), in a significant addition to the revised edition of *Imagined Communities*, notes that in many non-European contexts the maps, censuses, and museums 'imagined' by colonial managers 'have become powerful concretizations which have a powerful life . . . long after the colonial state has disappeared' (p. 185). Both Thomas Eriksen (1993: 161) and Markus Banks (1996: 186 ff.) conclude that ethnicity is 'created by' or is 'in the heads' of anthropologists. Thomas Eriksen (1993: 66–7, 116), further distinguishes the classification systems of academic or official observers, which tend to operate on a 'digital', 'inclusion/exclusion' basis, and the systems of local observers, which permit 'analogic' differences of degree. This study of identity goes far in confirming both the key role of state ethnographers in minting new and influential categories of identity as well as documenting a transition from relational forms of address to the 'digitization' of identity into exclusive forms.

The problem with using metaphors from contemporary computer science in order to situate national categories within a discrete data processor is that it draws attention away from what the relationship might be between the ethnographer-digitizer and the people who then reproduce his or her codes. One of the main conclusions of this book is that Soviet state ethnography was coded with a certain aesthetic admiration for economically viable and compact human communities with prescribed solidarity to certain institutions and spaces. That the product of this endeavour was discord is not so much a reflection on the quality of the ethnography as on the success of Soviet social engineers in designing a segmentary social space where it became useful for people to circulate identities overlapping with discrete territories and productive communities. This ethnographic account of how authorized identity is wielded on the Khantaika also demonstrates the complicating point that nationality categories are still performed, 'tuned', and inflated before ethnographers and state managers in a manner which suggests the relational strategies of the recent past. This nested relationship between ethnographers, state managers, *tundroviki* and ultimately tundra is closer to an ecological interrelationship than a set of classificatory divisions. If one must use a cybernetic metaphor, then identity seems to be rooted in a cybernetic relationship closer to that identified by Bateson (1972) than in a digital series of binary relationships. The tragedy of this account is that this intricate relationship, like many ecological relationships, could not withstand radical change in each of its three component elements simultaneously. The elimination of salaries and benefits attached to *kollektivy*, while simultaneously attempting to parcel out the tundra into private territories, led to an unfortunate attempt to draw attention to civic entitlements through the strategy of national inflation.

If the nationalist sentiment is rooted in contexts broader than both the categories and the categorizers, is there then any need for a single term to describe this interrelationship? Eriksen (1993), Banks (1996), and Barth (1994) defend a highly abstract concept of ethnicity to capture an expanding corpus of work examining chauvinistic relationships between people. Although it would be possible to render the large catalogue of terms used to classify people on the Khantaika as instances of 'ethnicity' (and then to explain what is really meant), this term distracts from the primary responsibility of an anthropologist to convey the local view. The category of 'ethnicity', which evokes a rather controversial literature, is doubly damned in the Russian north since it is understood as demeaning by representatives of the sparse peoples, as yet another attempt to make them even more diminutive [*etnicheskaia gruppa, etnichnost'*]. Although identity on the Khantaika is not usually described, but rather indicated practically, there is one important paradigm in everyday speech which does appear often: the evocative idea of 'belonging'.

The word 'belonging' has an ambiguous meaning in English perhaps second only to the idea of 'being'. In terms of specifying the relationship between a state ethnographer and her or his subjects, the term does not immediately suggest the direction in which authority flows. A herder can feel he 'belongs' to a certain nationality as much as a village secretary can decide that a 16-year-old girl 'belongs' to the Evenkis. The term has the strong advantage of coming closest to the way that identity is expressed on the Khantaika through possessive particles and possessive endings. In both Evenki and in the vernacular use of Russian there is a remarkable lack of abstract nouns for affixing relationships. Instead people prefer possessive pronouns [*nash* 'ours', *mende* 'mine'], adjectival forms of proper names indicating possession [*Vovanyi* 'Vova's', *Ustin gora* 'Ustin's mountain', *brigadny* 'brigade's], or Evenki possessive suffixes [*Oron nunganngiin bihin* 'Reindeer | he-<u>his</u> | is'], all of which translate clumsily into English. Thus, the term 'belonging', as used in this study, represents this subtle mix of possessive attributes which signal the relationship between a person and other people or a person and the land.

The idea of 'belonging' has also been used by two anthropologists in order to link interpretative and structuralist traditions in the study of community (Cohen 1982; 1985) and the analysis of citizenship within a social interaction paradigm (Borneman 1992). This ethnography also bridges the divide between official and vernacular identities by examining how people have been 'placed' [*ustroeny*] within territories or professions or 'registered' [*zaregistrirovany*] by nationality. I see these procedures as offering people bounded, authorized identities which they then take and hold (as one 'holds' a passport or 'holds down' a job). Thus, unlike both Borneman and Cohen, I have used the term belonging in its possessive mood rather than in the negotiated senses of 'constituting a meaningful subject' (Borneman 1992: 30) or as an 'awareness' of shared language, knowledge, or solidarity when 'standing at [a culture's] boundaries' (Cohen 1982: 3, 6). Instead of appealing to the language of Frederik Barth (1969) and Erving Goffman (1967) on how the self comes to freely discover and negotiate salient boundaries through interaction with others, I see identities to be pre-selected by administrative agents, although people do then use these identities in creative and often unexpected ways. In Hobsbawm's words, the territorial citizen-state provides 'an institutional or procedural landscape which . . . is the setting for [its inhabitants'] lives, which it largely determines' (1990: 86).

The category of 'belonging' is also appropriate in the sense that it evokes an idiom of interrelationship and reciprocity which is increasingly evident in aboriginal representations of identity. Evenkis tend not to use the language of rights when making claims on social actors but rather the language of 'feeding' and of 'taking'. By feeding the tundra, as with feeding kinsmen (or even bureaucrats), one cultivates a particular relationship with land or with people. 'Taking' implies putting reasonable claims on relationships; for one should not 'take' unless one holds the knowledge to use that object or opportunity properly. The sentient ecology of people and tundra cannot be imagined without the exchange of entitlements. Although entitlements can be glossed as 'rights', the way one becomes entitled is not through passive membership of a lineage or a state farm but through appropriate, sensitive action. As such, the ecology of entitlements evokes a civic metaphor more than a metaphor connected with contracts. In this sense the ambiguity in the word 'belonging' allows us to access levels other than contractual bonds in the relationship between people.

As Hobsbawm (1990: 86–90) identifies in his analysis of the nationalist sentiment, the political unit (which he happens to term a state) generates a notion of 'our own' which he terms the *patrie*. He notes that this notion seems so appropriate and natural that often the word nationality is used interchangeably with citizenship. If we adapt this thought to the case at hand where the segmentary nature of Soviet state-building has created a social space with many quasi-autonomous fragments, the idea of *patrie* nicely describes allegiances to *kollektiv*, territory or to nationality. The category of 'one's own' so evident in Evenki discourse points directly to what might be identified to be a civic entitlement within a North Atlantic metaphor. Here, and in another work, I have made the strong argument that the Soviet-era distinction between citizenship [*grazhdanstvo*] and nationality [*natsional' nost'*] should be taken seriously (Anderson 1996*b*). In an early and prescient study, d'Encausse (1978: ch. 6) also demonstrated that the citizenship complex in the former Soviet Union consolidated and created some peoples as much as it disorganized others to produce *apatrides*. Thus, in this state, and perhaps in others, citizenship is a binomial relation which is incomplete without a declared and duly authorized nationality. The anxiety over the power of the state to dissolve nationalities in the lower Yenisei valley was shown to encourage the possessive sense of belonging to this binomial category.

Without an understanding of the double-edged 'civic nationalism' of the former Soviet Union (Smith 1992: 61), the upsurge in nationalist sentiment indeed appears to be irrational or a product of a 'failed modernization' (Lane 1992; Cohen & Arato 1992: 621 n.; Hutchinson 1994: ch. 4; Barner-Barry & Howdy 1995: ch. 4). The analysis of the nationalist sentiment as civic nationalism also contributes to the debate on the 'creative' side of an imagined community (B. Anderson 1991: 6; Benthall & Knight 1993) while limiting the cynicism which is rife in exposés of identities as being merely invented (Friedman 1992). Furthermore, it explains away some of the puzzlement of Cold War analysts who had expected the unified political space of the former Soviet Union to generate its own homogeneous Soviet or Russian identity (Szporluk 1990; Young 1992: 87–9; Anderson & Silver 1983; Suny 1993: ch. 1, 124–31). Those two scholars who were clever enough or fortunate enough to 'predict' the rise of national rivalry in the former Soviet Union today emphasize the primacy of the ethnic or national relation over that of class (d'Encausse 1995; Moynihan 1993). Apart from a counter-revolutionary tendency to now purge class identities in this literature, the primacy of 'ethnicity' is defended by examples of loyalty to concrete places and concrete groups; a relationship which might be better styled as a sense of civic belonging.

The subtle relationship of belonging in these cases seems better analysed in recent literature on various forms of aboriginal autonomy within nation-states than in the classic literature on the nation. In contexts from around the world, indigenous peoples are articulating notions of 'alliance', 'self-government', or 'ethno-nationalist-autonomy' which are remarkable for their 'ambiguity' in terms of traditional paradigms. The Mohawk political scientist Gerald Alfred (1995) writes of a 'nested' form of identity and autonomy which goes beyond a 'one-way' transfer of information and authority. Charles Hale (1994), in his subtle analysis of Miskitu resistance to Sandinista socialism, writes of the drive for an 'ethnic autonomy' designed to guarantee the respect of local practice and skill which have come to be repressed within a system of power designed solely to negate class oppression. Recent work from Australia analyses how indigenist movements manage to co-opt tools of power and authority by means of cultural symbolism in order to negotiate spaces of resistance within highly colonized settings (Beckett 1988; Trigger 1992; Bird Rose 1996).

As entitlements become eroded through continued experimentation with the market relations, one can see implicit relationships of belonging becoming more explicit. The petitions by both newcomers and Dolgans for private ownership of lands propose to remove multiplexed nuances of belonging by making ownership sharp and clear. I see this instance of understanding 'land as a belonging' as equally imagined, abstract, and potent as the imagined communities which spur people to make nationalist claims. As with the imagined communities of Benedict Anderson, the rhetoric of possessive individualism now found in some fractions of the Khantaika is rooted within the experience of particular sites and the fading memory of extensive land-use. Sociologists like d'Encausse (1978) and Suny (1993) argue that the Soviet administrative and constitutional system was rife with inequities which made the dramatic nationalist events of this decade seem like 'the revenge of the past'. This case study also confirms the presence of cleavages within what was thought to be a uniform administrative matrix. However, the nationalist sentiment for land seems instead to be based on the anxiety that in the future the weak hold that persons and *kollektivy* gained over certain territories will be loosened instead of strengthened. In this respect, the past which seeks its revenge through contemporary nationalists is not the memory of travesties against pre-Soviet understandings of tenure but the worry that the dismantling of weak yet systematic controls on appropriation will herald the arrival of an even more inequitable regime.

Wild meat and the wild market

When people in Taimyr reflect today upon a decade of reform in the way that entitlements are negotiated, the images brought forth are apocalyptic. The fact that salaries have not been paid to employees in the state farm 'Khantaiskii' for years blends with complaints about the difficulty in getting consumer goods and observations upon the weather which has seemingly become warmer, damper, and difficult to predict. *Tundroviki* observe that the yearly migration of the Taimyr population of wild deer remains fickle with the deer arriving either late, or early, or completely bypassing regions which they had frequented previously. However, the reigning mood among urban administrators in Dudinka as well as *tundroviki* in the settlements is not one of resignation but one of hunger for new opportunities. Although living in a wild market ecology is stressful, it is not without its pleasant surprises.

Among the more unexpected results of ten years of reform is the stubborn persistence of the state farm 'Khantaiskii'. The enterprise has reoriented itself from a provider of meat and figures to the Department of Agriculture to a provisioner of statistics on its enormous debts to the Federal Tax Inspection Agency. In November 1997 the enterprise had compounded debts of over 1.5 billion [old] roubles, mostly through fines placed on its operating accounts for the failure to pay taxes on its capital resources, on its payroll, and for obligatory payments into the state pension fund. The enterprise remains intact only through the diligent accounting practices of the women in the Administrative Apparatus of the farm, who on their abacuses, calculate official registers of monthly debts to the tax inspectors. The most important aspect of their job is to ensure the accounts are postmarked before the required date, thereby avoiding liquidation of the enterprise under bankruptcy laws. (The fact that the ledgers may remain in the local post office for up to three months before a postal helicopter arrives is an unimportant detail.) Herders still play a significant role in defending the enterprise. Apart from the fact that two reindeer herds, now led by Viktor and Konstantin Utukogir, literally feed the village, the tundras upon which they travel are classified as 'pastures', thus avoiding the heavy burden of a land tax. There are several difficult catches in the new mechanism of the debt-economy. The first is the fact that the enterprise could be spared *all* taxes if it could prove that 70 per cent of the employees work 'on the land' (presently only 40 per cent are so employed). But to win this privilege would mean that there would be no one to file the reports which keep the enterprise from its debts. The second, more ingenious, regulation is the fact that should the farm be able to sell a large amount of fish, meat, or fur to a wealthy buyer for cash, this cash would have to go first to extinguish the billion rouble fines levied by the Tax Inspection Agency. In a creative manoeuvre to avoid this event, the senior accountant of the farm collected petitions from all of the farm's workers as to the 'failure' of the farm to meet its payroll obligations on time. These documents were then filed with the District Procurator by the same accountant *against* her own employer. If the farm were to 'win' its legal suit against itself, the workers would win the right to be paid first before the state collection agency. Although there is much in these examples to suggest that the substantive rural economy is unravelling, they do suggest that Khantaika Evenkis and Dolgans still 'know how to take' opportunities as they present themselves.

The fact that enterprise survives legally through the diligent sating of the various state inspection agencies does not explain how people are corporally fed. Since fines are calculated on the enterprise's operating account, employees are paid in services and in commodities. The farm's most important role is in maintaining the electric power plant and the central heating plant which provision the school, nursing station, post office, and the village house of culture. Since the City of Dudinka, which reimburses the farm for heating and lighting its agencies, also has little liquid cash, it arranges for the supply of services through a 'barter-arrangement' [*vzaimnootchet*] with a vendor in Noril'sk who periodically sends food and petrol to the Khantaika in exchange for credit with the City of Dudinka for its provision of transportation to the vendor. Employees of the farm are paid in portions of spaghetti, flour, vodka, and gasoline in proportion to their unpaid wages and in relation to 'prices' set by the director of the farm. This money-less economy has worked so well that this debtor enterprise was able to raise its 'salaries' by 15 per cent in 1998.

Although producers on the Khantaika, as in every settlement in Taimyr, live amongst large populations of 'wild' fish and venison which can enter into the market economy essentially 'free', one of the enduring ironies of the market transition is that the large urban population in Dudinka and Noril'sk is almost entirely fed on imported food. In Soviet times, a small part of the consumption needs of these cities was met with processed reindeer sausage from the native herders, wild deer meat culled during machine-gun harvests along the Piasina river, and various forms of canned and fresh fish harvested by local fishermen. Since the reforms, it has become more cost-effective to import lamb from New Zealand, chicken from the United States, and beef and sausage from Holland and Belgium (some of which was rumoured to be purchased at a discount from the United Kingdom). Distributors in the city of Noril'sk complain about the 'cost' of local production, by which they refer to the various licences, taxes, and payments to pension and employment insurance funds which must be paid to the state in order that they may be able to compensate local hunters or fishermen. Foreign meat comes into the economy without civic encumbrances. More perversely, local meat is not subject to a 'reasonable' profit margin, by which is meant a profit margin of between 150 per cent and 300 per cent. According to the Director of Provisions for the Noril'sk Factory, in 1997 it was possible using existing capital resources to process and sell up to 500 tonnes (10,000 head) of wild deer meat a year at a profit margin of 50 per cent. It was an idea that he was entertaining, since by making an application to the thin list of subsidies still available for aboriginal peoples by the Federal Committee of the North, he might be able to be reimbursed for the cost of the freight helicopters (which contributed to almost one half the cost of the meat).[4] He felt that if he could convince local producers to take a lower price in exchange for the free transport of goods (most likely vodka), the profit margin could be raised to 200 per cent. Nevertheless, this was far less than could be earned in other sectors of the 'wild' market.

The above example is just one of may examples of what is known variously as 'Russian *biznes* [business]' or 'wild capitalism'. The referent is simultaneously to Marx and Hobbes to describe the lack of order in the early days of 'primitive accumulation'. However, any ethnographic analysis of the actors involved in this wild sphere of commodity transactions immediately reveals a space populated by a variety of interest groups all trying to protect 'their own'. Rather than national identity, Russian merchants speak frequently of endogamous 'mafias' which often use the threat of violence to

[4] The rough figures for this example were the following: Assuming that raw wild deer meat could be sold in large quantities in Noril'sk markets at 18,000 [old] roubles per kg., at present prices the profit margin would be 6,000 roubles per kg. after covering costs of 6,250 r/kg. in helicopter time and 6,000 r/kg. in payment to Evenki and Dolgan hunters (helicopter time costs 8 million roubles per hour × 3 hours at a load of 4 tonnes). The director hoped to reduce the 6,000 r/kg. payment to the hunters and to have the helicopter time covered by the state.

protect exclusive access to lucrative markets. Within the regional economy of Taimyr, such as with the director of this Noril'sk enterprise, nationally defined indigenous people are perceived as one of many mafias who are trying to sell their powerlessness and exoticness in a market place over-populated with competing vendors. To return to the example of marketing wild meat, upon my suggestion that a Noril'sk meat-processing plant could appeal to international agencies which provide development assistance for indigenous peoples, the answer of the director was a hungry and enthusiastic offer of collaboration.

To this end, the best wild product that indigenous peoples control today is the image of 'wildness' itself. Among the most influential international capital providers of the region, apart from the Muscovite banks struggling for control of the Noril'sk Factory, is the World Wide Fund for Nature. Since 1993, this internationally funded agency has been increasingly interested in supporting and subsidizing institutions for the protection of pristine spaces (and the peoples who live in harmony with them). According to one public document published in 1993, the Taimyr is the homeland of the last free-ranging wild deer herd in Eurasia and thus should be the site of an internationally funded protected space for the preservation of this majestic population (WWF 1993). The fact that this chaotically exploding deer population is as much the product of the construction of parks and other exclusive spaces as it is a beneficiary of them is a point absent in this literature. Indigenous hunters have now been co-opted in plans for a 'bio-sphere reserve' where hunters will provide quaint insights on the place of people in the natural order and highly paid technicians will manage and monitor their former homelands (Klokov 1991; Syroechkovskii *et al.* 1994). According to recent information, the 'Big Arctic Nature Reserve', officially opened by Prince Philip in 1995, which is the first link in a chain of protected spaces on Taimyr, has been the subject of allegations of money-laundering in the Russian Press (Ustiugov 1997).

The final lever that indigenous political associations can use is the threat to use ecosystemic arguments to limit or eliminate industrial production altogether. As multinational corporations circle around the mining combine in Noril'sk, there will be a nervous interest among their agents that aboriginal claims to ore-bearing lands be clearly extinguished lest they encounter resist-ance of the type which has disrupted production in northern Canada or in Brazil. To this end, there has been a growing public consciousness of the international impact of heavy metal pollutants originating from the Noril'sk factory. Trace elements of these poisons have been identified in the breast milk of Inuit mothers in Canada (Arctic 1997; Jensen *et al.* 1997). Furthermore, there is an ironic (but unproven) allegation that this 'largest polluter in the world' is also one of the world's largest provisioners of platinum for use in ecologically purifying catalytic converters in automobiles (Taiga 1996).

The idea of selling indigenous interests in an international market place seems to be part of an expanding industry in the commodification of indigenous knowledge (Escobar 1996). This has been a strategy used to some success by Siberian intellectuals from a point of time preceding the market reforms through to recent appeals to international agreements for the protection of 'aboriginal rights' (IWGIA 1990; Kriazhkov 1994: ch. 5; Pika & Prokhorov 1994). The lineage of this strategy may be even older. Arguably, the structure of Soviet Siberian development policy itself was shaped by a Cold War competition over which bloc could best treat the indigenes. The modern rhetoric of building 'nature reserves' may be a clear and similarly contradictory cognate to the original Soviet policy of creating 'national reserves' for indigenous people in the 1930s. The appeal to indigenous knowledge and aboriginal rights may today represent the best fit to the nationalist sentiment appearing in native villages. The various vectors of belonging on the Khantaika lead to the unambiguous conclusion that demographically 'sparse' Evenkis and Dolgans deserve to be better treated *as peoples*. Since appeals to the ladder of culture within the former Soviet order are no longer effective, moral appeals to the international community on the basis of an endangered demography or an endangered ecology may present the next best opportunity to advertise their sense of entitlement. This potential transformation of the nationalist sentiment into a consciousness of an 'aboriginal right' may in a formal sense represent the 'exiting' of nationalism from the political landscape of the lower Yenisei valley, as Hobsbawm (1990) controversially suggests. However, it does not represent a very discreet exit, for it will always have one leg firmly planted in various ideas of belonging to a 'community of producers', a territory, and a nationality.

Unfortunately, although I can trace the meaning and the history of three senses of belonging on Taimyr, I cannot say with the same confidence that it is possible to alter the very clear preference for circulating authorized identities which has been evident over three generations on the Khantaika. I have been asked by some to decide if there is any future for Evenkis as a great nation. After a decade of study I can see no other viable path for self-conscious Evenkis than to encourage the type of knowing perfected by the *tundrovik*: the ability to make a home anywhere without relying on prefabricated structures or practices. In this book I have shown that the ideas of territories, nationalities, and *kollektivy* which now form the essence of Evenki national identity were indeed prefabricated in order to receive intelligence on the activities of people so as to support a peculiar system of social power. This system may have eliminated hunger and given each nationality and *kollektiv* a place in a complex industrial economy. It may also have given them very sophisticated organizational skills which now allow them to market their disempowerment to taxation agencies and international ecological conglomerates. However, these same skills have also set people on divergent trajectories which threaten the reproduction of those very skills and markers that these institutions were designed to support. Exclusive territories and bounded nationalities may still prove useful when negotiating the market relationship which is notoriously unforgiving of collective rights. However, the strength of the accumulated knowledge in this community is in the fostering of alliances between Russians, Dolgans, Evenkis, and eventually other circumpolar peoples. These alliances seem to be the most reliable way to take knowledge and to define common interests before a globalized yet parochial industrial economy.

Departure

In contrast to the ravaging blizzards of the winter, late August on the Khantaika was ominously calm. In autumn, the sun begins to disappear behind Treasure Chest [*sunduk*] Mountain just after midnight only to rise again after only an hour of dusk, casting the waters of the lake in hundreds of shades of orange and red. Transfixed by the deep colours pervading the silent settlement, I once praised the beauty of this place to my elderly neighbour Pana Khutukagir'. She was not so naively entranced as me by the lake's sleepy mood. It was below the still surfaces of these waters on a long summer night such as this one that her husband and child disappeared inexplicably from their boat while crossing to the opposite shore. 'It is a bad lake,' I was assured. This sad memory provoked another as she recalled her grief-stricken pilgrimage as a widow back to Chirinda, Evenkiia, to spend a few months with her cousins. Her kin gave her a puzzled reception since the only common language between them was Russian. Pana, who was born in the Evenki Autonomous District, was taken at an early age to grow up and marry into a Mountain Evenki lineage. Thus she spoke Yakut and Russian, but no longer understood her 'native' language. Pana explained to me that she still registers herself as *evenka* but she added with some sadness, 'I guess I've become Dolgan now since I can't speak with my relatives'. Her melancholic words were lost to pervasive silence of that autumn night.

August of 1993 was a particularly quiet month in the Khantaika. Due to yet another financial crisis in the farm, the diesel generator had ceased to power the televisions and cookers in the crowded flats. Many families had chosen to live out in the fish camps preparing nets for the hectic fishing period in September. Those who remained in the village gathered on door-steps to smoke, enjoy the freedom of a warm night without mosquitoes, or to cook on small open fires between the houses. I had joined these small groups to drink tea and to tell stories—at times forgetting my imminent departure. When there is no electricity in the settlement it is next to impossible to receive information on the mysterious plans of helicopter pilots. Like many travellers in this part of Siberia I accepted that a helicopter would arrive when I was fated to leave. In my field notes for that month I mused that I could now understand why the Yenisei Evenkis divided their annual calendar into two separate years. Experiencing a soft, warm summer after a windy, violent winter makes it seem as if you have lived two lives.

It would not be long before the siren's peace of the lake was shattered by the thunder of two helicopters from the city. The first arrived to remove a weak and burnt young child to the district hospital in Noril′sk. The second landed with a fire inspector charged with examining the burnt remains of two other children and their father who had perished in an early morning blaze. This house was shared by two families, although tragedy only struck one.

The official report said that the fire was caused by the husband, who in a drunken state attempted to fry meat on a propane cooker. He may have dozed off, or the frying-pan may have tipped over. The brittle timbers of the house caught fire instantly. In the half-hour that it took to burn to the ground, leaving only the brick chimney standing, the frightened children hid themselves under a bed. The bed was on one side of a wall. On the other side, a panicked family was frantically removing its possessions. Although the neighbours were calm and collected enough to wake all of their relatives to help remove their belongings before the flames reached their side of the house, no one had thought of helping the other family.

This tragedy was doubly suffered within the community. Although there are many deaths along the shores of this lake in all seasons, this was the first time that anyone could recall that people had *burned*. More significantly, the family that perished was Evenki while the one that survived, almost unscathed, was Dolgan.

Ritually, it was difficult to appease the grief of these deaths. The mother and wife of the victims, whether for better or for worse, was in Dudinka in the maternity hospital awaiting the birth of her fourth child. It was she who should have organized the wake—a task that was performed by her sister. The local rites demanded that the bodies be buried within five days wearing new clothes. However, the corporal remains left on this earth were few—and what remained were under police control. One old woman proudly devised a silk hat in which to wrap the man's skull. The children's remains were wrapped in new blankets. Following the burial, the relatives were to bring the personal belongings of each person to the grave site to be placed, broken, beside the cross. However, this family also had no remaining possessions to accompany them to the Upper World. Another woman decided that it would be best to affix a photograph on the cross. Every day the state farm operator patiently sat by the weak radio demanding to know when the authorities would arrive by helicopter to let the community bury the dead.

It was also difficult to make sense of this tragedy. The models which were suggested also reflected on the fragmented state of the settlement. Some Khantaika Evenkis recalled hearing a shaman's prophecy on television that when outsiders arrive in a community the local people slowly die out. Some of the more suspicious residents recalled that the matriarch of the Dolgan household had some Nia forebears. They accused her of using the dark powers of this mysterious people to curse the perished family for refusing to relinquish their side of the house. Others, more traditionally, recalled that the Evenki family should not have moved back into the same flat where they had lived some years before. It is considered to be a 'sin' to return to the same place where you once lived.

The helicopter that was fated for me arrived three days later. Without touching the ground, let alone stopping to speak to the people at the platform, the pilots deposited the fire inspector and immediately took off once again. The stern officer conducted his investigation and gave the death warrants to the head of the settlement administration. It was unclear where the pilots had taken the aircraft in such a rush, but the machine returned five hours later. This time there was an even greater crowd at the helicopter platform. Some had gathered to see me off. Others had hoped to travel to see a doctor or meet relatives in the city. Still others were looking for alcohol. Once again the pilots brought the machine barely to the ground, letting the rotors and turbines spin just below full force. The fireman pushed his way to the front of the crowd and clambered on board while the navigator attempted to slam the doors on all those scrambling to get in. 'No fuel!' he shouted, 'Get away!' It was all I could do to scream above the rotors that indeed I was a foreigner and that I needed to leave. After three attempts at dispelling his disbelief, the navigator pulled me in and decisively slammed the door. The huge machine fired up its motors, flinging dust into the eyes of those seeing me off. That was my last sight of the Khantaika.

As we flew over the settlement and along the lakeshore, I was puzzled at the collection of conspiratorial faces peering out at me from behind the supplementary fuel tanks. I was instructed to take a seat previously occupied with fly-fishing equipment. It was soon clear why this official flight was so short of fuel. Overloaded with one officer, one ethnographer, and eleven holiday fishermen, the pilots landed the helicopter three times at eddies along remote tundra streams so that these official holidaymakers could try their luck for grayling. I did not have the heart to fish, although I was offered a rod. Instead, I threw a coin at each site so that these new lands would be pleasantly disposed to me.

Appendix: Genealogical Charts

Legend for Charts 1 through 4

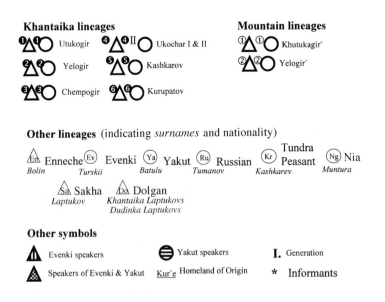

Khantaika lineages

❶△❶○ Utukogir   ❹△❹II○ Ukochar I & II

❷△❷○ Yelogir   ❺△❺○ Kashkarov

❸△❸○ Chempogir   ❻△❻○ Kurupatov

Mountain lineages

①△①○ Khutukagir`

②△②○ Yelogir`

Other lineages (indicating *surnames* and nationality)

⟨En⟩ Enneche   ⟨Ev⟩ Evenki   ⟨Ya⟩ Yakut   ⟨Ru⟩ Russian   ⟨Kr⟩ Tundra Peasant   ⟨Ng⟩ Nia
Bolin   *Turskii*   *Batulu*   *Tumanov*   *Kashkarev*   *Muntura*

⟨Sa⟩ Sakha   ⟨Do⟩ Dolgan
Laptukov   *Khantaika Laptukovs*
             Dudinka Laptukovs

Other symbols

△ Evenki speakers   ⊜ Yakut speakers   **I.** Generation

▲ Speakers of Evenki & Yakut   Kur`e Homeland of Origin   * Informants

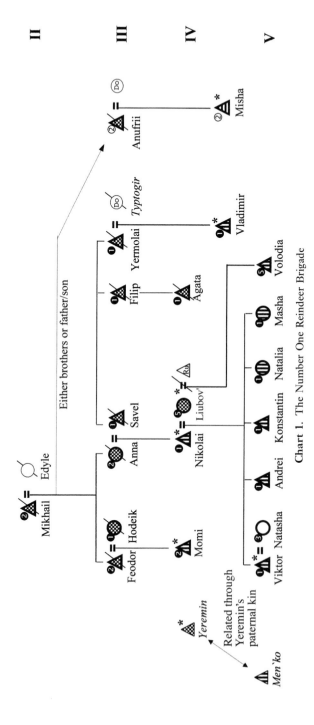

Chart 1. The Number One Reindeer Brigade

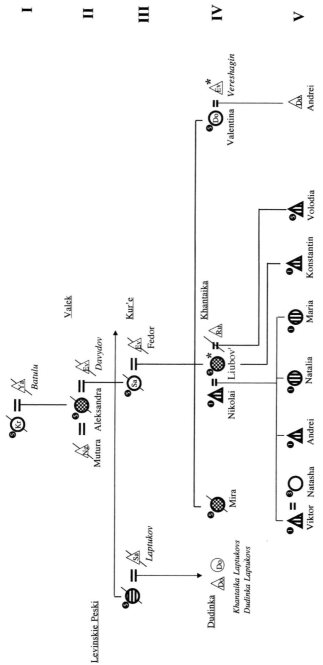

Chart 2. The extensive kinship of the Kashkarevs

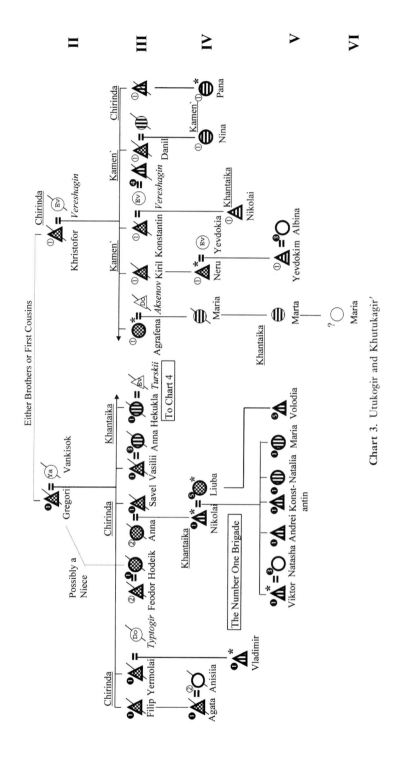

Chart 3. Utukogir' and Khutukagir'

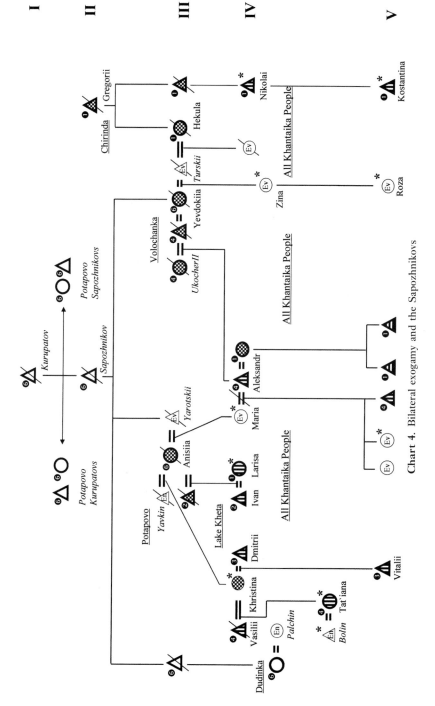

Chart 4. Bilateral exogamy and the Sapozhnikovs

REFERENCES

PUBLISHED SOURCES

ABEL, KERRY (1993). *Drum Songs: Glimpses of Dene History.* Montreal: McGill-Queen's University Press.

AFANAS'EVA, G. M. (1990). *Traditsionnaia sistema vosproizvodstva nganasan (problemy reproduktsii obosoblennykh populiatsii).* Moscow: Institut etnologii i antropologii AN SSSR.

ALEKSEEV, A. A. (1993). *Zabytyi mir predkov (Ocherki traditsionnogo mirovozzreniia evenov Severo-zapadnogo Verkhoian'ia).* Yakutsk: Sitim.

ALFRED, G. R. (1995). *Heeding the Voices of Our Ancestors: Kahnewake Mohawk Politics and the Rise of Native Nationalism.* Toronto: Oxford University Press.

ALIA, V. (1994). *Names, Numbers, and Northern Policy: Inuit, Project Surname, and the Politics of Identity.* Nova Scotia: Fernwood.

ANDERSON, B. (1991). *Imagined Communities: Reflections on the Origin and Spread of Nationalism*, rev. edn. London: Verso.

ANDERSON, B. A. and SILVER, B. D. (1983). Estimating Russification of Ethnic Identity Among Non-Russians in the USSR. *Demography* 20: 461–90.

ANDERSON, D. DZH. (1998). *Tundroviki: ekologiia i samosoznanie Taimyrskikh evenkov i dolgan.* Novosibirsk: Izd-vo Sibirskogo otdeleniia Rossiiskoi akademii nauk.

ANDERSON, D. G. (1991). Turning Hunters into Herders: A Critical Examination of Soviet Development Policy Among the Evenki of Southeastern Siberia. *Arctic* 44, no. 1: 12–22.

—— (1994). The Novosibirsk Stock Market Boom: Privatization and Accumulation in Russia. *Anthropology Today* 10, no. 4: 10–16.

—— (1995). Hunters, Herders, and Heavy Metals in Arctic Siberia. *Cambridge Anthropology* 18, no. 2: 35–46.

—— (1996*a*). National Identity and Belonging in Arctic Siberia: An Ethnography of Evenkis and Dolgans at Khantaiskoe Ozero, Taimyr Autonomous District. Unpublished Ph.D. dissertation, Department of Social Anthropology: University of Cambridge (UMI 9708211).

—— (1996*b*). The Aboriginal Peoples of the Lower Yenisei Valley: An Ethnographic Overview of Recent Political Developments in North Central Siberia. *Polar Geography and Geology* 19, no. 3: 184–218.

—— (1996*c*). Bringing Civil Society to an Uncivilized Place: Citizenship Regimes in Russia's Arctic Frontier, in C. M. Hann and E. Dunn (eds.), *Civil Society: Approaches from Anthropology*, 99–120. London: Routledge.

—— (1997). Intelligence Gathering and Possessive Performances on Evenki Lands in Arctic Siberia, in C. M. Hann (ed.), *Property Relations*, 64–84. Cambridge: Cambridge University Press.

ANISIMOV, A. F. (1936). *Rodovoe obshchestvo evenkov.* Leningrad: Izd-vo Instituta narodov Severa.

ARCTIC MONITORING AND ASSESSMENT PROGRAMME (1997). *Arctic Pollution Issues: A State of the Arctic Environment Report.* Oslo: AMAP.

ARMSTRONG, J. A. (1982). *Nations Before Nationalism*. N. Carolina: University of North Carolina Press.

—— (1992). The Autonomy of Ethnic Identity: Historical Cleavages and Nationality Relations in the U.S.S.R., in A. J. Motyl (ed.), *Thinking Theoretically about Soviet Nationalities: History and Comparison in the Study of the USSR* , 23–44. Oxford: Columbia University Press.

ASCH, M. (1984). *Home and Native Land: Aboriginal Rights and the Canadian Constitution*. New York: Methuen.

BAKHRUSHIN, S. B. (1955). Yasak v Sibiri, in A. A. Zimin (ed.), *S.B. Bakhrushin: Nauchnye trudy*, tom 3, chast' 2: 49–85. Moscow: Izd-vo Akademii nauk.

BAKHTIN, M. M. (1981). *The Dialogical Imagination*. Austin: University of Texas Press.

BALZER, M. M. (1983). Ethnicity Without Power: The Siberian Khanty in Soviet Society. *Slavic Review* 42, no. 4: 633–48.

BANKS, M. (1996). *Ethnicity: An Anthropological Construction*. New York: Routledge.

BARNER-BARRY, C. and HOWDY, C. (1995). *The Politics of Change: The Transformation of the Former Soviet Union*. New York: St Martin's.

BARTH, F. (1969). *Ethnic Groups and Boundaries: The Social Organization of Cultural Difference*. Boston: Little, Brown & Co.

—— (1994). Enduring and emerging issues in the analysis of ethnicity, in H. Vermeulen and C. Govers (eds.), *'Ethnic Groups and Boundaries'*. Amsterdam: Het Spinhuis.

BASKIN, LEONID M. (1970). *Severnyi olen': ekologiia i povedeniie*. Moscow: Nauka.

—— (1984). The Behaviour of Wild Reindeer as a Basis for Game Management, in E. E. Syroechkovskii (ed.), *Wild Reindeer of the Soviet Union*, 260–6. New Delhi: Amerind Publishing Co.

BASSO, K. H. (1984). 'Stalking With Stories': Names, Places, and Moral Narratives Among the Western Apache, in E. Bruner (ed.), *Text, Play and Story: The Construction and Reconstruction of Self and Society*, 19–55. 1984 Proceedings of the American Ethnological Society, Washington.

BATESON, G. (1972). *Steps to an Ecology of Mind: Collected Essays in Anthropology, Psychiatry, Evolution, and Epistemology*. London: Intertext Books.

BECKETT, J. (1988). The Past in the Present: The Present in the Past: Constructing a National Identity, in J. Beckett (ed.), *Past and Present: The Construction of Aboriginality*, 190–209. Canberra: Aboriginal Studies Press.

BENTHALL, J. and KNIGHT, J. (1993). Ethnic Alleys and Avenues. *Anthropology Today* 9, no. 5: 1–2.

BEREZOVSKII, A. I. (1930). Kak ratsionalizirovat' rybnoe khoziaistvo Turukhanskogo kraiia, in *Sovetskii Sever: Sbornik statei*, vyp. 2: 71–160.

BIRD-DAVID, N. (1990). The Giving Environment: Another Perspective on the Economic System of Gatherer-Hunters. *Current Anthropology* 31: 189–96.

BIRD ROSE, D. (1996). Histories and Rituals: Land Claims in the Territory, in B. Atwood (ed.), *In the Age of Mabo: History, Aborigines and Australia*, 35–53. Sydney: Allen & Unwin.

BLOCH, ALEXIA (1996). Between Socialism and the Market: Indigenous Siberian

Evenki Grapple with Change. Unpublished Ph.D. dissertation, University of Pittsburgh (UMI 9728658).

BOGORAZ-TAN, V. G. (1923). Ob izuchenii i okhrane okrainnykh narodov. *Zhizn' natsional'nostei*, kn. 3–4: 168–77.

—— (1925). Podgotovitel'nye mery k organizatsii malykh narodnostei. *Severnaia Aziia*, no. 3: 40–50.

—— (1933). Olenevodstvo. Vozniknovenie, razvitie, perspektivy, in *Problemy prois-khozhdeniia domashnikh zhivotnykh*, 219–251. Trudy laboratorii genetiki, vyp. 1. Leningrad: Tip. Akademii Nauk.

BOLDYREV, V. G. and GIRINOVICH, P. A. (1926). *Raionirovanaia Sibiri*. Novoniko-laevsk: Sibkraiizdat.

BORNEMAN, J. (1992). *Belonging in Two Berlins: Kin, State, Nation*. Cambridge: Cambridge University Press.

BOURDIEU, P. (1976). Marriage Strategies As Strategies of Social Reproduction, in E. Forster and P. Ranum (eds.), *Family and Society: Selections From the Annales*, 117–45. London: Johns Hopkins University Press.

—— (1984). *Distinction: A Social Critique of the Judgement of Taste*. London: Routledge & Kegan Paul.

—— (1990). *The Logic of Practice*. Cambridge: Polity.

BREMMER, I. (1993). Reassessing Soviet Nationalities Theory, in I. Bremmer and R. Taras (eds.), *Nations and Politics in the Soviet Successor States*, 3–26. Cambridge: Cambridge University Press.

BRIGGS, J. L. (1983). Le Modèle traditionnel d'Éducation chez les Inuit: Différentes formes d'Expérimentation face à l'inconnu. *Recherches Amérindiennes au Québec* 13, no. 1: 13–25.

BRIGHTMAN, R. (1993). *Grateful Prey: Rock Cree Animal–Human Relationships*. Berkeley: University of California Press.

BROMLEI, Yu. V. (1969). Etnos i endogamiia. *Sovetskaia etnografiia*, no. 6: 84–91.

—— (1983). *Ocherki teorii etnosa*. Moscow: Nauka.

BROWN, JENNIFER S. H. (1980). *Strangers in Blood: Fur Trade Company Families in Indian Country*. Vancouver: University of British Columbia Press.

BROWN, W. K. *et al.* (1986). The Distribution and Movement Patterns of Four Woodland Caribou Herds in Quebec and Labrador, in *Proceedings of the Fourth International Caribou and Reindeer Symposium, Whitehorse, Canada*. ed. A. Gunn, F. L. Millar, and S. Skjenneberg, 43–9. Rangifer Special Issue, 1.

BULAG, URADYN ERDEN (1993). Nationalism and Identity in Mongolia. Unpublished Ph.D. dissertation, Department of Social Anthropology: University of Cambridge.

BURCH, E. S. Jr. (1975). *Eskimo Kinsmen: Changing Family Relationship in Northwest Alaska*. New York: West Publishing Co.

—— (1991). Herd Following Reconsidered. *Current Anthropology* 32, no. 4: 439–44.

BYKOV, K. M. and SLONIM, A. D. (1960). *Issledovaniia slozhnoreflektornoi deiatel'nosti zhivotnykh i cheloveka v yestestvennykh usloviiakh*. Moscow and Leningrad: Izd-vo Akademii Nauk.

CAMERON, R. D., WHITTEN, K. R., and SMITH, W. T. (1986). Summer Range Fidelity of Radio-Collared Caribou in Alaska's Central Arctic Herd, in *Proceedings of the*

Fourth International Caribou and Reindeer Symposium, Whitehorse, Canada. ed. A. Gunn, F. L. Millar, and S. Skjenneberg, 51–5. Rangifer Special Issue, 1.

CERNEA, M. and GUGGENHEIM, S. (1993). *Anthropological Approaches to Resettlement: Policy, Practice and Theory.* Boulder, Colo.: Westview Press.

CHAMPAGNE, DUANE (1989). *American Indian Societies: Strategies and Conditions of Political and Cultural Survival.* Cambridge, Mass.: Survival International.

CHERKANOVSKII, A. L. (1876). Dopolnitel'nye svedeniia k karte reki Nizhnei Tunguski. *Izvestiia Imperatorskogo Russkogo Geograficheskogo Obshchestva,* tom 12, vyp. 5: 403–15.

CHESNAIS, J.-C. (1992). *The Demographic Transition.* Oxford: Clarendon Press.

CHICHLO, B. (1981). Les Nevuqaghmiit ou la fin d'une ethnie. *Inuit Studies* 5, no. 2: 29–47.

COHEN, A. (1982). *Belonging: Identity and Social Organization in British Rural Cultures.* Manchester: Manchester University Press.

—— (1985). *The Symbolic Construction of Community.* London: Routledge.

—— (1986). *Symbolizing Boundaries: Identity and Diversity in British Cultures.* Manchester: Manchester University Press.

COHEN, J. and ARATO, A. (1992). *Civil Society and Political Theory.* Cambridge, Mass.: MIT Press.

COLLINS, D. N. and URRY, J. (1997). A Flame Too Intense for Mortal Body to Support. *Anthropology Today* 13: 18–20.

Cruikshank, Julie (1998). Yukon Arcadia: Oral Tradition, Indigenous Knowledge, and the Fragmentation of Meaning, in Julie Cruikshank (ed.), *The Social Life of Stories,* 45–70. Vancouver: UBC Press.

CZAPLICKA, M. A. (1914). *Aboriginal Siberia.* Oxford: Clarendon.

—— (1917). On the Track of the Tungus. *Scottish Geographical Magazine* 33, no. 7: 289–303.

DAVIES, MAUREEN (1985). Aspects of Aboriginal Rights in International Law, in B. Morse (ed.), *Aboriginal Peoples and the Law: Indian, Metis and Inuit Rights in Canada.* Ottawa: Carleton University Press.

D'ENCAUSSE, H. C. (1978). *L'Empire éclaté: La Révolte des Nations en URSS.* Paris: Flammarion.

—— (1995). *The Nationality Question in the Soviet Union and Russia.* Oslo: Scandinavian University Press.

DOBROVA-YADRINTSEVA, L. N. (1925). *Tuzemtsy Turukhanskogo kraia.* Novonikolaevsk: Sibrevkom.

DOLGIKH, B. O. (1929). Naselenie poluostrova Taimyr i prilegaiushchego k nemu raiona. *Severnaia Aziia,* no. 2: 49–76.

—— (1949). Rodovoi i plemennoi sostav narodnostei severa srednei Sibiri. *Kratkie soobshcheniia instituta etnografii,* no. 5 (1): 70–85.

—— (1950). K voprosu o naselenii basseina Oleneka i verkhov'ev Anabary. *Sovetskaia etnografiia,* no. 4: 169–73.

—— (1952a). O naselenii basseinov rek Oleneka i Anabary. *Sovetskaia etnografiia,* no. 2: 86–91.

—— (1952b). O nekotorykh etnogeneticheskikh protsessakh (pereseleniiakh narodov i rasprostranenii yazykov) v Severnoi Sibiri. *Sovetskaia etnografiia,* no. 1: 51–9.

DOLGIKH, B. O. (1960). *Rodovoi i plemennoi sostav narodov Sibiri v XVII veke*. Trudy Instituta etnografii AN SSSR, NS tom 60. Moscow: Nauka.

—— (1963). Proiskhozhdenie dolgan, in B. O. Dolgikh (ed.), *Sibirskii etnograficheskii sbornik*, tom 5: 92–141. Trudy Instituta etnografii AN SSSR, NS tom 84. Moscow: Nauka.

—— (1993*a*). Naselenie raionov Krainego Severa Krasnoiarskogo Kraia, in S. I. Vainshtein (ed.), *Polevye issledovaniia*, vyp. 2, tom 1: 122–41. Moscow: Institut antropologii i etnologii RAN.

—— (1993*b*). Nekotorye voprosy natsional'noi politiki na Severe SSSR, in S. I. Vainshtein (ed.), *Polevye issledovaniia*, vyp. 2, tom 1: 142–53. Moscow: Institut antropologii i etnologii RAN.

—— and LEVIN, M. G. (1951). Perekhod ot rodoplemennykh sviazei k territorial'nym v istorii Severnoi Sibiri, in *Rodovoe obshchestvo: etnograficheskie materialy i issledovanniia*, 95–108. Trudy Instituta etnografii im. N. N. Miklukho-Maklaia, tom 14. Moscow: Izd-vo Akademii Nauk.

DOLGIN, V. N. and ROMANOV, V. I. (1983). Ekologo-faunisticheskaia kharakteristika malakofauny Khantaikskikh ozer. *Voprosy geografii Sibiri*, vyp.14: 68–72.

DORRIS, M. (1979). Twentieth-Century Indians: The Return of the Natives, in R. Hall (ed.), *Ethnic Autonomy—Comparative Dynamics: The Americas, Europe, and the Developing World*, 66–84. New York: Pergamon Press.

EIDHEIM, H. (1969). When Ethnic Identity is a Social Stigma, in F. Barth (ed.), *Ethnic Groups and Boundaries: The Social Organization of Cultural Difference*, 39–58. Boston: Little, Brown & Co.

EINHORN, B. (1993). *Cinderella Goes to Market: Citizenship, Gender, and Women's Movements in East Central Europe*. London: Verso.

ERIKSEN, T. H. (1993). *Ethnicity and Nationalism: Anthropological Perspectives*. London: Pluto Press.

ESCOBAR, A. (1996). Constructing Nature: Elements for a Poststructural Political Ecology, in R. Peet and M. Watts (eds.), *Liberation Ecologies: Environment, Development, Social Movements*, 46–68. New York: Routledge.

EVANS-PRITCHARD, E. E. (1958). *Witchcraft, Oracles and Magic Among the Azande*. Oxford: Clarendon Press.

FEIT, H. (1994). The Enduring Pursuit: Land, Time and Social Relationships in Anthropological Models of Hunter-Gatherers and in Subarctic Hunters' Images, in E. S. Burch and L. Ellanna (eds.), *Key Issues in Hunter-Gatherer Research*, 421–40. Oxford: Berg.

FIENUP-RIORDAN, A. (1990). Original Ecologists? The Relationship Between Yup'Ik Eskimos and Animals, in A. Fienup-Riordan (ed.), *Eskimo Essays*, 167–91. New Brunswick: Rutgers University Press.

FONDAHL, G. (1993). Siberia: Native Peoples and Newcomers, in I. Bremmer and R. Taras (eds.), *Nations and Politics in the Soviet Successor States*, 477–511. Cambridge: Cambridge University Press.

—— (1996). Contested Terrain: Changing Boundaries and Identities in Southeastern Siberia. *Post-Soviet Geography and Economics* 37, no. 1: 3–15.

—— (1998). *Gaining Ground? Evenkis, Land and Reform in Southeastern Siberia*. Boston: Allyn & Bacon.

FORSYTH, J. (1992). *A History of the Peoples of Siberia: Russia's North Asian Colony 1581–1990*. New York: Cambridge University Press.

FRIEDMAN, J. (1992). The Past in the Future: History and the Politics of Identity. *American Anthropologist* 94, no. 4: 837–59.

GEERTZ, C. (1963). *Agricultural Involution: The Process of Ecological Change in Indonesia*. Berkeley: University of California Press.

GEKKER, N. L. (1898). Umiraiushchaia narodnost' (tungusy). *Zemlevedenie*, no. 3–4: 162–70.

GELLER, M. KH. and VOSTRIAKOV, P. N. (1984). Interrelations Between Wild and Domesticated Reindeer, in E. E. Syroechkovskii (ed.), *Wild Reindeer of the Soviet Union (Proceedings of the First Interdepartmental Conference on the Preservation and Rational Utilization of Wile Reindeer Resources)*, 54–9. New Delhi: Amerind Publishing Co.

GELLNER, E. (1978). Scale and Nation, in F. Barth (ed.), *Scale and Social Organization*, 133–49. Oslo: Universitetsforlaget.

—— (1983). *Nations and Nationalism*. Oxford: Basil Blackwell.

GLAZER, N. and MOYNIHAN, D. P. (1963). *Beyond the Melting-Pot*. Cambridge, Mass.: Harvard University Press.

GLUCKMAN, M. (1965). *Politics, Law, and Ritual in Tribal Society*. Oxford: Basil Blackwell.

GOFFMAN, E. (1967). *Interaction Ritual: Essays on Face-to-Face Behaviour*. New York: Doubleday.

GORDON, B. H. C. (1975). *Of Men and Herds in Barrenland Prehistory*. Archaeological Survey of Canada Paper, 28. Ottawa: National Museums of Canada.

—— (1996). *People of Sunlight: People of Starlight: Barrenland Archaeology in the Northwest Territories of Canada*. Archaeological Survey of Canada Paper, 154. Ottawa: National Museums of Canada.

GOSKOMSTAT RSFSR (1991). *Sotsial'no-demograficheskie pokazateli, kharakterizuiushchie natsional'nyi sostav naseleniia kraia*. Krasnoiarsk: Krasnoiarskoe kraevoe upravlenie statistiki.

GOW, P. (1991). *Of Mixed Blood: Kinship and History in Peruvian Amazonia*. Oxford: Clarendon Press.

GRACHEVA, G. N. (1980). Taimyrskii poselok Ust'-Avam (preobrazovaniia v khoziaistve i etnicheskie protsessy), in *Etnograficheskie aspekty izucheniia sovremennosti*, 136–52. Leningrad: Nauka.

—— (1983). Poezdka k zapadnym dolganam, in *Polevye issledovaniia instituta etnografii 1979*, 59–68. Moscow: Nauka.

GRANT, B. (1993). Siberia Hot and Cold: Reconstructing the Image of Siberian Indigenous Peoples, in D. Diment and Y. Slezkine (eds.), *Between Heaven and Hell: The Myth of Siberia*, 227–254. New York: St Martin's Press.

—— (1995). *In the Soviet House of Culture: A Century of Perestroikas*. Princeton: Princeton University Press.

GRAY, A. (1997). *Indigenous Rights and Development: Self-Determination in an Amazonian Community*. The Arakmbut of Amazonian Peru, 3. Oxford: Berghahn Books.

GUMILEV, L. N. (1993). *Drevnie t'urki*. Moscow: Klyshnikov, Komarov, i Ko.

GUMILEV, L. N. (1990). *Etnogenez i biosfera zemli.* Leningrad: Gydrometeoizdat.

GURVICH, I. S. (1950a). K voprosu ob etnicheskoi prinadlezhnosti naseleniia Severo-Zapada Yakutskoi ASSR. *Sovetskaia etnografiia,* no. 4: 150–68.

—— (1950b). Sotsialisticheskoe pereustroistvo khoziaistva i byta yakutov baseinov rek Oleneka i Anabara. *Sovetskaia etnografiia,* no. 1: 107–23.

—— (1952). Po povodu opredeleniia etnicheskoi prinadlezhnosti naseleniia baseinov rek Oleneka i Anabara. *Sovetskaia etnografiia,* no. 2: 73–85.

—— (1977). *Kul'tura severnykh yakutov-olenevodov.* Moscow: Nauka.

HAJDA, L. and BEISSINGER, M. (1990). *The Nationality Factor in Soviet Politics and Society.* Oxford: Westview.

HALE, C. R. (1994). *Resistance and Contradiction: Miskitu Indians and the Nicaraguan State, 1894–1987.* Stanford, Calif.: Stanford University Press.

HALL, J. (1993). Nationalisms: Classified and Explained. *Daedelus: The Proceedings of the American Academy of Arts and Sciences* 121, no. 3: 1–28.

HALLOWELL, A. I. (1960). Ojibwa Ontology, Behaviour, and World View, in S. Diamond (ed.), *Culture in History: Essays in Honour of Paul Radin,* 49–82. New York: Columbia University Press.

HARUMI, B. (1993). *Cultural Nationalism in East Asia.* Berkeley: University of California Press.

HARVEY, D. (1989). *The Condition of Postmodernity: An Enquiry into the Origins of Cultural Change.* Oxford: Basil Blackwell.

HENRIKSEN, G. (1973). *Hunters in the Barrens: The Naskapi on the Edge of the White Man's World.* Toronto: Memorial University of Newfoundland.

HIRSCH, E. and O'HANLON, M., eds. (1995). *The Anthropology of Landscape: Perspectives on Place and Space.* Oxford: Oxford University Press.

HIRSCH, F. (1997). The Soviet Union as a Work in Progress: Ethnographers and the Category of Nationality in the 1926, 1937, and 1939 Censuses. *Slavic Review* 56, no. 2: 251–78.

HOBSBAWM, E. (1990). *Nations and Nationalism Since 1780.* Cambridge: Cambridge University Press.

HONIGMANN, J. J. (1966). Social Disintegration in Five Northern Canadian Communities. *Canadian Review of Sociology and Anthropology* 2, no. 4: 199–214.

HOROWITZ, D. L. (1992). How to Begin to Think Comparatively About Soviet Ethnic Problems, in A. J. Motyl (ed.), *Thinking Theoretically about Soviet Nationalities: History and Comparison in the Study of the USSR,* 9–21. Oxford: Columbia University Press.

HUMPHREY, C. (1979). The Uses of Genealogy: A Historical Study of the Nomadic and Sedentarized Buryat, in Équipe Écologie et anthropologie des sociétés pastorales, *Pastoral Production and Society,* 235–60. Cambridge: Cambridge University Press.

—— (1983). *Karl Marx Collective: Economy, Society and Religion in a Siberian Collective Farm.* Cambridge: Cambridge University Press.

—— (1989). Perestroika and the Pastoralists: The Example of Mongun-Taiga in Tuva ASSR. *Anthropology Today* 5, no. 3: 6–10.

—— (1993). Women, Taboo, and the Suppression of Attention, in S. Ardener (ed.), *Defining Females: The Nature of Women in Society,* 73–92. Oxford: Berg.

—— (1994). Remembering an 'Enemy': The Bogd Khaan in Twentieth-Century Mongolia, in R. S. Watson (ed.), *Memory, History, and Opposition Under State Socialism*, 21–44. Santa Fe: School of American Research Press.

—— (1998). The Domestic Mode of Production in Post-Soviet Siberia? *Anthropology Today* 14, no. 3: 2–7.

HUTCHINSON, J. (1994). *Modern Nationalism*. London: Fontana.

INGOLD, T. (1986). *The Appropriation of Nature: Essays on Human Ecology and Social Relations*. Manchester: Manchester University Press.

—— (1994). Hunting and Gathering as Ways of Perceiving the Environment, in R. Ellen and K. Fukui (eds.), *Redefining Nature: Ecology, Culture, and Domestication*, 117–55. Oxford: Berg.

INTERNATIONAL WORKING GROUP FOR INDIGENOUS AFFAIRS (1990). *Indigenous Peoples of the Soviet North*. Copenhagen: International Secretariat of IWGIA.

ISACHENKO, V. L. (1913). *Inorodtsy Turukhanskogo kraia, vykhodiashchie na bereg reki Yenisei v raione sela Dudinka stanka Osinovoi i ikh rybnyi i drugie promysly* Materialy po issledovaniiu r. Yenisiia v rybopromyslovom otnoshenii, vyp. 9. Krasnoiarsk: Tip. Abakakova.

JENSEN, J., ADARE, K., and SHEARER, R. (1997). *Canadian Arctic Contaminants Assessment Report*. Ottawa: Minister of Public Works and Government Services Canada.

KAISER, R. J. (1994). *The Geography of Nationalism in Russia and the U.S.S.R.* Princeton: Princeton University Press.

KARLOV, V. V. (1982). *Evenki v XVII—nachale XX v. (khoziaistvo i sotsial'naia struktura)*. Moscow: Izd-vo MGU.

KASTREN, M. A. (1860). Puteshestvie v Sibir' 1845–1849, in *Magazin zemlevedeniia i puteshestvii*, tom 6, chast' 2: 199–482. St Petersburg: Izd-vo Folovoi.

KENNEDY, J. C. (1985). *Holding the Line: Ethnic Boundaries in a Northern Labrador Community*. St John's, Newfoundland: Institute of Social and Economic Research.

KEPPEN (1845). Dopolnitel'naia instruktsiia gospodinu Kastrenu sostavlenno akademikom Keppenom. *Zhurnal' Ministerstva Narodnogo Prosveshcheniia*, no. 8: 114–28.

KHEIN, I. A. (1909). Dnevnik poiskovoi ekspeditsii, organizovan N.V. Astrasevoim v sistemu rek Nizhego Tunguska. *Izvestiia Krasnoiarskogo podotdela Vostochno-Sibirskogo Otdeleniia Russkogo Geograficheskogo Obshchestva*, tom 2, vyp. 5: 1–149.

KIUNER, N. B. (1961). *Kitaiskie izvestiia o narodakh iuzhnoi Sibiri, Tsentral'noi Azii i Dal'nego Vostoka*. Moscow: Izd-vo vostochnoi literatury.

KLEIN, D. R. (1971). Reaction of Reindeer to Obstructions and Disturbances. *Science*, 173: 393–8.

—— (1980). Conflicts between Domestic Reindeer and their Wild Counterparts: A Review of Eurasian and North American Experience. *Arctic* 33, no. 4: 739–56.

KLOKOV, K. B. (1991). *Traditsionnoe khoziaistvo narodov Severa i okhraniaemye territorii (k probleme sozdaniia tsentral'nosibirskogo biosfernogo rezervata)* Leningrad: GO SSSR.

KOCHNEVA, Z. I. (1990). *Evenkiisko-russkii systematicheskii slovar'*. Krasnoiarsk: Krasnoiarkskoe knizhnoe izd-vo.

KOSTROV, N. A. (1855). Eniseiskie Tungusi. *Moskovitianin*, vyp. 11, kn. 3: 27–48.

KOZLOV, V. I. (1992). Mezhdu etnografiei, etnologiei i zhizn'iu. *Sovetskaia etnografiia*, no. 3: 3–14.

KRIAZHKOV, V. A. (1994). *Status malochislennykh narodov Rossii: pravovye akty i dokumenty*. Moscow: Yuridicheskaia literatura.

KRIUKOV, M. B. (1989). Chitaia Lenina (razmysleniia etnografa o problemakh teorii natsii. *Sovetskaia etnografiia*, no. 4: 5–18.

KRIVOSHAPKIN, M. F. (1865). *Yeniseiskii okrug i yego zhizn'*. St Petersburg: Tip Bezobraza.

KUKLIK, H. (1991). *The Savage Within: The Social History of British Anthropology*. Cambridge: Cambridge University Press.

KUOLJOK, K. E. (1985). *The Revolution in the North: Soviet Ethnography and Nationality Policy*. Uppsala: Almqvist & Wiksell International.

KUPER, A. (1988). *The Invention of Primitive Society: Transformations of an Illusion*. London: Routledge.

KWON, HEONIK (1993). Maps and Actions: Nomadic and Sedentary Space in a Siberian Reindeer Farm. Department of Social Anthropology: University of Cambridge.

LANE, D. (1992). *Soviet Society Under Perestroika*, rev. edn. London: Routledge.

LAPPALAINEN, HEIMIO (1992). 'The Skills You Passed On', dir. Heimio Lappalainen and Jouko Aaltonon. Taiga Nomads: A documentary series about the Evenki of Siberia. Helsinki: Illume Ltd. Video Recording.

LAPTEV, K. P. (1851). Bereg mezhdu Lenoi i Yeniseem: zapiski Leitenanta Kh.P. Laptev. *Zapiski Gidrograficheskogo Departamenta Morskogo Ministerstva*, no. 9: 8–58.

LASHOV, B. V. and LITOVKA, O. L. (1982). *Sotsial'no-ekonomicheskie problemy razvitiia narodnostei Krainego Severa*. Leningrad: Nauka.

LEACH, E. R. (1964). *Political Systems of Highland Burma: A Study of Kachin Social Structure*. London: Athlone Press.

LEBEDEV, M. (1929). K voprosu o stroitel'stve olenevodcheskikh kolkhozov v Turukhanskom krae. *Pushnoe delo*, no. 10: 17–26.

LEBEDEVA, E. P. (1960). K kharakteristike severnogo narechiia evenkiiskogo yazyka (po materialam govorov B. Poroga i Agaty). *Uchenye zapiski Leningradskogo gosudarstvennogo pedagogicheskego instituta*, no. 167: 137–70.

LENARTOVICH, E. S. (1936). Tri goda raboty s korralami v Nenetskom olenevodcheskom sovkhoze. *Sovetskoe olenevodstvo*, vyp.7: 45–51.

LÉVI-STRAUSS, C. (1966). *The Savage Mind*. Chicago: University of Chicago Press.

LEVIN, M. D., ed. (1993). *Ethnicity and Aboriginality: Case Studies in Ethnonationalism*. Toronto: University of Toronto Press.

LEVIN, M. G. and POTAPOV, L. P. (1964). *The Peoples of Siberia*. Chicago: University of Chicago Press.

LITTLE BEAR, L., BOLDT, M., and LONG, J. A. (1984). *Pathways to Self-Determiniation: Canadian Indians and the Canadian State*. Toronto: University of Toronto Press.

MCCLELLAN, C. (1975). *My Old People Say: An Ethnographic Survey of Southern Yukon Territory*. (2 vols.) National Museum of Man Publications in Ethnology, 6 (1 & 2). Ottawa: National Museums of Canada.

MACPHERSON, C. B. (1962). *The Political Theory of Possessive Individualism: Hobbes to Locke*. Oxford: Clarendon Press.

—— (1978). The Meaning of Property, in C. B. Macpherson (ed.), *Property: Mainstream and Critical Positions*, 1–13. Toronto: University of Toronto Press.

MAUSS, M. (1969). *The Gift: The Forms and Functions of Exchange in Archaic Societies.* London: Cohen & West.

MICHURIN, L. N. and MIRONENKO, O. N. (1964). 'Osobennosti razmeshcheniia i ispol'zovaniia zimnikh pastbishch dikimi severnymi oleniami Taimyrskogo stada. *Trudy Vsesoiuznogo sel'skokhoziaistvennogo instituta zaochnogo obrazovaniia,* no. 2, vyp. 17, 89–96.

—— —— (1966). Rasprostranenie kopytnykh v gorakh Putorana, in *Trudy Nauchno-issledovatel'skogo Instituta sel'skogo khoziaistva Krainego Severa,* tom 14: 69–75.

MIDDENDORF, A. (1869). *Puteshestvie na Sever i Vostok Sibiri,* tom 2. St Petersburg: Tip. Imperatorskoi Akademii Nauk.

MILAN, F. A. (1980). The Demography of Selected Circumpolar Populations, in F. A. Milan (ed.), *The Human Biology of Circumpolar Populations,* 13–35. Cambridge: Cambridge University Press.

MILLOY, J. S. (1988). *The Plains Cree: Trade, Diplomacy, and War 1790–1870.* Winnipeg: University of Manitoba Press.

MORDVINOV, A. (1860). Inorodtsy v Turukhanskom Krae. *Vestnik Russkogo Geograficheskogo Obschestva,* vyp. 2, no. 28: 25–64.

MORGAN, LEWIS HENRY (1878). *Ancient Society, or Researches in the Lines of Human Progress from Savagery through Barbarism to Civilization.* New York: Holt.

MOYNIHAN, DANIEL PATRICK (1993). *Pandaemonium: Ethnicity in International Politics.* Oxford: Oxford University Press.

NAIRN, T. (1977). *The Break-Up of Britain.* London: Verso.

NAUCHNO (1976). *Nauchno-Issledovatel'skii Institut Sel'skogo Khoziaistva Krainego Severa and Taimyrskoe Okruzhnoe Statisticheskoe Upravlenie.* Spravochnik po ekonomike kolkhozov i sovkhozov Taimyrskogo Natsional'nogo Okruga. Dudinka: Izd-vo Sovetskii Taimyr.

NELSON, R. K. (1983). *Make Prayers to the Raven.* Chicago: University of Chicago Press.

NIKUL'SHIN, N. P. (1939). *Pervobytnye proizvodstvennye ob"edineniia i sotsialisticheskoe stroitel'stvo u evenkov.* Leningrad: Izd-vo Glavsevmorput'.

NUTTALL, M. (1992). *Arctic Homeland: Kinship, Community, and Development in Northwest Greenland.* Toronto: University of Toronto Press.

—— (1998). *Protecting the Arctic: Indigenous Peoples and Cultural Survival.* Reading: Harwood Academic Publishers.

O RABOTE V NATSIONAL'NYKH RAIONAKH KRAINEGO SEVERA (1932). *Sovetskii Sever,* no. 2: 47–8.

OKAMURA, J. (1994). Situational Ethnicity. *Ethnic and Racial Studies* 4: 452–63.

OPEKOKEW, P. (1982). *The First Nations: Indian Government and the Community of Man.* Regina: Federation of Saskatchewan Indians.

OSGOOD, C. (1936). *Contributions to the Ethnography of the Kutchin.* New Haven: Yale University Publications in Anthropology, 14.

OSHERENKO, G. (1995). Property Rights and the Transformation of Russia: Institutional Change in the Far North. *Europe-Asia Studies* 47, no. 7: 1077–108.

OSTROVSKIKH, P. E. (1902). Turukhansk. *Vostochnoe obozrenie,* no. 167: 380.

—— (1903). O polozhenii zhenshin u inorodtsev Turukhanskogo Kraia. *Izvestiia Krasnoiarskogo Podotdelia Russkogo Geograficheskogo Obshchestva,* tom 1, vyp. 5: 13–22.

OSTROVSKIKH, P. E. (1904). Poezdka na ozero Yessei. *Izvestiia Krasnoiarskogo Podotdela Vostochno-Sibirskogo otdela Imperatorskogo Russkogo Geograficheskogo Obshchestva*, tom 1, vyp. 6: 21–33.

OTDEL EKONOMIKI NIISKH KRAINEGO SEVERA (1961). *Spravochnik po ekonomike kolkozov i sovkhozov Taimyrskogo natsional'nogo okruga*. Dudkinka: Tipografiia Sovetskogo Taimyra.

PAINE, R. P. B. (1977). Tutelage and Ethnicity: A Variable Relationship, in R. P. B. Paine (ed.), *The White Arctic: Anthropological Essays on Tutelage and Ethnicity*, 249–63. St John's, Newfoundland: Institute of Social and Economic Research.

PATKANOV, S. (1906). *Opyt geografii i statistiki Tungusskikh plemen Sibiri na osnovanii dannykh perepisi naseleniia 1897 g. i drugikh istochnikov: Chast' I Tungusy Sobstvenno*, Zapiski Imperatorskogo Russkogo Geograficheskogo Obstshchestva po Otdeleniiu Etnografii, tom 21, vyp. 1, chast' 1. St Petersburg: Slova.

—— (1911). *O priroste inorodcheskago naseleniia Sibiri. Statisticheskie materialy dlia osveshcheniia voprosa o vymiranii pervobytnykh plemen*. St Petersburg: Tip. Imperatorskoi Akademii Nauk.

PAVLOV, P. N. O. (1964). O social'nykh otnosheniiakh na sobolinom promysle v Yeniseiskom krae v XVII veke. *Uchenye zapiski Krasnoiarskogo pedagogicheskogo instituta*, vyp.1, no. 26: 76–100.

PETRUSHIN, A. A. (1992). Korennye narody Taimyra i osnovnye pokazateli razvitiia traditsionnykh otraslei khoziaistva (kratkaia spravka) [manuscript available at Library of the Scott Polar Research Institute].

PIKA, A. I. (1993). The Spatial-Temporal Dynamic of Violent Death Among the Native Peoples of Northern Russia. *Arctic Anthropology* 30, no. 2: 61–76.

—— and Prokhorov, V. V. (1994). *Neotraditsionalizm na rossiiskom Severe*. Moscow: Institut narodnokhoziaistvenogo prognozirovaniia.

POPKOV, Iu. V. (1994). *Etnosotsial'nye i pravovye protsessy v Evenkii*. Novosibirsk: Sibirskoe otdelenie RAN.

POPOV, A. A. (1931). Poezdka k dolganam. *Sovetskaia etnografiia*, vyp.3–4: 210–13.

—— (1934a). Materialy po rodovomu stroiu dolgan. *Sovetskaia etnografiia*, no. 6: 116–39.

—— (1934b). Zatundrinskie krest'iane. *Sovetskaia etnografiia*, no. 3: 77–86.

—— (1935). Olenevodstvo u dolgan. *Sovetskaia etnografiia*, no. 4–5: 184–205.

—— (1937a). Okhota i rybolovstvo u dolgan, in I. I. Meshchaninov (ed.), *Pamiati V. G. Bogoraza (1865–1936): Sbornik statei*, 147–206. Moscow and Leningrad: Izd-vo Akademii Nauk.

—— (1937b). Tekhnika u dolgan. *Sovetskaia etnografiia*, no. 1: 91–136.

—— (1946). Semeinaia zhizn' u dolgan. *Sovetskaia etnografiia*, no. 4: 50–74.

—— (1954). Dolgany, in Maksim G. Levin and L. P. Potapov (eds.), *Narody Sibiri*, 742–59. Moscow: Nauka.

—— (1958). Perezhitki drevnikh doreligioznykh vozzrenii dolganov na prirodu. *Sovetskaia etnografiia*, no. 2: 77–99.

—— (1981). Shamanstvo u dolgan, in *Problemy istorii obshchestvennogo soznaniia narodov Sibiri i Severa*, 253–64. Leningrad: Nauka.

POPOVA, M. I. (1991). *Osnovy istorii kul'tury malochislennykh narodov Taimyra*. Dudinka: Dudinskaia tipografiia.

PULLIAINEN, E. *et al.* (1983). Seasonal Movements of the Wild Forest Reindeer (Rangifer Tarandus Fennicus) in Eastern Finland. *Acta Zoologica Fennica* 175: 15–16.

RAEFF, M. (1956). *Siberia and the Reforms of 1822.* Seattle: University of Washington Press.

Renan, E. (1990). What Is a Nation?, in H. K. Bhabha (ed.), *Nation and Narration*, 8–22. London: Routledge.

RIASANOVSKY, V. A. (1965). Juristic Customs of the Tunguses, in V. A. Riasanovsky (ed.), *The Customary Law of the Nomadic Tribes of Siberia*, 71–86. The Hague: Mouton & Co.

RIDINGTON, R. (1990). *Little Bit Know Something: Stories in a Language of Anthropology.* Vancouver: Douglas & McIntyre.

RYCHKOV, K. M. (1908). Ospa v Turukhanskom krae. *Sibirskie voprosy*, no. 19–20: 76–81.

—— (1914*a*). Poezdka v severovostochnye tundry Turukhanskogo Kraia iz selo Dudina. *Zemlevedenie*, vyp. 21, 4: 97–123.

—— (1914*b*). Stranitsa iz zhizni vymiraiushchego plemeni. *Sibirskii arkhiv*, no. 3–4: 162–5.

—— (1915). V Turukhanskom krae. *Sibirskii arkhiv*, no. 6: 268–73.

—— (1917; 1922–3). Yeniseiskie Tungusy. *Zemlevedenie*, tom 24: 25, vyp. 1–2 (1917); 1–2, 3–4 (1922–3): 1–67; 69–106; 107–49.

SAMOKVASOV, DMITRII I. (1876). *Sbornik obychnogo prava Sibirskikh inorodtsev.* Varshava: Tip. Ivana Noskovskago.

SCOTT, C. (1996). Science for the West, Myth for the Rest? The Case of James Bay Cree Knowledge Construction, in L. Nader (ed.), *Naked Science: Anthropological Inquiry into Boundaries, Power, and Knowledge*, 69–86. New York: Routledge.

SERGEEV, M. A. (1955). *Nekapitalisticheskii put' razvitiia malykh narodov Severa.* Trudy Instituta etnografii im. Miklukho-Maklaia. Moscow and Leningrad: Nauka.

SEROSHEVSKII, V. L. (1993). *Yakuty. Opyt etnograficheskogo issledovaniia.* Moscow: Rossiiskaia politicheskaia entsiklopediia.

SHARP, H. S. (1988). *The Transformation of Bigfoot: Maleness, Power and Belief Among the Chipewyan.* Washington: Smithsonian.

SHIDELER, R. T. *et al.* (1986). *Impacts of Human Developments and Land Use on Caribou: A Literature Review* (2 vols.). Division of Habitat Technical Report, 86–2. Juneau: Alaska Department of Fish and Game.

SHIROKOGOROFF, S. M. (1933). *Social Organization of the Northern Tungus.* Shanghai: Commercial Press.

—— (1935). *Psychomental Complex of the Tungus.* London: Kegan Paul, Trench, Trubner & Co. Ltd.

SHMELEV, N. and POPOV, V. (1990). *The Turning Point: Revitalizing the Soviet Economy.* London: Tauris.

SHTERNBERG, L. Ia. (1933). *Sem'ia i rod u narodov severo-vostochnoi Azii.* Leningrad: Izd-vo Instituta Narodov Severa.

SIBIRSKII KRAEVOI STATISTICHESKII OTDEL (1928). *Materialy pripoliarnoi perepisi v Sibirskom krae.* Novosibirsk and Krasnoiarsk: Izd-vo Sibirskogo kraevogo stat. otdela.

SIMARD, B. (1979). Éléments du comportement du caribou du nord Québéçois. *Recherches amérindiennes au Québec*, 9, nos. 1–2: 29–36.

SIMCHENKO, Yu. B. (1976). *Kul'tura okhotnikov na olenei severnoi Yevrazii: etnograficheskaia rekonstruktsiia*. Moscow: Nauka.

SIMINOV, M. D. (1983). Materialy po shamanstvu Symskikh Evenkov. *Izvestiia Sibirskogo otdeleniia Akademii nauk SSSR: Seriia obshchestvennykh nauk*, vyp. 3, no. 11: 102–12.

SIU, H. F. (1993). Cultural Identity and the Politics of Difference. *Daedalus: Proceedings of the American Academy of Arts and Science*, 122, no. 2: 19–43.

SKACHKO, A. (1923). K voprosu o kolonizatsii okrain. *Zhizn' natsional'nosti*, no. 2: 13–19.

—— (1930). Organizatsiia territorii malykh narodov Severa, in *Sovetskii Sever: Sbornik statei*, vyp. 2: 5–68.

SLEZKINE, Y. (1994). *Arctic Mirrors: Russia and the Small Peoples of the North*. Ithaca, NY: Cornell University Press.

SLOBODIN, R. (1966). *Métis of the Mackenzie District*. Ottawa: St Paul University.

SMELE, J. (1997). *Civil War in Siberia: The Anti-Bolshevik Government of Admiral Kolchak*. Cambridge: Cambridge University Press.

SMITH, A. D. (1986). *The Ethnic Origins of Nations*. Oxford: Blackwell.

—— (1992). *Ethnicity and Nationalism*. Leiden: Brill.

SNEATH, D. (1993). Social Relations, Networks and Social Organisation in Post-Socialist Rural Mongolia. *Nomadic Peoples*, 33: 193–207.

SNOW, A. H. (1921). *The Question of Aboriginals in the Law and Practice of Nations*. New York: Putnam.

SNOW, R. E. (1977). *The Bolsheviks in Siberia, 1917–1918*. London: Associated University Presses.

SSORIN-CHAIKOV, N. (1991). Historia and Ulo: A Critique of Sociological Reasoning with a Siberian Evenk Epistemology. Unpublished M.A. thesis, Department of Anthropology: Stanford University.

STALIN, I. V. (1913). Natsionalnyi vopros i sotsial-demokratiia. *Prosveshchenie*, nos. 3–5.

STATICHESKOE UPRAVLENIE TAIMYRSKOGO NATSIONALNOGO OKRUGA (1967). *Sel'skoe i promyslovoe khoziaistvo Taimyra*. Taimyrskoe Statupravalenie: Dudinka.

STEPANOV, A. P. (1835). *Ocherki istorii: Yeniseiskaia guberniia*. St Petersburg: Tip. Konrada Vingebera.

STOCKING, G. W., ed. (1986). *Malinowski, Rivers, Benedict and Others: Essays on Culture and Personality*. History of Anthropology, 4. Madison: University of Wisconsin Press.

—— ed. (1991). Maclay, Kubary, Malinowski: Archetypes From the Dreamtime of Anthropology, in *Colonial Situations: Essays in the Contextualization of Ethnographic Knowledge*, 9–74. History of Anthropology, 7. Madison: University of Wisconsin Press.

SUNY, R. G. (1993). *The Revenge of the Past: Nationalism, Revolution and the Collapse of the Soviet Union*. Stanford, Calif.: Stanford University Press.

SUSLOV, I. M. (1927). Okhota u tungusov. *Okhota i pushnina Sibiri*, no. 1: 44–9.

—— (1928). Sotsial'naia kul'tura u tungusov basseina Podkamennoi Tungusski i verkhov'ev r. Taimury. *Sovetskii Sever*, no. 1: 55–62.

—— (1930). Raschet minimal'nogo kolichestva olenei, potrebnykh dlia tuzemnykh khoziaistv. *Sovetskii Sever*, no. 3: 29–35.

—— (1952). O natsional'noi prinadlezhnosti sovremennogo naseleniia severo-zapada Yakutskoi ASSR. *Sovetskaia etnografiia*, no. 2: 69–72.

Suslov, M. (1884). Putevoi zhurnal missionera Suslova pri poezdke k ozeru Yessei. *Yeniseiskiia eparkhal'nyia vedomosti*, no. 13: 182–5; no. 14: 207–11; no. 19: 262–9; no. 20: 275–9; no. 21: 292–6.

Syroechkovskii, E. E. (1984). Overview of the Problem of Wild Reindeer in the Soviet Union, in E. E. Syroechkovskii (ed.), *Wild Reindeer of the Soviet Union (Proceedings of the First Interdepartmental Conference on the Preservation and Rational Utilization of Wild Reindeer Resources)*, 6–44. New Delhi: Amerind Publishing Co.

—— (1990). Reindeer in the USSR: Problems of Protection and Rational Use, in *Proceedings of the Sixth International Caribou and Reindeer Symposium*, 423–33. Rangifer Special Issue, 3.

—— Rogacheva, Ye. V., and Rogacheva, E. V. (1994). *Bol'shoi Arkticheskii zapovednik i problemy okhrany prirody Arktiki*. Moscow: Institut ekologii i evoliutsii RAN.

Szporluk, R. (1990). The Imperial Legacy and the Soviet Nationality Problem, in L. Hajda and M. Beissinger (eds.), *The Nationality Factor in Soviet Politics and Society*, 1–23. Oxford: Westview.

Taiga Rescue Network (1996). Hotspots in the Taiga: Noril'sk, Krasnoyarsk. *Taiga News*, 19:6.

Tanner, A. (1979). *Bringing Home Animals: Religious Ideology and Mode of Production of the Mistassini Cree Hunters*. St John's, Newfoundland: Institute of Social and Economic Research.

—— (1983a). *The Politics of Indianness: Case Studies of Native Ethnopolitics in Canada*. St John's, Newfoundland: Institute of Social and Economic Research.

—— (1983b). Introduction: Canadian Indians and the Politics of Dependency, in A. Tanner (ed.), *The Politics of Indianness: Case Studies of Native Ethnopolitics in Canada*. St John's, Newfoundland: Institute of Social and Economic Research.

—— (1993). History and Culture in the Generation of Ethnic Nationalism, in M. D. Levin (ed.), *Ethnicity and Aboriginality: Case Studies in Ethnonationalism*, 75–96. Toronto: University of Toronto Press.

Taras, R. (1993). Making Sense of Matrioshka Nationalism, in I. Bremmer and R. Taras (eds.), *Nations and Politics in the Soviet Successor States*, 513–38. Cambridge: Cambridge University Press.

Terletskii, P. E. (1951). Eshche raz k voprosu ob etnicheskom sostave naseleniia severo-zapadnoi chasti Yakutskoi ASSR. *Sovetskaia etnografiia*, no. 1: 88–99.

Tilly, C. (1990). *Coercion, Capital, and European States, AD 990–1990*. Oxford: Blackwell.

Tonkin, E., McDonald, M., and Chapman, M., eds. (1989). *History and Ethnicity*. London: Routledge.

Tret'iakov, P. I. (1869). *Turukhanskii krai, ego priroda i zhitelei*. St Petersburg.

TRIGGER, D. S. (1992). *Whitefella Comin': Aboriginal Responses to Colonialism in Northern Australia.* Cambridge: Cambridge University Press.

TROSHEV, Z. (1993). Taimyrskaia tragediia: fragment rukopisi. *Krasnoiarskii rabochii* vyp. 12–go oktiabria.

TROSHEV, Z. H. (1998). *Taimyrskaia Tragediia.* Moskva: Slovo.

TUGARINOV, A. Ya. (1919). Ocherki Turukhanskogo kraia. *Sibirskie Zapiski*, no. 1: 48–61; no. 2: 53–65; no. 3: 75–84.

—— and LAPPO, D. E. (1927). *Tuzemtsy Prieniseiskogo Severa.* Biblioteka prieniseiskogo kraevedeniia, vyp. 6. Krasnoiarsk: Izd-vo biuro kraevedeniia pri Kras. otdel. RGO.

TUGOLUKOV, V. A. (1963). Khantaiskie Evenki, in B. O. Dolgikh (ed.), *Sibirskii etnograficheskii sbornik*, tom 5: 5–32. Trudy Instituta etnografii AN SSSR, NS tom 84. Moscow: Nauka.

—— (1985). *Tungusy (Evenki i Eveny) Srednei i Zapadnoi Sibiri.* Moscow: Nauka.

UBRIATOVA, E. I. (1966). O yazyke dolgan, in V. A. Avrorin (ed.), *Yazyki i fol'klor narodov sibirskogo Severa*, 41–68. Moscow: Nauka.

—— (1985). *Yazyk noril'skikh dolgan.* Novosibirsk: Nauka.

USTIUGOV, BORIS. Zakon turukhanskoi taigi. *Moskovskie Novosti*, 2 Feb. 1997: 18–19.

VAINSHTEIN, S. I. (1970). Problema proiskhozhdeniia olenevodstva v Yevrazii (Saianskii ochag odomashnivaniia olenia). *Sovetskaia etnografiia*, no. 6: 3–14.

—— (1993). *Polevye issledovaniia 1 (2).* Moscow: Institut antropologii i etnologii.

VAKHTIN, N. (1994). Native Peoples of the Russian Far North, in Minority Rights Group (ed.), *Polar Peoples: Self-Determination and Development*, 29–80. London: Minority Rights Publications.

VALKENBURG, P., DAVIS, J. L., and BOERTJE, R. D. (1983). Social Organization and Seasonal Range Fidelity of Alaska's Western Arctic Caribou—Preliminary Findings. *Acta Zoologica Fennica* 175: 125–6.

VASIL'EV, V. I. (1963). Lesnye entsy (ocherk istorii, khoziaistva i kul'tury), in B. O. Dolgikh (ed.), *Sibirskii etnograficheskii sbornik*, tom 5, 33–70. Trudy instituta etnografii AN SSSR, NS tom 84. Moscow: Nauka.

—— and SIMCHENKO, Yu. V. (1963). Sovremennoe samodiiskoe naselenie Taimyra. *Sovetskaia etnografiia*, no. 3: 9–20.

—— and TUGOLUKOV, B. A. (1960). Etnograficheskie issledovaniia na Taimyre v 1959 godu. *Sovetskaia etnografiia*, no. 5: 128–41.

VASIL'EV, V. N. (1908). Kratkii ocherk inorodtsev Turukhanskogo kraia, in *Yezhegodnik Russkogo Antropologicheskogo Obshchestva*, tom 2: 57–87. St Petersburg: Sankt Peterburzhskii universitet.

—— (1968). In the Districts of the Far North. *Soviet Education*, 10, no. 3: 7–13.

VASILEVICH, G. M. (1972*a*). Nekotorye voprosy plemeni i roda u evenkov, in *Okhotniki, sobirateli, rybolovy*, 160–72. Leningrad: Nauka.

—— (1972*b*). Zaselenie tungusami taigi i lesotundry mezhdu Lenoi i Yeniseem, in *Voporosy yazyka i folklora narodnostei Severa*, 183-238. Yakutsk: Institut yazyka, literatury i istorii.

—— (1931*a*). K voprosu o tungusakh, kochuiutshchikh k zapadu ot Yeniseia. *Sovetskii Sever*, no. 10: 133–45.

—— (1931*b*). Symskie tungusy. *Sovetskii Sever*, no. 2: 132–51.

—— (1946). Drevneishyie etnonimy Azii i nazvaniia evenkiiskikh rodov. *Sovetskaia etnografiia*, no. 4: 34–49.

—— (1951). Yesseisko-chirindinskie evenki (po kollektsiia V.N. Vasil'eva, MAE no. 1004), in *Sbornik Muzeia antropologii i etnografii*, tom 13: 154–86.

—— (1969). *Evenki: Istoriko-etnograficheskie ocherki (XVIII–nachalo XX v.)*. Leningrad: Nauka.

—— (1970). Vopros o plemeni i rode u tungusov. *Trudy Sed'mogo Mezhdunarodnogo kongressa antropologicheskikh i etnograficheskikh nauk*, tom 10: 460–74.

—— and LEVIN, M. G. (1951). O klassifikatsii i proizkhozhdenii osnovnyikh tipov sibirskiogo olenevodstva. *Sovetskaia etnografiia*, no. 1: 63–87.

VERDERY, K. (1991). *National Identity Under Socialism: Identity and Cultural Politics in Ceausescu's Romania*. Oxford: University of California Press.

—— (1993). Ethnic Relations, Economies of Shortage, and the Transition in Eastern Europe, in C. M. Hann (ed.), *Socialism: Ideals, Ideologies, and Local Practice*, 172–86. London: Routledge.

VITEBSKY, P. (1990). Centralized Decentralization: The Ethnography of Remote Reindeer Herders Under Perestroika. *Cahiers du monde soviétique* 31, nos. 2–3: 345–56.

—— (1992). Landscape and Culture Among the Eveny: The Political Environment of Siberian Reindeer Herders Today, in E. Croll and D. Parkin (eds.), *Bush Base, Farm Forest: Culture, Environment and Development*, 223–46. London: Routledge.

VSEROSSIISKII TSENTRAL'NII ISPOLNITEL'NII KOMITET (1927). Vremmenye Polozheniia ob upravlenii tuzemnykh narodnostei i plemen Severnykh okrain RSFSR. *Severnaia Aziia*, no. 2: 85–91.

WATKINS, M. (1977). *Dene Nation: The Colony Within?* Toronto: University of Toronto Press.

WATSON, M. (1990). *Contemporary Minority Nationalism*. Oxford: Routledge.

WENZEL, G. (1991). *Animal Rights Human Rights: Ecology, Economy, and Ideology in the Canadian Arctic*. Toronto: University of Toronto Press.

WOLF, E. (1982). *Europe and the Peoples Without History*. Berkeley: University of California Press.

WORLD WIDE FUND FOR NATURE—ARCTIC PROGRAMME (1993). *Nature Reserves on Taimyr*. Oslo: WWF-Norway.

YAKUSHKIN, G. D. *et al.* (1971). Eksperiment na Piasine. *Okhota i Okhotich'e khoziaizstvo*, no. 7: 10–12.

—— (1984). Biological Principles of Commercial Utilization of Wild Reindeer in Northern Krasnoyark Region, in E. E. Syroechkovskii (ed.), *Wild Reindeer of the Soviet Union (Proceedings of the First Interdepartmental Conference on the Preservation and Rational Utilization of Wild Reindeer Resources)*, 225–9. New Delhi: Amerind Publishing Co.

YOUNG, M. C. (1992). The National and Colonial Question and Marxism: A View from the South, in A. J. Motyl (ed.), *Thinking Theoretically about Soviet Nationalities: History and Comparison in the Study of the USSR*, 67–98. Oxford: Columbia University Press.

YOUNG, T. K. (1994). *The Health of Native Americans: Toward a Biocultural Epidemiology*. Oxford: Oxford University Press.

ZASLAVSKY, V. (1991). Nationalism and Democratic Transition in Postcommunist Societies. *Daedelus: The Proceedings of the American Academy of Arts and Sciences* 121, no. 2: 97–121.

ZIKER, J. (1996). Problems of the North. *Michigan Discussions in Anthropology*, 12: 59–75.

ARCHIVAL SOURCES

Archival documents in the former Soviet Union are referenced by means of a five-part classification system which sorts documents into progressively smaller units. This system has been simplified here to make it less cumbersome for in-text references. The initial acronym refers to the name of the archive. The acronym is followed by three numbers separated by dashes. The first number represents the *fond*. The second number refers to the *opis*. The final number represents the *delo*. If an individual page is cited (or *list*), it is separated from the classification numbers by a colon. This reference list gives the full titles of the archives, *fondy*, and *dela*. The citations are grouped by city, archive, and *fond*.

Dudinka

♦ *GATAO* [Gosudarstvenyi Arkhiv Taimyrskogo avtonomnogo okruga]

Fond: *Zemel'nogo otdela pri RIK Dudinskogo raiona.*
GATAO 2–1–3 [1937]. 'Dokhody kolkhozov Dudinskogo raiona za 1937 po otrasliam'.
GATAO 2–1–4 [1937]. 'Proizvodstvennye plany artelei Dudinskogo raiona 1937–38'.
GATAO 2–1–8 [1937]. 'Svodki, spiski, vedomosti, svedeniia o sostoianie kollektivi-zatsii v kolkhozakh Dudinskogo raiona'.
GATAO 2–1–11 [1937]. 'Dokumenty o zagotovke ryby'.
GATAO 2–1–12 [1937]. 'Godovye otchety po kolkhozam Dudinskogo raiona 1937'.
GATAO 2–1–27 [1939]. 'Vedomost' nalichia olenei po Khantaiskomu kochsovetu'.

Fond: *Khantaiskogo sel'skogo soveta.*
GATAO 73–2–1–25[1958–78]. 'Pokhoziaistvennye knigi Khantaiskogo sel'skogo soveta'.

Fond: *Okruzhnoi zemel'nyi otdel 1934–1953.*
GATAO 85–1–2 [1936]. 'O livkidatsii integral'noi kooperatsii'.
GATAO 85–1–22 [194?]. 'Zakreplenie voduemy po rybzavodam'.

Fond: *Sovkhoza Khantaiskii.*
GATAO 92–1–1 [1969]. 'Akt perescheta olenei'.
GATAO 92–1–6 [1970]. Rosliakov, A. 'Postanovlenie Taimyrskogo RIK Protokol No. 3'.

Irkutsk

♦ *GAIO* [Gosudarstvenyi Arkhiv Irkutskoi Oblasti]

Fond: *Vostochnogo-Sibirskogo Komiteta Severa.*
GAIO R538–1–196 [1929–30]. 'Materialy ekspeditsii v Khatangsko-Anabarskii raion Turukhanskogo Kraia'.

Krasnoiarsk

♦ *GAKK* [Gosudarstvenyi Arkhiv Krasnoiarskogo Kraia]

Fond: *Isponitel'nogo komiteta Turukhanskogo Kraevogo Soveta.*
GAKK R1303–1–121 [1923]. 'Spisok rodov, kochuiushchikh v raione Ilimpiiskoi tundry'.

Fond: *Otdela Severa Kraiispolkoma.*
GAKK R1386–1–3820 [1960]. 'Materialy o razvitii ekonomiki i kul'tury narodnostei Severa'.

Fond: *Otdel Severa i Artiki Krasnoiarskogo Kraevogo Ispolnitel'nogo Komiteta.*
GAKK R1386–1–3820 [1960]. Strakach, Yu. B. 'Nekotorye vyvody i predlozhenia po materialam etnograficheskii ekspeditsii 1960 v T.N.O.'

Fond: *Krasnoiarskogo Komiteta sodeistviia malym narodnostiam okrain Sibiri.*
GAKK R1845–1–5 [1926]. Savel'ev 'Tablitsa kochevogo tuzemnogo naseleniia na vnov' ustanovlenykh granitsakha v 1922 g.'
GAKK R1845–1–210 [1929?]. 'Instruktsiia po spisaniiu dolgov s bedniatskogo tuzemnogo naseleniia Turukhanskogo Kraia'.
GAKK R1845–1–224 [1929]. Shmyrnov; Artem'ev 'Svodka o sostoianii Sovetskoi raboty v Tuzemnykh RIKakh i rodovykh sovetakh Turukhanskogo Kraia'.

Fond: *Krasnoiarskogo kraevogo zemel'nogo upravleniia.*
GAKK R2275–1–22 [1929]. 'Svedeniia o raspredelenii olenei po khoziaistvennym gruppam Dudinskogo raiona'.
GAKK R2275–1–83 [1932]. 'Spisok o kulakskikh khoziaistvakh po Yesseiskomu kochsovetu'.
GAKK R2275–1–143 [1934–5]. Davydov 'Istoricheskii ocherk ekonomista Khantanskoi ekspeditsii o sostave naseleniia Khatankogo raiona'.
GAKK R-2275–1–144 [1930]. Usol'tsev, I. S. 'Otchetnyi doklad Khatangsko-Anabarskoi ekspeditsii'.
GAKK R2275–1–144 [1934]. 'Predvaritel'nyi proekt po pervonachal'nomu zemleustroistvu kochevykh sovetov Taimyrskogo okruga (Khantanskogo raiona)'.

♦ *KTsKhIDNI* [Krasnoiarskii Tsentr Khraneniia i Izucheniia Dokumentatsii Noveishei Istorii]

Fond: *Krasnoiarskii kraikom KPSS.*
KTsKhIDNI 28–1–24 [1930]. Popov, A. A. 'Doklad orgkomitetu kompleksnoi ekspeditsii isledovanii AN'.
KTsKhIDNI 28–1–26 [1931]. Dudinskii raikom KPSS 'Instrukstii integralsoiuzu, svodki, doklady, direktivnye pis'ma'.
KTsKhIDNI 26–34–98 [1958–61]. 'Godovye statisticheskie otchisleniia i dvizheniia komunistov'.

Fond: *Taimyrskii Okruzhnoi Komitet VKP(b).*
KTsKhIDNI 28–2–28 [1932]. 'Politsvodka Vossibkraia o politicheskikh sobytiakh v Avamskom i Khantanskom raione'.

Fond: *Taimyrskii okruzhkom KPSS.*
KTsKhIDNI 28–4–7 [1935]. 'Direktivnye pis'ma okruzhkomu, partiinoym i

sovetskim organam po voporosam provedeniia natsional'noi politiki sredi narodov Severa'.

Moscow

♦ *TsGARF* [Tsentralnyi Gosudarstvenyi Arkhiv Rossiiskoi Federatsii]

Fond: *Ministerstvo sel'skogo khoziaistva RSFSR. Upravlenie raionov Krainego Severa.*

TsGARF (RSFSR) A310–18–20 [1932–4]. 'Materialy pervonachal'nogo zemleus-troistva Avamskogo raiona Krasnoiarskogo Kraia 1932–1934'.

TsGARF (RSFSR) A310–18–21 [1932]. Kopylov, I. P. 'Materialy Dudinskoi zemlevoduustroitelnoi ekspeditsii Vostochno-Sibirskogo Kraevogo zemel'nogo upravleniia po pervonachal'nomu zemlevoduustroistvu Dudinskogo raiona Krasnoiarskogo Kraia za 1932'.

TsGARF (RSFSR) A310–18–37 [1933]. 'Pervonachal'noe zemlevodustroistvo Dudinskogo Raiona'.

TsGARF (RSFSR) A310–18–67 [1934–35]. 'Materialy pervonachalnogo zemleus-troistva Avamskogo raiona Krasnoiarskogo Kraia 1934–1935'.

Fond: *Komitet sodeistviia narodnostiam severnykh okrain pri Prezidiume Vsesoiuznogo Tsentral'nogo Ispolnitelnego Komiteta (1924–1935).*

TsGARF (Okt. Rev.) R3977–1–214 [1927]. Simonova, L. A. 'Otchet o poezdke v Ilimpeiskuiu tundru po marshrutu Bolshoi Porog, oz. Niakmiagda, oz. Tembenchi, oz. Vivi i kult'baza'.

♦ *RTsKhIDNI* [Rossisskii Tsentr Khraneniia i Izucheniia Dokumentatsii Noveishei Istorii]

Fond: *Sekretariat VKP(b).*

RTsKhIDNI 17–114–305 [1932]. 'Postanovlenie Biuro VosSib Kraikoma VKP(b) o polozheneni v Taimyrskom okruge'.

Fond: *Sekretariat VKP(b).*

RTsKhIDNI 17–114–305 [1932]. Meerzon; Sakhlinova 'O rabote sredi narodov Krainego Severa'.

Novosibirsk

♦ *GANO* [Gosudarstvenyi Arkhiv Novosibirskoi Oblasti]

Fond: *Zapadno-Sibirskii Komitet Severa.*

GANO R354–1–118 [1930?]. Dobrova-Yadrintseva 'Sovremennoe sostoianie, problemy natsional'nogo raionirovaniia malykh narodnostei Sibirskikh okrain'.

GANO R354–1–156 [1927]. Dobrova-Yadrintseva 'Doklad o formakh khoziaistva tuzemtsev Krainego Severa'.

GANO R354–1–238 [1928]. Dobrova-Yadrintseva 'Pis'mo k mestnym komitetam Severa'.

Fond: *Ispolnitenl'nyi Komitet Zapadno-Sibirskogo Kraevogo Soveta.*

GANO R47–1–1089 [1930]. Bazovskii; Vetrov 'Pis'mo v Prezidium VTsIK'.

GANO R1072–2–3 [1926–8] 'Otchety doklady i perepiski o Severnoi torgovle i zemleustroiste v Krasnoiarskom Krae'.

St Petersburg

♦ *ARAN* [Arkhiv Rossiiskoi Akademii Nauk—Sankt-Peterburskoe otdeleniie]

Fond: Institut po Izucheniu Narodov SSSR.

ARAN 135–1–330 [1919–29]. 'Plany, zapiski i perepiski po nauchnym i nauchno-organatsionnym voprosam Sibirskogo otdeleniia KIPSa'.

ARAN 135–2–305 [1923]. Tugarinov, A. Ya. 'Poiasnitelnaia zapiska k etnograficheskoi karte Turukhanskogo Kraia'.

♦ *AMAE* [Arkhiv Muzeia Antropologii i Etnografii im. Petra Velikogo]

Fond: *Ekspeditsionnye materialy po ekonomike Taimyrskogo Natsional'nogo Okruga (H.M. Rymgan).*

AMAE K2–1–118 [1900–39]. 'Statistiki po naseleniiu i raionirovaniiu'.

AMAE K2–1–124 [1900–39]. 'Ob"iasnitel'naia zapiska k proektu zemleustroistva olennogo sovkhoza'.

AMAE K2–1–127 [1900–39]. 'Pervonachal'noe zemleustroistvo Khantaiksogo-Evenkiiskogo tuzemenogo soveta'.

AMAE K2–1–128 [1900–39]. 'Proekt zemleustroistva kolkhoza RKKa'.

AMAE K2–1–129 [1900–39]. 'Godovye otchety za 1938 g.'

AMAE K2–1–130 [1916–39]. 'Statistiki po olenovodstvu'.

Fond: *Boris Osipovich Dolgikh.*

AMAE K5–1–291 [1938–39]. Dolgikh, B. O. 'Predvaritel'nyi otchet etnografa severnoi ekspeditsii Krasnoiarskogo Kraevogo Muzeia'.

Fond: *Andreia Aleksandrovicha Popova.*

AMAE 14–1–42 [1936–8]. 'O Plakhino-evenkiiskom Tuzsovete, Khantaisko-evenkiiskom tuzsovete (i polevye zapiski iz Norl'iska)'.

AMAE 14–1–89 [1930–1]. Popov, A. A. 'Polevoi dnevnik ekspeditsii k dolganam'.

AMAE 14–1–134 [1930]. Popov, A. A. 'Skhematicheskie karty rybolovnykh mest Noril'skogo raiona. Polevye zapisi'.

AMAE 14–1–141 [1932]. Popov, A. A. 'Dolgany (stat'ia—Tri varianta s zamechaniiami Levina i Potapova)'.

AMAE 14–1–149 [1930]. Popov, A. A. 'Otchet po dolganskoi etnograficheskoi poezdke za vtoruiu polovinu 1930 g.'

AMAE 14–1–151 [1932]. Popov, A. A. 'Zapiski o dolgano-yakutskom naselenii raiona mezhdu rr. Yeniseem i Khatangoi (na osnovanii ekspeditsionoi poezdki 1930–31 gg)'.

♦ *AIV* [Arkhiv Instituta Vostokovedeniia Rossiiskoi Akademii Nauk]

Fond: *K. M. Rychkova.*

AIV RAN 49 [1907–13].

♦ *ARGO* [Arkhiv Russkogo Geograficheskogo Obshchestva]

Fond: *Khatanskoi ekspeditsii Russkogo Geograficheskogo Obshchestva V.N. Vasil'eva.*

ARGO [1905].

INDEX

Italic numbers refer to illustrations and charts.

orthography v, 180; spoken with Yakut
    (Dolgan) 67, 105, 108, 112–13, 131;
    terms for reindeer 28, *30*, 30–1
location and population 7–9, *77*
pedagogy 6, 20, 26–7, 33–7, 120–2, 195–6
post-Soviet era v, 17, 27, 73, 98, 194
Potapovo Evenkis 24–7, 48, 49, 112–13, 169
reindeer herding, *see* herding; Number One
    Reindeer Brigade; reindeer; Utukogir
    family
relations with Dolgans 22, 67–73, 90, 180,
    186
relations with Enneches 25, 180
settlements 15, 37, 39, 41, 62–7, *134*
trade *134*, 135–47
and Tsarist state 44–5, 46; *see also yasak*
see also Chapogir people; ecology; *khempo*;
    kinship; lower Yenisei valley; Number
    One Reindeer Brigade; resettlement;
    women
Evens (*eveny*) 7, 84, 91

Federal Tax Inspection Agency (of the Russian
    Federation) 211–12
'feeding' 209
    dylbiltik (thread) 127, *128*
    fire 44, 122, 125, 126 n., 142
    land 43–4, 65, 66, 127, 202, 209, 218
    settlement 20, 43–4, 167, 196, 212
    society 43, 46, 48, 51, 52, 202, 209, 212
    see also reciprocity; ritual
Feit, H. 127 n.
Fienup-Riordan, A. 127 n.
fishing 190–1; *see also* Khantaiskii state farm;
    kollektivy; Russian local identities
Forsyth, J. 142 n.
Fort McPherson Indian Band 4

Gellner, E. 55, 206
Girinovich, P. A. 153
Glazer, N. 206
Goffman, E. 209
Gordon, B. H. C. 141
Gracheva, G. N. 5
Grant, B. 18
Gumilev, L. 204 n.
Gurvich, I. S. 88 n.
Gwich'in 4, 205

habitus 36
Hale, C. 210
hamanil 7, 118; *see also* shamans
helicopters 2, 27, 131, 216–18
Henriksen, G. 127 n.
herding 18–19, 27–33, 48, 93, 105, 117–31,
    166 n., 192
    olen'sovkhoz (Reindeer Farm) 49–50

productive herds 30, 31, 60
state nomadism 28, 30, 35, 37–8, 41–2, 117,
    167; resistance to 31, 111, 144
technology 20, 25, 31, 37–8
use of corrals 31–2, 39, 41, 99, 166 n.
yearly round 39–42, 93, 167
see also reindeer
Hertzen Pedagogical Institute 104 n., 192
Hobbes, T. 213
Hobsbawm E. 205, 209, 215
Humphrey, C. 30, 48 n., 181, 185, 195

identity:
    aboriginal v, 11, 75–6, 135, 168–9, 202, 205,
        210, 215; *see also* mixed descent
    assimilation of 75, 83, 88, 89, 93, 185; *see also*
        Khatanga Way
    authorized (or digitized) 74, 76–9, 76 n.,
        82–6, 98–109, 185–6, 207, 208–10,
        215–16; administrative 'clan' 17 n.,
        45 n., 49, 81–2, 91, 99, 173; cultural-
        economic types 85, 92–3; identities as
        'monuments' 3, 98–9; Sperkanskii's
        system 79–80, 132, 149 n., 172; *see also*
        Dolgans: ethnological classification of;
        national identity; registration; state
        ethnographers
    circulation of 92, 99–101, 109–10
    multiple or multiplex ('analogic') 11, 72, 85,
        90–3, 205, 207, 210
    performed 70–3, 108, 110–11, 113, 207–8
    relational 6, 90–6, 98–101, 107–8, 116
    and territory 17, 97, 149–50, *152*, 154
    'tuning' 106–7, 207
    wielding 97, 99, 206–7
    see also Khantaika; mixed descent; national
        identity; state ethnographers; territorial
        formation
Igarka, city of 13, 15–16, *16*, 51, 136
Igarka Industrial County 15, 170
Igarka Pedagogical School 192, 196
Ilimpei County, *see* Evenki Autonomous District
Imagined Communities 207
industry:
    development, effects of 4, 42, 62, 63; *see also*
        Khantaika hydroelectric reservoir and
        station; pollution
    precious metals 14, 74, 80, 214
    see also energy corridors; wild deer: migration
        of
Inuit 98–100, 127 n., 141, 205
Isachenko, V. L. 87 n.
'intelligence' 44, 47, 50, 148, 170
    accounts of property 38, 47, 69–70, 144–5,
        167–8
    census 47–8
    economic gravitation 152–9, 161